The Whole Machinery

SERIES EDITOR

Riché Richardson, Cornell University

FOUNDING EDITOR

Jon Smith, Simon Fraser University

ADVISORY BOARD

Houston A. Baker Jr., Vanderbilt University

Leigh Anne Duck, The University of Mississippi

Jennifer Greeson, The University of Virginia

Trudier Harris, The University of Alabama

John T. Matthews, Boston University

Tara McPherson, The University of Southern California

Claudia Milian, Duke University

The Whole Machinery

THE RURAL MODERN IN CULTURES OF
THE U.S. SOUTH, 1890-1946

Benjamin S. Child

The University of
Georgia Press
ATHENS

Parts of chapters 1 and 2 first appeared in *American Literature* and are republished here by permission of the copyright holder, Duke University Press. Chapter 5 contains elements of an essay that originally appeared in *Faulkner's Geographies*, edited by Jay Watson and Ann J. Abadie, copyright © 2015 by the University Press of Mississippi.

Paperback edition, 2024
© 2019 by the University of Georgia Press
Athens, Georgia 30602
www.ugapress.org
All rights reserved
Set in 10/13 Kepler Std. by Classic City Composition LLC, Athens, GA

Most University of Georgia Press titles are
available from popular e-book vendors.

Printed digitally

Library of Congress Cataloging-in-Publication Data

Names: Child, Ben, author.
Title: The whole machinery : the rural modern in cultures of the
   U.S. South, 1890–1946 / Benjamin S. Child.
Other titles: New southern studies.
Description: Athens [Georgia] : The University of Georgia
   Press, [2019] | Series: The new southern studies | Includes
   bibliographical references and index.
Identifiers: LCCN 2019008112| ISBN 9780820356013 (hardback :
   alk. paper) | ISBN 9780820356006 (e-book)
Subjects: LCSH: American literature—Southern States—History and
   criticism. | Rural conditions in literature. | Civilization, Modern,
   in literature.
Classification: LCC PS261 .C45 2019 | DDC 810.9/975—dc23
   LC record available at https://lccn.loc.gov/2019008112

Paperback ISBN 978-0-8203-6708-8

For Katie

CONTENTS

ACKNOWLEDGMENTS   ix

INTRODUCTION   Limning the Land   1

Part I. Cultures of Black Agriculture

CHAPTER ONE   "The True Reconstruction of the Country" in *Iola Leroy* and the Plantation Poems of Paul Laurence Dunbar   21

CHAPTER TWO   "Strange Vicissitudes": Dirt, Progress, and the Modern   49

Part II. Other Agrarian

CHAPTER THREE   Making It Old in the New South; or, The Leisure Agrarians Cultivate the Folk   91

CHAPTER FOUR   Disinherited Speech Acts: The Body as Archive in Labor Agrarianism   121

Part III. Migratory Modernism

CHAPTER FIVE   Station to Station: New York City and the Returns of the Rural   159

CODA   Uneven Ground   201

NOTES   215

WORKS CITED   243

INDEX   269

ACKNOWLEDGMENTS

I want to begin by thanking my friends and colleagues in the Colgate English Department. In the interest of space, I name only those who have contributed to this project, but my gratitude extends more widely: Greg Ames has been a terrific source of moral support; Michael Coyle has thickened these arguments in all kinds of ways; the junior-faculty study group—John Connor, Christian DuComb, Amelia Klein, Nimanthi Rajasingham, and Lenora Warren—also provided important insights at a crucial stage. Linck Johnson deserves special mention for invaluable proofreading and editing, strategizing and reassurance. Love and appreciation to Kezia Page (and Andrew Fagon) as well for long-lost sibling support. I need to acknowledge others who have directly shaped this work, sometimes unknowingly: Peter Balakian, Susan Belasco, Kristin Bluemel, Lindy Brady, Daniel Buehner, Debra Rae Cohen, Erin Drew, Eric Eliason, Ann Fisher-Wirth, George Handley, Katie McKee, Susan and William Nicholas, Ted Ownby, Peter Reed, Riché Richardson, Lynn Staley, Dan Stout, Annette Trefzer, Kenneth Warren, Caroline Wigginton, and Ian Wittington. There are others, I'm certain, but I'll have to thank you in person. I can openly thank, in the aggregate, my students at Colgate and the University of Mississippi, who have broadened and sharpened me in all kinds of ways. And at the University of Georgia Press, I owe major gratitude to Walter Biggins for seeing this project through, and to Jon Smith for critical input on its final shape.

Bottomless thanks and respect are due to Jay Watson, whose thoroughness, generosity, friendship, and staggering intelligence have done so much to build this project. Jay has provided my most lasting template of excellence in scholarship and teaching. I am similarly indebted to Leigh Anne Duck, who taught me new ways of seeing both modernism and southern literature, and who has been a tireless mentor; to Adam Gussow, who always refined my thinking through peerless line-editing; and to Deborah Barker, for the timely reminder to never bury the lede. And my acknowledgments to Elizabeth Payne for introducing the work and legacies of Myrtle Lawrence and Louise Boyle.

I'm also grateful to Ivo Kamps and the University of Mississippi's College of Liberal Arts for the dissertation fellowship, and to the University of Mississippi's Graduate Student Council for funding a Nashville research trip. At Colgate, grants from the dean's office and the Research Development Council arrived at just the right moment. I'd like to express appreciation to the interlibrary loan offices at both Colgate and the University of Mississippi as well as the staffs at Cornell's Kheel Center for Labor-Management Documentation and Archives, the Special Collections and University Archives at the Vanderbilt University Library, and the Bountiful Branch of the Davis County Public Library. My gratitude as well to the participants and organizers of conferences at which early versions of this material were presented: Faulkner and Yoknapatawpha, Society for the Study of Southern Literature, Association for the Study of Literature and the Environment, the Modernist Studies Association, and the Modern Language Association. Eddie Lang, Brian Eno, and Tsequé-Maryam Guébrou, too, for late nights and attention-setting sounds.

My biggest debts are to family: to my parents and in-laws—as well as my siblings and siblings-in-law—for their endless love and encouragement. And to Hank, Louis, and Billie—for coming into the world alongside this project and for making everything better. Most of all, love and gratitude to Katie for her patience, smarts, never-ending support, and exacting editorship. She's a better best friend and coconspirator than I've ever deserved. This work, and all other, is dedicated to her.

The Whole Machinery

INTRODUCTION

Limning the Land

Joseph Mitchell is likely the most celebrated prose portraitist of urban life in U.S. cultural history. The profiles of New York City variegation he produced in the middle decades of the twentieth century created indelible templates of literary reportage. Marked by a large-hearted, melancholy scrutiny, they cast light on a clutch of enduring, nearly totemic, characters, places, and scenarios. A partial list includes McSorley's Old Ale House; Mr. Flood, the self-declared "seafooditarian," who plans to live 115 years on a diet of fish, bread, and whiskey; the bearded Lady Olga; Sloppy Louie's restaurant; King Cockeye Johnny, leader of a band of Romani travelers; the Fulton Fish Market; George Hunter, the chair of an African Methodist church board of trustees and child of an escaped slave who haunts his own future grave in Sandy Ground, Staten Island; the city's prodigious harbor rats; Joe Gould, the homeless, Harvard-educated bohemian who claimed to be recording the sprawling *Oral History of Our Time* on the pages of dime-store notebooks and diner napkins.

Though his own prose style is lauded for its crystalline communicativeness, Mitchell evidently found his models in the work of James Joyce: in the way that Joyce's Dublin revealed itself in intricate layers, in the author's affection for the playfulness and unpredictable profundity of spoken language, in his belief in the inexhaustible significance of the everyday and the ordinary. Late in Mitchell's career, he commented ruefully on a long unwritten novel—conceived "under the spell" of *Ulysses* and shaded by his own biography—about a homesick "country Southerner" trying to navigate New York City.[1] An "obsessive reader of *Finnegans Wake*" and longtime member of the James Joyce Society, Mitchell also shared valences with more recognizably modernist writers of the period.[2] At the outset of his career he appeared alongside several such figures—William Faulkner, Robert Penn Warren, William Carlos Williams, E. E. Cummings, Jean Toomer, Erskine Caldwell—in a pair of yearbooks designed to anthologize the best American writing.[3] And in a review of the 1943 collection *McSorley's Wonderful Saloon*, Mitchell received the imprimatur of prominent critic Malcolm Cowley, who helped parlay the canonization of a raft of mainline American modernists—Fitzgerald, Hemingway, Faulkner, and Sherwood Anderson among them. According to Cowley, Mitchell's reporting was "more imaginative than anything to be found in recent novels."[4] Perhaps Mitchell's most identifiably modernist trait, and the reason his sensibility aligns so readily with the writers mentioned above, was the nagging sense of loss he brought to his depictions of worlds eclipsed—some bit by bit, others all at once—by modernization.

Not incidentally, Joseph Mitchell was also an irreducible southerner. He came from an obscure corner of cotton and tobacco country in the south-central coastal plain of North Carolina, a town called Fairmont in Robeson County, where his father rose to prominence as a cotton planter. Mitchell's childhood, recounted in a posthumously published excerpt from an unfinished memoir, was spent wandering the banks of the Pittman Mill Branch, examining the local flora with the same level of attention he would later bring to his urban subjects. In 1939, after making the transition from beat reporter at the *New York World-Telegram* to full-time staff writer at the *New Yorker*, Mitchell published as much short fiction in the magazine as he did nonfiction, offering a handful of stories, pieces such as "The Downfall of Fascism in Black Ankle County" and "Uncle Dockery and the Independent Bull," set in a rural South that bore close resemblance to Robeson County.[5] "It is odd, to begin with," Mitchell wrote in his memoirs, "that I ever had any connection with New York City at all."[6]

Unlikely as it may have seemed to Mitchell in retrospect, his work has come to exemplify New York in the first half of the twentieth century. Yet even the lauded dispatches from the city bear the imprint of the rural South. Take the profile of street preacher Rev. Mr. James Jefferson Davis Hall in 1943's "A Spism and a Spasm." It depicts a "garrulous old southerner" whose ministry has roots in his evangelical upbringing and whose whole persona, as Mitchell tells it, is a product of his origins in the South: "He developed a quality of hysteria years ago in Alabama by going deep into a cypress swamp for an hour or so a day and screaming warnings of one kind or another at an imaginary crowd."[7] New York City provided a new kind of crowd. "Hall's outlook on life is a product of the grayness of the Reconstruction period in the South," Mitchell explains, and it's easy enough to see what he means: Hall belongs to another place and, to draw on Peter Osborne's model, to a different temporality of modernity.[8] Elsewhere, Mitchell opens his 1938 profile of Charles Eugene Cassell, proprietor of Captain Charley's Private Museum for Intelligent People, by looking back at a scene from his rural childhood in which the tackle used to hoist a soon-to-be-butchered cow collapsed, burying Mitchell himself at the bottom of the pile: "That is the way I feel after I have listened to Captain Charley for a little while. I feel as if I had been hit on the head with a cow."[9]

The episode provides the story's title, "Hit on the Head with a Cow," but it could double as a description for any number of characters and scenarios documented in the author's city reporting, as the density of bodies and sensations swirling around the metropolis gain momentum and energy through contrast with the relative quiet of his rural South. Mitchell did as much as anyone to forge literary images of New York City in the modernist period, and yet his sensory descriptions of the urban experience derive from a conceptual vocabulary that was resolutely rural.

A familiar story holds that modernization radiates out from metropolitan origins.[10] *The Whole Machinery* explores representations of people and places, objects and occasions, that reverse that trajectory, demonstrating how modernizing agents move in a contrary direction as well—from the country to the city. In a crucial reversal, these figures aren't pulled by or into urban modernity so much as they post alternate—and transformative—iterations of the modern, often bringing them to the urban world itself. My work here aims to upend the U.S. South's reputation as retrograde and unresponsive to modernity by showing how the effects of national and transnational exchange, emergent technologies, and industrialization animate environments and bodies associated with, or performing, versions of the rural. It also encourages new ways of imagining the politics of rurality, particularly as it considers models of action that emphasize collectivity and cross-racial alliance. To this end, I search out the shadow side of the cosmopolitan modern by investigating the rural sources—the laboring bodies and raw materials—that made such urban spaces possible. The result is a geography of modernism that includes a striking suite of landmarks, both actual and imagined: Twisted Oak, Arkansas, and Tukabahchee County, Alabama; Manhattan, Manchester, and Moscow; Tuskegee and Gobbler's Knob, North Carolina.

My readings of literature and other forms of cultural expression from roughly 1890 to 1946, what has been identified as the "core" of the modernist period, use examinations of the rural U.S. South to refine an expanding sense of *how*, *when*, and—perhaps most pointedly—*where* the modern occurs.[11] Early in *Up from Slavery*, describing the institution's ability to degrade labor, Booker T. Washington makes reference to "the whole machinery of slavery" (14), a phrase that captures its malign totality, the searching violence of its material and psychological scope. With acknowledgments to recent scholarship on the connections between the making of the modern world and southern cotton economies by figures such as Edward Baptist, Sven Beckert, Walter Johnson, Joshua Rothman, and Caitlin Rosenthal, my argument here is that any literary-critical assessment of *the whole machinery of modernity* must of necessity include rural forms and figures, rural histories and phenomena.[12] As Sven Beckert concludes in his magisterial survey of cotton's global influence on the emergence of capitalist modernity, "Although our historical imaginations are usually dominated by cities, factories, and industrial workers, we have seen that much of the emergence of the modern world occurred in the countryside."[13] One of *The Whole Machinery*'s primary goals is to use expressive cultures of the U.S. South to think through modern worlds that rise from southern countrysides, recasting these spaces as sites of fluidity, diffusion, and profound political unrest. For Clyde Woods, at the end of the twentieth century, the plantation was the "settlement institution" that established "modern capitalist slavery" in the cotton South.[14] Such work is perhaps inevitably an amplification and elaboration of Cedric J. Robinson's crucial argument that slavery and the slave trade were "integral to the modern world economy." "[T]heir relationship to capitalism," Robinson holds, "was historical and organic rather than adventitious and synthetic."[15] Even further back, in 1944, Eric Williams introduced the broad outlines of this discussion when he demonstrated the essential part slave labor played in the expansion of the Industrial Revolution. Slavery, Williams explained, "produced the cotton to serve as a base for modern capitalism." In the adjoining sentence, he makes an equally profound, if perhaps less commonly contested, claim: "[Slavery] made the American South."[16] Not surprisingly, imaginative literature, expressive culture, and discourses of modernism have by and large escaped the purview of these studies.[17] By focusing on a slightly later period and tending to a different set of questions, I address this lacuna by examining cultural products that also uncover modernity's rural southern roots. Janet Casey has recently called for greater attention to rurality and modernity as "mutually constitutive" forces, with astute and bracing analysis that asserts the centrality of women to rural modes of modernity.[18] Although her work occasionally looks southward, particularly in a chapter that takes up "Women and/in Photography," she is predominantly focused on the Midwest and therefore not occupied by the South's place in the production of capitalist modernity. Because the agricultural South has always been on the vanguard of North Atlantic economic modernity, however, *The Whole Machinery* argues for the region's centrality to any discussion of cultural and literary expressions of the rural modern in the United States.[19]

While several critics have assayed modernism/modernity's attention to rural people and places in the United States, *The Whole Machinery* is the first book-length study of the various ways that cultural products both mirror and shape the rural modern in the American South.[20] Thadious Davis's *Southscapes* (2011), for instance, contains arguments against popular notions of the region as premodern, yet it is primarily a treatment of southern black writers and the development of literary postmodernism in the second half of the twentieth century. *The Whole Machinery*'s task is to expand upon the suggestive—but brief—statements in *Southscapes'* introduction about generative bonds between the rural, modernity, and race in an earlier period.

Leigh Anne Duck's *The Nation's Region* (2009) provides an incisive examination of the coexistence of the South's perceived anachronism alongside its contributions to a modernizing nation. Although Duck's explication of "southern modernism" deeply informs my work, her book doesn't detail how exactly the "rural" functions in these formations—an opening *The Whole Machinery* investigates.[21]

For his part, Mark Storey has produced an illuminating survey of Gilded Age "rural fiction" guided by the "single question" of how such texts address the "intimately connected processes of urbanization and modernization."[22] It's an essential undertaking, and one that occasionally overlaps with my task in *The Whole Machinery*. But while this study proceeds with a wider chronological and generic scope, it also requires a narrower geographic one that allows me to address two questions: How does *modernism* play into these equations? And how can cultural productions reveal a reverse trajectory by which the modern is both embodied and generated by rural figures? Maria Farland explicitly argues that "heightened attention to the rural as a diverse and dynamic category can restore our sense of the forces of marginalization and exclusion that transcend regional and even national borders."[23] I agree, and one of *The Whole Machinery*'s major projects is to imagine a broadly configured rendition of the "rural" as crucial to both new modernist and new southern studies.

As an investigation of the rural modern that considers multiple media and forms of technology, *The Whole Machinery*'s readings range widely, encompassing a spectrum of texts and their networks of transmission, reception, and signification. These include novels, poems, and short stories but also radio broadcasts, sound recordings, political pamphlets, and photographs; magazine articles, newspaper reports, and agricultural bulletins. Folding such expressive artifacts into my larger arguments, I consider how they both reflect *and* form modern(ist) culture. While federally funded industrial efforts such as the Tennessee Valley Authority (1933) and the Rural Electrification Act (1936) provide an important backdrop to my analysis, the book is primarily scaled to the individual and to the individual's relation to the collective. Reckoning with the political turbulence of the period, *The Whole Machinery* inspects the rich legacies and textual productions of insurgent agricultural movements in the South, particularly the Southern Tenant Farmers' Union of the 1930s. It gauges the response of rural subjects to identifiably modern devices such as the steam engine and the tractor, just as it seeks out the modern in technologies that operate at slower speeds and lower volumes: the hoe, the plow, and the handwritten letter. These responses convey diverse desires for escape or entrenchment, often in the same conflicted voice, resulting in multivalent performances of rurality that are, in their way, as thoroughly modern as those of more widely canonized urban figures.[24]

Consequently, I highlight ways in which depictions of the rural intermediate, as well as revise, standard notions of what constitutes both modernity and modernism, for as Dilip Gaonkar reminds us, "When viewed from different perspectives, modernity appears to have an almost iridescent quality; its contours shift depending on the angle of interrogation."[25] Following Gaonkar, I examine figurations of the rural modern that call forth the varied, often innovative, representational grammars used to describe these spaces and their inhabitants. Note the diction: following Walter Benjamin's preference for *die Moderne*, I present "modern" with care here for the way that it floats between modernism (a matter of aesthetic and philosophical expression) and modernity (a category that tracks economic, industrial, and social development). Under *The Whole Machinery*'s angle of interrogation, the shape of the rural modern becomes clear in the vast reach of the agricultural South's systems of labor and cultural capital, and in the region's participation in increasingly smooth networks of both national and transnational exchange.

Mary Louise Pratt's formulation of the spatialized power dynamic that flourishes under colonialism presumes two groups: "the subordinated or marginal" and the "dominant or *metropolitan*."[26] How might this dyad, in which the metropolitan pairs so easily with the dominant, come apart? Placed within matrices of sociopolitical, economic, and cultural exchange, my objects of study emblematize the startling spaces and temporalities brought into being by capitalist modernity. For instance, by tracing the diffuse trajectories of the products—material, cultural, political—of the southern cotton trade, the book shows how twentieth-century returns of the nineteenth century unearth deep connections between southern agriculture and urban modernity. To be more specific: whereas Benjamin notes that the rise of the Paris Arcades—his ultimate repository of *die Moderne*—marks the emergence of an early nineteenth-century, U.S. cotton-fed "boom in the textile trade,"[27] I describe ways in which the (re)sources of both modernity and modernism create a well-lubricated, two-way path from the rural U.S. South to the urban North Atlantic, exposing a tangled skein of the "old" and the "new" wherein the material interdependence of the southern margin and the northern center takes on a temporal dimension. My aim is not to permanently bracket expressions of the rural modern as "rural modernism," a category always distinguishable from modernism qua modernism, but to correct a tendency to read the urban and metropolitan as definitive signs of the modern. More broadly, the project is guided by the distinct but related aims of conceptualizing the period and place from a macro perspective while considering how its complexities played out—and continue to play out—in the expressions and experiences of historically specific individuals.

The Whole Machinery's visions of the rural modern thus assess Perry Anderson's contention that modernity is "neither economic process nor cultural vision but the *historical experience* mediating the one to the other."[28] Focusing on rural spaces and figures, I argue that both "economic process" and "cultural vision" are essential to the kinds of "historical experience" that Anderson posits, and that these experiences and the multiplicities of meaning they produce are plainly not restricted to urban areas. Indeed, the force of their mediating contrast may be more readily apparent in relatively underdeveloped rural spaces. So while critics such as Dilip Gaonkar and Dipesh Chakrabarty describe links between the modern and the postcolonial by uncovering "alternative modernities" that arise along the margins of colonized and formerly colonized spaces, I look for them along the edges of the nation of the United States.[29] In a similar vein, David Harvey parses the transformative, global effects of World War I in a manner that also applies to the rural peripheries of the long twentieth century: "[T]he world's spaces were deterritorialized, stripped of their preceding significations, and then reterritorialized according to the convenience of colonial and imperial administration."[30] Harvey's teleology of modernization presumes the existence of a foundational culture undone by the global marketplace, one whose reconfiguration will show how "capitalism became embroiled in an incredible phase of massive long-term investments in the conquest of space."[31]

These conquered spaces, I contend, include the rural regions of the postbellum South. Of course, the notion of a unified, "traditional" southern culture irrevocably warped by the Civil War and the onset of industrial modernization is a trope that runs throughout literary productions of the South, from the full array of plantation romances—Thomas Nelson Page's *Red Rock* (1899) on one end; Margaret Mitchell's *Gone with the Wind* (1938) on the other—to the writings of the Nashville Agrarians and neo-agrarians such as Wendell Berry. It's a powerful idea, and one that has contributed to the immense strength of southern conservatism and lost causism. And while this particular version of the South is mostly fantasy, it's also true that processes of industrial modernization did have transformational effects on the environmental profile of the region, on its social and political composition, and on its varied modes of cultural production. In sum, the notion that modernization has changed the rural South isn't exclusive to the "lost cause"; as *The Whole Machinery* contends, however, there are concrete ways in which the rural South itself changed modernization. Those changes shore up the less-obvious idea that you can't believe in the lost cause if you believe that the rural may in part have possessed germinating modernizing energies.

In calibrating this study's figurations of the rural modern, I follow Rosi Braidotti's resourceful construction of "figuration" as "a politically informed account of an alternative subjectivity" by arguing that when critics privilege the urban and the industrial as the purest forms of the modern, rurality arrives as a kind of "alternative subjectivity," one with its own constellation of political concerns and responses.[32] I also embrace "figuration" for its suggestive possibilities—it can appear in the guise of persons but also thoughts, performances, actions, objects, and landscapes. Jon Smith has recently diagnosed the shortsighted consequences of a common Americanist preference for "antimodern escapes" into "populist worlds," one that too easily reinforces familiar polarities of the rural and the urban.[33] With this in mind, *The Whole Machinery* works against the grain of the "metronormative" to generate fresh interpretive categories, new and complex meanings in cultural zones often regarded as static, depthless, and "primitive."[34]

While I don't plan to permanently dislodge the privileged position of the urban in studies of modernism, I do hope to call attention to the blind spots that accompany its scholarly treatment. And since I aim to elaborate and expand upon current models, my analysis requires a deliberate definition of terms. The "rural," for one. Raymond Williams acknowledges that popular images of the country signify "old ways, human ways, natural ways," while the city stands for "progress, modernisation, development." But he is likewise interested in how "we use the contrast of country and city to ratify an unresolved division and conflict of impulses"—a tenebristic conflict present at both sites and across geographies of development more generally.[35] Inasmuch as these images help manage a "division and conflict," they do the important cultural work of helping people code spaces with stable meanings in a world of discordant flows. Yet an emphasis on contrast rather than points of contact can perpetuate a false sense of how and why these forms signify in the ways that they do, contributing to binary formations of modern/antimodern that make it all too easy to find the modern in the metropolitan alone. These are unsteady foundations, however. As Barbara Ching and Gerald Creed wisely suggest, rurality is always an elastic condition. One person's backwater can be another's metropolis since "almost any inhabited place can be experienced as either rural or urban," a statement that suggests the inescapable contingency of familiar notions of the country and the city.[36]

As *The Whole Machinery* investigates conditions wherein the fate of the soil is sealed to the fate of its inhabitants, it drifts into the domain of ecocriticism. Accordingly, my interests in landscape, labor, and phenomenologies of place make it possible to address questions about sustainability, land ethics, and environmental justice—to explore the functions of ecologies in unnoticed places. In his lauded attempts to develop a "theory of ecological criticism," Timothy Morton aims at a site beyond self-limiting definitions of "nature" and their reification in the critical practices of ecocriticism. According to one especially damning passage, "Ecocriticism is too enmeshed in the ideology that churns out stereotypical ideas of nature to be of any use."[37] The

Whole Machinery avoids this tendency by seeking out a more elemental formation: the shaping functions that nonhuman actors play and that the earth itself plays in arrangements of land-bound human labor.[38] If this seems, à la Morton, a less-than-forthright approach to the "environment," much less ecocriticism, it may be worth recalling Lawrence Buell's foundational contention that an "environmentally minded work" will of necessity include "[s]ome sense of the environment as a process rather than as a constant or a given."[39] Just such processes are evident in nearly all this book's subjects of analysis: it is committed to evaluating their meanings in the foreground, through the background, and all across the uneven ground it inspects.

What, precisely, are the connections between recognizable concepts of modernization, modernity, and modernism? Patricia Chu, for one, opposes the tendency to label "'modernist' any work written within a particular span of years," insisting that, above all else, "[m]odernism was an aesthetic commitment."[40] I take Chu's point about formal intentionality, but it's also important to recognize the extent to which aesthetics is never cleanly divisible from history and geography, from politics and economics. What if the same qualities recognized as strategies of "aesthetic commitment" are just the best, most immediate means by which a person can communicate her modern reality? If psychic fragmentation, to take one readily referenced characteristic of modernism, is a standard condition of modernity, then won't it inevitably, if sometimes unconsciously, feature in the expressive culture of the period? More to the point, what do we do when something looks like a modernism but lacks a manifesto? Chu's well-reasoned critique of "common approaches" to delineating modernism prompts a series of pressing questions: Can an artifact or a performance be unintentionally modernist? If modernism is the incorrect label for "the ways in which an author's work aesthetically resembles the work of authors whose place in the modernist canon is unchallenged," where should we look for a better one?[41] Can we avoid endlessly instantiating "modernism" as a series of predetermined aesthetic gestures and affects? To be sure, my work here won't definitively answer these questions. But I will present readings that evaluate the deep and tangled associations between processes of *modernization* and practices of *modernism*, claiming along the way that figurations of the rural "modern"—a descriptor that allows for the "rethinking of relations among the key terms *modernism, modernization,* and *modernity*"—deserve to be recognized as a central contribution of new modernist studies.[42] While my examinations of the rural modern might occasionally drift into canons of modernism, they will also acknowledge that the rural modern maps a distinct range of responses to the onset of development—reflexes enacted by individuals grappling with such emergent conditions as industrialism, market capitalism, modern thought (e.g., Darwinism, Marxism, Freudian psychology), mechanization, abstraction, standardization. Put bluntly, the modern is not always something you choose to embrace—sometimes you are interpellated by it. Yet artistic and intellectual reactions to the emergence of capitalist modernity and industrial development constitute a form of modernism, even when that reaction may signal a retreat to the provincial or to an imagined past.

Interactions between the period's increasingly standardized national economies and infrastructures as well as technological innovations such as the newswire and the radio, telephones and telegraphs, trains and automobiles present one essential node in my analysis. When Ulysses S. Grant published the second installment of his memoirs in 1886, he proposed the Civil War itself as the great modernizer, a force that shifted its participants' horizons beyond the local by way of advances in cartography and transportation that exposed them to an enlarged national landscape. For Grant, the war and its conclusions prepared the United States for the industrial age by unleashing a "spirit of independence and enterprise" and by encouraging a "commingling of the people" that pushed the nation toward "the eve of a new era," one in which regional differences would encourage rather than impede economic and industrial development.[43] Grant's optimism is unburdened by specifics, but it does tap into late-century discourses about unity and progress that forward unification-via-standardization as an inevitable outcome of modernization.[44] These discourses necessarily include discussions of labor practices as well. Consider, for instance, the Fordist ethos of the assembly line, with its emphasis on specialization toward the goal of creating replaceable parts for every machine and a uniform set of practices for assembling it. The centripetal forces of modernization here begin at the nation and spiral down to the consumer good.

The urge to create a more solid center also contributes to a pronounced articulation of the margins. And in the early decades of the twentieth century, with the frontier declared "closed" and urbanization on the upswing, the national margin began to look more and more like the rural countryside. This wasn't always the case. While Jefferson's belief that the republic is best served by independent, farming landowners continues to hold sway in certain corners of the popular imagination, it was an article of faith for many citizens and policymakers in nineteenth-century America. Pedaling back to the late eighteenth century, Crèvecoeur's *Letters from an American Farmer* (1778) configures the rustic terrains of the American continent as a locus of the modern.[45] And not just because the influence of the church ("ecclesiastical dominion") and the throne was attenuated there: rural America was modern because it lacked the very signs that typically gave the category its composition—"no great manufacturers employing thousands, no great refinements of luxury."[46] The protofactories of Europe were, in Farmer James's view, already enervated, no longer on the leading edge. "If you recede still farther from the sea," Farmer John records, "you will come into more modern settlements": the inland farming frontier presides over the text as the location of modern culture.[47]

Flash-forward to the turn of the twentieth century and Charlotte Perkins Gilman's *Women and Economics* (1898), in which she argues that progressive ideas and experiences of gender develop at wide removes from the metropolis: "In the country, among the peasant classes, there is much less sex-distinction than in cities, where wealth enables the women to live in absolute idleness.... It is from the country and the lower classes that the fresh blood pours into the cities."[48] By the early decades of the new century, however, things had changed. H. L. Mencken's oft-referenced 1917 denunciation of the South as "the Sahara of the Bozart" is just the most famous expression of a widely held attitude that coded the rural—and the rural South in particular—as a bastion of backwardness. While the agricultural South was constantly negotiating modernity vis-à-vis material and economic development, modernism as a matter of cultural communication and capital took on a persistently urban flavor.[49] Never mind that many of its chief purveyors in the United States bore traces of the provincial: Ezra Pound hailed from Hailey, Idaho, and Zora Neale Hurston from Eatonville, Florida; Frost's New England was carefully and deliberately posed in contrast to the urban North, as was Faulkner's Mississippi.

So while it's plainly impossible to draw the ultimate map of modernism, one feature that recurs throughout prominent modernist geographies is a meridian distinguishing country from city. To reckon with the pattern, I propose more locally conceived iterations of the division between core and periphery that are central to Immanuel Wallerstein's "modern world-systems." In Wallerstein's expansive model, developing countries act as peripheries to developed countries' cores, with economic advantages continually flowing back to the centralized powers.[50] I argue here that a similar dynamic is at work within the national borders of the United States, as urban spaces broadly serve as core to the rural province's periphery. In short, divisions between the country and the city in the twentieth century do correlate to a hard reality—the rural South's position as a zone of uneven development serves as evidence and crystallizes this book's concerns—yet that unevenness extends to the permeable border itself. While it's fair to say, for instance, that economic power and cultural capital are largely pooled in the city, the city itself is pocketed with spaces of underdevelopment and poverty just as the impoverished countryside features sectors of vast wealth. Moreover, the southern plantation's imbrication in the Caribbean and Latin America makes it an exemplary manifestation of what Wallerstein himself, in an account of the rise of the modern world-system authored with Aníbal Quijano, called

"Americanity": "There could not have been a capitalist world-economy without the Americas."⁵¹ In other words, what looks like the periphery can, when narrated from the perspectives embodied in the texts I examine, reconstitute itself as the core, a point relevant to Amy Clukey's model of circum-Atlantic "plantation modernity." According to Clukey's essential reading, "Plantation modernity effectively reorders the interdependencies of core-periphery relations and dismantles binaries that pit the cosmopolitan and global against the local and parochial,"⁵² an observation that cashes out as an explanation of the cross-currents of Irish and southern colonialisms in *Gone with the Wind*. In that vein, I suggest that such reorderings occur across and beyond the shadow of the plantation South. For though this dividing line is bound to the material, it is also, to invoke an infamously complex concept, cultural—a site of continual negotiations, exchanges, and performances of ideas, objects, and images.⁵³

Since the South is the great variable throughout so many of my readings, it's important to clarify how the region appears in this project. In recent scholarship, popular notions of regional-national relationships generally meet greater skepticism than transnational and postnational approaches, and for good reason: critics note how older forms of southern studies have often reproduced rather than challenged received images of the space and its culture. On the other hand, scholars who have recently approached the South as multiple, as an intricately spun web of diverse social, cultural, and economic interests, have dramatically revised common notions of what and how the region means.⁵⁴ In particular, their efforts show that the politics of the southern cultural landscape were always engaged with the global, were always in flux, and that the untold histories of largely subaltern populations confound the region's supposedly stable geographies of place and culture. The problem isn't inherent to the regional frame; the task is to reposition the frame. Harilaos Stecopoulos, exploring the possibilities for postnational Americanists, has recently argued that regionalism's "seemingly outmoded geographic fictions not only yield indispensable historical information ... about power; they also offer us insight into the relationships that obtain between center and periphery."⁵⁵ Within southern microregions and between the South as a whole and the cultural centers of the Northeast, these relationships form a major dynamic of my analysis.⁵⁶

One flashpoint here appears in the painful histories of labor and race that surround sites of plantation slavery and postslavery tenancy. Although both slavery and segregation are most accurately understood as national rather than strictly regional practices, it is evident that the composition of the physical landscape—the "thick, dark, and naturally rich soil" of the Black Belt described by Booker T. Washington (52)—and the region's role as a source of raw materials contributed in essential ways to the force and persistence of these institutions. The viability of the agricultural South, in turn, depended on vast tracts of land to produce industrial-sized yields of cash crops such as cotton (particularly inland varieties of short-staple cotton), corn, rice, sugar, and tobacco. Of course, these conditions proved ideal for slavery's expansion in the plantation system of the antebellum period and encouraged the persistence of sharecropping and tenant farming after the war. And while tenancy in the period wasn't exclusive to the South—it was widespread throughout the lower Midwest as well—it lingers in the popular imagination as a mostly southern phenomenon. (The association was solidified, no doubt, by a string of haunting images of rural southern poverty produced during the Depression by such Farm Security Administration photographers as Walker Evans, Marion Post Wolcott, and Dorothea Lange.) The South's nexus of labor and landscape creates a dense and peculiar history of modernization, marked by struggles for and against organized labor, by the arrivals of mechanization, and by dramatic patterns of uneven development. It is a history contingent upon other histories, driven by reactions and impulses that transcend any single region. And yet residues of regional inscription remain.

With this particular reading, one juncture at which modernization and the South cross is segregation. The revised edition of Lillian Smith's memoir, *Killers of the Dream* (1963), includes a dedication to the author's parents, who "valiantly tried to keep their nine children in touch with wholeness even though reared in a segregated culture."[57] The dream of the book's title, it seems, is the achievement of a psychic and social wholeness, a goal nullified in Smith's environment by the presence of segregation—that "symbol and symptom of our modern, fragmented world."[58] Smith's diction reveals a knotty ambiguity: Is segregation a consequence of modernity, or is U.S. modernity itself a consequence of the logic of segregation? Can it be both at once? Her description contains some rich possibilities: "fragmentation," a condition so commonly recognized as the ontology of modernism, is offered as a source for segregation. This because segregation operates as a political manifestation of industrial impulses to identify, order, and rank segments of a world that increasingly turns on vertiginous exercises in diffusion and mixture.[59] Making much the same point as Smith, Grace Elizabeth Hale has highlighted the collaboration between science, industrial modernity, and systems of segregation, exposing the deeply sunk problems that state-sponsored apartheid was designed to solve: "Hierarchical structures founded in the personalized social relations of specific localities lost their authority in an increasingly mobile and rapidly changing society. How would people know who they are within this spinning abstraction, the newly economically integrated, industrialized nation-state?"[60] Emerging from the tension between disorder's increased influence and the ordering functions of post-Reconstruction industrial and political powers, segregation acts as both a protection against modernity and an expression of its brutally innovative forms of systems management—a symbolic reaction, to second Smith, and a symptomatic defense.

No surprise, then, that the milieu of the modern is unmistakable in journalist-activist Ida B. Wells's accounts of U.S. apartheid during the Jim Crow period.[61] This is particularly true in her representations of space, with their uneasy descriptions of regional mixture and exchange. For instance, according to Wells, the "mob spirit" that propels urban racial violence migrates inward from the rural margins: "It has left the out-of-the-way places, where ignorance prevails, has thrown off the mask and with this new cry stalks in broad daylight in the large cities, the centres of civilization."[62] The edge is contaminating the center, and Wells's readiness to see violence as a portable problem with rural origins is a quality that, in one instance at least, the writer shares with her antagonists: in order to unveil the racism of the southern media, Wells's pamphlet *Southern Horrors* (1892) quotes a *Memphis Ledger* story detailing a "miscegenation" case in which the reporter castigates a young white mother and her mixed-race child. Although the woman is a resident of Memphis, over and again the article makes her an outsider, observing that "[s]he is a country girl," fresh from "her father's farm."[63] The marker "country girl" denotes both the girl's ignorance and her deviance, a kind of deviance-through-ignorance of the strictures and behaviors essential to the maintenance of a segregated society. Such gestures of identification attempt to hold the woman apart for both her uncomfortable congress with blackness and for her rural identity.

Otherness is not formed by racial or ethnic lineage alone then; it can derive from where one stands, spatially, in relation to the dominant culture—a matter of geographic lineage. And, as Wells's reporting suggests, the very creation of otherness may be brought to a head through collisions so typically recognized as characteristic of modernity. More precisely, the troubling mixtures represented by the nonwhite child become quintessential emblems of the very forces segregation was designed to thwart, and they turn both her and her child into agents of an alternative modernity arrived up from the country. Under this logic, the article's opprobrium for violations of the color line suggests that, in Jim Crow Memphis at least, the city is actively buttressed *against* arrivals of the modern. These sorts of combinations, and their unwieldy consequences, are a major feature of *The Whole Machinery*, and they arrive in many forms throughout the project, as I expose a modernity of rusticity within the period's overlapping concerns with economies, ecologies, and race.

The Whole Machinery is divided into three broad sections. Part 1 ("Cultures of Black Agriculture") comprises two chapters exploring representations and experiences of African American agricultural labor at the turn of the twentieth century, as the post-Reconstruction moment flows into the century of the color line. Chapter 1 argues that while recent trends in ecocriticism multiply the political meanings of African American ecologies, this emphasis was always already shaping black discourse, particularly in the years following Reconstruction.[64] Building on Margaret Ronda's important essay on Paul Laurence Dunbar and the georgic tradition, I argue for the recognition of a differently articulated georgic in Dunbar's work, one in which, *pace* Ronda, pessimism is tempered by optimism and black agricultural labor in the post-Reconstruction era is at once a burden and an opportunity to forge newness.[65] My analysis then turns to Frances E. W. Harper's novel *Iola Leroy* (1892) and engages recent arguments on behalf of the emancipatory potential of African American connections to the rural landscape.[66] Despite southern agriculture's histories of violence and oppression via slavery and tenancy, I consider how these texts imagine black farming in the period as possible sources of autonomy—especially when read alongside the late-century actions of agricultural collectives such as the Colored Farmers' Alliance. Finally, the chapter contends that both Dunbar and Harper propose ways of transforming plantation spaces through a past-conscious, postplantation poetics of reclamation that illuminates the unfinished nature of nature and of history in the black South at the turn of the century.

While scholars have vigorously analyzed the "debate" between Booker T. Washington and W. E. B. Du Bois that plays out in *Up from Slavery* (1901) and *The Souls of Black Folk* (1903), chapter 2 seeks a largely unexamined corner: their varied interests in the relationship between nature and cultures of labor, a subject that has distinct implications for both men's impacts on the global arrival of capitalist modernity. Attention to the land, its products, and the work of black bodies remained a major theme in Du Bois's transnational concerns beyond *Souls*; Washington's efforts at Tuskegee provided a model for both colonized subjects seeking self-determination and colonizers pursuing access to the cotton trade. Throughout this chapter, I use intersecting representations of landscape and labor in *Up from Slavery* and *Souls* to evaluate the distance between the two thinkers and their visions for African American participation in the modern nation. I conclude with a reading of Du Bois's 1911 novel, *The Quest of the Silver Fleece*, that mediates that gap by at once affirming the redemptive potential of southern soil *and* the importance of classical education and fully integrated citizenship.

Part 2 ("Other Agrarian") uses rubrics of the modern to synthesize varieties of the agropolitical in the South of the 1930s. For instance, when critic Michael Kreyling cast "southern literature" as a creation of the Nashville Agrarians, he highlighted the extent to which they crafted the category to match their own image—white, male, "southern," deeply invested in the entropy of tradition.[67] As a practical matter, though, the conditions of agriculture in their place and time were abstracted beyond recognition: in *I'll Take*

My Stand (1930), for example, farming acts above all else as a literary conceit. Chapter 3 thus juxtaposes the deliberate conservatism of the Agrarians in that book, as well as the distributionist tendencies of the later collection *Who Owns America?* (1936), with the work of their leftist contemporaries in the Highlander Folk School to theorize a position I call *leisure agrarianism*. I focus most specifically on the writings of Highlander cofounder Don West, whose work at Highlander and beyond pushed directly against the Twelve Southerners. While these two parties tended toward opposed ends of a bipolar political spectrum, they each represent differently directed evocations of the "folk" and the "traditional" as responses to modernity's ruptures. The chapter concludes by proposing ways in which these formulations provide a pointedly modern theory, if not practice, of the agri-cultural.

Counterposed against the leisure agrarianisms of the previous chapter, chapter 4 inspects alternate modes of expression that take into account the material realities—and the wide range of voices—present in the work of *labor agrarians* of the farming South, a group primarily composed of women and African Americans. I find one such mode in an archive unearthed by historian Elizabeth Payne and heretofore neglected by literary critics: photographer Louise Boyle's images of Southern Tenant Farmers' Union member Myrtle Lawrence.[68] In contrast to similar documentary projects from the late 1930s and early 1940s (*You Have Seen Their Faces* [1937], *Land of the Free* [1938], *An American Exodus: A Record of Human Erosion* [1939], *Let Us Now Praise Famous Men* [1941], *12 Million Black Voices* [1941]), Boyle's pictures reroute the medium's visual grammar to collapse the distance between the object of the photograph and the photographic subject: Lawrence herself participated actively in the creation of the images, offering up pictures of her body in its physical environment both as an act and text of protest against the sharecropping system. Drawing on the thinking of Roland Barthes, Susan Sontag, and Michael Warner, I present these STFU images alongside the group's 1936 pamphlet *The Disinherited Speak* and a series of letters from rural children responding to Eleanor Roosevelt's radio broadcasts and newspaper articles as artifacts of embodied discourse that allow their audiences to both *see* and *feel* the subaltern "speaking" between the lines. Moreover, I argue that these texts underline the irrefutable existence of other Souths and other experiences of the modern.

Part 3 ("Migratory Modernism") consists of a single expansive chapter that braids together several strands introduced across the book to create a designation I call *migratory modernism*. Throughout this chapter, I evaluate the benefits and the burdens of contact zones formed through flows of bodies, images, and language from the rural South to New York City, flows that delineate race-based vectors of uneven mobility. Here I investigate both canonical fictions and less-frequently read ones, positioning Rudolph Fisher's clutch of migration stories of the 1920s beside Zora Neale Hurston's "Story in Harlem Slang" (1942) to theorize the terminal hegiras of black characters. I also use Ellen Glasgow's novel *Barren Ground* (1925) to investigate the horseshoe-shaped movements of their white counterparts. Since a major segment of the city's modern profile was cast by its role in the Cotton Triangle connecting crops of the Mississippi Valley to ports in England, the fictional figures I analyze serve as metaphors for systems of exchange and embeddedness that reach back into the nineteenth century. Ultimately, I demonstrate how each of these narratives uses representations of migrants of the southern diaspora and their interpenetrating movements to deterritorialize familiar notions of the country and the city, of the North and the South, of the modern and the antimodern.[69]

Finally, in a brief coda, I consider the recent, and unpredictable, popularity of two texts to underscore *The Whole Machinery*'s contemporary relevance: in 2014 *New York Times* critic Dwight Garner's laudatory reappraisal of *All God's Dangers* (1974)—a decades-old oral history of Alabama tenant farmer Ned Cobb—sent the book to the top of Amazon's nonfiction list, temporarily bumping Thomas Piketty's *Capital in the Twenty-First Century* (2013) to the number-two spot.[70] What does it mean to have two texts—which each, in its own way, revisits intellectual and physical terrains readily linked to the modernist period—gain such traction in a postmillennial moment? In this section, I use *All God's Dangers*' curious proximity to Piketty's contemporary study of global income inequality to develop an unflagging point: the contradictions that modernity forces on society and its individual subjects remain unresolved. But this sharp lack of resolution, underscored by the recurrent presentness of a resilient tenant farmer's life and language, exposes a deep cultural current that continues to deposit signs, practices, and histories of the rural into the contemporary structures of capitalist modernity. More broadly, my reading of *All God's Dangers* also provides an opportunity to test *The Whole Machinery*'s concluding statements about the constitutive role of the *rural-in-the-modern* as well as its obverse—but complementary—formation, the *modern-in-the-rural*. The task of tracing the products and perils of these kinds of movements, in and across a diversity of spaces and through the distinct perspectives of a variety of texts, is the work of this book. We'll visit some unexpected places.

PART I

Cultures of Black Agriculture

CHAPTER ONE

"The True Reconstruction of the Country" in *Iola Leroy* and the Plantation Poems of Paul Laurence Dunbar

Of all the public appearances and celebrity encounters recorded in Booker T. Washington's *Up from Slavery*, the most suggestive may be a benefit staged at Boston's Hollis Street Theater in early 1899. According to the text, Washington made an address, W. E. B. Du Bois read an early version of *The Souls of Black Folk*'s profile of Alexander Crummell, and Paul Laurence Dunbar recited four poems (123). The occasion for the meeting was to pay tribute to the Tuskegee Institute, symbol of both Washington's educational philosophy and the system of labor that would soon emerge as a major point of contention with Du Bois. While none of the poems Dunbar read that afternoon ("When Malindy Sings," "The Party," "When de Co'n Pone's Hot," "An Antebellum Sermon") directly reference Tuskegee or Washington—he debuted the explicit tribute, "To Booker T. Washington," a year later, at the Denver Ministers' Alliance—they are all celebrations and expressions of African American achievement and the function of double-voiced discourse.[1] Most salient to my purposes are the opening lines of "When de Co'n Pone's Hot":

> Dey is times in life when Nature
> > Seems to slip a cog an' go,
> Jes' a-rattlin' down creation,
> > Lak an ocean's overflow (57)

The occasion for such disorder ("When yo' mammy says de blessin' / An' de co'n pone's hot") is perhaps less important than the poem's readiness to imagine a condition wherein "Nature," reverently capitalized despite the otherwise nonstandard dialect, "Seems to slip a cog," to unfix and disastrously liquefy, throwing all expectations for the exterior world out of joint. Dunbar's keen sense of the untenable order of putatively elemental things—"Nature" but also history, culture, language, and race—allows him to triangulate the Washington–Du Bois continuum through the interpretive tools of imaginative literature. This is especially true of Dunbar's work that asserts forms of black agropolitics, a category emphasizing the emancipatory potential of agriculture and one that exists in concert with strains of black populism exemplified in this period by organizations like the Colored Farmers' National Alliance and Cooperative Union and the Colored Agricultural Wheel.²

Questions about what black labor—agricultural labor in particular—could mean for African Americans in the new century were of high priority to many of the period's most prominent black thinkers and artists, among them the subjects of *The Whole Machinery*'s first two chapters: Paul Laurence Dunbar and Frances E. W. Harper in the first case, and Booker T. Washington and W. E. B. Du Bois in the second. Specifically, in this chapter I augment the familiar combination of Du Bois–Washington with a less common pairing: Dunbar's poems of the plantation and farm (mostly published in the 1890s) and Harper's *Iola Leroy, or Shadows Uplifted* (1892). Taken together, these texts set the stage for the "debate" that played out between the Washingtonian and Du Boisian positions, a conflict predicated on the unavoidable interdependence of land and labor in black America at the turn of the twentieth century. Consequently, over the course of this two-chapter sequence, images of the organic (soil, plant matter) replace the mechanical, and "slow" technologies such as the mule-drawn plow supplant the speedy as tokens of the modern, a move that draws out agropolitical potential for economic and cultural self-determination. Rather than revisit the dispute staged by Washington's *Up from Slavery* and Du Bois's *Souls*, then, I will consider ways in which these various texts demonstrate how political subjecthood develops in combination with plant matter, with the products of agricultural labor in particular. Such a view conveys potentially radical processes of black subject formation wherein the agricultural gives rise to new mergers of epistemic and incarnate selfhood and where the sign "reclamation" achieves a rich polysemy.³

Writing the Agropolitical: Modernism/Modernity and the Georgic

Agriculture remains a common, even overdetermined, presence in southern studies. But what does it have to do with investigations of modernist cultures? Bruno Latour prominently identified "translation" as one of modernity's two signal characteristics: a "set of practices [that] creates mixtures between entirely new types of beings, hybrids of nature and culture."⁴ Latour's "work of translation" is always in unresolved competition with his other definitional property of modernity: the "work of purification," which insists upon the reality of "two entirely distinct ontological zones: that of human beings on the one hand; that of nonhumans on the other."⁵ Because these contending commitments have never been successfully integrated, Latour can claim, as his study's title has it, that "we have never been modern." I'm less interested here in affirming Latour's conclusion than I am in tracing the lineaments of his categories—particularly as they relate to the kinds of agriculture that prevailed in the late nineteenth and twentieth centuries and that necessarily abide in the interstices of nature and culture. Is it possible, under Latour's model, that the tension born of modernity's irreconcilable parts could be fundamental to modern(ist) thought and expression? If so, agriculture would seem to offer an ideal venue for the interpretation and representation of such tensions.

It's obvious enough that "nature" has often functioned as a filter through which Euro-American thinkers and artists have viewed and, in doing so, composed their most idealized versions of themselves and their surroundings. The work of dismantling and problematizing such concepts has preoccupied ecocritics of every stripe. Yet nature has not been fully absolved of its place as an essential component in a series of biotic relations that can yield both the needful ingredients of human subsistence (e.g., food, clothing) and the surplus values associated with the bourgeois epoch. We have never been fully free from nature. In turn, there's good reason that the signs "agricultural" and "revolution" have been repeatedly paired at historical inflection points: the political ramifications of the agricultural remain inescapable. Hence the rhetorical resonance but practical impossibility of Fredric Jameson's famous description of the "process of modernization" as one that narrows toward the permanent "disappear[ance] of nature."[6] In a Jamesonian turn, the validity of this claim depends on how one historicizes the concept "nature," since agriculture—even at its most industrialized, rationalized, and abstract—remains impossible without the marshaling of some other-than-human—read: *natural*—resources. If the presence of southern cash crops (rice, tobacco, and, most especially, cotton) on the global market placed the region on the advance guard of capitalist modernity, then the literary significance of the forms of production that yielded them remains worthy of analysis. The stakes matter because these are the terms of our shared materiality—places where human and nonhuman stage fateful collaborations, molded by forces of modernization and providing, in Latour's thinking, a matrix for modernity writ large. I contend that cultural products which narrate and comment on the agricultural operate in the theater of what Jedediah Purdy has recently called "environmental thought," a classification containing "reminders that democracy is not just the stripping away of old hierarchies; it means making the world together, including taking responsibility for our mutually shaping interaction with nature."[7]

With this in mind, I want to suggest that the georgic provides a conceptual vocabulary for assessing how the objects and actors I study in this section interacted with the kinds of "modern commitments" Purdy mentions. More specifically, to flesh out these agropolitical visions, I contend that African American writers of the "nadir"—shorthand for that low point when lynching and other acts of race-based terrorism occurred with the greatest frequency—reframed cultures of black agriculture by using the georgic as a modern mode.[8] According to Lawrence Buell, any discussion that considers "an ethos of rurality or nature or wilderness over against an ethos of metropolitanism" tends toward the pastoral.[9] Yet, as many critics have long argued, the pastoral's reliance on bucolic, idealized landscapes obscures hard realities of both scarcity and labor shaping cultures of agriculture.[10] Better suited to my task is the georgic, which runs in the opposite direction. Jeffrey McCarthy has recently explored this terrain as it relates to modernist studies, maintaining that the "georgic can help interpret modernism where pastoral falls short ... offer[ing] a tradition of social protest where pastoral's story is one of aristocratic cooptation."[11] The essence of the classical georgic is perhaps best provided by an oft-cited passage from Virgil's *Georgics* of the first century of the common era: "Toil subdued the earth / Relentless toil, and the prick of dearth in hardship" (1.145–46). Expanding upon this emphasis on labor and pain, translator Kimberly Johnson considers the *Georgics*' role as an agricultural manual, noting that it "emphasizes variegation and experimentation ... promoting ambiguity and uncertainty in place of didactic conviction."[12] Unlike the pastoral, which most often presents an agricultural tableau scrubbed of signs of human exertion, the georgic foregrounds work, striking an ambivalent balance between the knowledge and power that labor imparts and the physical and mental tolls that it exacts.[13]

For Raymond Williams, the tensions inherent in the "Virgilian pastoral" are pitched "between the pleasures of rural settlement and the threat of loss and eviction."[14] Another word for this complex of responses is, of course, "georgic," as the reference to Virgil underscores. Williams further notes the occasional drift into an "idealising tone" in regard to nature's beneficence, recognizing it most strongly in the "idyllic" anticipation of "the future: of a restoration, a second coming, of the golden age; one that is even politically imminent."[15] The possibilities of eviction and the unpredictable realities of other-than-human forces rest, uneasily at times, alongside the hope for a future wherein the basic logic of farming is cashed out as the rights of citizenship—that seeds and soil, time and toil, might produce something politically usable. While it's true that, say, the Nashville Agrarians might be said to have veered toward the georgic in their emphasis on a restoration of (imagined) worlds lost to industrialization, the crucial difference is that the golden age of the black georgic must be invented along different ideological axes, with an alternate set of images and associations. For African Americans in the post-Reconstruction/pre-Migration South, agriculture and its potentially traumatic associations with both plantation past and present can neither be ignored nor straightforwardly embraced, and the writers I discuss in this section evince a georgic ethos not of restoration but of imaginative *reclamation*.

Margaret Ronda's important investigation into Dunbar's poems argues that the conventions of the georgic best capture images of post-Reconstruction plantation life. In Dunbar's georgics, according to Ronda, agricultural labor inevitably appears as "a struggle that necessarily ends in disappointed failure."[16] While I share Ronda's contention that the frustrations and disparities of the nadir make the georgic an ideal optic for viewing black rural writing in the period, this chapter aims to amplify and develop Ronda's analysis by examining the modality's wider expressive contours: it considers the georgic's philosophical disposition as one in which pessimism is tempered by optimism, charting georgic appearances in texts that span an ideological spectrum. I'm not claiming, as Sarah Wagner-McCoy does in her marvelously fine-grained reading of Chesnutt's invocations of Virgil's *Eclogues* and *Georgics*, that any of the writers covered in this section were openly alluding to Virgil but that they were operating within an avenue of expression wherein "loss is the central experience of those who work the land."[17] Classicist Christine Perkell established the pattern for such readings: "As life has joy and grief, so [the *Georgics*] reflects the real tensions of most human experience."[18] Following Perkell, I theorize a distinctly black georgic that simultaneously captures the burdens, benefits, and contradictions of African American life on the land during the nadir.

In such writing, the plantation is deconstructed and reconstructed, evacuated and reoccupied; it is remembered, repudiated, sublimated, and ironized, often all in the same text. And it becomes not just a locus for the production of commodity crops that have propelled capitalist modernity but also an imaginative matrix for black modernism. The representations of southern agricultural spaces in Dunbar and Harper reflect, in short, a postplantation poetics of reclamation that simultaneously narrates and overruns the constricting pressures of "nature" and of "history" on slavery's former territories in the modernist period. Throughout this chapter, I also analyze how attempts to understand expressions of black agropolitics arise from multiple historical and material tensions, forces that make comprehensible the ecocritical, even posthumanist, resonances found in the depictions of rural landscapes and black bodies of Dunbar and Harper. None of this is without complications, however. Why, to draw on a phrase of Wendell Berry's, is it so difficult to imagine a continuous harmony for black agricultural subjects? Or, to put it another way, why do contemporary discourses of the posthuman and the biopolitical rest so uneasily alongside this chapter's figures of post-Reconstruction rural blackness on the land? While moves toward the posthuman have frequently touted the liberatory possibilities of conceptually uniting abstract bodies with the landscape or with effacing differences between abstract humans and abstract animals, this is much less simply done when considering bodies historically coded black, bodies that centuries of racist thought and action have vigorously separated out as incompletely human. Zakiyyah Iman Jackson, for one, is rightly cautious that "appeals to move 'beyond the human' may actually reintroduce the Eurocentric transcendentalism this movement purports to disrupt."[19] Surveying the influence of Agamben and Foucault, Alexander Weheliye makes a similar point: "Bare life and biopolitics discourse not only misconstrues how profoundly race and racism shape the modern idea of the human, it also overlooks or perfunctorily writes off theorizations of race, subjection, and humanity found in black and ethnic studies."[20] Flesh, these thinkers remind us, is not a universally neutral value.

I make the case below that the master image of agricultural labor in these texts from Dunbar and Harper, Washington and Du Bois, allows a broad rethinking of the relations of body and land that form the substrate of both slavery and tenancy, that they help demonstrate how in the post-Reconstruction New South a connection with the land makes possible claims not just on citizenship but on new forms of subjecthood itself. Thinking about *Iola Leroy* and Dunbar's poems through the conceptual language of the georgic, with its emphasis, as Johnson explained, on "ambiguity and uncertainty," provides a more bracing view of the possibilities of the black agricultural. In these texts, the black georgic promotes imaginative spaces where subjecthood and nationhood are inscribed on the ground itself, where people in their physical environments create another meaning and encounter history afresh, directing an ontologically modern reflex toward the rural landscape. If, as Benjamin rightly noticed, the Paris Arcades yielded particular forms and expressions of modern *European* consciousness in the nineteenth century, it's essential to explore legacies of modern *African American* consciousness that were forged in and through New World plantation spaces, to hear the reverberations produced at these junctures of creolization and to consider the new modes of being they engendered.

"Plant of Freedom Upward Sprung": Paul Laurence Dunbar's Plantation

For Dunbar, conclusions about how the land signifies and what black agricultural labor can mean never settle onto a single track. And whereas both Du Bois and Washington have received prominent, though contested, attention for their role as modernists, critics often classify Dunbar as a residual figure from the premodern tradition of dialect poetry. Geoffrey Jacques, for one, recognizes Dunbar as "an important modernizer of American lyric language," but he stops short of classifying the poet as a modernist.[21] James Smethurst's recent thinking about Dunbar highlights the modernist resonances of the poet's output, yet he is, by his own admission, pushing back against a sense that "Dunbar and his work have been generally very poorly treated by scholarship"—which is another way of saying that he has been tied to aesthetic practices perceived as less than modern and perhaps less than serious.[22] I take cues, however, from Susan Stanford Friedman's generous definition of modernism as "the loosely affiliated movements and individuals in the arts and literature that reflect and contribute to the conditions and consciousness of modernity."[23] Under this logic, it's hard to deny that Dunbar's work and his open "affiliations" with Du Bois and Washington both "reflect and contribute" to the conditions of African American modernity—the complex of experiences, ideas, and material products created by black subjects in the rapidly industrializing, postslavery United States. Friedman's model productively corresponds with the "alternative modernities" proposed by Dilip Gaonkar wherein "modernity is incomplete and necessarily so"; it makes it possible to draw together modernity as a sociological classification and modernism as an aesthetic one to examine different combinations of categories.[24]

Counterintuitively, it's possible to recognize Dunbar's modernist impulses in his attention to rurality. Assessing the poet's legacy in a 1907 lecture, future New Negro impresario Alain Locke noted his ability to make a "contribution . . . to English literature" by way of the "crude thoughts of a negro farm."[25] Locke's diction reveals something about how he processed Dunbar's achievements: the poet channeled not just the human voice of the black farmer but of a more broadly construed network of "negro" human/nonhuman objects and subjects—the farm itself. In this appreciation for the earthbound and the rural, Locke biographer Jeffrey Stewart detects the influence of Irish modernists such as Yeats—Locke had "no doubt" studied Yeats and his compatriots during his Harvard years—who felt that the Irish people "needed imaginative literature, not sociological or political treatises, to incite them to dream a new future for themselves."[26] As Locke himself wrote, "Harlem has the same role to play for the New Negro as Dublin has had for the New Ireland."[27] And Locke wouldn't be the last black intellectual to look—against expectation, perhaps, given the often troubled relations between Irish Americans and African Americans in the nineteenth and twentieth centuries—to the Irish writers of the modernist era for precedents in handling the formation of a national literature positioned away from the dominant identity of the nation-state, one that attempted to get in front of history by appealing to folk, even mythic, motifs. In the preface to his monumental anthology, *The Book of American Negro Poetry* (1922)—a collection that leads with Dunbar—James Weldon Johnson appeals to John Millington Synge and his work on rural Irish peasants: "What the colored poet in the United States needs to do is something like what Synge did for the Irish; he needs to find a form that will express the racial spirit by symbols from within rather than by symbols from without."[28]

I don't bring any of this up to submit Dunbar to an is-he-or-isn't-he litmus test but to acknowledge that even if the poet didn't scale the formal heights of the high modernists, his sensibility was so thoroughly trained by the conditions of late nineteenth-century modernity that he can be comfortably—and usefully—approached through discourses of modernism. Dunbar's discursive flexibility allows him to try out different voices, to wear not just *the* mask but a bold assortment of masks: the slave, the former slave, the nostalgic old man, and the versifying Romantic among them. A version of Keatsian negative capability, this stance creates opportunities to inhabit other subjectivities, other historical indices, and other historical possibilities "without any irritable reaching after fact and reason."[29] While it's a move that complicates the project of sorting out readers' expectations about where the values and loyalties of an ex-slave should lie, in some larger sense, the ambiguity is the point. Yet as scholars and theorists of the period consistently remind us, this sort of ambivalence—the sense of a self in irrevocable conflict with itself, with its own community and history—is a hallmark of both modernist and, as Kimberly Johnson posits, georgic expression.

Dunbar's poems of black agriculture, however, most frequently address the challenges of modernity through the materials of the past, one saturated by memories of the plantation. While critics have often puzzled at the atmosphere of nostalgia that permeates much of Dunbar's work, we might also read these representations as a means of reshaping trauma and asserting a level of imaginative ownership over the plantation spaces themselves—to "brush history against the grain," as Benjamin proposes.[30] In his pioneering study of memory and the Civil War, David Blight forwards a collection of black "attitudes" toward the age of slavery and the Civil War that include "the slave past as a dark void," "a celebratory-accommodationist mode of memory," "an African American patriotic memory," and "a tragic vision of the war" as the fiery force that cleared the ground for a more perfect union.[31] Dunbar's poetic evocations of the plantation, which willfully mingle fact and imagination, have no easily identifiable place in Blight's model. Closer to the bone, perhaps, is another celebrated passage from Benjamin: "To articulate the past historically does not mean to recognize it 'the way it really was.' It means to seize hold of a memory as it flashes up at a moment of danger."[32] The reconstructed plantation of Dunbar's poems conceives both the space's historical significance and its meanings in the poet's own moment of great "danger"—the nadir of American race relations. Pointedly, the past is rearticulated through representations of the plantation itself as a zone of black appropriation. A site of contended meanings and histories, it becomes a poetic evocation of what Washington was aiming for with Tuskegee: the transformation—indeed, the reclamation—of the plantation space into an alternate "institute" and an alternate institution. If, as Marxist tradition is quick to remind us, working the land grants one greater claim to ownership than inheritance or legal deed, then all these nostalgic former slaves might be staking out a place in the social imaginary, unwriting plantation history by centralizing the labor of African Americans as a legitimate, if legally nonbinding, deed.

Accordingly, Dunbar provides a rubric for remembering that identifies the undeniable relationships among southern soil, slavery, and freedom, effectively asking the questions: When a formerly enslaved person weeps because his or her ex-master's plantation is in ruins, can they reset their position in the historical narrative? What's the practical effect of conjuring up a differently signifying version of memory? It's tempting to dismiss these moves as blanching optimism or outright erasures, but they might also work a degree of parity into a sharply unbalanced arrangement of power. And, appearing within the vicinity of what George Handley identifies as the New World's "poetics of oblivion," we sense Dunbar's acknowledgment that, when representing traumatic histories, "language of necessity fails." This is not, to Handley's mind, "cause for lamentation but rather an opportunity to pay homage to those histories that can never be summed up."[33] I suggest that the poems also offer the empty plantation as a *geography of oblivion*, a site in which the silences of the historical record generate additional, less oppressive meanings.

One of Dunbar's most evocative poems, "The Haunted Oak" (1903), grimly indexes the geography of oblivion. Lapsing into prosopopoeia to dramatize dialogue between a tree that has recently served as the site of a lynching and a credulous observer, the poem makes the tree itself a victim of the horror: "why, when I go through the shade you throw, / Runs a shudder over me?" the passerby asks. The tree answers by relating its distinct sensory reaction to the violent event: it "*saw* ... [a] guiltless victim's pains" and it "*hear[d]* his sigh" (emphasis mine). And although time has passed, the lingering corporeality of the lynching victim continually inscribes the tree's "body" in the present tense:

> I feel the rope against my bark,
>> And the weight of him in my grain,
> I feel in the throe of his final woe
>> The touch of my own last pain. (220)

The victim's torture and his death are both shared by the tree in a remonstrance of mob violence that solidifies a bond, forged through suffering, between a black body and a fatally damaged plant. A spectral body killed by the "curse of a guiltless man" (220) who had been held on rape charges ("the old, old crime" [219]), the tree is obligated to bear his weight forever as it watches the prominent citizens who carried out the deed enjoy their freedom — the judge and the doctor, the minister and his son. The tree is dead; it still speaks. By denying the silencing techniques of lynching, the poem becomes a countermonument to the crimes of the (neo-)Confederacy at the very moment that lost cause memorials were proliferating. In Dunbar's ironic poetic economy, it falls on the tree—an object without language—to voice ghostly witness to murder because, unlike black subjects in the period, its testimony to the terrors of white violence doesn't carry the threat of retaliation. The tree must speak in this poem because the human victims cannot. A supernatural blend of human and plant matter, and hence a scrambling of common separations of object and subject, becomes the most appropriate register through which to apprehend the fantastic brutality of Jim Crow.[34]

"The Haunted Oak" also functions as an essay on concepts of ownership that prevailed in plantation slavery and throughout its repetitions in post-Reconstruction tenancy: the slaveholder/planter presumes violent control of the enslaved/tenant body, the labor of the enslaved/tenant, and the landscapes they inhabit. This concatenation of body-labor-land rests at the center of "The Haunted Oak," as the poem figures the collapsing distance between black bodies and the nonhuman world. In asking questions about what and how exactly the slaveholder/planter owns, the poem answers by pressuring the triad of body-labor-landscape, allowing the land—synecdochally present in the tree—a chance to announce resistance in a startling voice. It imagines a legible archive for the nonhuman just as it achieves something like cross-species communication. Dunbar's human subject isn't simply dissolved into "nature" to achieve new levels of (decidedly human) perception (i.e., the transparent eyeball that presides over Eurocentric American Romanticism): his powers of perception are extinguished along with his life in a burst of violence that imparts human forms of expression on the nonhuman. Plant and person combine in a jarring comment on the mutual exploitation of southern landscape and black body.

Ultimately for Dunbar, the land acts as a cipher through which the contradictions of historical memory are processed. On one hand, it's obvious that African American labor—both during and after slavery—is worthy of recognition:

> Upon thy brow the cross was laid,
> And labour's painful sweat-beads made
> A consecrating chrism ("Ode to Ethiopia" 15–16)

On the other hand, to confront the link between southern soil and black bodies is to engage legacies of violence, coercion, and dissociation. For all his optimism about agricultural labor, then, Dunbar's poems of soil, dirt, and clay approach the subject with an impulse that prefigures Du Boisian twoness. "To the South—On Its New Slavery," a meditation on debt slavery and the convict-lease system, draws the "cold unam'rous sod" and flirts with the image of the black rapist ("Our fathers left to till th' reluctant field, / To rape the soil for what she would not yield" [217]) to make a statement about the deleterious effects of a perversion of agriculture on both the land and its workers.³⁵ The ground can be forced to produce, through violence, but the long-term consequences of these actions cannot be contained. To rape the land, in other words, is to betray its bid for futurity, and the new slavery of the poem's title finds multiple applications, referring at once to human bodies driven to labor and to the ground itself, the "groaning land." The attribution of this combination of tropes—reluctance, rape, verbal protest—to the soil grants the natural world a measure of sentience generally reserved for the human: "its" new slavery becomes the one that the South practices and that is practiced *upon* it—another striking reorientation of familiar positions of subject and object. Still, tellingly, nonhuman subjectivity is meted out through victimization: as in "The Haunted Oak," the natural landscape in these poems is never so alive as when it's being abused or when it is absorbing the abuse of others.

Similarly, Dunbar's Civil War rumination "The Colored Soldiers" presents the ground as a venue for uncanny racial mixture in which the black speaker indicates to his white listener the precise spot where "their blood with yours commingling / Has enriched the Southern soil" (51). To the elaborate social and legal boundaries established by paranoia about racial mixing in the white South—to the specters of "miscegenation" and the "one-drop rule" that animated the lost cause—the poem offers the ultimate retort: the war itself produced these biracial sites of eternal rest, battlefields that forever enshrine the impossibility of "pure" blood.

> There is no holier spot of ground
> Than where defeated valor lies,
> By mourning beauty crowned.³⁶

So wrote Henry Timrod in "Ode," an elegy sung during the 1867 decorating of Confederate graves at the Magnolia Cemetery in Charleston, South Carolina. The holiness isn't entirely effaced in Dunbar's poem; it is reimagined as biological regeneration, as the miracle of the soil. "The Colored Soldiers" thus concretizes a paradoxical relationship between dirt's reproductive properties and its burial function—its ability to assimilate life's material remainders and to create new life—by linking these to the combination of hope and hopelessness that marks postbellum black lives. In refutation of what is perhaps Timrod's most famous work ("Ethnogenesis" [1861]), "The Colored Soldiers" calls up a post-Reconstruction "ethnogenesis," the birth of a new nation that denies the supremacy of whiteness by using unexpected material remainders of black bodies (blood) to claim old landscapes and to re-present ontologies of humanness that recognize the mutual constitution of organic matter.

Blood and soil mix freely in Dunbar's imagination. In what is perhaps his most open evocation of the classical georgic, blood feeds the very ground that yields the region's agricultural wealth. Virgil's *Georgics* presented itself as a poetic agricultural manual, but arriving after the fifteen years of Roman civil war that followed the assassination of Julius Caesar and at the dawn of a new empire led by Octavian, it also acts as a meditation on the effects of war and the failures of the republic; it is a "reconstruction" document of a different era. In one of its most celebrated passages, the poet observes a powerful storm and recalls the tumult of war, as "Roman troops / clash[ed] sword with fellow sword among themselves" (1.489). But still he casts hopefully toward the future:

> Surely time will come when in those fields
> the farmer drudging soil with his curved plough
> will turn up scabrous spears corroded by rust
> or with his heavy hoe strike empty helmets
> and gape at massive bones in upturned graves. (1.493–97)

Artifacts of violence run in sedimentary layers throughout the ground upon which a new world will be constructed: material remains and implements of war striate Virgil's soil. In Dunbar's poem, it's permanently stained by blood. Just as Virgil looked to agriculture and the signifying potential of the natural world in his post–civil war moment, so did Dunbar; just as Virgil's poem signals uncertainty by using the soil to model what Richard Slotkin famously called "regeneration through violence," so does Dunbar's.[37]

For all this uneasiness about the soil, however, in 1902's "Tuskegee Song" the land signs benevolently, bending back toward its black workers: "The fields smile to greet us," the poet explains in an unabashed endorsement of Washington's agricultural project.[38] At the same time that it presents progress's movement "onward and upward," it also recognizes Tuskegee's efforts to strike a balance whereby labor displays the "worth of our minds *and* our hands" (333, emphasis mine). Coming a year after *The Souls of Black Folk*'s iconoclastic take on Washington and Tuskegee, "Tuskegee Song" rejects the either/or logic that so frequently codes Washington as southern black body, Du Bois as northern black mind. More broadly, Dunbar's poetry argues that progress may well be configured as "upward" movement, but it also depends on the reoccupation—and possible usurpation—of narratives that lump the South, rurality, and the plantation together in subordinate positions.

Dunbar treats this impulse toward reoccupation in several poems that display an unsettled strain of southern homesickness. I'll focus on two: "The Deserted Plantation" (1895) and "To the Eastern Shore" (1903), each of which finds the locus of African American life in the rural South, and each of which seeks to remediate popular representations of plantation culture. For instance, while conceding the mixed quality of Dunbar's work, Henry Louis Gates Jr. celebrates the rhetorical nimbleness with which the poet "[s]ignified upon the received white racist textual tradition and posited in its stead a black poetic diction."³⁹ This racist textual tradition, of course, includes minstrelsy. Take Stephen Foster's ubiquitous "My Old Kentucky Home, Good-Night!" (1853): with crudely drawn racialisms and a heavy dose of Victorian sentimentalism, Foster's lyric mourned the absence of a plantation's black workers—their actions, their bodies, their voices.⁴⁰

> They hunt no more for the possum and the coon
> On meadow, the hill and the shore,
> They sing no more by the glimmer of the moon,
> On the bench by the old cabin door.⁴¹

Although in an early iteration ("Poor Uncle Tom, Good-Night!") the song functioned as a response to *Uncle Tom's Cabin* that dramatized Tom being sold away from the Shelby plantation, "Old Kentucky Home" never reveals the exact source of the absence. It's easy to presume that the speaker refers to separations caused by the slave trade ("The time has come when the darkies have to part / Then my old Kentucky home, good-night!"), but that doesn't do much to explain why an entire antebellum plantation seems emptied of its slaves. The absent referent in "Old Kentucky Home" is not the laboring black bodies but the cause of their absence. Eric Lott, discussing the function of Foster's plantation songs on the minstrel stage, has suggested that their persistent interest in the separations, deaths, and disappearances of the enslaved "supervised the elimination of black characters" to such an extent that "what was being symbolically eliminated and put to rest was the whole lamented business of slavery in the United States, by means of the elimination of black people themselves."⁴² The plantation idyll is more than disrupted; it is vanished, along with the peculiar institution and the people whose enslavement provided its peculiarity. In other words, the vagaries of the plantation past—which was emphatically *not* past in Foster's 1853—are not so much enshrined as they are absorbed in melancholy's numbing embrace. The song promotes a fixed and carefully staged peek at the past that consciously elides the trauma of the present.

At the center of Margaret Ronda's analysis of Dunbar's georgics is an illuminating reading of "The Deserted Plantation," a piece she calls "the most controversial poem of Dunbar's oeuvre." While Ronda convincingly argues that the text's participation in the georgic mode consists in a "diagnostic frame" that is "ultimately tragic rather than accommodationist or subversive," it's also possible to recognize, through its depictions of a plantation in decline, a series of rhetorical strategies that directly confront—and overturn—the pastoral conventions of minstrelsy's plantation melodies.⁴³ Indeed, the poem consciously reverses the tropes of the minstrel ballad so thoroughly that, I argue, it becomes a kind of modernist plantation countermelody, deliberately unstitching the seams that give the genre its distinctive shape.

Heard in this key, the sweet melodies of Dunbar's turn-of-the-century songs of the South take on a different tonality: ironic, earthy, and doubled; this is a music that one senses through its extramusical *absence* in the text rather than through the presence of sound. In its broadest dimensions, "The Deserted Plantation" is fundamentally formed by, and becomes a meditation on, (un)musical representations of slavery and its aftermaths. And we might recognize the silence that permeates "The Deserted Plantation" as a sign of its georgic commitments, for as Juan Christian Pellicer forcefully claims, "There is no such thing as georgic song."[44] In stony contrast to the pastoral's cheery music, the georgic refuses to sing.

While Foster's "Old Kentucky Home" introduces a scene in which the "corn top's ripe and the meadow's in the bloom," where "the birds make music all the day," Dunbar's "The Deserted Plantation" reverses the scenario—all in the kind of dialect that provides minstrelsy its common currency: "In de furrers whah de co'n was allus wavin', / Now de weeds is growin' green an' rank an' tall"—and untamed plants overrun the verdant expanse of the minstrel plantation. Perhaps the poem's firmest evocation of minstrelsy and its material culture arrives in the appearance of the banjo whose "voice is silent in de qua'ters" (67). A New World adaptation of stringed instruments traditional in Africa, the banjo's link to minstrelsy was solidified by the ascendancy of Dan Emmett's Virginia Minstrels in the mid-nineteenth century, when the instrument became a central element of that group and nearly every troupe that followed.[45] Its sound is conspicuously unheard in "The Deserted Plantation."

At every turn, in fact, the poem's soundscape denies convention, bringing its point of reference directly into the 1890s: "D' ain't a hymn ner co'n-song ringin' in de air" (67). Songs of spiritual consolation and endurance are missing, but so too is the "coon song," a genre that infiltrated the American mainstream in the early 1880s and retained popularity through the first decade of the twentieth century. Composed by some of Tin Pan Alley's most celebrated songwriters—including a young Irving Berlin—the idiom drew heavily on racist caricature: watermelons and chickens, razors, dice, and whiskey all circulate widely through a still-vibrant plantation world. Why, then, does the speaker reference a genre that consciously performs anachronism if not to empty out its conventions in the contemporary moment? Here is a picture of the plantation that denies the representational authority of the coon song— it doesn't, it can't, exist on the grounds of the deserted plantation. If coon songs emasculate and humiliate in order to intimidate and coerce black citizens, then the speaker makes clear that their sound simply doesn't carry in Dunbar's post-Reconstruction imagination.

The loudest sound on the plantation, in fact, is the silence of emptiness and decay: the hoe "a-rustin' in de co'nah," the plow "a-tumblin' down in de fiel'" (67). Curiously here, the participial construction of the verbs, particularly in the image of the plow ("a-tumblin'"), freezes the process of decomposition, creating a scene in which the disintegration of the plantation happens—and continues to happen—in an unbroken series of present-tense repetitions. The vision of black agropolitics worked out in "The Deserted Plantation" is perhaps less about vaunting the redemption of agricultural labor than imagining the phenomenological possibility of claiming lands formerly possessed by slaveholders through an agropoetics of waste and decay. The central conceit of "Old Kentucky Home" is that the plantation's slaves are, mysteriously, no longer present. But Dunbar's decision to revive, and revise, that scenario in a post-Emancipation context offers a peculiar instance in which the sole human inhabitant of the decaying plantation space is a (former) slave. Where the plantation of Foster's imagination was oddly drained of blackness, Dunbar's lacks any defined trace of white influence or coercion to labor. So much so, in fact, that the narrator redirects his attention and loyalty to "de othah Mastah"—God, whose presence here is more apprehensible than that of the old plantation master (68).

Two years before he arrived at its conceptual counterpart, "The Deserted Plantation," and forty years after "Old Kentucky Home" first appeared, Dunbar published "Goin' Back" (1893), a poem that explicitly signifies on Foster's work by reimagining the overwrought picture of a fecund southland with "bluegrass medders an' fiel's o' co'n" through the prism of a past trained on emancipation. Distilling the plantation's legacies in the history of a single ex-slave, it draws on the wide vein of melancholy produced in Foster's song at the same time that it relocates its sources and tensions, effectively undoing the vague yearning of minstrelsy's environments. Dunbar writes the black subjects back into the scenario, picking up the story from their position by imagining an old man reminiscing on his time at a plantation while "standing beside the station rail" of a major city, preparing to board a train that will take him "Back to my ol' Kaintucky home, / Back to the ol' Kaintucky sights" (317). He has been in the city for thirty years, having presumably fled the South after Emancipation ("I caught the fever that ruled the day"), and although he admits that "[t]har was lots of things in the North to admire," the poem magnifies its speaker's doubleness, providing an extended rumination on the joys of his plantation youth and the drawbacks of city life:

> They said that things were better North,
> An' a man was held at his honest worth.
> Well, it may be so, but I have some doubt,
> An' thirty years ain't wiped it out. (317)

The poem also offers a glimpse into the moment just before the empty plantation of Foster's imagination, with its weeping mothers, hard times, and empty cabin doors, is about to be reanimated by an emancipated slave. But then, unlike "The Deserted Plantation," it pulls away. Deferring the triumph of an actual reoccupation, "Goin' Back" maps the geography of oblivion onto the old plantation, just as it implicates the North in both the suffering of ex-slaves and in the cruel discursive practices of the minstrel stage. By using dialect to reclaim Foster's famed chorus as "My ol' Kaintucky home," the poem underscores Dunbar's larger project of showing that poetic ownership of these spaces belongs to the black southerners who endured slavery and benefited by emancipation, and to those whose labor ushered the modern world into its current form. Silences and hauntings, anthropomorphized trees and blood-fed plots of soil, a ground that coughs up voices: for Dunbar these openings expose the range of experiences—the overlapping planes of the psychic and the physical—that embody rural black lives in the nadir, sculpting the possibilities of post-Reconstruction being and its claims on history.

Visiting the Settlement: Frances E. W. Harper's Garden

Most attempts to configure cultures of black agriculture during the nadir have focused on the experience and thinking of black men. There are practical explanations for this imbalance: farming is often represented as a mostly masculine affair, and African American women's writing from the period is, in general, more interested in models of ascendancy *up from*, rather than *down* or *back to*, the farm. The significance of Harper's *Iola Leroy*—published in 1892, a full decade before Du Bois publicly responded to Washington—is apparent not just in its status as one of the earliest novels by an African American woman but also in its varied representations of black womanhood in the postbellum period. These representations include crucial encounters with the agricultural. And so *Iola Leroy*'s depictions of black women's ties to the land and farming make it possible to begin untangling the role that rural spaces and identities play in Harper's imagined solutions for the future of her race, her gender, and a burgeoning black middle class. While the novel's conclusions on the meanings of African American rurality are often inconsistent, Harper recognizes that modern black citizenship in the United States must address the stubborn significance of agricultural labor.

Iola Leroy details the title character's attempts to redeem the injustices of slavery through the restoration of a family fractured by war, violent taxonomies of race, and both spatial and psychological dislocation. A young mixed-race woman, Iola begins her life as a privileged member of a Mississippi plantation household. But when her white father unexpectedly dies of yellow fever, she is snatched into slavery. Although Iola regains her freedom in the post-Emancipation North, she refuses to pass as white, declining the relative comforts of marriage to a northern physician in favor of a tortuous quest to search out lost relatives, to reclaim and carefully define her own blackness, and to improve the conditions of her native South and its people. Like so many of her peers in the postbellum United States, Iola's personal reconstruction is bound up in the larger Reconstruction of the region and the nation. In the end, she marries Dr. Latimer, a light-skinned African American who likewise refuses to pass, and moves to North Carolina, accompanied by Harry, her brother, and Robert Johnson, a long-lost uncle, to serve the community as an educator.

Although the geographic scope of the novel is wide, stretching south, north, and then south again, it insists that, oddly enough, the greatest opportunities for educated African Americans like Iola and her family exist within the borders of the former Confederacy. Despite the horrors of the region's recent past as well as its Jim Crow present, the novel argues that prospects for progress are written upon the southern landscape itself, a fact that comes clear in a sharply drawn scene wherein the slave Tom Anderson learns the alphabet by tracing out letters in the bark of his plantation's trees and on the banks of its streams. These images are conveyed secondhand, through a conversation between Robert Johnson and a white army officer in which Robert describes Tom's assiduous attempts at learning. While Robert admires Tom's diligence, he can't recommend his method: "[He] never got very far with his learning" (45), Robert explains. Still, though Tom could scarcely read a book, "[h]e was well versed in the lay of the country" (33). The impasse here points up the text's larger uncertainty about a life on the land in conflict with the uplift narrative's essential commitments to education and literacy. It also offers a less hopeful revision of a famous scene from the ur-text of American racial ascendancy, *Narrative of the Life of Frederick Douglass* (1845). Having learned to read, Douglass comes to understand that further possibilities for securing mobility and freedom arrive through the production of texts: "I wished to learn how to write, as I might have occasion to write my own pass," he relates, mindfully detailing the steps he took to gain literacy. Like Tom, Douglass uses his local environment as a tablet; unlike Tom, however, Douglass's environment is Baltimore, a distinctly urban space: "my copy-book was the board fence, brick wall, and pavement; my pen and ink was a lump of chalk."[46] Reading these accounts across one another, the message may well be that the very texture of rural spaces impedes literacy.

Nevertheless, much like *The Souls of Black Folk* in the following decade, Harper's novel argues that the richest expressions of black culture arise from the remains of slavery and within its territories. There is, it seems, no path forward for black Americans that doesn't lead through the rural South. And so, paradoxically, when Iola speaks of moving up from slavery, her geographic orientation points down. Nevertheless, these interpenetrating movements—between South and North, from the Civil War to the nadir—

create a pattern that agrees with the novel's larger themes of reconciliation and restitution. Considering the novel's explorations of bloodlines and genealogies scrambled by slavery, George Handley notes that its sense of "national unity" is "accomplished through metaphors that forge competing and overlapping imagined communities."[47] And these communities are often delimited through representations of spoken language. To this point, Hollis Robbins makes the case that *Iola Leroy* presents "dialect as a performance of community rather than a marker of difference."[48] Yet the forms of dialect present in the novel are part of an untamed compound of voices, one that encompasses Iola's boarding school–polished English alongside the nonstandard speech of Tom Anderson; it seems specifically designed to use different registers of language to call up something like common purpose. More precisely, when the text's characters change names and speak in slave-specific codes, *Iola Leroy* becomes a novel about the unifying effects of the secret language, a creolized lingua franca designed to create what Robert Johnson forcefully calls "a people" (34). If it's true, as historian Walter Johnson has recently suggested, that "[s]laveholders' control of literacy... provided them with a safe channel for privileged communication: a code," then *Iola Leroy* offers firm examples of an alternate literacy—a code—that binds black bodies through (often surreptitious) defiance.[49] Conversations among the enslaved that use the freshness of butter, eggs, and fish to communicate developments on the battlefront provide one prominent example.[50] In such ways, the novel's linguistic qualities outline the stakes of its elaborate pictures of publics and counterpublics destabilized by war and reconstruction.

The text's most vital statements on the meanings of black agropolitics occur at the edges of the proscenium. Its opening scenes show a wartime meeting of slaves, gathered in a wooded hiding place and considering their next move as a vanguard of Union troops draws near. Most eagerly anticipate making the break to freedom, but Uncle Daniel, an elderly member of the group, declines, choosing to stay behind and tend his master's farm. Although Daniel may appear unduly submissive, his decision to remain on the plantation provides a rare opportunity to work the land at a distance from the constant gaze of white authority, a desire that emphasizes the value of rural districts as sites of strategic inaccessibility. Following Lawrence Levine, we recognize Daniel's choice as a chance to materialize the "necessary space" created by slaves' folk practices as an actual plot of ground.[51] While the novel declines to condemn Daniel's decision, it's of two minds about farming: on one hand, the text's standard-English-speaking characters—Iola, Dr. Latimer, Robert Johnson—have access to middle-class employment options that overturn the idea that the only labor black subjects can sell on the modern free market is agricultural; on the other, the novel performs a series of maneuvers meant to wrest agricultural labor from the stranglehold of white control, as we see in working-class characters such as Uncle Daniel. Though *Iola Leroy* never insists, as Washington will in *Up from Slavery*, that a life in the "country districts" is the surest way to establish a vibrant future, neither does it argue that farming in the South unequivocally earns its reputation for oppression. Its georgic visions are necessarily doubled; its affirmative tendencies at cross-purposes.

More broadly, in fact, the divisions of labor worked out in the text predict Du Bois's later conception of a "talented tenth," albeit one that incorporates age into the equation. And, perhaps understandably, farming seems to miss the cutoff for desirable professions. Tom, one of the novel's rustic black heroes, appears to speak for the text as a whole when he yokes Iola's refinement and her elemental appeal to an aversion to manual labor: "Her han's look ez ef she neber did a day's work in her life," he comments approvingly (41). Likewise at the novel's highly idealized conclusion, Robert Johnson creates an agricultural utopia in which he resembles nothing so much as a wealthy patron to worthy former slaves: "He bought a large plantation ... which he divided into small homesteads, and sold to poor but thrifty laborers, and his heart has been gladdened by their increased prosperity and progress. He has seen the one-roomed cabins change to comfortable cottages, in which cleanliness and order have supplanted the prolific causes of disease and death" (280). The diction here is worth noticing: the novel poses concepts like "comfort," "cleanliness," and "order" over against scare words such as "death" and "disease," all at the site of slavery's most harrowing dispossessions. This is perhaps where Houston A. Baker Jr.'s characterization of the novel as a "mulatto utopia" feels most appropriate:[52] Robert has remade the plantation but upheld its basic architecture, retaining the hard line that separates the "poor ... laborers" from a light-skinned managing class, and framing the whole system with a genteel ethos of racial uplift.

Iola Leroy offers a more radical version of such a scenario, however, in the figure of Aunt Linda. One of the novel's most lively and effusive characters, Linda is part of an aging generation, but she remains marked by a roughly drawn feminism and a pugnacious independence. When Robert and Iola meet up with her, Linda has bought a plot of land on her old plantation from an interloping Jewish investor. (The novel makes conspicuous mention of that fact that the area's long-established white settlers have refused to sell to ex-slaves.) As Robert revisits the site of his former slavery, his erstwhile mistress describes "the great changes" that have occurred in the area, how the prominent plantation owner Mr. Gundover died an ignominious death, and how "a number of colored men have banded together, bought his plantation, and divided it among themselves" (152). Among those *colored men* is Aunt Linda. When Robert and Iola visit this collectivist settlement, they note that "the gloomy silence" of the old plantation grounds has been "broken by the hum of industry," see that "the school-house had taken the place of the slave-pen and auction block," and encounter a formerly desolate landscape renewed by "a garden filled with beautiful flowers, clambering vines, and rustic adornments" (153). Aunt Linda tends the garden.

Although the novel celebrates her newfound freedom and "industry" (a concept that functions as both a material description and as the sign of a valorous, thrifty disposition), it also works hard to underscore Linda's ignorance by animating her with a thick dialect, her illiteracy becoming, in her own rendering, a function of the agricultural life: "sence freedom's com'd I'se bin scratchin' too hard to get a libin' to put my head down to de book" (156). (At one point, Linda's husband, John Salters, admits that the very act of handling a book is enough to put him to sleep—"But wen it comes to gittin' out a stan' ob cotton an' plantin' corn, I'se dere all de time" [173].) Oddly enough, the novel's descriptions of the physical environment Linda inhabits conform, with almost startling exactness, to moonlight-and-magnolia conventions: "The air was soft and balmy. The fields and hedges were redolent with flowers. Not a single cloud obscured the brightness of the moon or the splendor of the stars. The ancient trees were festooned with moss, which hung like graceful draperies" (175). However, if Aunt Linda's words and the world they craft veer uncomfortably close to the regional stereotype, her actions represent the novel's most fully realized attempt to upend the old order, to unwrite the conventions of the plantation romance by allowing an elderly black woman—a former slave, in fact—to assume the responsibilities of a plantation master. The centrality of black land ownership—either collective or individual—is among the narrative's most persistent motifs. As Linda herself claims, in an unsurprising conclusion, "I'd ruther lib on a little piece ob lan' ob my own dan a big piece ob somebody else's" (173).

Although the novel presents formal education and the adoption of middle-class values as a sure path to black elevation in the modern United States, Aunt Linda is just the most prominent of the many characters that exhibit a different cast of knowledge, a competing epistemology that tracks the values of a pointedly rural African American counterpublic. "[H]er fingers had not lost their skill" (164), the novel explains, forwarding a model of skillfulness and productivity that isn't limited to the mind—that is, in fact, contained and given its fullest expression in the black body. In Russ Castronovo's incisive presentation of *Iola Leroy* as "an allegory of citizenship," Aunt Linda's connection to "the folk" and her disconnection from the discriminating ethos and *conversazione* of its light-skinned heroes render her "forever unfit for African American citizenship" in an ex-slave counterpublic guided by notions of "Victorian respectability and professional status."[53] I won't argue with Castronovo's description here. But I do wonder if it's possible to acknowledge that even as the novel privileges the model of uplift embodied—quite literally—in Iola, its vivid descriptions of Linda and her world make visible a related, if distinctly agropolitical, counterpublic—a modern counter-counterpublic, as it were. According to my reading, Linda's role in the narrative is to retain a hold on the importance of physical work, its rootedness in the rural South, and to show how the terrors of slavery and forced labor can be physically, even ecologically, undone, as the "gloomy silence of the woods" that edged Gundover's plantation—presumably a large-scale cotton or corn outfit—gives way to a decidedly more cheerful, ostensibly more biodiverse environment in which flowers and vines abound (153). And so, as in Dunbar's poems, the novel presents an alternate take on who lays claim to the land and its products, and how these slavery-era spaces and practices will appear in the present.

To this point, in one telling scene the once-enslaved Uncle Jack explains, in the third person, the process whereby he alone cleared the land and cultivated the wheat crop on his enslaver's property: "an' den wen it war all done, he hadn't a dollar to buy his ole woman a gown" (136). So he "took"—and sold—a bag of wheat. While seemingly at odds with the novel's polite sense of propriety, transforming a bag of wheat yielded by slave labor into cash cannot register as a crime in *Iola Leroy*'s moral economy. Similarly, in the novel's early war scenes, when a group of slaves speculate on a world without masters, Tom Anderson poses a sharp-edged rhetorical question, "[W]ho plants de cotton and raises all de crops?" Robert Johnson answers with a snippet of verse that succinctly captures the inequities of forced labor's products and their participation in the global market: "They eat the meat and give us the bones, / Eat the cherries and give us the stones" (17). Under slavery's exploitative logic, where there's no such thing as compensation, there's also no such thing as theft.

In a further complication of the novel's balance of racialization and morality, Aunt Linda may well be its secret hero of black female independence, but, in a series of troubling speeches, she also acts as a sieve designed to strain out the less-desirable elements—a group she deliberately, and repeatedly, labels "the niggers." Linda's denunciation of the ex-slave "who will spen' his hard-earned money in dese yere new grog-shops" (160) allows the narrative to land its blows on behalf of temperance from a different, "blacker" angle. She acts, in effect, as a separate screen upon which to project the values of the 1890s reformer. So if the text encases broader uncertainties about New World blackness, its future, and its histories of labor and landscape, it also foregrounds Linda's deep dialect and her undeniable connection to the southern soil as traits that lend a new degree of credibility to the uplift narrative, just as they legitimize a more grounded form of black modernity. While the farm can stand as a source of strength for certain African Americans, it's important to recognize the colorist associations between rurality and darker, seemingly unmixed forms of blackness.[54] On some uncomfortable level, then, *Iola Leroy* threatens to portray the farm as a lightly modified reservation for working-class, darker-skinned African Americans.

If farm labor fails to find unqualified favor in the text, however, it's worth considering how and why exactly *Iola Leroy* insists upon endorsing the rural South as the best way forward. For one thing, the text works hard to map spaces of black liberty back onto the region, unsettling late nineteenth-century schemes of national reconciliation that allowed northern and southern whites to reunite through the mutual suppression of emancipated African Americans. To reclaim the South, as Harper's black characters do, is to destabilize the balance in a national economy of space and power deliberately tilted in its white citizens' favor.

In the novel's final scenes of reconciliation and resettlement, the contours of a modern black georgic arise, presenting the rural South as a series of spaces and economies that allow for independence beyond the pressing weight of white supervision and control—though not necessarily from the restrictions of class control or the vagaries of the natural world. So although Harper's optimism occasionally clashes with contemporary realities of Jim Crow, her novel suggests that there are reasons to believe that rural black southernness offers the most viable options for collective African American autonomy, however provisional it may be. Peter Schmidt, for instance, notices the novel's interest in the "indispensable role a new educational system for blacks must play to prepare [them] to resist the depredations of Jim Crow and build protective communities."[55] In much the same way, *Iola Leroy* claims the region's underdeveloped rural spaces as sites for the fabrication of just such "protective communities." Hazel Carby makes a similar observation: "The overall structure of *Iola Leroy* progressed increasingly toward a complete separation of the black community from the white world and thus implicitly accepted the failure of Reconstruction."[56] To the extent that the machinations of Jim Crow behave as "sovereign" power, however, it's possible to fit *Iola Leroy*'s models of independent production on the rural margins into what Foucault identifies as a tactic for abjuring the sovereign's influence: "if economic practice or economic activity, if the set of processes of production and exchange elude the sovereign geographically, so to speak, ... [they] fix a sort of frontier to the exercise of his power."[57] It's a problem of space, and *Iola Leroy*'s frontier is located, intriguingly, on abandoned plantations; independence doesn't exist in slave labor or in tenancy but, as both Dunbar and Harper demonstrate, in the act overcoming the plantation's traumas. As a result, the space's deep connections to the rise of capitalist modernity are converted into something both politically and aesthetically productive.

To adapt a contemporary phrase, the farther off the grid one ventures, the easier it becomes to elude containment. Edward Ayers's account of the

Atlanta Riot of 1906, for example, holds that one precipitating factor in the conflict was anxiety about the influx of African Americans from the rural districts: "'Bad niggers' were supposedly flowing into Atlanta from the countryside, their past crimes unknown, their proclivities toward vice unchecked."[58] It's conceivable that the impression of country people as dangerously unrestrained was nothing more than a product of Jim Crow hysteria. But it's also possible to read between the lines of Ayers's analysis and see the signs toward which Harper gestures: although the city is commonly figured as the most promising space for post-Emancipation African Americans, it may be easier to picture modern black sovereignty along the rural peripheries than in the cultural centers, where both surveillance and segregation are increasingly enforced. The rural black modern, in other words, doesn't always figure by riding the wave of urbanization; sometimes it pushes back.

At several points in the novel, Harper seems to foretell Washington's decision in *Up from Slavery* to present Tuskegee as both fortress and training ground for Jim Crow–era African Americans. Yet the community Harper envisions centers around the work and virtue of a young, black, and ambitiously middle-class woman. Still, according to the standards of late nineteenth-century femininity, the nature of Iola's womanhood is curiously mixed: she meets expectations in her generosity of spirit, her conspicuous modesty, and her unceasing willingness to submit and serve; those standards, however, contend with an intense loyalty to her race that sends her down the social scale rather than upward toward white gentility. Although the novel strains to synthesize these oppositional elements at its too-tidy conclusion, they refuse, leaving the text with an unresolved sense of duality. Paul Gilroy has argued that in 1903, *The Souls of Black Folk* opened up the "genre of black modernist writing ... [with its] self-consciously polyphonic form."[59] It's possible, however, to look at an earlier work like *Iola Leroy* and hear a slightly different kind of modern music, less self-conscious perhaps, but no less committed to braiding together disparate melodies: dialect and standard English, for instance, as well as distinct modes of discourse such as poetry and public lecture, sermon and debate—all within the body of a single novel that attempts, in Elizabeth Ammons's perceptive reading, "to reach toward a new form."[60] These formal concerns match the psychological dualism that infuses the novel's content, the doubleness cited by Du Bois as the de facto position of the "American Negro."

In James Smethurst's elegant argument, this ontological scenario of the self-divided-against-the-self makes post-Reconstruction African Americans the first true American modernists, and it's a condition that manifests throughout *Iola Leroy*.[61] A good example appears in the episode in which Iola denies the advances of her white northern suitor, Dr. Gresham, by explaining that she has "no home but this in the South." The adjoining sentence complicates this statement: "I am homeless and alone" (60). She has no home but her home in the South, and yet she remains homeless. The contradiction here is symptomatic of the modernist motif of an individual's inability to attain lasting psychic stability: we see the subject ever reaching for but never grasping a permanent sense of belonging and homeland. Still, *Iola Leroy* aims to fill this gap with a distinctly, if differently, romanticized variant of the rural South. Contrary to the unabashedly white-supremacist messages that often shaped the fiction of her contemporaries who treated the region, Harper emphasizes the positive products of black and white intimacy as well as the pleasures and profits of exclusively black communities. Likewise, in its attention to the physical properties of the agricultural South, the novel offers hope for a new century that also recognizes the shadows of slavery; it presents a modernist geography wherein the ground, at least in the experience of its human inhabitants, remains divided against itself.

One way to account for the novel's valorization of the rural South is to view its representations of the region through the matrix of national reconciliation presented by historian Nina Silber. In theorizing a "romance of reunion," Silber proposed that whites of the middle and upper classes—northerners in particular—sought to reestablish national unity through the production of "metaphors and cultural images of reconciliation [that have] less to say about the real-life South and more to say about the ideal and desired South."[62] The difference in Harper's narrative, of course, is that it configures these desires along altogether different nodes, emphasizing instead the reconstitution of ex-slave families and calling for the reoccupation of their ancestral spaces in the New World. This impulse to bind up slavery's familial wounds is, according to Eric Foner, a signal characteristic of postbellum African American migration: "Of all the motivations for black mobility, none was more poignant than the effort to reunite families separated during slavery"—those "remnants of broken families" the novel consistently foregrounds (179).[63] In *Iola*'s South, the broken families are healed, and the national project of romanticizing southern spaces takes on a whole new valence of meaning. So while the text's optimism might fail to harmonize the brutal realities of Jim Crow, it offers a romance of intraracial, intergenerational, cross-class *black* reunion(s) and imagines the kinds of counterpublics, the metaphors of alternate social reality, necessary to apprehend the shape of things to come in the rural black South.

Black Georgic and the Rural Future

In the pastoral mode, labor is a lacuna. In the georgic sensibility of so much black writing from the nadir, labor equals a hard-earned sense of ownership that contravenes the claims of landlords who, as Marx wrote, "love to reap where they never sowed."⁶⁴ For both Dunbar and Harper, rurality and agricultural labor can be redrawn as sites of resistance that recalibrate the legacies of the plantation spaces. Yet the image of a plantation reclaimed by the very bodies it was designed to repress wasn't a motif arrayed by black writers alone. In the decades that followed, it was of serious interest to at least two of the region's most prominent white writers—Margaret Mitchell and William Faulkner. The year 1936, of course, saw the publication of a pair of texts that have defined distinct, and in many ways oppositional, sectors of the South's literary treatment: *Absalom, Absalom!* and *Gone with the Wind*.⁶⁵ In *Absalom*, Faulkner's most sustained exploration of the destructive consequences of the plantation and its legacies, Thomas Sutpen's crumbling monument to triumphant whiteness, Sutpen's Hundred, is ultimately possessed by one of his "black" descendants—Jim Bond, the mentally disabled grandson of Sutpen's son Charles Bond. Violent, tangled histories of incest, fear, internecine contention, and fratricide: such is the afterlife of the plantation in Yoknapatawpha County. It appears to the reader much as it does to Byron Bunch, who, late in *Light in August*, achieves a view of the valley holding the Joanna Burden property: "Like a shallow bowl the once broad domain of what was seventy years ago a plantation house lies beneath him.... But the plantation is broken now by random negro cabins and garden patches and dead fields erosiongutted and choked with blackjack and sassafras and permission and brier."⁶⁶ The plantation is broken now, and the gaps that emerge, the level planes of the "dead fields," are reclaimed in tandem by native flora and African American settlers.

Although Mitchell's plantation drama lacks some of the psychological density of Faulkner's, *Gone with the Wind* also addresses the destabilizing effect of black bodies occupying formerly white plantations. When Scarlett O'Hara returns to Tara after a long tenure in Atlanta, she takes great interest in the "County news," particularly as it relates to Reconstruction's reversals of antebellum conventions of race and space: "[T]here were negroes living in the old Calvert house! Swarms of them and they actually owned it! They'd bought it at the sheriff's sale. The place was dilapidated and it made you cry to look at it."⁶⁷ The disbelief is obvious: white spaces are now black spaces; the long-established, intricately maintained sense of order is unraveled through, of all things, a legal process ("the sheriff's sale").

While the plantation's meanings multiply across culture and time, it appears in black texts of the nadir as an inescapable feature of the present moment, not just a shaping device that casts a troubling shadow over contemporary concerns; it points toward what Paul Outka calls the "traumatic pastoral" of slavery's residues.⁶⁸ In this same vein, Lewis Simpson's reading of William Gilmore Simms shows that when the pastoral runs up against "modern history," it reveals the extent to which "African chattel had come into the Southern garden of paradise as an intruder, dispossessing the garden of the Western pastoral imagination ... and threatening to transform the South into an image of a completely nonpastoral character."[69] Michael Bennett further argues that "a main current within African American culture has ... expressed a profound antipathy toward the ecological niches usually focused on in ecocriticism: pastoral space and wilderness," asserting that an African American version of the pastoral is best expressed as "anti-pastoral."[70] This may be true in a broad sense, but exceptions like Dunbar's plantation poems and *Iola Leroy* deserve a different designation.

The presence of African American histories of slavery and anguished black bodies clearly undermines the southern pastoral. But if the georgic offers a more generative conceptual optic, I also recognize that any coherent theory of a black georgic will need to account for those same tortured histories and those same black bodies—and from a more fully felt, more deeply conflicted subject position, one that encompasses the full range of possibilities tied to black farming in the post-Reconstruction South. Ultimately, to theorize a New World black georgic is to rescore European conventions according to the distinct rhythms of African American experience; it is to hear black voices signifyin(g) on a whole series of familiar images and tropes. Sometimes those voices sign darkly, other times hopefully, but always with full and wary consciousness of the consequences of unruly blackness.

The tensions that emerge around these issues of representation, however, are not just posed between black and white but also between competing registers of blackness. From Du Bois to the Harlem Renaissance on, observers have most readily associated African American modernism and modernity with urban life—a strain of thinking that Riché Richardson discovers within both academic and popular culture. As Richardson posits, "urban-centered epistemologies of blackness belie the continuing significance of the U.S. South and its rural contexts as factors in shaping black identity" and thus its interactions with the modern.[71] Under this light, the specific challenges facing black farmers are forced to the background, as their lives and livelihoods are filtered through a method of cultural accounting that equates authentic black life with the young and the urban.

So is the rural South the ground upon which to build a productive black future? The fact that the conversation stretches from the postbellum period into the present day suggests something of the question's potency as well as its controversy. It's the potency of the question, measured against a heightened environmental awareness, that causes radical black feminist bell hooks at the beginning of the twenty-first century to voice a sentiment similar to that of *Iola Leroy*'s Aunt Linda: "Collective black self-recovery takes place when we begin to renew our relationship to the earth."[72] As hooks further explains, "it has been easy for folks to forget that black people were first and foremost a people of the land, farmers.... [T]hat at the first part of the twentieth century, the vast majority of black folks in the United States lived in the agrarian south."⁷³ I won't attempt any concrete conclusions about what kind of difference this observation can or should make to contemporary black Americans, but recent attention to the *Pigford* case offers a useful endpoint. Class-action claimants in *Pigford v. Glickman* (1999) successfully brought suit against the U.S. Department of Agriculture for discriminatory practices in the dispersal of loans and other forms of assistance between 1983 and 1997.⁷⁴ In one interview, John Boyd—a black farmer from Virginia and a plaintiff in the case—made an explicit connection between his experience and that of his predecessors, bluntly calling the USDA "the last plantation" for its past devotion to white dominance.⁷⁵ And with over one billion dollars committed to compensation, the "largest civil rights settlement in history" intersects directly with histories of black agriculture.⁷⁶

If there's any one point upon which this chapter's subjects agree, it's that African American progress is bound up in a need to somehow move through plantation-coded spaces and to redirect the narratives they represent. Although both Dunbar and Harper occupy distinct ideological positions, the black rural South of their texts is not created out of whole cloth but is, instead, an uneven patchwork of existing cultural materials, practices, and performances. The postplantation poetics of each writer is filled with clefts and vacancies, improvised performances that leave visible fingerprints on the objects of historical narrative; they are scattered with hoes and shovels, plowlines and turnrows, mules and cabins and creekbeds, all r*eplaced* as the stuff from which the future proceeds. In this sense, the "true reconstruction of the country" that *Iola Leroy* proposes toward its conclusion may have less to do with the nation-state than with the rural, and the regional, environment (236)—it aims toward a restoration of the land itself, a land riven and ruined by destructive agricultural practices and race-based terrorism. This reconstruction may also signal a subnational engagement with the past and a productive encounter with what Ernst Bloch provocatively called the "unfinished world," a world conceivable only through the creation of a new kind of earth and a new way of working it.⁷⁷ Thus the millennialist streak that runs hard throughout *Iola Leroy*: it "can't come soon enough," reports one character (174). Yet the redeeming angel in these texts of the nadir can only be realized through a penetrating, and visionary, backward gaze that recognizes the extent to which plowshares are always already given to serve as swords. To redeem a painful history is to imaginatively embrace its original conditions and, in that embrace, to transform them. *Iola Leroy*'s narrator closes the opening chapter by claiming that, under the influence of slavery, the entire

"Nation ... failed to read aright the legible transcript of Divine retribution which was written upon the shuddering earth" (14). Once again, at the beginning and the end, it's a matter of land and literacy. Poised outside the opening edge of the twentieth century, Dunbar's poems and Harper's novel offered a chance to reread the earth and try to get it right.

CHAPTER TWO

"Strange Vicissitudes"

Dirt, Progress, and the Modern

When Booker T. Washington first went to Europe, he couldn't stop looking at cows. "The thing that impressed itself most on me in Holland," he writes, "was the thoroughness of the agriculture and the excellence of the Holstein cattle.... It was worth a trip to Holland ... just to get a sight of three or four hundred fine Holstein cows grazing in one of those intensely green fields" (126). Washington was evidently less interested in Old World cradles of civilization than in the cultivation of the Dutch landscape and livestock, a sensibility that informs his assessments of post-Reconstruction black America as well. As I suggested in the previous chapter, the use and abuse of the southern soil was an unavoidable topic for African American writers of the 1890s, and it retained prominence at the turn of the century, functioning as a flashpoint in the arguments about the possibilities of modern black labor and education that played out between Washington's *Up from Slavery* (1901) and Du Bois's *The Souls of Black Folk* (1903).

Mindful of the extensive critical tradition that has compared these two texts, my readings will consider specific intersections of the modern and the agricultural, not so much to resolve the tension between Washington and Du Bois—or, for that matter, to enter what James Smethurst calls the "old and complicated debate of whether Washington was an accommodationist with or trickster guerilla against Jim Crow"[1]—but to reevaluate our sense of how and where these familiar figures engaged the modern world and thereby forged new iterations of modernism, how they wrote into existence a theory and an etiology of the land itself. Rereading Washington–Du Bois with this in mind, it's possible to draw a clearer picture of contrasts and commonalities, to inject a specific unit of analysis into a conversation that can easily drift into generalities, and to come to a fuller understanding of the agrocentric models of education and labor worked out in Du Bois's 1911 novel, *The Quest of the Silver Fleece*. These observations matter because the agricultural was, and remains, political. As both Washington and Du Bois prove, land and land-bound labor yielded a vibrant set of claims and counterclaims, images and counterimages.

The work of this chapter, then, is to explore how textual manifestations of black encounters with the agricultural, so frequently construed as outmoded remainders of oppression via slavery or tenancy, become apertures that allow a vision of turn-of-the-century African American literature meeting formations of the modern. Such views highlight the reality whereby modernism and modernity are not experienced or produced in the same way across subject positions, an observation that rings a sharp truth for black citizens in the nadir South. To that end, I analyze images of the agricultural to situate interchanges of fact and fiction at the limits of precarity. In particular, I continue the pattern of the previous chapter by using the georgic to probe connections between soil culture and politico-economic culture, reading Washington's attention to the redemptive properties of the farm (*Up from Slavery*) as well as Du Bois's representations of sterile plots of dirt (*Souls*) and a fecund swamp (*Quest*) as metaphors for different strains of turn-of-the-century black political possibility.

"A New Earth": *Up from Slavery*'s Farm

Owing perhaps to Du Bois's powerful critiques in *Souls* or to the echoes of the Atlanta Exposition Address in the separate-but-equal decision of 1896's *Plessy v. Ferguson*, Washington's reputation as a well-meaning, if misguided, compromiser persists.[2] In Michael R. West's sophisticated analysis, for instance, Washington's willingness to work within the strictures of Jim Crow, under the aegis of his invention of "race relations," represented a fatal concession to American democracy, offering whites a way to maintain segregation while still supporting a program of incomplete African American economic and social development.[3] This assessment mostly centers on Washington's relationship with white culture and capital, his work at the Tuskegee Institute, and his promotion of industrial education. However, to speak of Washington in this chapter is to reference the sign "Washington" as developed in *Up from Slavery* and, to a lesser degree, its sequel, 1904's *Working with the Hands*. That's not to say that the material, historical presence of Washington or Tuskegee is without consequence in my reading, but I do want to underscore the implications of autobiography as a rhetorical performance through which a textual persona, and a philosophy of progress, emerge. My intention isn't to rehabilitate Washington's reputation as a historical figure but to consider the polyvalent representations of post-Reconstruction race and space that pervade his writing in the first decade of the twentieth century.

Agriculture was foremost among the projects encapsulated by discourses of industrial education—Tuskegee's nickname, "the farm," indicates as much—and farming at the institute is both embraced *as* "industry" and *for* its industrial potential. But when it takes its place alongside other, more obviously mechanical expressions of modernity like the factory and the mill, the position of the farm as a throwback to traditional culture is overturned.[4] Joel Williamson put a distinct frame around this discussion when he claimed that "Washington's program was designed for the agrarian order of the nineteenth century."[5] That may be true, but, as I hope to show, it is an agrarian order positioned to meet the historically specific challenges of a rural black citizenry in the turn-of-the-century South.

Contrary to its reputation for unreasonable optimism, then, *Up from Slavery*'s view of the role of industrial education in the post-Reconstruction black South is often startlingly realistic. Andrew Zimmerman captures the common sentiment regarding vocational training when he holds that Tuskegee "represented an attempt to redirect African American efforts at self-education into channels supportive of the political and economic status quo."[6] Donald Spivey's assessment is harsher, as telegraphed in the title of his 1978 study, *Schooling for the New Slavery*. Yet *Up from Slavery*'s representations of opportunities for black Americans and their relationship to U.S. society at large—a cultural environment that biographer Robert J. Norrell has broadly described as "white nationalism"[7]—present African Americans as colonized subjects whose most welcome contribution to the presiding power is labor, by which they struggle to carve out autonomous spaces and practices without attracting the violent attention of white authorities. In post-Reconstruction Alabama, to maintain a benign appearance is essential to survival, a reality that churns quietly beneath the surface of *Up from Slavery*.

While Washington's stress on the potential of land and labor to provide autonomy looks toward Jeffersonian ideals of agrarian republicanism, it might also prefigure a set of problems that Frantz Fanon would present, sixty years later, in spaces of decolonization. This is a world that, for black subjects at least, bears striking resemblance to conditions in post-Reconstruction Alabama. It's useful here to note the multiple histories of colonization and decolonization that pertain to the U.S. South: as with other parts of the continent, the South has been occupied by white settler-colonizers who squeezed out indigenous populations, but it has also featured the forced colonization of enslaved peoples pulled from their countries of origin, the federal occupation of Reconstruction, and the brutal recolonization of African Americans during the nadir. Without extending unwarranted sympathy to the planter class, it's possible to note that the region has played host to a collection of colonizing agents and colonized subjects whose political and economic interests have often been at cross-purposes. So when Fanon explains that, "[f]or colonized people, the most essential value ... is first and foremost the land" because it can "provide bread and, naturally, dignity,"[8] he is speaking of concepts that carry weight for a range of prominent southerners—both real and imagined, from Scarlett O'Hara and John Crowe Ransom to Booker T. Washington. Moreover, in each of these scenarios it's possible to configure colonized spaces as sites where the distillation of violence acts as the most powerful currency for maintaining the existent power structures.[9] And *Up from Slavery*'s peculiar response to this turbulence is to erase it, to disarm terrorism by refusing to acknowledge it.

Labor's potential to stand in for violence as a means of claiming subjectivity, of claiming dignity, provides one of *Up from Slavery*'s most penetrating analyses of slavery. Every aspect of slavery, Washington holds, "was constructed so as to cause labour, as a rule, to be looked upon as a badge of degradation, of inferiority" (14). The text's overriding goal, in a Fanonian turn, is to wrench labor away from slavery by reappropriating and valorizing it, to reinscribe work with the "dignity of labor."[10] This might appear as an act of appeasement, but it may also mark the practical value of independent labor. For all his talk in the Atlanta address about the natural contributions of black labor to white capital, the Tuskegee of Washington's autobiography discreetly highlights opportunities for white capital to fund black self-determination via agriculture. The bifurcated rhetoric of *Up from Slavery*—the twoness often read as its distinguishing tonal feature—derives from Washington's attempts to both reassure his white readers and to claim, subtly, labor's potential to grant sovereignty to his black audience.

It's not simply Washington's interest in agricultural labor that finds an analogue in Fanon: the later thinker also shares Washington's appreciation of the distance between rural spaces and urban-consumer culture, a distance that threatens to collapse under the influence of capitalist modernity. A stated aim of Washington's education project, for example, is "to be careful not to educate our students out of sympathy with agricultural life, so that they would be attracted from the country to the cities, and yield to the temptation of trying to live by their wits" (60). In picturing a grassroots organization of the de/colonized, Fanon similarly fears a scenario where the "towns and villages are deserted, the unaided, uneducated, and untrained rural masses turn their backs on an unrewarding soil and set off for the urban periphery."[11] Such scrambling of dominant geographic codes—reimagining the rural as the core and the urban as the periphery—becomes a powerful manifestation of Washington's spatial imagination. As he puts it in a passage extolling agricultural education in the European travelogue *The Farthest Man Down* (1912), "most of the problems that arise in the cities have their roots in the country."[12] By implication, to create favorable racial conditions in the country provinces is to see the benefits migrate cityward. Consequently, in Fanon's estimation, anticolonialists "should reside in the rural areas" so that resistance might "be decentralized to the limit."[13] The best way to thwart the impulses of nadir-era colonization, then, is to embrace a program of decentralization that reverses the order of the dominant culture, that establishes a community beyond the purview of the city's officiating logic. To create, in the manner of the Maroons who escaped plantation slavery, a society beyond the grasp of the enslavers.

According to the defensive spatial economies proposed by both Fanon and Washington, the fields and farms are the cultural center; the city is the marginalized—and marginalizing—periphery. It's here, in celebrations of the rural over the urban, that *Up from Slavery*'s georgic tendencies assert themselves most loudly. In book 2 of the *Georgics*, Virgil denounces the violence of the city while praising agricultural virtues: "O blessed farmers! doubly blessed if they should recognize / their blessings!" (2.458–59). In a similar sort of gesture, Washington draws a bright line between the city and the country, as in the description of his first visit to Richmond, Virginia: "When I reached there, tired, hungry, and dirty, it was late in the night. I had never been in a large city, and this rather added to my misery. When I reached Richmond, I was completely out of money. I had not a single acquaintance in the place, and being unused to city ways, I did not know where to go. I applied at several places for lodging, but they all wanted money, and that was what I did not have" (26–27). It's the money economy that produces the city ways that prove so disorienting to Washington: he is adrift in a system wherein a preference for the material and the hands-on unfastens from its foundations. Modern capitalism's fatal final condition, as Marx and Engels describe it, is one in which the material becomes immaterial. In the midst of just such a free fall, Washington seeks to reattach himself to the ground: he curls up and sleeps on the dirt beneath the sidewalk, the safest—Washington might say the *realest*—available option. It's clear that both Washington and Fanon view the yearning to inhabit the centers of modernity as a barrier to progress and the establishment of a sovereign society. Better instead, as the wretched *of* the earth, to build up opposition *from* the earth.

Given the book's spatial values, it's altogether appropriate that at *Up from Slavery*'s conclusion, Washington has triumphed over Richmond. He communicates victory in the final chapter, marveling to find himself an invited speaker in a city that not only mistreated him during his first visit but "which only a few decades ago was the capital of the Southern Confederacy" (145). If the book drifts toward resolution and reconciliation, *Up from Slavery* also quietly works to position Washington as conqueror: through his savvy intervention, the text asserts, it's not just the country districts but also the capitals of southern history and identity formation that have been altered by crusading visions of postslavery rural blackness.

To get a sense of Washington's broad influence as a public figure, it's worth considering another early twentieth-century image of Washington that appeared in popular culture: Gus Cannon's string-band recording "Can

You Blame the Colored Man?," released in 1927 under the name Banjo Joe. The song imagines Washington's much-noticed dinner with Theodore Roosevelt—an event that occurred in October 1901, the same year *Up from Slavery* was published—and in combination with Cannon's bright, descending banjo lines, the lyrics portray Washington as a mindful minstrel, whose bulging eyes and barrelhouse laugh conceal a deeper, more profoundly uncertain reaction to the situation. Arriving at the door, the singer records, "He almost changed his color / when Roosevelt said to come in." Though it's hard to tell whether this statement indicts Washington as an accommodationist, as an actual *shade*-shifter, or simply acknowledges the improbability of a black man finding such intimate audience with the president, the line encapsulates the wider ambivalence of the song's narrative. Carrying all the weight of slavery's history and the federal government's complicity in Jim Crow, blackness necessarily wavers as it crosses the threshold of the White House.

After imagining Washington "drunk on wine," taking in a late-night, post-dinner carriage tour of the capital, the song's chorus probes its protagonist's behavior with a provocative question directed squarely at the listener: "Could you blame the colored man for making them goo-goo eyes?" How else, the song asks, should a black man born into slavery process the absurdity of such a visit at the nadir's deepest trough? In "Can You Blame the Colored Man?" it's not simply Washington's words but his very body, with its "goo-goo eyes" and improbable chromatic fluctuations, that expresses itself through strategies of what I'll call double-bodied discourse. Cannon's depiction harmonizes in this regard with Norrell's interpretation of Washington as a "master of indirection, of the hidden hand of action."[14] He's not just, as Houston Baker once argued, sounding the minstrel mask; he's enfleshing it—and to great effect.[15] Here again, as Washington infiltrates the nation's centers of culture anew, he's able to claim a sly, provisional form of ownership.[16]

Since the practice of agriculture is an essential feature of the black autarky, Washington's program in *Up from Slavery* seeks to expand opportunities to go to work. And against the separate-spheres ideology that we might expect from Washington, he readily extends participation to women. "[W]e now train a number of girls in agriculture each year," he writes, describing how "[t]hese girls are taught gardening, fruit-growing, dairying, bee-culture, and poultry-raising" (142). *Working with the Hands* expands this dynamic, devoting an entire chapter to "Outdoor Work for Women." The list of tasks included above likewise suggests that contrary to its label, models of agriculture in Washington's industrial education don't simply result in the mass production of a single commercial crop but in a more carefully constructed, biodiverse—and gender-diverse—approach to farming. In its history of Tuskegee, *Up from Slavery* notes the difference between the privation of the school's early days, when residents depended on the "merchants in town" to provide their food on credit, and its present state of relative prosperity and food independence, when the institute hosts alumni dinners featuring "tempting, well-cooked food—largely grown by the students themselves" (75). In *Working with the Hands*, Washington carefully draws out the contrast between the home-grown and the commercial: "No pease, no turnips, radishes nor salads taste so good as those which one has raised and gathered with his own hands in his own garden. In comparison with these all the high-sounding dishes found in the most expensive restaurants seem flavourless."[17] It's not solely a matter of economic and cultural independence, of avoiding debt and bringing about "food justice"; you can actually taste the superiority of garden food.[18]

The transition from external to internal food source, then, is rightly presented as a sign of Tuskegee's success, and its biodiversity as a model for other rural communities. In 1901, when German colonial authorities sought advice from four Tuskegee representatives about the establishment of a cotton production outpost in Togo, Washington sent a note to one of the project's overseers: "I should very much hope that your Company will not make the same mistake that has been made in the South among our people, that is, teach them to raise nothing but cotton. I find that they make much better progress financially and otherwise where they are taught to raise something to eat at the same time they are raising cotton."[19] Setting aside Washington's potentially unnerving alliance with European colonizers, the message conveyed here is a valuable one: cash crops alone cannot ensure the health of a burgeoning community.

It's worth scanning back at this point to one of the most disheartening details of Washington's first trip to Richmond: the inaccessibility of food-as-commodity. "I passed by many foodstands where fried chickens and half-moon apple pies were piled high and made to present a most tempting appearance" (27), Washington writes. These items remain out of reach because, for a young black man and a former slave, cash is nearly impossible to come by. Here the text narrates the insidious immobility built into a structure of exchange that controls cash flow to restrict participation in the broader economy. Money is both the means and the mode of mobility in the city, and it only trickles down to black subjects at the will of white authority. At this early stage in the narrative, then, Washington is constantly reaching for but never fully possessing the objects of modernity. By the end, however, when Tuskegee finally appears as a fully functioning source of strength, the text redeploys the signifier "tempting," making it hover, triumphantly, over the "well-cooked" products of black labor at the alumni dinner. Cash has been replaced by food-as-commodity, a reality borne out in the text's descriptions of Tuskegee donors who make their bequests with agricultural products, as in the case of an impoverished seventy-year-old woman who donates a half-dozen eggs (62).

Representations of food serve multiple purposes in the text. For instance, Washington repeatedly underlines its use as a social marker, decrying the diet of fatback, cornbread, and black-eyed peas so common in the postbellum black South. Degraded food, in Washington's estimation, benchmarks more serious forms of social and cultural degradation (54). He likewise sees both corporate malevolence and a disposition of wastefulness in ex-slaves who buy high-priced foods in town when "the land all about the cabin homes could easily have been made to produce nearly every kind of garden vegetable that is raised anywhere in the country." Of the planters, Washington claims that "[t]heir one object seemed to be to plant nothing but cotton; and in many cases cotton was planted up to the very door of the cabin" (54). The draw of cotton as a cash crop crowds out all other considerations, stripping the ground of its ecological functionality and deepening its black inhabitants' reliance on oppressive food sources. For Washington, food sovereignty is at the base of politico-economic sovereignty.[20]

Washington's denunciation of the excesses of a cotton economy complies with his larger ecological and economic vision for Tuskegee. This because cotton monoculture, notorious for depleting southern soils in the plantation and sharecropping systems, is dangerously counterproductive to a community that favors self-sufficiency over participation in a cash economy. In this regard, Tuskegee more closely resembles a large-scale subsistence farm than a cash-crop factory. And as it declines to abstract food crops into commodities on the national marketplace, Tuskegee participates in what David Nicholls calls a form of "political modernity": "To those seeking autonomy through agricultural production, subsistence farming was seen as a workable option and not simply a return to an idyllic past. This fact elaborates the transition narrative of modernization by showing that supposedly superseded modes of production may yet yield political modernity."[21] Thus the "new earth" of Washington's imagination necessarily appears as a product of the old ways.

Tuskegee's thrust for more sustainable modes of farming resounds in the work of its most notable faculty member, George Washington Carver, whose experiments in agriculture represent an attempt to align the economic necessities of the South's farmers, the region's own ecological needs, and scientific innovation. In his recent "environmental biography," Mark D. Hersey lauds Carver as "a prophet of sustainable agriculture,"[22] showing that it was precisely this concern for local ecologies that led Washington to aggressively recruit Carver to Tuskegee. Such facts rest uneasily against Scott Hicks's recent contention that Washington's work, particularly in the Atlanta Compromise speech, simply "celebrates environmental degradation and exploitation past and present."[23] Though Hicks offers insightful readings of Richard Wright's ethics of ecology, his take on Washington and Du Bois enacts a familiar critical reflex in which Washington becomes Du Bois's less canny, less beneficent foil. While Washington may not qualify as a thoroughgoing conservationist when stacked against his Progressive Era peers, in *Up from Slavery* he writes himself as a pragmatist above all else, and his agricultural program represents a full expression of this temperament, as farming and soil conservation are, finally, practical imperatives: "We began farming," Washington explains, "because we wanted something to eat" (65).

The degree to which the institute actualized this principle is apparent in the extensive survey of Tuskegee's agricultural production contained in *Working with the Hands*. In a chapter entitled "The Experimental Farm," Washington details the effects of crop rotation at Tuskegee and proposes a model for a soil-healthy forty-acre homestead. The plan includes an acre devoted to a private garden and orchard on which to grow "vegetables of various kinds, peaches, pears, plums, figs, strawberries, blackberries, grapes, etc.," with thirty-six acres committed to marketable crops such as hay, cowpeas, sorghum, potatoes, and sweet potatoes.[24] Conspicuously absent from this list is cotton, the product most readily associated with the crop-lien system, a condition that forms, in Washington's estimation, the "curse of the Negro." "It is the mortgage structure," Washington continues, "which binds him, robs him of independence, allures him and winds him deeper and deeper in its meshes till he is lost and bewildered."[25] What Washington describes was, as the 1900 Census of Agriculture confirms, a condition designed for post-Emancipation black workers: "[T]he negro has become the true basis of the tenant system that has grown to large proportions in the South."[26]

In this way, the independent production of food alongside other cash crops, and over against industrial-scale cotton farming, provides his community an opportunity to escape the circuits laid down by a white-supremacist culture and economy, to step outside an American mainstream increasingly guided by national codes of consumption.[27] If cotton acts as a primary source for adaptations of a global market economy that persistently disadvantages black tenants in the U.S. South, Washington's alternate modernity runs on food.

A tight bond between space and its functional capabilities prevails in Washington's economy. In elaborating *Up from Slavery*'s spatial values, we might graft Washington's anxieties about the metropole onto Ian Baucom's explanation of Fanon's interest in the connections between colonial desire and modernity: to the colonized, modernity appears as a substance "seen, glimpsed, partially approached, but still 'distant'"; it presides in spaces "brightly lit but held apart, on the far side of the color-, poverty-, anger-line."[28] Washington's suspicions about urbanity's drive toward consumption over production underlie his larger proposal for postbellum African American self-sufficiency and his attempts to recraft the modern. Under this model, the Tuskegee of *Up from Slavery* isn't simply antimodern; its patterns of resisting

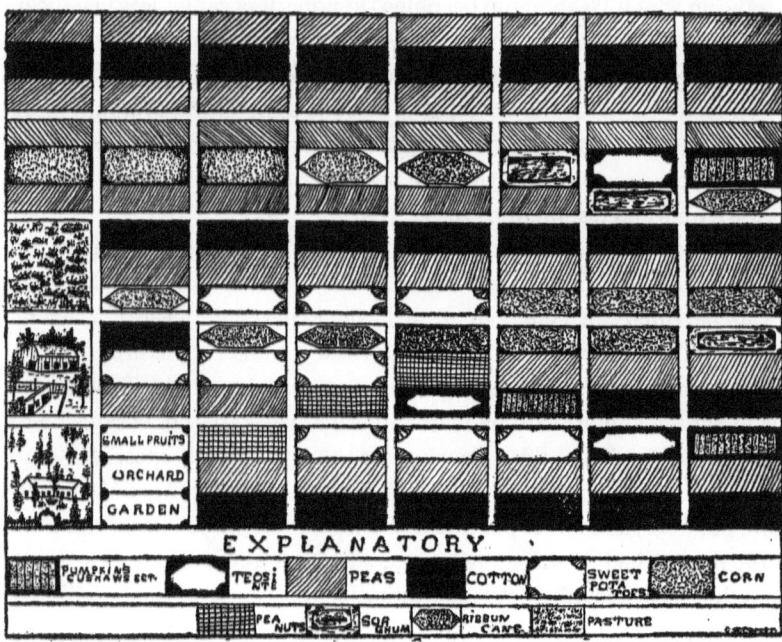

Washington's "experimental farm," *Working with the Hands*, 1904.

the desire for capitalist modernity provide opportunities for attempting, for daring, to desire it differently, an observation that inevitably colors the text's engagement with discourses of modernism itself.

The most famous discussion of Washington and modernism belongs to Houston Baker. In an analysis of Washington he later recanted, Baker reads the Washington of *Up from Slavery* as practicing a form of modernism that "blend[s]...class and mass—*poetic* mastery discovered as a function of deformative *folk* sound—[which] constitutes the essence of black discursive modernism."[29] In other words, Washington found himself in a "tight spot," and the voice he developed to navigate it contains multiple orbits, each of which is artful enough to signify differently to different audiences. Despite his clearly Victorian tendencies—the several passages emphasizing the importance of hygiene and cleanliness provide one obvious example—we recognize a twinge of the modern in Washington's attitudes toward a world undergoing swift and wrenching transformations. As Baker elsewhere describes, it was "*change*...in what could be taken as unquestionable assumptions about the meaning of human life" that prompted the shift into modernity and modernism, changes that Washington at once welcomes and refuses.[30]

For instance, *Up from Slavery* goes to great lengths to emphasize the usefulness of certain technologies: large chunks of Washington's narrative depend on his experiences with train travel, and the toothbrush—an item that entered mass production just six years before the book appeared—commands special attention throughout. Yet the text also reveals a deep unease with much of industrial society, a characteristic that places it squarely within the modernism of mixed responses limned by Marshall Berman: "All forms of modernist art and thought ... are at once expressions of and protests against the process of modernization."[31] A similar impulse guides Washington's wish that he "might remove the great bulk of these people into the country districts and plant them upon the soil ... where all nations and races that have ever succeeded have gotten their start,—a start that at first may be slow and toilsome, but one that nevertheless is *real*" (44–45, emphasis mine). Real in that it addresses the immediate needs of a community in crisis, and real in that it forces an engagement with the biological realities of survival via food production. In its theory that farming requires a recognition of one's deeply rooted ties to the natural world—both human and nonhuman—*Up from Slavery*'s Washington would appear to agree with postwar conservationist Aldo Leopold: "[T]here is value in any experience that reminds us of our dependency on the soil-plant-animal-man food chain."[32]

More pointedly, Washington's prescriptions for the black community include a form of agro-communalism positioned away from the temptations of the city and the power structures it represents. The country districts might lack certain amenities, but they can also provide a space apart from white supervision, a germinal site for an alternative modernity wherein the landscape of the plantation can be reordered—reconstructed even—in the image of black sovereignty. Audible, if slightly muted, in these passages is the more radical voice of prominent black journalist T. Thomas Fortune, who protested the debt-slavery of tenancy by advocating for the abolishment of private property in *Black and White: Land, Labor, and Politics in the South* (1884), a text published in precisely the same period that he entered Washington's inner circle as a confidant and occasional ghostwriter. "No man is free," wrote Fortune, "who is debarred in his right, to so much of the soil of his country as is necessary to support him in his right to life, for without the inherent right to unrestrained access to the soil he cannot support life."[33] With this message in the foreground, the precise means by which Washington used the Tuskegee Institute itself to materialize principles of black autonomy in a hostile region come into focus.

When South African educator and politician D. D. T. Jabavu visited Tuskegee in 1915, he kept a diary in which he speculated on the degree to which Washington's character was formed through a need to superintend the menace of white violence. According to Jabavu's account, Washington's "overpowering responsibilities" included not just the financial management of Tuskegee but also the mighty task of maintaining "social relations with the venomous

"Teach the Child Something about Real Country Life," *Working with the Hands*, 1904.

Southern Whites who might, on any false step of his, any unguarded utterance, not hesitate to blow up the Tuskegee Inst. with bombs, lynch him and his students in a single night, demolish and annihilate the whole Industrial city."[34] In Jabavu's estimation, Tuskegee is no expression of "plantation black abjection"[35]; it's a defensive redoubt, and its progenitor's every "utterance" is shaded by the threat of violence (bombs, nighttime raids, lynching). Conscious of this climate of intimidation, Kenrick Grandison examines the specific ways that Washington, by building the campus on the site of a former plantation accessible by a single, barely passable road, used space at Tuskegee to establish a compound beyond the scope of white surveillance. Even the placement of the campus buildings, Grandison shows, made the institution a real and practical bulwark against outside invasion. Women, for instance, occupied the barracks on the interior, while the male students were housed around the perimeter, "where they could potentially serve as a first line of defense in the case of hostile intrusion."[36] In Washington's view, then, the country districts provide not only the best working conditions but also the safest place to dig in.

Similarly, at several turns in *Up from Slavery* Washington's interest in agriculture allows the ground itself an almost preternaturally regenerative energy. The occasion for this regeneration is physical interaction with the land, a trope that recurs consistently: expanding on the connections between persons and spaces, the text probes a thin line separating people from the places they inhabit. The term "Black Belt," for example, common to both *Up from Slavery* and *Souls*, reveals a nexus of group identity, space, and the soil itself. Though it originated as a description of the dark fertile soils of middle Alabama and northeast Mississippi, by the time Washington wrote *Up from Slavery* it had come to "designate the counties where the black people outnumber the white" (52), an instance of slippage that highlights the extent to which public discourse attempted to weld African Americans to their physical environments. The shifting significance of "black" is particularly important as the distance between landscape, labor, and perceptions of the black subject's body and "place" gives way, with the sign "black" becoming a meeting point for all three: bodies, soil, farm labor. This is a principle fleshed out by the figure of Washington presented in *Up from Slavery*. As Peter Coclanis puts it, "Whether one points to the earthen kitchen floor he slept on as a slave boy or his squalid Malden house, the stench and filth of the salt furnaces and coal mines, or his legendary night under the sidewalk in Richmond, Booker was one with dirt."[37]

Despite Coclanis's language, what's notable in *Up from Slavery* is how *soil* acts as an ennobling, enriching locus of blackness at the same time that *dirt* often serves as an impediment to bodily and domestic cleanliness; it is a contaminant that must be dispatched with an almost obsessive thoroughness. In one memorable passage, Washington insists upon the necessity of "absolute cleanliness" in the project of racial uplift (80). And the same chapter that contains the Richmond sidewalk scene also includes the famous vignette in which Washington painstakingly sweeps the Hampton Institute recitation room, prompting one of his sharpest lectures on cleanliness: "I sometimes feel that almost the most valuable lesson I got at the Hampton Institute was in the use and value of the bath" (31). At the same time that Washington stands as a former slave refusing the role of the black beast by conflating civilization with near-sterility, he is also fundamentally invested in soil-bound labor. The paradox is perhaps irresolvable, but it's consistent with the contradictory impulses of the georgic mode and altogether appropriate for a signing figure whose rhetoric is distinctly, and consistently, doubled.

The overwhelming interest in dirt and cleanliness also points out Washington's position as an archmaterialist: in a world where skin is race is destiny, surfaces matter. "[H]ow I wish that our schools and colleges might learn to study men and things!" Washington exclaims (30). He elaborates further in a passage from *Working with the Hands* that explores a division in forms of knowledge: "When talking to a farmer, I feel that I am talking with a real man and not an artificial one—one who can keep me in close touch with the *real things*."³⁸ Real things versus artificial ones; the material versus the abstract: Washington proposes a tactile, object-oriented epistemology that trumps the textual, the literary, the academic. "There has been almost no thought of connecting the educated brain with the educated hand," Washington complained in a passage from *Working* that makes a strong case against the mind-body split which so often orders pedagogy, gesturing instead toward the value of embodied cognition.³⁹

At the book's conclusion, the soil again provides one of *Up from Slavery*'s most poignant images. While taxed by public engagements, administrative business, and fundraising efforts, Washington explains his practice of seeking solace by working the ground: "When I can leave my office in time so that I can spend thirty or forty minutes in spading the ground, in planting seeds, in digging about the plants, I feel that I am coming into contact with something that is giving me strength for the many duties and hard places that await me out in the big world" (121). While Washington's physical attachments to the land both foreshadow and parallel Heideggerian notions of autochthony, the plantedness Washington envisions arrives less as the result of a generation-spanning national identity than by way of claiming ground for oneself in the present. He becomes an Antaeus of the industrial era whose strength derives from contact with the southern soil of the Black Belt. In Washington's georgic, labor is synonymous with progress: you get to the end of the line by guiding the plow, however rocky the soil. And as a complement to the emphasis on "routes" over "roots" embedded in Paul Gilroy's model of black modernism, Washington proposes an African American encounter with the modern that hinges on manufactured roots and rootedness.⁴⁰ From this perspective, the ground becomes the material out of which a self-determined history and a productive present are imagined—it comes to represent the precise spot where, as Washington promised in the Atlanta Exposition Address, the South itself is revitalized as "a new heaven and a new earth" (102).

"Shadow of a Marvelous Dream": *The Souls of Black Folk*'s Tenant Tract

If *Up from Slavery* recognizes formations of black agri-culture as a way forward, *The Souls of Black Folk* registers greater skepticism. Acute anxiety about African American occupations and how they might modulate the meanings of racial progress permeates *Souls*, a sign of the burden placed on black labor when it's required to act as a symbol of the race's potential. As with Washington, Du Bois's questions about what progress means for both the black South and the nation at large depend on the shape and character of work itself. Yet in *Souls*, agricultural labor simply can't offer the same redemptive opportunities present in *Up from Slavery*. Although commentators such as Anne Raine and Michael Belifuss have recently measured the pastoral qualities of Du Bois's work from the period, I argue that the georgic, with its careful attention to both the costs and the benefits of life on the land, is a more productive metric.[41] In the autobiographical *Dusk of Dawn* (1940), Du Bois himself gestured toward the black georgic by proposing a painful link between labor, race, and rural space. Commenting on his tenure as an itinerant schoolteacher in the "country districts" of Wilson County, Tennessee, during the mid-1880s, Du Bois explained, "I saw the hard, ugly drudgery of country life and the writhing of the landless peasants." Summing up the scene, he concludes, "I saw the race problem at nearly its lowest terms."[42]

Souls includes a reflection on this same episode in an affecting chapter entitled "Of the Meaning of Progress" wherein Du Bois uncovers concrete connections between agriculture, landscape, and a case of tragic retrogression in the "hills of Tennessee" (46). Foremost among its several subjects, the chapter includes the portrait of twenty-year-old Josie, dramatizing her family's struggle to scrape out a living in an inclement environment: "it was a hard thing to dig a living out of a rocky hill-side" (47). Revisiting the area a decade later, Du Bois learns of both Josie's death—"We've had a heap of trouble since you've been away," her mother explains—and the family's move from the farm on the hillside to a location "nearer town" (51). The text also presents Doc Burkes, a black farmer who works ceaselessly to purchase the "seventy-five acres of hill and dale where he lived." However noble this project might appear, it prompts plenty of doubt: "people said that he would surely fail, and the 'white folks would get it all'" (49). In his wider survey, Du Bois notes students pulled away from their studies by the cycles of the growing season and the demands of the landowners; he describes women and men wasting away under the same kind of labor extolled by Washington. Contra Washington, farm work dulls and starves minds rather than quickening and fertilizing them. And as the soil's demands halt education, history, time, and "progress," *Souls* supplies a vision of the black agricultural as a battle against both the natural world and the white world that too frequently threatens to collapse into something close to slavery. In total, the result is a blow-by-blow account of incremental degradation across generations shared by both black bodies and the lands they work. It is, to call up Rob Nixon's apt phrase, a study in "slow violence" that can quicken with little warning.[43]

Du Bois's language turns most explicitly toward images of slavery and violence in the assessment of the Freedmen's Bureau and Reconstruction-era politics of *Souls*' second chapter. Former slaveholders, according to Du Bois, were "determined to perpetuate slavery under another name" (28), and his analysis of the period relies on familiar metaphors of soil and cultivation as well as probing questions about the material realities of postslavery labor and land use. In its brief history of the Civil War's aftermath, *Souls* figures the ever-present "problem of the color-line" as a native property of southern ground itself: "No sooner had Northern armies touched Southern soil than this old question, newly guised, sprang from the earth,—What shall be done with Negroes?" (17). It takes nothing more than physical contact with the "soil" to ramify the inescapable dilemma of what it means to actually grant freedom to a newly freed people.

The government's first pass at a solution came in 1865, through a branch of the War Department called the Bureau of Refugees, Freedmen, and Abandoned Lands. Typically shortened to Freedmen's Bureau, the longer official title captures a greater measure of the organization's strategy and its philosophy. There was, in the opening stages of Reconstruction, a convenient and instant connection between the "abandoned lands" of the slaveholding plantations and the scores of freedmen in the South, most of whom, it was assumed, were well trained and eager to assume the role of independent farmer. Many were—and many, as Paul Cimbala's description of former slaves in Ogeechee, Georgia, attests, were ready to embrace "communal" approaches to agricultural production: "They continued to farm the land productively 'in concert' instead of working on the individual plots to which they were entitled."[44]

Du Bois himself highlights such developments: "large quantities of land were leased in the Mississippi Valley, and many Negroes were employed," but, he notes, these "new regulations were suspended for reasons of 'public policy'" (21). In 1870, five years into the project, Freedmen's Bureau commissioner O. O. Howard wrote a letter to Congress,[45] lamenting the obstacles facing freedmen engaged in farming: "Many were afraid to remain on the same soil that they had tilled as slaves lest by some trick they might find themselves again in bondage. Others supposed that the government would either take the entire supervision of their labor and support, or divide among them the lands of conquered owners, and furnish them with all that might be necessary to begin life as independent farmers."[46] Just as contact with the southern soil instantly dredged up visions of slavery for Union troops, so too for former slaves, who fear that "some trick"—perhaps something about the practice of agriculture itself, perhaps something inherent to physical and emotional investment in that tainted ground, perhaps the intricacies of credit finance—might reinstall slavery and strip them of their newfound freedoms. Howard's letter buttresses Du Bois's basic argument as it pertains to both farming and the southern landscape: there is no coherent, productive way for emancipated slaves to interact with spaces and modes of labor so strongly associated with their erstwhile bondage.

That's not to say that Du Bois doesn't appreciate the "vision of 'forty acres and a mule'" or "the righteous and the reasonable ambition to become a landholder." But the abandoned properties ostensibly managed by the bureau rarely fell into the possession of former slaves, and, as Howard's letter indicates, the promise that they might inhabit the "lands of conquered owners" was, in Du Bois's words, "destined . . . to bitter disappointment" (28). One obvious source of friction was the bureau's inability to manage unresolved animosity between blacks and whites in the South. Eric Foner has argued that northerners associated with the Freedmen's Bureau mistakenly considered the hostility between freedpeople and white planters on the plantations an "irrational legacy of slavery that would disappear as soon as planters and freedmen absorbed free labor principles."[47] This kind of optimism toward free labor and its contributions to the free market calls up the larger question about how the sign "free" functions in Reconstruction discourse. In its large and unruly semantic field, "free" indicates freedom from physical and mental bondage at the same time that it suggests the acquisition of something without paying for it. In Du Bois's assessment of Reconstruction, "free labor" too often means something close to *free labor* for the white planter class. Better than the promise of "free land" or a vague hope in the redeeming power of "free labor," then, is the "planting of the *free school* among the Negroes" (28, emphasis mine). Note the verb: it's not crops but schools that must be rooted to enrich the southern environment.

The problem of the color line in farming the South remained visible after Reconstruction. Through the 1880s and 1890s, a movement to reestablish agriculture as the province of white Americans appeared in the southern branch of the Farmers' Alliance, that precursor of the national Populist Party, which was thoroughly devoted to segregation. According to Theodore R. Mitchell, the alliance's intention of bringing together farmers from the South and the North was undone by the persistence of racism: "[T]he race question proved the greatest ideological hurdle of all, and it proved ultimately insurmountable."[48] (Black farmers formed their own organization, the Colored Farmers' National Alliance and Cooperative Union [Colored Farmers' Alliance] in 1886.) In Joel Williamson's view, the depression of 1892–93 sparked action by white farmers in the Black Belt against black tenants as the most desirable lands were "most often tenanted by the freedmen and their descendants." Williamson further reasons that white farmers were made vulnerable by the vigor and determination of their black peers: "[T]here are suggestions in agricultural statistics that black farmers, so recently out of slavery and beginning almost literally only with the clothes on their backs, farmed their lands . . . more intensively than their white contemporaries."[49] And thus arose organizations like the Whitecaps, created by disgruntled whites seeking to "terrorize Negroes off farms rented from landlords and country merchants."[50] Black farmers also felt the pinch borne of an economy in transition, as a shift from agricultural-industrial to mechanized-industrial production took shape in the 1880s and 1890s. According to James Cobb, business and political interests were determined to prevent any cross-racial alliance between white and black farmers who might feel mutually disserved by emergent industrialism. In Georgia, the southern state *Souls* explores most carefully, Cobb explains that "New South leaders proved especially effective in fusing the goals of white supremacy and industrial development with the ideals of the lost cause and presenting themselves as the champions of all three," a configuration that conspicuously excludes African Americans who work the land.[51] In a New South ideology that merges progress and nostalgia, black farmers were pushed both out of place and out of time.

Given this white hostility to African American farming, it's easy to understand some of *Souls'* anxieties about black agriculture. As a student of Hegel, Du Bois recognized that advancement depends on change and exchange, creation and destruction. To the extent that synthesis yields newness, of course, it also creates obsolescence, an undercurrent that swamps simple notions of progress. In "Of the Meaning of Progress," the site of the writer's former employment acts as a powerful illustration: "My log schoolhouse was gone. In its place stood Progress; and Progress is necessarily ugly." The schoolmaster's cabin is absent, but its foundation stones remain; the "blackboard had grown by about two feet," but the "seats were still without backs." Observing the cast-off detritus of forward motion—broken windowpanes, chunks of a broken stove—that litter the scene, Du Bois reports that "[a]s I . . . looked on the Old and the New I felt glad, very glad, and yet—" (52). One way to account for the note of uneasiness in this trailing sentence is to recognize that it signals an awareness of the casualties of progress and all the contradictory paths it follows. The dash indicates an aporia, a gap between progress as a conceit of the Enlightenment—wherein it is presumed to grant ever-increasing levels of growth, wellness, and truth—and its darker affiliations with creative destruction. The author's expression of gladness, it seems, cannot proceed without qualification. As Du Bois himself puts it earlier in the text, there is a "curious double movement where real progress may be a negative and actual advance be relative retrogression" (37). The pattern matches Du Bois's reading of Washington's project: he never doubts the motive driving the Tuskegee model, yet he is concerned with its broader transformative capabilities. Using the abandoned schoolhouse as an illustration, *Souls* argues that "Progress" has converted the world of small, independent farms into a landscape of ruin and deprivation. Correspondingly, the text never denies the important role that agriculture has played in African American cultural history; it just never achieves the elevated position it holds in Washington's economy.

Perhaps *Souls'* most sustained examination of black agriculture and rural life comes from "Of the Quest of the Golden Fleece," in which Du Bois zeroes in on the material conditions created by a southern cotton economy in Dougherty County, Georgia.[52] This is, the author is quick to point out, the realization of an intensive, rationalized theory of monocrop cultivation. With an unswerving emphasis on maximizing profits and a basic disregard for the conditions of workers and their environments, it represents a startling southern expression of modernization, one that appears and originates in the rural districts.

Although Sherman's orders extended a guarantee of land and livestock to freed slaves after the war, Andrew Johnson quickly revoked the policy. By the time Du Bois turned his attention to the region in the 1890s, tenancy had largely restored slavery's ratios by holding the labor force in place through debt. The promise unfulfilled, black farmers encountered a scheme wherein "the crop-lien system, the deterioration of the land, and the slavery of debt" assures that the "position of the metayers has sunk to a dead level of practically unrewarded toil" (101). In Du Bois's analysis, then, the realities of black agriculture appear as an unbroken cycle of rents and obligations, abusive labor and inhospitable conditions.

Southern ecologies paid a steep price as well. Marking the end of the Civil War as "the beginning of a second period in the history of cotton culture in the South," the 1900 Census of Agriculture makes an unfavorable comparison: "The destruction of the soils by the methods of cultivation prior to the war was worse than the devastation of the war. The post-bellum farmer received as an inheritance large areas of worn-out and generally unproductive soils."[53] Decades after the publication of *Souls*, in 1938, the Department of Agriculture commissioned a study seeking out the causes of soil exhaustion and concluded that generations of contracts upholding tenancy "were developed during a period when the soil was exploited as a matter of course" and that they "naturally reflect a policy of ignoring, in large degree, the growing problem of soil maintenance and restoration."[54] More broadly, the authors argue that a fundamental disregard for the fate of the land by both tenants and landowners promotes these abusive practices: "The uncertainties of his occupancy and the requirements of his lease dictate quite definitely what crops he can grow and what livestock he can keep to advantage. Hence he is largely a producer of cash crops such as cotton, tobacco, corn, and small grain, and he is not concerned that these crops are hard on most soils."[55] But it was cotton, the very crop that placed such stringent demands on both the land and its laborers in Du Bois's narrative, that gave the South entrée into international markets and that orchestrated an economic, if not a racial and social, integration of the country's two halves.[56]

Even as *Souls* examines cultures of black agriculture, a distance always mediates Du Bois's involvement in the text. For better or worse, through all his impassioned critique, there remains a gulf between Du Bois, an African

American sociologist who has already transitioned to an information/service economy, and the manual labor of his rural subjects. Commenting on what might be called the rural urbanization of the overpopulated sharecroppers' quarters, Du Bois writes, "*We* have come to associate crowding with homes in cities almost exclusively. This is primarily because we have so little accurate knowledge of country life" (91, emphasis mine). The first-person plural "we" curiously implies an absence among the text's readers of anyone with an intimate "knowledge of country life," and the differences between pictures of black rural life in Du Bois and Washington become appreciable if you recognize Du Bois as a dismayed outsider looking in—looking in at the rural and, perhaps more distressingly, at the race itself. Gabriel Briggs has recently argued that Du Bois's account of reading, singing, and picking flowers alongside his pupils in the country districts of Tennessee evinces a "tone" that suggests that "there is no longer a distinction between Du Bois and these rural folk.... [He] is no longer an educator or an outsider; he is part of a community."[57] Whatever part he played in the community, however, was temporary. Du Bois may, in key passages, stop representing himself as an outsider, but he never remains on the inside, and he certainly never recuses himself from his role as an educator. Unlike Washington, he is never consciously *of* the earth. To that end, Andrew Scheiber makes the point that because of Du Bois's background and professional orientation, "the South comprised something like a foreign country" to him, and, although he understands the region as the locus of African American cultural production, the "location of his own soul's voice in the collective expression of these southern 'black folk'" is a problem that threatens to undermine his entire project.[58] One doesn't have to subscribe wholly to Scheiber's reading to recognize that when it comes to agricultural labor, Du Bois is speaking from an observational position rather than an experiential one. It's also clear that *Souls* grapples with an unnerving sociocultural paradox whereby the sites of the most material misery also provide the most aesthetic beauty and the greatest cultural value. This is the underside of *Souls*' position as what Gayatri Spivak calls the "prototype... vision of metropolitan Cultural Studies"[59]: contrary to its best intentions, in the text's assumptions of urban authority, in its basic metropolitanism, forms of knowledge and power exist that may well be complicit with the very patterns of colonization and imperialism that the text seeks to unravel.

And so for all the diverse contexts in which images of dirt, clay, and soil occur, Du Bois's approach to the subject is fairly consistent. In the chapter "Of the Black Belt," Du Bois holds that the "Negro problem [lies] in its naked *dirt* and penury" (80, emphasis mine); in the short story "Of the Coming of John," protagonist John Jones is swept up, when attending a concert in New York, by a "deep longing [that] swelled in all his heart to rise with that clear music out of the *dirt* and *dust* of that low life that held him prisoned and befouled" (147, emphasis mine). Elsewhere, we read a sardonic voice pointing out "the scarred and wretched *land*; the ruined mansions, the worn-out *soil* and mortgaged acres.... This is Negro freedom!" (100, emphasis mine). In the autobiographical chapter "Of the Passing of the First-Born," Du Bois observes a grotesque hue in the southern dirt that prevents him from burying his deceased child there: "We could not lay him in the ground there in Georgia, for the earth there is strangely red" (133). The text further describes the fall of Atlanta during the Civil War as a "vision of empire fade[d] to real ashes and *dirt*" (55, emphasis mine), and, in the famous final chapter, the singer of sorrow songs is a *"toiler"* out "transfigur[ing] his fatalism ... amid the *dust* and *dirt*" (161, emphasis mine). In each of these examples, earth is the element of enforced humility and degradation, and, in stark contrast with its role as a source of power in *Up from Slavery*, it stands as something to be transcended in *Souls*. (As mentioned above, Washington likewise decries dirt's sullying properties in *Up from Slavery*, but he consistently reveres soil.) Although *Souls* works out an admirable ecological ethic, these images of the earth are emphatically not ecological because they are manifestly disconnected with the living process—they offer decay without regeneration; all dirt, no soil.

But in accordance with the "neo-Hegelian dialectic" that Stanley Brodwin recognizes as crucial to the text's patterns of meaning-making, southern dirt is finally synthesized into something new toward the conclusion of *Souls*.[60] In "The Sorrow Songs," Du Bois sits in his office listening to the sounds of the Fisk Jubilee Singers, "fresh young voices welling up to me from the caverns of brick and mortar below" (163). Du Bois's elevated station— literally, as an academic in a lofty office—is upheld, according to his own metaphor, by bricks crafted from the dirt and clay linked to southern histories of slavery and violence. He is held at a physical remove from his subject by the same material that gave rise to the very culture, most starkly emblematized in the sorrow songs, that he celebrates. This isn't just true of Du Bois alone, of course. The shape of modern America, particularly in the South, owes itself to the labor of African Americans and to the suffering bound up in the southern soil. Consequently, tropes of bricks and brickmaking figure prominently throughout Reconstruction discourse, as evidenced in Albion W. Tourgée's 1880 novel, *Bricks Without Straw*, and, compellingly for this chapter, *Up from Slavery* itself, which includes a detailed explanation of Tuskegee's history of brickmaking and the role of the brick-as-commodity in Washington's exchange with the wider, white economy: "We needed these [bricks] for use in connection with the erection of our own buildings; but ... [t]here was no brickyard in town, and in addition to our own needs there was a demand for brick in the general market" (70).[61] Soil becomes "mud" in Washington's account (70), the needful ingredient for the construction of a new physical and social infrastructure.

For Washington, the bricks come to represent a medium of productive exchange between "the two races of the South," and a black-controlled means by which hostile whites sought out the products of autonomous black labor. The result, in *Up from Slavery*, is a territory of economic integration: "As the people of the neighbourhood came to us to buy bricks, we got acquainted with them; they traded with us and we with them. Our business interests became intermingled" (71). *Souls'* investment in the future of black America and, more specifically, its investment in the construction of the black academy and intellectual class—the group for whom Du Bois was the most prominent and gifted spokesperson—depends on a differently motivated double infrastructure: the material and economic, on one hand, metaphorized in the bricks and mortar; and the cultural and aesthetic on the other, encapsulated in the "sorrow songs," performances wherein "soul" becomes the strongest token of cultural capital.

Accordingly, the synthesis the text reaches for at its conclusion is a hallmark of its intertwined innovations in both content and form. For instance, critics such as Brodwin argue that *Souls'* status as a modernist landmark turns on its incorporation of Hegel, and so in addition to underscoring the author's staggering erudition, this quality might also account for certain of its distinguishing textual features. Paul Gilroy, for one, presents *Souls* as a "polyphonic" mélange that "supplement[ed] recognisably sociological writing with personal and public history, fiction, autobiography, ethnography, and poetry."[62] The tendency toward multiplicity but also dividedness results in an asymmetrical set of unresolved formal and thematic tensions, a series that includes *Souls'* ultimate uncertainty about the meanings and possibilities of the rural South as well as its wariness toward the southern soil.

Hence the text's georgic undercurrents. Working with Raymond Williams's "structures of feeling" to arrive at a lens of "presentness" through which to perceive unheralded or perhaps invisible histories, Kevis Goodman draws attention to the "immanent, collective perception of any moment as a seething mix of unsettled elements." She specifically aims to imagine the georgic as a tool that unearths history's claims on the present, revealing ways in which "historical presentness is often 'turned up' by georgic as *unpleasurable* feeling: as sensory discomfort, as disturbance in affect and related phenomena that we variously term perceptive, sensorial, or affective."[63] Looking back at the description of the Burkes' farm in "Of the Meaning of Progress," it's clear that descriptions of suffering and privation excavate both the ground and farm labor's persistent connections to slavery, as the peculiar institution's horrific past becomes present through the press of the plow. Most pointedly, the girl Josie is dead. In a literalization of Patricia Yaeger's notion of "place-as-crypt," Josie's absorption in the southern dirt contributes to the "creation of landscapes loaded with trauma unspoken, with bodies unhealed or uncared for, with racial melancholia."[64] But the chapter also attends to the discomfort of living, laboring black bodies in duress: the "gaunt father who toiled night and day... his massive frame... showing decline"; the mother, whose "lion-like physique of other days was broken." In a move of distinctly georgic ambivalence, Du Bois notes, "The farm was fat with the growing crop," but the valley is shadowed by a "strange stillness"—death. Even when the farm is productive, *Souls* can't help but notice that the same ground which brings a bountiful harvest also holds the body of young Josie: "How shall man measure Progress there where the dark-faced Josie lies? How many heartfuls of sorrow shall balance a bushel of wheat?" (53). Although Du Bois presents an exceptionally discordant version here, this is a figure played on repeat throughout black writing in the nadir: the southern soil's famous fertility owes itself to the suffering—and even at times to the physical decomposition—of black bodies.

Yet the text appears to be asking an adjoining question as well: Does the rural South simply crystallize the problem of the color line, or does it contain the seeds of a solution? According to Michael Belifuss, *Souls* includes marked "celebrations of pastoral and wilderness," but "in the end, the land cannot be reclaimed by African Americans as long as they are barred from the opportunities for social and economic mobility."[65] No surprise, then, that *Souls* is most openly skeptical about opportunities for black advancement in the country districts. Still, the text's overarching investment in the region's fertile cultural practices creates an internal dialogue that is, appropriately enough, divided against itself—"two warring ideals in one dark body" (11). Such are the fruits of what Du Bois elsewhere calls the "Negro's double environment."[66]

According to scholars like Gilroy and Smethurst, articulations of African American psychological dualism are another sign of *Souls*' intricate modernism. If, however, we follow the suggestions of Houston Baker's more recent work and try to configure black modernism along more sociological lines, we see that Du Bois's text fulfills those requirements as well. Black modernism, Baker explains, "signifies the achievement of a life-enhancing and empowering public sphere mobility and the economic solvency of the black majority... coextensive with a black citizenship that entails documented mobility."[67] Likewise for Du Bois, whose problem of the color line can only be remediated by greater, and more varied, opportunities for African Americans as full citizens. It demands, foremost, the recognition of democratic subjects free to follow any channel the modern world provides. And the constitution of modernity, modernism, and all the social values they represent are intrinsically tied to rural African American labor, an enterprise that, in turn-of-the-century America, retains deep roots.

"Bold Regeneration": *The Quest of the Silver Fleece*'s Swamp

Souls doesn't contain Du Bois's last words on the matter of southern soil. In the years leading up to its publication, Du Bois contributed "The Negro in the Black Belt" and "The Negro Landholder of Georgia" to the Department of Labor's *Bulletin*, articles that act as rural counterparts to his 1899 urban ethnography, *The Philadelphia Negro*, and prove that Du Bois's interest in the state of the race spanned regional and demographic demarcations.[68] Later, in a 1912 edition of *Publications of the American Statistical Association*, he published "The Rural South," a "sharp warning" against "favorable signs of advance in the rural South." It's a data-bound study showing that an uptick in the "accumulation of landed property in the hands of black folk" doesn't necessarily translate into dramatic improvements for African Americans in the region.[69] Between these pieces—and eight years after *Souls*—appeared Du Bois's first novel, *The Quest of the Silver Fleece*, a text that draws on the expressive latitude of fiction to reimagine the soil and toil of black folks in the cotton South. Most importantly, as I argue below, it narrates an iteration of the rural modern that finds common ground between *Up from Slavery* and *Souls*, binding the physical reclamation of a plantation swampland to the rising agropolitical power of its black characters, thereby asserting the value of both agricultural labor *and* the liberal arts in the lives, histories, and imagination of New South African Americans.

A densely plotted, thickly populated narrative, *Quest* centers on the relationship of two young black southerners, both, in Du Boisian parlance, "gifted": Zora, a resident of Colonel Cresswell's plantation in the imagined town of Toomsville, Alabama, and the bearer of a "strange sixth sense" (163) that recalls both *Souls*' "gift of the Spirit" (162) and its "second-sight" (10); and Blessed "Bles" Alwyn, a transplant from Georgia whose "intelligence, broad sympathy, [and] knowledge of the world" position him as one of the "exceptional men" poised to lead the race.[70] In the swamp at the edge of the Cresswell plantation, Zora and Bles collaborate to cultivate a preternatural cotton crop (the titular "silver fleece"), and though they briefly cohere romantically, Bles leaves when he learns that Zora was sexually abused by one of the Cresswells, whereupon they each exit Alabama—Bles, for Washington, and Zora, for Atlanta, New York, and, finally, Washington. Alongside the actions of its black protagonists, the novel also narrates the machinations of powerful white families—the Cresswells of Alabama and the Taylors of New England—who corner the global cotton market by promoting favorable political policy in Washington, managing the labor force in the South, and seeking to control production everywhere. The narrative concludes when Zora returns to Toomsville to complete her work in cooperative agriculture and education, a project that hastens the dissolution of the Cresswell Cotton Combine and communicates the value of voluntary attachment to southern soil. With the help of Bles and Miss Smith, the white New Englander who runs a school for black students, as well as the local African American community, Zora buys the swamp and establishes it as a sovereign space of black economic production and cultural achievement. Buffeted by violent opposition from a white mob, Zora's vision is actualized just as she and Bles reconcile: he admits his mistake, and the text ends with *her* proposal of marriage.

The novel occupies a minor place in Du Bois's corpus. Even the author himself tended to minimize its importance: *Quest* warrants just a single sentence in his 1940 autobiography, *Dusk of Dawn*, and no mention at all in 1968's *Autobiography*. In the earlier book, Du Bois even downplayed *Quest*'s very status as a novel, insisting that it "was really an economic study."[71] How can fiction function as "economic study"? What is the precise relation of the world of the text to the sociologist's world on the ground?[72] *Quest* is tellingly not set in Georgia, the focus of Du Bois's most sustained treatment of the rural South, but in a fictional town one state west—Toomsville, Alabama. Since parts of both Alabama and Georgia fall within the Black Belt and under the same regime of agricultural production and exploitative labor, the decision to swap one for the other may seem fairly unremarkable. Yet it is difficult to deny the significance of Alabama's ironclad associations with Washington and Tuskegee. By 1911, Washington's influence in the broader public had been largely eclipsed by Du Bois's actions with the Niagara Movement (1902–1909) and the NAACP (established in 1909). Still, it's hard not to see traces of *Up from Slavery* in *Quest*'s images of a sovereign, rural cooperative that gains greater economic, political, and cultural freedoms as it plies wider markets with goods and services produced by rural, black Alabamians.

A useful point of contrast: in 1935 Tuskegee graduate George Wylie Henderson published *Ollie Miss*, a novel that valorized, in Washingtonian fashion, the pronouncedly rural milieu of its title character, a female farmhand in an all-black town in Macon County, Alabama (the county that houses Tuskegee). The whole text could, according to J. Lee Greene, "be considered a southern black folk idyll."[73] But, unlike Zora, and in accordance with the idealized values of Tuskegee outlined above, Ollie inhabits a small-scale black nation unto itself. For all her material and romantic trials, the trail of Ollie's conflict never leads her into the white world, and the crucial difference between the Tuskegee novel *Ollie Miss* and *Quest* may boil down to the presence of white people in Du Bois's dramatis personae.

Curiously enough, however, the real-world basis for one of *Quest*'s most prominent white characters, Miss Smith, is likely unimaginable without Washington. As Herbert Aptheker notes, the novel's fictional geographies expanded on Du Bois's own 1906 fieldwork studying the conditions of black citizens in Lowndes County, Alabama.[74] Here Du Bois found the prototype for

Miss Smith's project in the Calhoun Colored School, an institution founded on the Hampton-Tuskegee model in 1892 by Charlotte Thorn and Mabel Dillingham, two white New England women operating under Washington's direction.[75] Using this unexpectedly favorable treatment of a school committed to industrial education as just one example, *Quest* sweeps across the partitions so often ascribed to Du Bois's thinking; it offers vivid images of a politically productive engagement with capitalist modernity and black modernism by following it across environments of both blackness *and* rurality.[76]

Quest's figurations of the rural modern come into earshot in the novel's opening scene. While searching for Miss Smith's school, with night falling all around, Bles stumbles into a "strange land," crossing into the swamp that lines the Cresswell property and finding himself frightened when "of a sudden up from the darkness came music." It's not just the unexpected intrusion of sound but also the music's sonic qualities—its "wildness and *weirdness*" (1, emphasis mine)—that disquiet Bles. Submitting this scene to a wider view, the descriptor "weird" appears as a surprising halo to several examinations of African American "folk" music during the period. Most prominent perhaps is Du Bois's own in the "The Sorrow Songs" of *Souls*. Explaining the hybrid epigraphs that knit musical notation from a "Negro spiritual" to a snippet of text, Du Bois describes the "haunting echo of these *weird* old songs in which the soul of the black slave spoke to men" (154–55, emphasis mine). But since Du Bois sets himself up as an avatar of American blackness, and since he proposes these songs as the black *folk*'s most important cultural legacy, it's fair to ask, Whence the weirdness?

For one thing, in Du Bois's reading, these melodies originate in slavery, an institution he—unlike Washington—never experienced firsthand. Second, and more important, the songs "came out of the South unknown to me, one by one, and yet at once I knew them as of me and mine" (155). They are at once indispensable to Du Bois's sense of black self ("at once I knew them . . .") and "unknown"—distant in both geography and culture, for given Du Bois's background and training he stands, in Eric Sundquist's memorable phrase, as something of a "folk parvenu."[77] Writing of the affective consequences of the sorrow songs, Jonathan Flatley holds that they "signal missing histories, absent worlds."[78] I contend that such histories go missing and worlds become absent because the songs themselves—even when dressed up by the Fisk Jubilee Singers—remain imbricated in forms of rural southern labor to which Du Bois had only partial access. So while in *Souls* he confidently asserts that the "Negro folk-song" represents "the singular spiritual heritage of the nation" (155), Du Bois still experiences it through the veil of weirdness.

Such responses aren't contained by the color line. By way of contrast, I would point to an interview from the provocatively named white minstrel Ben Cotton that looks back, in 1897, on the beginnings of a career that peaked in the years directly following the Civil War. Cotton claims here to have both observed and participated in performances of African American music while working on an antebellum Mississippi riverboat: "I used to sit with them in front of their cabins, and we would start the banjo twanging, and their voices would ring out in the quiet night air in their *weird* melodies. They did not quite understand me. I was the first white man they had seen who sang as they did; but we were brothers for the time being and were perfectly happy."[79] Aside from Cotton's fantasies of cross-racial consanguinity, the most striking detail of this account is its link to *Souls* through the adjective "weird." Cotton contends, against the distancing effect carried by the word, that his appreciation of and participation in music making creates a bond ("we were brothers") at the same time that it uncovers signs of separation: "They did not quite understand me." In a description that distills the logic of blackface ventriloquism, Cotton expresses confidence that he actually could "s[i]ng like they did," proposing a collaborative performance of "weird melodies" that can undo racial difference—but only temporarily, and always under full control of the white participant. To Cotton's great advantage, the black mask is removable. Flirting with an origin myth of minstrelsy, Cotton hopes, by dint of his whiteness, to have avoided Ralph Ellison's trenchant description of the racial imitator who "becomes in fact that which he intends only to symbolize."[80] Lest I seem eager to yoke Du Bois to a white minstrel, I'll point out that in *Iola Leroy*, published several years before any of the texts above, the title character's black mother also sings "*weird* and plaintive melodies which she had learned from the plantation."[81] Another prominent example: the purported "weirdness" of black vernacular music appears as a central feature in the signal passage from bandleader and songwriter W. C. Handy's autobiography—his private Genesis of "the blues." At a late-night train station in Tutwiler, Mississippi, Handy comes across a "lean, loose-jointed Negro" playing "the *weirdest* music I had ever heard"—a slide-guitar figure beneath the vocal refrain, "Goin' where the Southern cross the Dog."[82] In Handy's telling this all happened in 1903, the year *Souls* appeared in print.[83]

As the descriptions above indicate, the air of weirdness often emerges from rural sites of surveillance and control via slavery (the fields, the slave quarters) and in spaces of geographic liminality (train stations, riverboats), with the larger message that someone needs to translate the essential estrangement of the music, to make it and the unspeakable histories it contains somehow intelligible. For both Handy and Cotton, that required adaptation into more digestible forms such as minstrelsy or dance-band music; Du Bois's task as the author of *Souls* was to promote the sorrow songs as world-historical art. In *Quest*, it falls to Zora. And the novel—an extended, imagined narrative instead of a sociological or historical study—allows Du Bois to propose a direct, untranscribed encounter with the source of the sound itself, a sound as trance-inducing as it is startling. One point of apparent paradox is that the noise emanating from Zora/the swamp, the "formless, boundless music," affiliates fairly easily with a modernist soundscape, "formless" and "boundless" acting as appropriate designations for the experiments in tonality and compositional structure associated with the modern concert music of, say, Anton Webern, Charles Ives, and Arnold Schoenberg, all in the avant-garde of the early twentieth century. The implication here is that the "folk"—so often made synonymous with rural blackness—might effectively double, parallel, and perhaps even give rise to characteristic innovations of sonic modernism.

Thus the music rises, unbidden, "up from the darkness" (1)—from spaces (the swamp) and bodies (Zora's) distinctly coded black. The significance of darkness in this scene introduces a motif developed throughout *Quest*: darkness/blackness become an expressive register that allows for new chances at communication and community building. So while Bles expresses fear of the "black dark" in the novel's opening pages (3), Zora "love[s] night" (3). There are also, the novel explains, practical advantages to blackness. In a crucial moment from the penultimate chapter, when a violent mob attempts to intimidate Toomsville's increasingly assertive black population by attacking the schoolhouse under the cover of night, a mob member exclaims, "I wish I could see a nigger" (232). Although phenotypic differences worn on the skin often cause "race" to manifest as a kind of hypervisibility in the light of day, this scene runs that familiar formation backward, in an Ellisonian turn whereby blackness makes invisibility possible.

Moreover, when matched to their white counterparts, modes of blackness given body, voice, and movement by *Quest*'s characters—by Zora in particular—come to represent an alternate, radical epistemology. The novel consistently explores what the characters know, how they know it, and the material, political consequences of these distinct canons of knowledge. So much so, in fact, that one effect *Quest* creates—and one allowed by the novel as a genre more broadly—is a series of conversations between competing, frequently raced, epistemologies and literacies. When Zora dances into the novel's frame in the opening scene, the narrator comments approvingly on the "poetry of her motion" (2), foregrounding a poetics that depends on embodiedness rather than language alone. Yet the difficulty of sounding—or visualizing—this poetry across hermeneutic divisions poses often-insurmountable problems. John Taylor, the Yankee businessman oriented by calculations, capital, and chronometric time, is blind to the "poetry of Toil . . . in the souls of the laborers" (25), while his sister, Mary, is temporarily transfixed when Bles introduces her to the intricate beauties of labor and the growing cycle: "The poetry of the thing began to sing within her" (12). However, none of this is enough to change Mary's notions of what counts as culture: "culture and work—were they incompatible? At any rate, culture and *this* work were" (34).

Under Mary Taylor's definition, then, culture is a single thing—it is reliably white and concomitant with modes of labor decidedly *not* agricultural. One feels the novel's radical impulses most acutely when it stages expressions of black, rural culture that are empowering and productive rather than oppressive and alienating, cultures of black agriculture that pose a direct challenge to the white overclass. The severity of the challenge is evident in an exchange between Harry Cresswell and his sister, Helen. Harry is hoping to make Helen's introduction to Mary:

> "By the bye, Sis, there's a young lady over at the Negro school whom I think you'd like."
> "Black or white?"
> "A young lady, I said. Don't be sarcastic."
> "I heard you. I did not know whether you were using our language or others'." (51)

Our language, our culture, our land, our image of "lady"—each demands protection. And the key to advancement, as Bles quickly recognizes, is to break the stranglehold through education. Hence Bles insists that Zora's own grammar of expression and communication—her own nonstandard literacy—meet the dominant forms. For her part, Zora needs convincing: "Don't white folks make books? ... I knows more than they do now—a heap more" (20). This isn't a statement the novel seeks to overturn. In fact, Mary Taylor, warning Miss Smith of Zora's disruptive potential, makes essentially the same case: "she knows too much" (33). Yet Zora projects a different sense of what counts as power: "No, no. They don't really rule; they just thinks they rule. They just got things—heavy, dead things. We black folks is got the *spirit*. We'se lighter and cunninger; we fly right through them; we go and come again just as we wants to. Black folks is wonderful" (20, italics in original). Bles doesn't disagree, but still he holds to the importance of standard literacies and knowledge: "Even if white folks don't know everything they know different things from us, and we ought to know what they know" (20). In its concluding chapters, the narrative bears out Bles's intuition. Zora's full potential can arrive only through a distinctly Hegelian merger of "things" and "spirit" that reveals the interpenetrating *spirit* of book learning and *thingness* of physical labor at the same time that it valorizes the object matter of education and the very poetry of work.

A synthesis of spirit and thing across a common geographic axis won't, of course, produce a common response. The *Dreamworlds of Alabama* (2007) recently proposed by sociologist Allen Shelton are activated by the death of Major John Pelham, a Confederate officer killed in a skirmish at Kelly's Forge who becomes the book's presiding spirit, shaping both the consciousness and unconscious of the region's human and nonhuman environments. A different dreamworld of Alabama appears in *Quest*, and it takes its cues from Zora. While Bles spends his first night near the swamp in a "dreamless sleep" (2), we watch as Zora lapses into a "daydream," speaks "dreamily" and asserts that "behind the swamp is great fields full of dreams" (4). Zora's dreamworld isn't compelled by the ghosts of dead Confederates but by an unseen horizon of material and political opportunity. Later, she and Bles pull that future in a little closer as they prepare to put out a cotton crop, allowing Zora to claim the swamp itself as the place "where the Dreams lives" (38). And the narrator presents this place, the "*black* swamp" (183), in a consistently achromatic color, marked by its "*black* lake" and soil "virgin and *black*" (38, emphasis mine); elsewhere we glimpse the "*black* waters of the lagoon" alongside a "*black* patch of rich loam" (47, emphasis mine). Likewise, the uncanny cotton-seeds the couple obtains from Zora's mother—a conjure woman, the novel is at pains to point out—are not "the green-white seed which Bles had always known, but small, smooth *black* seeds" (50, emphasis mine). This physical landscape, much like the postbellum racial landscape, is marked by almost pure potential, an observation that aligns neatly with economic reality. When it comes to cotton production, one antebellum commentator wrote, "two millions of acres of swamplands are worth four millions of upland," providing one is willing to "take *time and expense* of cultivation into account."[84] Zora is far less driven by the undying psychic legacies and physical remainders of white loss that haunt Shelton's pictures of rural Alabama than she is the sovereign production and equitable dispersal of capital via agriculture and the generative powers of black femininity.

Dreams are converted into reality-shifting material in a black space charged with oppositional energies. And the novel's representation of this liminal territory is illuminated by Monique Allewaert's handling of "ecologies of resistance" in the swampy "plantation zone" of the late eighteenth century.[85] Building on Michael Warner's concept of the "citizen-subject of print culture," Allewaert argues that "instead of simply producing subjects who gained power through an abstract and abstracting print culture, the plantation zone witnessed the emergence of agents who gained power by combining with ecological forces."[86] Zora becomes a hybrid citizen-subject/ecological-collaborator: exemplifying "mixtures between entirely new types of beings, hybrids of nature and culture," she acts as both arbiter and epitome of Bruno Latour's "translation."[87] Consequently, the swamp, with its ecological dynamism and its opposition to white rule, appears as a sure matrix of the African American rural modern.[88] And its correspondences to dominant, urban varieties of the modern first become visible, unexpectedly and all at once, to Zora. When Zora makes it to New York, as an assistant to the aging socialite

Mrs. Vanderpool, she intuits a link between northern industrial development and the southern countryside. Looking out from a Fifth Avenue hotel room, her "inarticulate questioning found words, albeit strange ones": "It reminds me of the swamp. . . . I mean, it is moving—always moving . . . always restless and changing" (133). Bles comes to share Zora's visions. After being betrayed by his grasping fiancée, Caroline Wynn, in Washington, he looks out the window "at the city he once found so alluring" and catches a similar connection: "Somehow it looked like the swamp, only less beautiful" (173). The relations aren't restricted to Zora alone, then, but she is most completely and productively energized by them.

While Dunbar's poems poetically reclaim plantation grounds, Du Bois's novel stages a more literal reclamation, enacted in the style of Progressive Era reformers for whom, in Jedediah Purdy's words, "Conservation was the principle and technique of eliminating waste."[89] In 1908, as horticulturalist Liberty Hyde Bailey was convening the Commission on Country Life—a Roosevelt-administration group designed to make U.S. rurality amenable to "the general readjustment of modern life"[90]—Du Bois corresponded with Bailey, stressing "the extreme importance that the real condition of Negro farmers be gotten at" and warning of the excessive power of "the great landlords."[91] If the commission's report, issued the same year as *Quest*, wasn't exhaustive on the troubled states of race and tenancy in the rural South, it had plenty to say about swamp reclamation, particularly as it relates to the interdependence of humans and nonhuman environments.[92] It's worth noting here, then, that *Quest*'s "bold regeneration of the land" proceeds in the rationalized style of Progressive conservationists: it must be "carefully studied out, long thought of and read about," submitted to a "plan of wide scope" (218). Tellingly, however, the manipulation and recomposition of a plantation's waste places are achieved not through federal- or state-sponsored intervention but through the efforts of Toomsville's black citizens, as the novel attaches the reclamation of black land—from "swamp" to "swamp in name only" (234)—to the reclaiming of black lives.

The most pointed example, of course, is Zora, whose full capability as an expressive figure and as a political actor takes shape in another dreamworld, this one rising through her immersion in northern libraries: "She was in dreamland; in a world of books" (136). Counterintuitively, to redeem the plantation's disregarded margins, Zora must absorb the traditions of a print-culture public. Through a sequence of paragraphs outlining Zora's education-via-reading, the narrator scans the breadth of Western history and mythology, making Zora both witness to and participant in the creation of archetypal narratives of North Atlantic identity. In a deeply provocative gesture, an African American woman reared in plantation environments of abuse and indifference serves as testimony, repository, and culmination of

Western culture: "She gossiped with old Herodotus across the earth to the black and blameless Ethiopians"; she is on the scene with Demosthenes, Cornelia, "the drunken Goths"; visits "the Paris of Clovis, and St. Louis"; weeps with the prophet Jeremiah and clasps hands with Mary of Scotland and Joan of Arc (136).

In his insightful examination of the novel's transnational engagements, Peter Schmidt has argued that through *Quest*, "Du Bois continues his long-standing dispute with Booker T. Washington and other promoters of 'industrial' education."[93] I would suggest, however, that the sharpest edges of the "dispute" are mostly absent in the novel, folded into a more layered, more optimistically drawn depiction of agricultural labor in the black rural South. In what is perhaps the novel's most direct address of *Souls'* criticisms of the Washingtonian model, *Quest* stages several scenes that pointedly allow for the value of both physical labor *and* the liberal arts. For instance, after Zora and Bles reunite at the swamp in the narrative's final act, she gives him a tour: "They looked at the land, examined the proposed farm sites, and viewed the living-room and dormitory in the house" (218). She shows her home and "den," a separate building hosting the kind of curricular material that could have lined Du Bois's own shelf in 1911: Plato's *Republic*; Maxim Gorky's 1906 call for broad-based collectivism, "Comrade"; a "Cyclopaedia of Agriculture"; Balzac novels, Herbert Spencer, and a volume of Tennyson. Political and economic theory, poetry, fiction, and an agricultural resource mingle freely.

Given the breadth of texts mentioned by the narrator, I want to suggest that the bookcase metaphorizes the novel's larger commitments to dialectic as a driver of political and intellectual development. The obvious clue may be *The Republic*, a pioneering model of dialectical inquiry. But even beyond that, the separate volumes display internal contradiction re-created as forward action—the "concrete" in the Hegelian triad *abstract-negative-concrete*. For instance, although Spencer's interest in the economic and social power of vivid individualism is antithetical to Gorky's flinty critiques of a world where the "strong were the rich" and "the weak should, without murmuring, submit themselves to the strong," the narrative resolves this disagreement in the figure of Zora, whose strength as an individual is undeniable but who never spends her power toward personal gain alone.[94] By the novel's conclusion, her personal advancements are never wholly distinguishable from the achievements of her community: just as, while working as an assistant to the wealthy white Mrs. Vanderpool, Zora masters the social manners and the habits of mind of the bourgeoisie—Vanderpool has recently asked Zora, with no apparent irony, if "she'd like to be ambassador to France" (136)—she declares, "I'm going back South to work for my people" (161). An "educated woman" who doesn't just return to the rural South but to the hands-on labor of southern agriculture (216), Zora represents a constructive step beyond the impasse of *Up from Slavery–Souls. Pace* Washington, there is nothing absurd about a young black agricultural worker studying a French grammar. But neither is there anything inherently tragic about working one's way out of an oppressed position through agricultural labor. "This is my university," Zora explains, in a statement that demonstrates how thoroughly she has "transformed" the plantation of her birth (218). She has transformed it through physical labor, through the courts, through confrontation with an angry mob, through Miss Smith's school: transformed it into the loftiest plane of higher education. The novel's discrete dreamworlds combine in its image of the cabin's library, as the spirit flows through the material object of the text and texts themselves arise from the dirt floor. Taking in Zora's accomplishments and the full spectrum of her experience, Bles realizes that, by following her lead, he was "being revolutionized" (218); he is, like the rest of Zora's observers, "startled" over and over again by the continual "newness of the girl" (13). Although the novel repeatedly emphasizes *becoming* across a range of characters, it is Zora who most fully defies "classification" (34). She is her world's most complete epitome of newness, an agropolitical subject drawn up to realize Anna Julia Cooper's contention that "the ground work and starting point of [the race's] progress upward, must be the black *woman*."[95]

As *Quest* makes clear, Du Bois isn't afraid to embrace the didactic. "I stand in utter shamelessness and say whatever art I have for writing has been used always for propaganda for gaining the right of black folk to love and enjoy," he famously declared in the 1926 manifesto, "The Criteria of Negro Art."[96] Under this light, Zora's constitution as an idealized social and political energy remains central to Du Bois's novelistic project. Pointedly, it is one key feature that fiction affords. In a 1901 article entitled "The Negro Landholder of Georgia," Du Bois approvingly commented on "socialistic experiments" among black farmers in the rural districts but noted that "[t]here was too little experience and intelligence to allow such experiments to be successful generally."[97] Fiction, then, builds Du Bois's visions of agropolitical possibility by conjuring a character with the exact *experience* and *intelligence* it would take to pull off such an endeavor. Imaginative literature bridges a gap in the archive, allowing Du Bois to build a new kind of political actor within the plantation-as-proscenium, a protagonist so vividly dynamic as to appear "inhuman" to at least one of her white observers (211).

However, *Quest* isn't didactic in any simple or final way. As it dramatizes solutions, the novel never fails to acknowledge the conflict, the profound risk, carried in its depiction of the settlement's establishment. What Zora creates in the Toomsville swamp is nothing less than a sovereign black agricultural collective. And though this emphasis on collectivity is not altogether surprising given Du Bois's attraction to socialism and, later, the Communist Party, the geographic setting is striking: measured against the blood-red, often sterile ground of Georgia surveyed in *Souls*, the black soil of *Quest*'s swamp is a fecund source of strength and independence.[98] Collectivity, however, is possible in the novel's post-Reconstruction Alabama only through land ownership: "We must have land—our own farm with our own tenants—to be the beginning of a free community" (198). Proposing to break tenancy's cycles of debt and rent, the community will include "a few" privately held twenty-acre parcels anchored by a "central plantation of one hundred acres for the school," land preserved "for the public good" (221). Here again is an oblique point of agreement with Washington, who repeatedly argued, as I noted above, for the abolishment of the crop-lien system and for the centrality of black ownership.[99] Bles, pitching the idea to a crowd of Cresswell's black tenants, emphasizes the richness of the physical environment ("the best land in the county") and the potential for autonomy represented by the swamp, promising a "little hospital," a "cooperative store for buying supplies," a "cotton-gin and a sawmill," all under control of the collective, with every member—including "the women and girls and school children"—redeemed through labor (221).[100]

"Rescue your own flesh and blood—free yourselves—free yourselves!" (202–3), Zora importunes during an impassioned speech at a local church. Free yourselves through labor, land ownership, *and* education? Through participation in national and transnational markets? Consciously or not, the overlap with Washington's Tuskegee—in geography, in concept, in rhetoric—runs deep as Zora's swamp presents a chance to create a sovereign space, dependent on agriculture, with a school at the center. According to Arnold Rampersad, the novel reveals Du Bois's "ideal state" as fundamentally "agrarian in its economic and social base"[101]—a vision that transmits fairly smoothly with Washington's. And, alongside *Up from Slavery*, the novel recognizes the need for participation from women and children as well as a necessary diversity of tasks—"we want all sorts of industries," Bles explains (221).

Even as it promotes diverse modes of production, the novel remains committed to exploring the characteristics and consequences of the "global cotton production complex."[102] Rather than promoting alternatives to cotton, as Washington does in *Working with the Hands*, *Quest* presents images of racial redemption that centralize the crop. In Jarvis McInnis's exquisite reading of *Quest*, "Du Bois attempts to extract cotton from the market economy to explore its potential values as an aesthetic and sacral object outside of the exchange-value/use-value binary."[103] I take McInnis's point—there's no question that cotton achieves striking aesthetic and sacral values—but I think it's also important to recognize that although the novel is sometimes scant on details, there is every indication that the cotton produced by the collective is still milled and taken to market; the crop represents not so much a total break from capitalist modernity as an attempt to reengineer it in miniature.

Critics often place the novel within a genealogy of Progressive Era fictions designed to expose the casualties of early twentieth-century extractive industries: Frank Norris's treatments of wheat (*The Octopus* [1901] and *The Pit* [1903]); Upton Sinclair on meat, coal, and oil (*The Jungle* [1906], *King Coal* [1917], and *Oil!* [1927]); and James Lane Allen on hemp (*The Reign of Law: A Tale of the Kentucky Hemp Fields* [1900]).[104] Of all these, Du Bois's attention to cotton is perhaps most significant, for as Sven Beckert has brilliantly demonstrated, cotton was ab initio the raw material that catalyzed the Industrial Revolution and solidified the bond among modern global markets. It also, as Du Bois frequently argued, put black southern cotton tenants at the base of a global economic force.[105] To calibrate these scalar relationships, the novel pans out to the macro—underlining cotton's place in a tightly woven, transnational network of capital flows and unprocessed materials—just as it zooms in on the micro, presenting a social and ecological condition where everything is reducible to cotton: "Cotton was currency; cotton was merchandise; cotton was conversation" (99); it was "the very life and being of the land" (16). Such descriptions ascribe cotton a dimensionality that meets Timothy Morton's explanation of the "hyperobject": it is "massively distributed in time and space relative to humans." While the growing cycle of any individual crop obviously falls well within a single human life span (well within a single year in fact), the aggregate "cotton" "involve[s] profoundly different temporalities than the human-scale ones we are used to."[106] It arches across capitalist modernity in such a way that it eludes containment within any one place or time.

Cotton necessitates a global perspective just as surely as it demands the exploitation of land and the manipulation of laborers, as any benefit produced by the cotton industry in the nineteenth century could be realized only by force. In 1853 the *American Cotton Planter* put it this way: "[I]t is idle to talk of producing Cotton for the world's supply with free labor. It has never yet been successfully grown by voluntary labor."[107] If postbellum tenancy represents the possibility of making free labor *un*free, then the *American Cotton Planter*'s antebellum formula carries through to *Quest*'s historical setting at the turn of the twentieth century. Miss Smith, for one, recognizes that "the bounty of Southern hospitality" (54) on exhibit at the Cresswell mansion was "built on a moan" (73). Yet the novel's basic premise holds that even as cotton can oppress, it might also be inverted toward freedom.[108] Such a turn, however, is possible only through unbending toil, through victory in the courts, and through canny defense against the realities of white violence.

"The cry of the naked was sweeping the world" (25) begins an early chapter entitled "Cotton," flashing through an image chain that scans distressed people around the world—in Russia and London, Africa and Alaska. If nakedness is the problem, then cotton—increasingly inexpensive and available to far-flung markets in the early twentieth century—is a partial solution, yet the passage also calls up a global stream of sounds ("the cry of the naked") made audible by modern technologies like the telephone, the telegraph, the phonograph, and the newswire. In details both large and small, the novel's picture of the cotton-industrial complex proceeds with an inherently global reach—a prominent Briton serving as an adviser to the Taylor-Cresswell Cotton Combine makes "quite eloquent" comparisons between the peasant class in India and the black tenant farmers of Alabama (77), for instance. But it's also true that new methods of communication and representation help the narrative's subjugated figures carve crosshatching microchannels of opposition, channels that gain depth and velocity through intersecting flows of information. I note one example, present only at a glance: the narrator relates that each room in the center for Zora's "settlement work"—a country cabin—contains a phonograph (163). The further significance of these machines is unremarked, but their suggestive presence, as objects of considerable expense in a humble environment, demands greater attention. Useful here is Michael Denning's recent argument that in the late 1920s phonographic technology produced a "vernacularization of music" that tied together the ports and byways of the colonial world and became "fundamental to the organization of social order, to creating social space and social solidarity."[109] In Denning's thinking, the combination of hardware (the gramophone itself) and software (commercially circulated 78-rpm discs) retrained the sensorium in a way that ultimately loosened the colonizer's grip. Although Denning is writing of a slightly later moment, the suggestive presence of the phonograph may well prove John Taylor's complaint that "the modern idea of taking culture to the masses" is "too socialistic" (28). It binds together the world in ways that prove inconvenient, perhaps even fatal, to the novel's ruling class. If it's true that cotton makes possible the emergence of dominant versions of industrial and capitalist modernity, then *Quest*'s account of liberation-via-cotton yields a fresh vision of the modern, one that draws strength from agricultural labor and the uneven ground of the Black Belt.

A 1907 agricultural manual published by German Kali Works, *Value of Swamp Lands, or, How to Make Unproductive Black Soils More Valuable*, gets at the very physical conditions described in *Quest*: in the swamp, "Nature has locked up great treasures of plant food."[110] But the missing element—potash, according to the text—must be injected. The black soils of the swamp will never bear without human intervention, without hands on the world. And since trust in "natural" processes isn't an option—"natural" so often functioning as a cloak to disguise racist thought and action—this reordering of the ecological status quo parallels, in many key ways, the political obligations of black subjects seeking to overturn an abusive planter class. In Virgil's *Georgics*, the other-than-human world's unpredictability and frequent destructiveness demand that the farmer, out of necessity, "ever disciplines his earth"

(1.99). "[A]ll things incline to worse," the poet explains, using a simile that compares the farmer to a desperate oarsman, "if perchance he slack his arms, sternward / the coursing water drags him down the rapids" (1.199). It's only by constant, consistent effort that agricultural workers avoid being swept under—an assessment reinforced throughout Du Bois's novel. These combinations of work and ecological intervention are central to *Quest*'s role as a georgic novel, and they appear throughout its depictions of labor. Despite the narrative's triumphalist impulses, these aren't images of labor's simple victories. The sweat and the blood, the failures and false starts, are too vivid throughout. Yet work is, ultimately and despite everything, ennobling. Distraught at being abandoned by Bles, Zora worries aloud to Miss Smith that she'll never be able to move beyond her distress. "Work is the only cure for such pain," Miss Smith responds (98). And, on Smith's suggestion, Zora's work focuses on the cultivation of the Silver Fleece. In a configuration that changes the psychological and, ultimately, material terms of black tenancy, grief can be subsumed through agricultural labor. It's tempting to dismiss such a notion as broadly romantic, but it complements the novel's larger project of redrawing scenes of rural modern abjection in politically resourceful ways.

Quest's investments in the reparative politics of imaginative literature arrive most fully in its opposition to the conventions of the plantation novels popular to the period. Many critics have noticed as much.[111] But I would offer the more granular point that Du Bois's reclamation project extends to remaking the nadir-era lost cause fictions on a point-by-point basis. For instance, *Quest* goes to great lengths to overturn the patriarchal sexual logic undergirding white-supremacist narratives such as Thomas Dixon Jr.'s *The Clansman: An Historical Romance* (1905). "You should have *died!*" Bles exclaims (90, italics in original), when Zora explains her past as a victim of sexual abuse at the hands of prominent members of the planter class, voicing a sentiment that aligns uncomfortably with Dixon's infamous set piece (broadcast throughout the world via D. W. Griffith's adaptation in *The Birth of a Nation* [1915]) wherein fifteen-year-old Marion Lenoir, duty-bound as a young white woman, throws herself from a cliff after being sexually assaulted by Gus, a freedman who wholly fits the image of the black beast rapist. Zora obviously doesn't die in *Quest*; she stands proud as the narrative's redeeming figure, and the novel's final scene allows Bles to recant: "She is more than pure" (238). Furthermore, unlike images of vigilante justice promoted in *The Clansman*, mob violence is revealed for what it is in *Quest*—destructive, and self-destructive, terrorism carried out under cover of night to control the laboring class and to protect a vulnerable sense of racial superiority. And the novel dismantles the threat of rape that underpins lost cause fiction by arguing that the true victims of sexual predation are young black women such as Zora and Emma.

Perhaps the most sustained response to lost cause fiction, however, arrives in *Quest*'s treatment of interregional marriage. As Maurice Lee has suggested, Du Bois's treatment of the post-Reconstruction double-marriage plot also denies a "central device of reconciliation romances."[112] Specifically, the double wedding that pairs Harry Cresswell–Mary Taylor and John Taylor–Helen Cresswell is a clear revision of a similar device organizing Thomas Nelson Page's *Red Rock* (1898).[113] In *Red Rock*, the unions of both the ex-federal officer and southern belle and of the Confederate gentleman and northern lady signaled not just the national unification of formerly warring factions but also the adoption, by certain right-minded northerners, of Jim Crow racial codes and a general amiability about the war. (In a passage satirizing the necessity of "mutual understanding," for example, Harry claims, "Both [sides] were right" [78].) These marriages make up *Red Rock*'s conclusion, acting as resolution of both narrative and national conflict. In *Quest*, by contrast, the double marriage occurs at the end of the first act, bringing together a different set of interests: speculative finance of the North and the declining social-cultural order tied to cotton production in the South. Where *Red Rock* used the marriage plot to create harmony within the families and between regions, *Quest*'s marriages ultimately sow discord and dissolution. Both Cresswell and Taylor grow rich in the Cotton Combine, but the union radically alters the social, domestic, and physical landscape: John Taylor betrays Colonel Cresswell in his legal dispute with Zora; Harry is unfaithful to Mary throughout their marriage; industrialized mills overrun and ruin the local environment. Even the prospect of unification through new birth is frustrated as the process of delivering a stillborn child renders Mary infertile. Indeed, Mary herself is so enervated by her embrace of southernness-via-marriage that the meanings of white womanhood—the container of white racial integrity in lost cause economies of sex and reproduction—are made over as something repulsive to behold: the narrator makes special mention of Mary's "ill-shaped head," the "sunken hollows of her face," and her "faded" hair (185). In the end, there is no productive (re)union among white elites in the novel. And these descriptions reveal the extent to which the rise of a modern nation belongs to Zora and Bles, African Americans from and of the rural South.

In its own way, however, *Quest* does invite the possibility of interregional alliances formed along lines of common economic interest. And in what is perhaps the novel's most dramatic step beyond the *Up from Slavery–Souls* binary, these alliances cross the color line. They are present, without question, in Miss Smith's school and in Mrs. Vanderpool's $10,000 gift, but the novel also points out the political potential of collaboration between black and white members of the working class, mill and field workers who all receive a similarly scant return on their efforts.[114] Upon crossing paths with Zora, the "gaunt, overworked" wife of a millworker gets her attention: "Durned if I don't think these white slaves and blacks had ought ter git together." Zora concurs: "I think so, too" (216). The prospect of white slavery makes common cause unavoidable. On the next page, a recently fired "northern spinner" makes much the same point to his white coworkers as he heads toward a leaving train: "It's none o' my business, of course. I've been fired and I'm damned glad of it. But see here: if you mutts think you're going to beat these big blokes at their own game of cheating niggers you're daffy. You take this from me: get together with the niggers and hold up this whole capitalist gang" (217). While it acknowledges that the "landlord and the white laborer" worked together toward "renewed oppression" (215), the novel voices these expressions of mutual defiance through its northern white characters. The chapters that follow will further develop the suggestion, present only in passing in *Quest*, that the greatest possibility for allaying the abuses of tenancy was a coordinated attempt at common redress made by a unified, biracial working class.

Once asked about the relative absence of white characters in her fictions, Toni Morrison explained how her own place in the culture informed her project: "I stood at the border, I stood at the edge, and *claimed* it as central, . . . and I let the rest of the world move over to where I was."[115] I suggest that *Quest*, like *Up from Slavery*, performs a similar work of reorientation, rerouting expectations about space, culture, and politico-economic activity. It includes excursions into zones of U.S. political and cultural power (Washington, New York City); it offers glimpses into the inner workings of white spheres of influence, with appearances by financiers and merchants, cotton kings, philanthropists, social scientists, educators. But the novel's undisputed center—and the epicenter of African American political action in the narrative—is a neglected piece of swampy ground at the corner of a cotton plantation in a small Alabama town. And the novel's undisputed hero—its most fully formed and forceful human actor—is a disregarded black woman who claims, to borrow Morrison's language, her own place as central.

In an insightful consideration of *The Souls of Black Folk* by Anne Raine, the problem of "negotiating the cultural divide between the Northern intellectual and the Southern 'folk'" is addressed through Romantic tropes and rhetorical modes.[116] The reading of *Souls* worked out above, however, highlights places where such negotiations break down, where Du Bois is confounded by rural subjects because they appear simultaneously anterior and essential to the modern. It's a pattern of reading corrected, with great care, in the author's first novel. And so *The Quest of the Silver Fleece*, a book scarcely claimed by its own author and rarely considered by contemporary readers, confounds the discursive split that so often attends accounts of Du Bois and Washington. In its fictive presentation of farming in the Black Belt, it recasts as politically radical an old and familiar relationship to the earth. Understood correctly, understood as another branch of the liberal arts, agriculture offers an unpredictably productive way of inhabiting and producing modern black subjecthood. Though posthuman models of "transversal subjectivity" such as those considered at points in these two chapters may well "restructure the processes of . . . racialization,"[117] such projects meet their limits when faced with circum-Atlantic histories that cannot justly overlook the indissoluble realities of racialized violence. These realities are the New World plantation's steepest legacy. In Baker's singular definition, "United States black modernism" is achievable only through "black public-sphere mobility and fullness of United States black citizenship rights of locomotion."[118] The plantation, by contrast, is a deliberate zone of "designated black or African *immobilization*" that leads directly to the carceral structures which continue to flourish in the present day.[119] While I don't dispute Baker's definitions or the range of his analysis, the agropolitical texts discussed throughout this section figure something different: modes of resistance, liberatory subjectivities, and affective responses that rise from the plantation itself. They acknowledge that in tending to problems ordered to the magnitude of slavery's life and afterlives, literature's highest calling is to cultivate our sense of what is possible—both within and beyond the human—from the ground up.

PART II
Other Agrarian

CHAPTER THREE

Making It Old in the New South

Or, The Leisure Agrarians Cultivate the Folk

Alongside an intensified ascendancy of digital culture, the early decades of the twenty-first century saw renewed interest in the local, the homegrown, and the handmade, often expressed, ironically, through digital media. Contemporary localist movements lack an official politics, though their loosely shared set of values—the hope to create a sustainable economic and agricultural ecoscape, and to recover qualities of regional distinction ("local") through networks of consumption like the farmers market or the CSA (Community-Supported Agriculture)—are typically assumed to have drifted in from some leftward quarter. Threaded throughout this collection of voices, however, we hear echoes of movements from the early twentieth century, and this latest variant begins to sound like the contemporary repetition of a prominent phenomenon in modernist America.

In a string of acclaimed titles by figures such as Michael Pollan, Bill McKibben, Barbara Kingsolver, and Joan Dye Gussow, the localist counterculture of the early 2000s frequently positioned itself against the corporate, the commercial, the industrial. And yet high costs, in both time and money, ensure that the practice of localism is too often a luxury afforded to the professional class alone, limitations that may have impinged its political possibilities as well. In a review of Matthew Crawford's 2008 ode to the hands-on work ethic, *Shop Class as Soulcraft*, the *New Yorker*'s Kelefa Sanneh perceptively recognized a loose allegiance between twenty-first-century localism and a brand of individualist conservatism. "Agrarianism, like environmentalism, hasn't always been considered a progressive cause," Sanneh writes—an observation that may feel like understatement to students of southern literature.[1]

The conservative instincts of the Twelve Southerners' 1930 manifesto, *I'll Take My Stand*, of course, display proudly. According to Michael Kreyling's famous reading, the Agrarians crafted a version of the South built "out of strategies for seizing and retaining power (cultural, political, sexual, economic, and so on) that are then reproduced as 'natural.'"[2] *I'll Take My Stand* is not simply a defensive reaction to modernity but an aggressively conservative one that, in its darkest logic, upheld the rationale of southern segregation. As a polemical document it has exhibited an outsized influence on both the construction of a regional identity and the shape of American literature and criticism since the overlapping interests of the Fugitives, the Agrarians, and the New Critics created a steep shadow for succeeding generations of writers and critics to cross, sidestep, or flee.[3]

In summoning the term "agrarian," I want to be clear that I am not attempting to sentimentalize or valorize conditions of agricultural labor that prevailed in the Depression-era rural South, nor am I interested in bolstering recent efforts to claim any of the Nashville Agrarians as "harbingers of the American environmental movement," as "groundbreaking proponent[s] of localism, slow foods, and sustainability."[4] Despite the presence of "agrarian" as a descriptor, I hope to avoid charges of neo-agrarianism by considering how a study, however incomplete, of the expressive history of agricultural laborers in tenancy can replace Agrarian narratives of declension ("decline-and-death," to use Jon Smith's phrase) with differently inflected expressions of protest—with narratives of radical ascension and transformation.[5] Though "agrarian" has justifiably lost respect as an analytical term, I am interested in accessing its early definitions as "the theory, advocacy, or practice of equal division of land; the redistribution of landed property, or reform of the conditions of tenure of land" (*OED*), all in order to recover the aesthetics and energies of Depression-era leftist agricultural insurgency, to place these in a modern lineage, and to show how they unwrite Nashville Agrarian fantasies of race, place, and history.[6]

In this chapter, my chief example is the life and work of Don West. West was a writer-educator-minister who, like the Nashville Agrarians, sought to gain political purchase from industrial modernity's interactions with rurality and who, like the Nashville Agrarians, used the images and ethos of the rural "folk" as a tool to both theorize and aestheticize forms of southern labor most commonly described as agrarianism. While neither party depended, in any consistent way, on farming for their livelihood, they were each committed to exploring the political and aesthetic meanings of an early twentieth-century ethos of agricultural labor. In pointed contrast to the "radical conservatism" of the Twelve Southerners, however, West's work provides an essential rubric for an other, radically progressive agrarianism.[7]

Born in Devil's Hollow, Georgia, to impoverished sharecropper parents, West made a decades-long career of advocating for civil rights and class equality in the South. Provocatively, he also passed through coordinates both spatial (Vanderbilt University; the mid-South) and temporal (1930s) shared by the Twelve Southerners. That moment also yielded the work for which West is most widely recognized: the establishment, along with activist Myles Horton, of the Highlander Folk School (HFS) near Monteagle, Tennessee, in 1932. The school came into being when Horton, a native Tennessean and student of Reinhold Niebuhr at Union Theological Seminary, collaborated with West to promote the Danish folk school model (*folkenhojskole*) as a means of preserving local Appalachian culture and addressing the area's economic disadvantages. While West's involvement with Highlander was short lived (he left within a year to establish the Southern Folk School and Libraries in Kennesaw, Georgia; HFS remains most readily associated with Horton), his writings of the 1930s and 1940s comprise the most lasting literary record of what I broadly call the "Highlander Project"—a term designed to encompass the rural-based social justice work embodied both cooperatively and separately by Don West and the HFS. And like the Twelve Southerners, West's work to enact a deliberate rusticity against the advance of industrialization bears modernist stress marks.

Not only do rural and agricultural images dominate West's writing, but his early connection to the HFS carries preeminently agri-cultural qualities. According to historian John M. Glen, Myles Horton's ideal for HFS was that the "school would be located on a farm, where students and teachers would have time both to reflect and to raise food."[8] The emphasis here on "time" existing on a balance between agricultural labor and "reflection" opens a concern that binds West's work to that of the Twelve Southerners: the meaning and value of leisure. As John Crowe Ransom, in a piece summarizing a major tenet of *I'll Take My Stand*, explained, "The good life depends on leisure ... on a prevailing magnanimity which scorns personal advancement at the expense of the free activity of the mind."[9] For the Twelve Southerners, perhaps the greatest promise of the new agrarian order was the increase in leisure time; such was, Ransom argued, an essential element to the "culture based on European principles" that he identified in the U.S. South.[10] With this in mind, I argue that, despite their vast political differences, West's work places him alongside the Agrarians in a classification I call "leisure agrarianism." This may seem counterintuitive given West's personal connection to leftist advocacy and his less privileged position within literary and academic professions. But it's one nevertheless supported by definitions contemporaneous to the period, definitions that undergird both West's art and his activism, and that expose the contested consequences of leisure in the 1930s. For instance, Thorstein Veblen's *The Theory of the Leisure Class* (1899) stipulates that "'leisure' ... does not connote indolence or quiescence. What it connotes is nonproductive consumption of time."[11] Leisure, in other words, is any work that doesn't directly bear a measurable economic output, and by this standard, the HFS's focus on extracurricular adult education places it squarely within the realm of leisure. In a 1928 study entitled *Leisure and Its Use*, Herbert L. May and Dorothy Petgen elaborate this very point, explaining that "in Europe adult education, cultural pursuits, and even political study and activity are considered a 'recreational' use of leisure."[12] Under this definition, the varieties of political instruction and activism practiced in the European-modeled Highlander Project—tedious, partial, and exacting as they were—fall under the technical classification of recreational leisure.

This chapter will assess the forms and functions of leisure agrarianism by reading Nashville Agrarian manifestos alongside West's essays and poems contained in such collections as *Crab-Grass* (1931), *Between the Plough Handles* (1932), *Toil and Hunger* (1940), and *Clods of Southern Earth* (1946). Analyzing these texts in conversation unveils the category's surprisingly wide political and aesthetic span; it showcases the divergence and convergence of messages about agriculture, ecology, and modern capitalism, the construction of "folk" regionalisms, and modernist inflections of time and space during the Depression. My analysis isn't designed to put the HFS and the Nashville Agrarians on an identical plane; it's aimed at considering the development of rural political action by identifying the actors and assessing their cultural output.

If politics is an attempt to translate the world of one's internal desires into a tangible, shared external reality, it's clear that the rural South of the 1930s and 1940s functioned as a political proving ground that brought into contest questions about agency and responsibility, history and futurity. Accordingly, this chapter is also designed to set the stage for a discussion in the following chapter about the cultural products of "labor agrarians" enmeshed in southern sharecropping and tenant farming systems. Over the course of this sequence, I highlight the generic differences between leisure and labor agrarianisms by exploring alternate modes of expression on display in the agricultural South of the 1930s. While both lodge protests against industrial agriculture and modern capitalism writ large, they proceed along separate, often contravening routes and toward disparate goals. In their products, principles, and legacies, they voice distinct articulations of the rural modern.

A/ agrarianism and Modernism

To establish this chapter's orders of analysis, it's important to consider the manifestations and meanings of various strains of antidevelopment, backward-looking modernism that sprung into being throughout the early decades of the twentieth century. Under this rubric, it's possible to connect Dilip Gaonkar's attention to the plural modernity of settler colonies along the (post) colonial margins—"not one but many... not new but old and familiar"— with Patricia Chu's interest in the "'anti-colonialist' regionalist rhetoric" of the Agrarians, which resulted in a "masculine, agrarian, and 'high' or New Critical modernism."[13] Such a formation uncovers the extent to which New

Critical reading practices and Nashville Agrarian philosophies of space, race, and history issued from the cultural and material pressures that produced both other forms of modernism and, I suggest, other forms of agrarianism.

This much of the story is familiar: where the city was widely recognized as the locus of the modern, making processes of modernization synonymous with urbanization, the contributors to *I'll Take My Stand* found the most viable aesthetic, economic, and cultural possibilities in the provinces. For all its distance from Nashville Agrarianism, the Highlander Project grew out of a similar principle. And like other rural subjects investigated in *The Whole Machinery*, their response to the overwhelming presence of industrial capitalism constitutes a particularly modern mode of protest. Still, when reading the Agrarians' essays of the 1930s alongside West's literary products of the same period, the relative absence of qualities widely associated with aesthetic modernism encourages the question: how might they function as modernist texts?

Seth Moglen's configuration of "two modernisms" provides a useful model. According to Moglen, the most widely canonized of the modernists "produced literary works that are structured by the presumption that collective resistance to the damaging forces of modernization was impossible." This group includes luminaries like Eliot, Faulkner, Hemingway, Fitzgerald, Cather, and Toomer. Conversely, the other major strand of modernists held that the "most corrosive forces at work in American life might be altered and ameliorated, and that the human capacities that seemed most constrained might somehow be enabled to flourish in the future," a possibility instantiated in the writing of Hurston, H. D., Tillie Olsen, Langston Hughes, and William Carlos Williams.[14] In short, a split rises between those who believe the experience of modernity to be unsalvageable and those who hew toward redemption; those for whom modernization equals despair, and those who embrace the interconnected political and aesthetic potential of the moment to work out what Jessica Berman evocatively labels "modernist commitments."[15] And, as I explore the advantages and disadvantages of an agricultural ethos in this chapter, it may be helpful to consider how this split follows the rift dividing figures who subscribe to a classical liberal model of selfhood, with its emphasis on individual modes of agency and subjectivity, and those who stress collective configurations of identity, personality, and action.

Although Moglen's analysis is primarily interested in the cultural work done by narrative fiction, his belief that certain American modernists could potentially "bring into being a social order in which the human potentialities imperiled by modernization might be revived or made anew" matches the stated aims of this chapter's subjects.[16] Whereas literary artists — many guided by Ezra Pound's famous exhortation to "make it new" — mounted formal experiments, the Agrarians theorized alternative approaches to living and economics; Don West, on the other hand, used the spirit of innovation as a basis for revolutionary action, for cross-class, cross-racial movement building.

Despite its binary claims—North or South, industrial or agricultural, progress or tradition—*I'll Take My Stand* is a tangled text with an irregular sense of its own message. It is an anthology that openly performs modernity's unevenness. And it is of at least two minds about what agricultural labor actually ought to be: the yeoman farmer or the gentleman planter (or, as the text frequently prefers, the "squireocracy"). For Mary Weaks-Baxter, this disagreement creates a deep and irresolvable contradiction in the text and is the primary reason that it "remains an enigma."[17] Consequently, as a document designed to articulate a consistent political philosophy, the very fact of the text's multiplicity brings the Agrarians up short. But its internal disagreements might also register as a kind of modernist multivocality, with the text itself a skein of unresolved fragments appealing beneath and beyond rationality, veering toward the kind of mythopoetic pastoral that so many of the symposium's contributors revered in high modernist touchstones such as Eliot and James Frazer. It makes sense, then, that the more doctrinaire constituents, Donald Davidson in particular, were often unnerved by the divergence of the text's messages. This multiplicity in the face of forceful uniformity, however, highlights the inevitable diversity of responses forced by the onset of industrial modernity, such that even within a narrowly selected group of participants—and it's hard to imagine a more evenly peopled group: all white, southern men of a shared ideological bent and, for the most part, a shared class background and professional orientation—it's virtually impossible to encounter the tumult of the modern without having one's vision refracted.

West's writerly persona proceeds according to a similar sort of paradox. Though he undoubtedly had firm connections to the millhands and dirt farmers populating his literary imagination—West worked intermittently on his parents' vegetable farm in Douglasville, Georgia—the decision to dress a radical message in the husk of the white southern vernacular creates an internal strain that often veers toward contradiction. Negotiating his own political identity in a hostile environment, West finessed his position in ways that, at the very least, signaled the inevitability of arriving at an impasse with one's own self and history. "I returned to the South to be a state organizer of Georgia for the Communist Party!" (32), West exclaims in 1934's "Georgia Wanted Me Dead or Alive." Two decades later, under pressure from conservatives to resign from a local newspaper, West sought to clarify an admittedly tricky position: "Those who read *The Southerner* or have heard me speak, know my public and voluntary statements that I am NOT a communist" (54). Careful, temporalizing diction—"am not" rather than "was not"—notwithstanding,

West's objections prove that even on the level of the individual biography, to meet the prism of capitalist modernity and its political discontents is to be separated out into discrete, often conflicting, parts.

How, then, does this particular constellation of texts engage discourses of modernism? Susan Stanford Friedman's deconstruction of the common lexigraphy concedes that whatever else modernism might represent, it is undoubtedly concerned with the turbulence of cultural rupture. Yet, as responses to this turbulence are translated into politically motived cultural products, they project their own kind of authority, against which emerging innovators must rebel: "The impulse to order is the product of chaos," she explains of modernism's uncanny ability to extinguish and reinvent itself in concert with capitalist modernity's ceaseless cycles of creative destruction.[18] Although Perry Anderson expressed doubt about the efficacy of "modernism" as a meaningful period descriptor, his begrudging definition does make possible a discussion of how the rural boundaries of the "modern" meet the rustic subjects addressed by both the Nashville Agrarians and Don West. Modernism, in Anderson's view, "arose at the intersection between a semi-aristocratic ruling order, a semi-industrialized capitalist economy, and a semi-emergent, or -insurgent, labor movement."[19] Anderson's emphasis on the incompleteness of the ruling order, of industrialization's capitalism, and of an inchoate labor movement captures the discordant tensions stippling both the Twelve Southerners and the Highlander Project. It's a world in which cultural and economic power are ostensibly up for grabs, and so it's unavoidable perhaps that for both parties the "imaginative proximity of social revolution," to use Anderson's phrase, becomes an animating force. West, in fact, embraced the inevitability of revolution well into the 1950s in essays such as "We Southerners Have a Rendezvous with Destiny" (1956), wherein he claimed a central role for working-class southerners in the imminent upheaval. The Agrarians, on the other hand, imagined the great social transformation as a process of radical retrogression and restoration. In "The South—Old or New?" John Crowe Ransom argued that the "American community" can only avoid the shipwreck of commercial and cultural industrialism by "remaining Southern in the pure, traditional, even sectional sense."[20] And, as Ransom and other of the Agrarians specify, this notion of purity was inextricable from the sense that, as Robert Brinkmeyer succinctly puts it, "southerners were the world's last Europeans."[21] Of course, to buttress a sense of European identity in decline is to recognize that what the essay implicitly calls for—and what *I'll Take My Stand* as a whole tends toward—is the forceful imposition of a uniformly Eurocentric culture.

West's work was mostly published with regional presses in limited-run editions, and although he has never found his way into any major canon of modernism, the warp and weft of the rural modern provides his poems of the 1930s and 1940s their distinctive patterns. I'm not interested in arguing that his work harmonizes stylistically with high modernism, or even that it belongs in the same corral as that of more celebrated vernacular-lyric modernists from the period, like Sterling Brown, William Waring Cuney, or Langston Hughes (the latter a friend and acknowledged influence for West). More important to me are the possibilities of his writing as politically activated iterations—and inventions—of the "folk." And by putting it into conversation with the work of Allen Tate, the most prominent Agrarian poet, the sound of West's verse in a widened theater of modernism becomes audible. Partly, and most obviously, this is a study in contrasts: to compare Tate's baroque aestheticism with West's seemingly untrained, deliberately demotic voice is to gain a firmer sense of how far from the circles of elite poetry West traveled.[22] It's also a matter of aesthetic philosophy: as Alfred Kazin wrote in 1942, literature's value for Tate was "precisely [that] it had no social relations at all," a marked contrast to West's position as activist-artist.[23] Where Tate understood literary production as necessarily separate from civilization, as material suitable for preservation and dissection with the new critical tools of university classrooms, West published in partisan outlets such as the *Liberator*, *New Masses*, and the *Daily Worker*, staged readings that drew working-class audiences, and often personally circulated his chapbooks.[24] Yet a comparison of the two poets also gathers a cluster of subjects they share—land, history, inheritance—and reveals some fundamental differences in the scope and values of the two parties' competing visions as well as the divergent ways that they experienced and represented an agrocentric modernity.

Tate's 1931 poem "Emblems," an extended meditation on the pull of ancestry across space and time, bears directly on several salient topics. The first stanza outlines the poem's topographic and biogeographic terrain:

> Maryland, Virginia, Caroline
> Pent images in sleep
> Clay valleys rocky hills old fields of pine
> Unspeakable and deep.

The proper-noun state names (Maryland, Virginia, the Carolinas) stack up as "pent images," carrying mythic associations that wait to spring into consciousness. As a swirl of name-signs and ecological textures strung together on a single unpunctuated line, the places cohere as historical associations: the eastern rim of the continent, where the Tidewater crosses the Fall Line and drains into the Piedmont, and where the speaker imagines Anglo settlers first establishing themselves. In the next stanza, these spaces—"clay valleys rocky hills old fields of pine"—become the very "source of time" toward which the speaker's "farthest source of blood / Runs strangely to this day" (36). The full reach of Tate's conflation of native ground, history, and culture becomes clear as both *time* and the speaker's own transgenerational identity—his "blood"—originate from *space*, from a plot of holy ground. And the blood runs "strangely" but surely back to its source on the mid-Atlantic seaboard. No surprise, then, that "the fathers," "unkempt" though they be, continually "waste in solitude / Under the hills of clay." In "Emblems," the ground is a crypt that keeps on giving.[25]

The thematic shifts in the poem's first section match its modulations in rhyme scheme across the first three stanzas: stanza 1 introduces the poem's milieu in a tight *abab* form, while stanza 2—where the southern soil assumes a clutch of numinous associations—torques that same pattern through slant rhyme ("blood" and "solitude"). In stanza 3, however, as the subjects move "Far from their woe fled to its thither side / To a river in Tennessee" (36), the pattern breaks into an irregularity (*abcbaab*) that signals the poem's final focal turn toward the speaker's own lived trajectory. Mapping onto Tate's biography the "alien house" and the "river in Tennessee" to which the speaker and his family decamp, it's likely that the poem looks to the poet's "farm," Benfolly, located on the banks of the Cumberland River in Clarksville, Tennessee. A gift from his brother that served as the site of countless Agrarian parties and weekend retreats, it was here that Tate styled himself, according to biographer Thomas Underwood, "as not so much a farmer, but as a cultivated country squire—as one of the gracious plantation owners he associated with the antebellum era."[26] This particular rural space offered Tate a proscenium within which to reenact the relations and roles of an eclipsed society, a lived experiment to lend some heft to the Twelve Southerners' poetic reveries.

In an undated essay, Davidson argued that it was the poetry of Allen Tate, not Eliot, that most fully met the criteria of "Tradition and the Individual Talent," for unlike Eliot, Tate had no trouble "locat[ing] a tradition to which to cling." His claims were, unmistakably, on the "tradition" of the white patrician South. "It is not surprising," Davidson explains, "to find in Tate's poems a certain quality of firmness and assurance that Eliot does not consistently exhibit."[27] "Emblems" evokes that tradition through the repetition of a common theme, especially prominent among the melancholic modernists described by Moglen: the ancestors are everywhere present but nowhere more visible than in the palimpsest of one's homeland. So the air of alienation that pervades the piece aligns with its messages of displacement, as the speaker recognizes the persistence of his predecessors' woes in his own condition, discovering, in his present moment, "their breath to be / All that my stars betide—" (36). An elegy for the present, populated by men who "must die forever," the poem fondles a knot of psychic and physical threads that tie the speaker to his forbears. These bonds are formed through conjunctions of death and landscape, as the speaker extends his gaze back toward the opening phalanx of Anglo settlers, in "the East where life began," ruminating on his ancestors' place there. It was out beyond, along the banks of some unidentified "great river," that these "forefathers ... carved out / Deep hollows of memory on a river isle" (37). The westering movement of American society signals decline, not progress, to the speaker: his is a vision of the land that will always escape its basic materiality, conjuring a site where memory assumes form and substance more real than the ground itself. And therefore the land, established as the source of time and identity early in the poem, unlatches, dissipating in a violent vortex of brilliant remembering.

The poem ultimately stands as an exercise in what Edmund Wilson, writing for the *New Republic* in 1931, identified as an article of faith to the "Tennessee Agrarians": the attempt to "revive the old myths of the family." This move, in Wilson's estimation at least, provides a calculated response to between-the-wars modernist ennui: "as lacking in a religion or a common ideal as their compatriots of New York or Paris, they try to find one in ancestor worship."[28] Although Tate's readiness to hypostatize historical memory suggests a space unhitched from the force and tempo of modernity, "Emblems" remains a deeply, even paradigmatically, modernist response.

While West's work is similarly preoccupied with family lineage, his approach to the subject is neither as haunted nor, tellingly, as defeated as Tate's. In "Mountain Boy"—a poem included in "Knott County, Kentucky: A Study," the 1932 thesis West submitted at Vanderbilt—the speaker directly addresses the titular mountain boy, dispensing valedictory bromides ("Turn your thoughts free" and "Nourish your imagination") while also essaying the confluence of people, place, and politics. "Love the soil," the speaker urges, "Your father's blood / Made it rich" (27–28). We're onto an image here that West shares with Paul Laurence Dunbar—the ground made arable ("His sweat caused fruit to grow") through bodily enrichments of suffering. In opposition to "Emblems," however, the human figures in "Mountain Boy" don't carve memories out of riverbanks; they posit a more direct, concrete relationship with the ground:

> Sift the coarse soil
> Between your fingers.
> Exult when it runs between your toes (28)

Another point of contrast: unlike Tate's, this poem never presumes the obligation to return to some pure vision of a past that was never as ancient as it needed to be. West doesn't recognize "the East" as the place "where life began"; his survey of ancestry reaches back only a single generation, not to "the fathers" of Tate's "Emblems" but to the singular father, remaining unclouded by misty evocations of Anglo contact with the New World. And his ground is biologically productive: instead of housing the dead who are continually dying, it yields fresh organic life, forwarding an image that calls forth Tate's famous tour of a Civil War graveyard ("Ode to the Confederate Dead") filled with "inexhaustible bodies that are not / Dead, but feed the grass row after rich row" (20). The signal difference in West's poem, however, is that the body-as-fertilizer is turned toward an agricultural product ("fruit"), not a wide field of cemetery grass.

Another important difference: read against Tate's studied formalism, "Mountain Boy" evinces a deliberately rough edge, with short, blocky lines, general inattention to rhyme and meter, and a willingness to court the language of sentimentality. While there's no reason to believe that Tate ever commented on, or even encountered, West's work, it's not hard to imagine his response: West's transparent politics and his unvarnished, colloquial voice would likely register as doggerel to Tate. Vulgarism that swaps aesthetic value for ideology, the well-wrought urn for common clay. But the poem itself anticipates just such a response by seeking definitions of poetry that stray from Tate's formal preoccupations and beyond the strictures of the text itself. "Yours is the poet's life," says the speaker to the mountain boy:

> You rhyme the soil,
> Dig and plant
> And watch the corn grow. (28)

Images of the plowboy poet go back at least to European Romanticism, but the idea of a poetry crafted through manipulation of the elements—through an ability to blend the lingual and the physical to "rhyme the soil"—boldly mingles language and the material world. It also signals the extent to which West sought to wrest literature from the experts, to unlock its political potential by merging physical action and the expressive grammars of poetry.

It may be that both Tate and West ask similar questions about how one occupies the present in an age where time has achieved new and disorienting fluidity. But, as expected, they arrive at divergent answers. In "Emblems," the response is simple enough: the sensation of perpetual decline, of a never-fading "sunset," is unbreachable, and the wounds of remembering are best addressed by ever more vivid remembering and a deeper imaginative connection, such that the sound of moving water reports "the ghost of a shout" and its sight, a "deep and populous grave" (37). In "Mountain Boy," by contrast, the past is never allowed to dominate the present. The accent is on futurity—on what the ground will yield going forward, on youth and the education of the mountain boy.

Tate may have remained unaware of West and his work, but West wrote with the Agrarians at his elbows. His decision to shift his academic focus at Vanderbilt, from English (his course of study at Lincoln Memorial University) to religion, is just one sign. West's most full-throated rejection of the Twelve

Southerners, however, came as a poem, 1940's "They Take Their Stand—For Some Professional Agrarians."

> Some poets live in Dixie Land
> > Who never to themselves have said
> We'll wash the star-dust off our hand
> > And wipe the cobwebs from our head. (129)

In a taunting singsong meter, "They Take Their Stand" proposes two related problems with Nashville Agrarianism. First, the group's insistence on the greatness of pastness, not just their readiness to proffer "Praise to a system dead and gone" but also the steady inclination to "sing of ancient Greece and Mars" while ignoring the "starving kids today." It's a sensibility that runs the entire project aslant the direction of social progress. There are, the poem reminds us, ethical failures in any configuration of culture and history that finds its models in the antebellum South, foremost among these being the elevation of white supremacy, an accusation the poem levies directly at the Agrarians:

> In Dixie Land they take their stand
> > Turning the wheels of history back
> For murder, lynch and iron hand
> > To drive the Negro from his shack. (130)

The second problem proposed by the poem is that just as the professional Agrarians "never delve in politics," neither do they delve into the ground itself. Suspended in physical inaction, they become "ass[es] / Braying loud in every school," public figures whose identities are tied to the image and idea of the land and agriculture, yet tellingly they never actually "*see* the growing grass / That might be had by every mule" (emphasis mine). "They Take Their Stand" ultimately posits an argument about how forms of labor and experience determine the limits of perception: what is everywhere apparent to the farmworker can be invisible to the commentator who presumes to speak for him. For example, the poem's final stanza, where the speaker implores the reader, "Come sift the star dust off their stars— / *See* coal-dumps where our children play" (emphasis mine), shines a light on the coal-shaped hole that bothers *I'll Take My Stand*'s survey of rural southern labor and landscape. Because it can't contribute to a picture of either antebellum squiredom or Jeffersonian yeomanry, the human and ecological plunder of industrial coal mining never enters the text. Hence the concluding gesture of West's poem: folding in his audience with the plural pronoun, the speaker imagines a mutually enacted corrective to the Agrarian vision, a call to collective demonstration. Against the individualist motto "*I'll take* my stand," West declares, "*We'll show* them starving kids today!" (130, italics in original). Lillian Smith, one of the Agrarians' most perceptive critics, insists that "they knew" of southern depravation but that "something had blunted their imaginations for they had only a contactless association with it."[29] What I want to highlight is how the symmetry of sensibilities connecting the authors of *I'll Take My Stand* and Don West extends so far, and then no farther. Like the Twelve Southerners, West recognizes industrial development in the region as a problem, particularly when it eventuates in the "coal-dumps." But, unlike his Agrarian counterparts, he knows what he's seeing because he's seen it.

Uprooting the Folk

The messages of West's "They Take Their Stand" continued to ring in the introduction to his most widely read collection of poems, 1946's *Clods of Southern Earth* (a slightly different version had also opened 1940's *Toil and Hunger*). In the introduction, West makes a case for the significance of his own poetry against the "minor themes" of the "little clique of the 'highly literate' elite," a group whose limited perspective determines that "[t]hey see neither the dirt and misery nor the beauty and heroism of common *folk* life" (3, emphasis mine). For West, gauging the space between the "elite" and the "folk" is a way of addressing the conditions of a rural working class: in the introduction he invites us to consider the importance of the "folk" as a grouping with both sociological and aesthetic consequences, one that includes proximity to both "dirt and misery" and "beauty and heroism" as its compositional features. It's also a reminder that for all their disagreements, Don West shared more than geography with the Twelve Southerners during the 1930s and early 1940s. In ways both direct and indirect, each party evinced an active interest in the cultural, political, and aesthetic possibilities of the "folk" as a category that pushed off of an American society guided by industrialization, militarization, mechanization, and standardization. But where past models often made the folk a metonym for the nation at large (eighteenth-century German philosopher Johann Gottfried von Herder's *volk*, to cite just one prominent example, was deliberately crafted to supply the image of German national identity), invocations of the folk for the leisure agrarians covered in this chapter delimit a series of subnational, regional concerns.[30]

For both the Highlander Project and the Nashville Agrarians, the folk provided a fruitful way to measure, and even create, rural distance from the northeastern metropole. In "A Mirror for Artists," Donald Davidson proposes that one can best access the state of the "folk-arts" in the South of the 1930s, sequestered in "mountain fastnesses and remote rural localities," through the region's "ballads, country songs and dances, in hymns and spirituals, in folk tales, in the folk crafts of weaving, quilting, furniture making." While he acknowledges that such practices are "merely surviv[ing]" in the South-under-siege and that they carry a hard distinction from the "sophisticated arts," these expressions of the folk are nevertheless "indicative of a society that could not be termed inartistic" (55). It's unclear whether Davidson's double-negative was damning with faint praise or earnestly attempting to grapple with common divisions between the high and the low, but his description most certainly accentuates a *folk difference*. The meaning of this folk difference recurs with striking consistency throughout *I'll Take My Stand*. In Frank Owsley's estimation, for instance, there's a direct line between early twentieth-century rural culture in the South and the "yeomanry" of the region's colonial settlers, who hailed "from rural England with centuries of country and farm lore and folk memory" (69). It's a resonant phrase, "folk memory," suggestive of a dimly conscious, scarcely visible set of images that can only be called up by those with the proper lineage, the correct claims of blood and soil. You've either got it or you don't.

What does "folk memory" look like in the modernist moment? For Andrew Lytle, it's Sacred Harp singing and the performance of "fiddlers' tunes" like "Leather Breeches," "Rats in the Meal Barrel," and "Hell Amongst the Yearlings" in an age of "canned music and canned pleasure" (232); it's the "[c]harms, signs, and omens" that represent "folk attempts to understand and predict natural phenomena" (224). These are, in Lytle's estimation, equivalent to the "same attempts which come from the chemist's laboratory in an industrial society" yet "far wiser," since unlike the arrogant "hypotheses of science," they operate with a recognition of their own limits (224). In *I'll Take My Stand*, then, the "folk" appear as firmly rural, resolutely organic, and purely Anglo-European.

When Don West leveraged the "folk" at the Highlander Folk School in 1931, he did so in combination with a signifier that glances in roughly the same direction as the Agrarians: "highlander." Indeed, the figure of the Appalachian highlander had uncommon currency during the modernist era. In 1899 William Goodell Frost published "Our Contemporary Ancestors in the Southern Mountains," in which the author, evidently mindful of Frederick Jackson Turner's 1893 pronouncements on the end of the frontier, discovered in the "highland stock" of the Appalachian regions "a contemporary survival of that pioneer life which has been such a striking feature in American history."[31] Conservationist Horace Kephart, whose 1913 account of life in the mountain South, *Our Southern Highlanders*, was revised and reprinted in 1922, presented the region as a "mysterious realm" with inhabitants so radically distant from the mainstream that any nonnative visitor would appear as "foreigner, outlander."[32] Yet, as in Frost's essay, the Appalachian rim of American culture still warrants the pronoun "our," a construction that rhymes with Waldo Frank's 1919 manifesto, an investigation of Whitman's pluralist nation that celebrates the "spiritual pioneering" of its own moment, the "many

Americas" that congeal as *Our America*.³³ The "our" in the accounts of both Frost and Kephart assumes that their highlanders are somehow both one of the nation's belongings and yet always operating with an unimpeachable degree of autonomy: they are constituted both within and without the nation, an overarching entity that nevertheless contains multitudes. In her landmark history of "our South's" role in the creation of a national literature, Jennifer Rae Greeson has recently argued that from the colonial period on, the entire region "South" has functioned as an essential "conceptual structure" that forms "an *internal other* for the nation, an intrinsic part of the national body that nonetheless is differentiated and held apart from the whole."³⁴ To draw on another tense of the plural pronoun, we know what we are because we know what we're not. On a smaller scale and within a more narrowly constructed historical frame, this same dynamic props up the earlier explorations of our southern highlander.

In 1908 John C. Campbell, operating under the commission of the Russell Sage Foundation, set out on an ethnographic project similar to Kephart's. It was an effort that stretched across a decade and culminated with the publication of *The Southern Highlander and His Homeland* in 1921, two years after his death. Campbell, struggling to establish a set of identifiable characteristics for the "southern highlander," echoes Kephart, noting a common feeling of antagonism between residents in the mountain regions and "travelers from urban centers in the South, or from Northern states where urban life has a prevailing influence."³⁵ Setting aside the Scots-Irish mythos that has so often provided an ethnic basis for Appalachian distinction, Campbell draws upon a spatioregional sense of difference that countervails the urban. Whatever else a southern highlander might be, that person is distinctly rural. Campbell's devotion to Appalachian folkways provided one template for the Highlander Folk School: in 1925 his widow, Olive Dame Campbell, founded the John C. Campbell Folk School in Brasstown, North Carolina, an institution that predates the Highlander Folk School by six years and that operated on a similar set of principles. It too was based on the Dutch folk school tradition, emphasizing instruction in local, rural practices as "an alternative to the higher-education facilities that drew young people away from the family farm"; it too was an attempt to reset institutionalized learning along a distinctly agri-cultural axis.³⁶

According to Glen, when the Highlander Folk School opened in 1932, it proceeded with a parallel collection of goals but with "more politically radical interests."³⁷ And curiously enough, it led with the sign "highlander." In his biography of West, James Lorence explains that Myles Horton originally proposed to name the institution the "Southern Mountain Folk School"; it was West and his wife, Connie, who lobbied for the more specific designation — "Highlander," in service of the "mountain culture and people that were to be their central concern."[38] Pointedly, Lorence's story of West's involvement at Highlander casts West as motivated by a "more regional ... perspective" that dragged at times against Horton's "cosmopolitan outlook."[39] It was almost inevitable that the partnership dissolve. But during their time together, and compelled by the significance of the term "highlander," the pair established the base of one of the United States' most productive civil-rights organizations and the most consequential of the American folk schools that arose in the twentieth century. How is such a thing possible? Just as the stress on "highlander" appears to feint toward a coherence that is narrowly cultural in its composition, in the Highlander Project it also expands out beyond any single ethnic or racial boundary, resulting in a figure of the highlander—so consistently offered as inventive, rugged, and unmistakably white in ethnographies of the period—that moves in a contrary direction, toward undermining the region's predominant racial and economic orders. From its conception, in fact, HFS imagined itself as a venue where "small groups of young southern men and women, black and white, could meet for three to five months at a time to learn 'how to take their place intelligently in the changing world.'"[40]

Broadening the view, it's clear that the sign "folk" would eventually operate within the HFS in much the same way as "highlander." In the 1930s, when—as both Karl Hagstrom Miller and Erich Nunn have recently demonstrated in discerning commentaries on American music in the period—discourses on the folk worked to reinforce the segregation of white ("Anglo-Saxon") and black ("Negro") vernacular cultures, the HFS used the same rubric to fight, in ways both actual and symbolic, against any such division.[41] So much so that by the next decade press reports on the HFS increasingly noted "the School's role in race relations in the South."[42] Contrary to *I'll Take My Stand*, "folk" in the Highlander Project sheds itself of ethnic and racial essentialisms.

Does folk have any sturdy meaning that transmits between these two groups? The significance of space, broadly configured, might provide an answer. In a 1930 article entitled "American Folk," Mary Austin offered a useful definition: "To be shaped in mind and social reaction, and to some extent in character, and so finally in expression, by one given environment, that is to be Folk."[43] Later Alan Dundes, an essential figure in the academic study of folklore in the mid-twentieth century, argued that "folk" signifies with an almost ungraspable capaciousness; it "can refer to *any group of people whatsoever* who share at least one common factor."[44] For the Highlander group, with its deliberately cross-racial mission, it may well be that the single common factor is a sense that the metropolitan world functions at a different pace and according to a different set of values, a condition of rural alterity (the "one given environment" referenced by Austin) imagined vis-à-vis an urbanized, mechanized

America. How do these two signifiers in combination—*highlander* and *folk*—call up freshly conceived antiracist social spaces? Most vitally they create distance, staunchly rural distance, between the folk school and an American mainstream that seemed bent upon actualizing what Walter Susman, in a widely cited overview of the 1930s, identified as the "American Way of Life." Such a way, Susman argued, rose from "cultural visions" of a unified, even uniform, national identity preoccupied with "questions of life-style, patterns of belief and conduct, special values and attitudes that constitute the characteristics of a special people."[45] The Highlander Project's elevation of the folk is both validation of an other-than-cosmopolitan ethos and a way of translating that otherness into political action. In this way, the HFS's proud evocation of the folk—and redefinition of its possible meanings—provides an early example of a practice that would become standard in the progressive environs of the late-1950s, early-1960s folk revival, in Greenwich Village, say, or Chicago's Old Town Folk Music School. It's the same impulse that led North Carolina attorney Bascom Lamar Lunsford to establish Asheville's Mountain Dance and Folk Festival in 1928 and, a generation later, polymath Harry Smith—one of Lunsford's most important boosters—to label his indispensable 1952 compilation of commercially released rural music the *American Folk Music*.

HFS exists in contrast to Owsley's notion of organic "folk memory" at the same time as it anticipates midcentury debates about the theory of folklore that played out between Benjamin Botkin and Richard Dorson. Botkin, a "popularizer," pushed for larger, more expansive renditions of the folk (Dorson labeled him "the treasury manufacturer" in a dig at the success of such books as 1944's *A Treasury of American Folklore*); and Dorson insisted that the science of folklore revolve around unselfconscious orality. Under this definition, folk expression loses its essence the instant it conceives of itself as "folk."[46] The HFS, on the other hand, operates on the assumption that the folk can be taught, codified, and institutionalized; it can be performed as identity, and those performances carry transformative political charges.

Consequently, the embrace of the folk in West's work at HFS and beyond contributes to efforts to legitimate an adjacent "culture" at a time when, according to Susan Hegeman, that concept carried an especially poignant meaning. Alongside Hegeman, it's possible to recognize how the fabrication of a new kind of agrocentric folk culture might "answe[r] a particular descriptive need in the modernist moment, when older conceptions of history and temporality had begun to seem, for various reasons, no longer adequate to explaining the specific experiences of alienation and difference Americans felt from others in their communities, their nation, the world."[47] These "experiences of alienation and difference" obviously follow close upon common descriptions of the crisis supposedly addressed via aesthetic modernism and the political, economic, and social structures of modernity. The impulse to recognize the concordance of the "folk" and the "modern" is, as Robin D. G. Kelley notes, an essential one since both are "mutually dependent concepts embedded in unstable historically and socially constituted systems of classification. In other words, 'folk' has no meaning without 'modern.'"[48] It has no meaning because the folk, as an analyzable, recognizable sign of distinction—the folk as an essential designation of difference—derives from the same motivation that indelibly marks the modern, and these categories act as differently motivated articulations of a shared condition.

If we refuse to equate the folk with simple notions of tradition or cultural purity, if we counter the move of the Agrarians, how might it fit within political taxonomies of the left? To put a finer point on it: can the "folk" and the "proletariat" act as synonyms, as Constance Rourke once claimed? In a widely celebrated 1933 *New Republic* article, "The Significance of Sections," Rourke disputed claims that under capitalist modernity society has effectively erased regional distinction, and that this erasure will hasten the ever-looming revolution. As Rourke has it, "Even if revolution starts in a tenth-floor loft in New York or in the textile mills of a Southern village or a plant on the River Rouge, a knowledge of these regional differences would seem essential for the enterprise of initiating the class struggle on any broad scale."[49] To deny that such is the case, she argues, is to miss the "social coherence" of regional cultures. She is talking here about a political instrumentality of "coherence" that runs against the one heralded in *I'll Take My Stand*, which anticipates, in Rourke's view, the mobilization of the radical working class: "So far as social coherences have developed among us, these seem to have appeared mainly in geographic sections; and they have been shown for the most in that class which the Marxian is most concerned. Call this the folk or the proletariat: the two have been pretty consistently identified in all countries."[50] One doesn't have to go the full distance of Rourke's argument—the revolution still looms—to recognize her larger point about the folk's resonance within, or closely astride, Marx's proletariat. It's a vision roughly consonant with West's own: his attempts to recruit rural workers to the Communist Party and other labor groups are well documented, and by moving in the opposite direction of the Nashville Agrarians, by refusing to assign the folk any definitive racial or ethnic criteria, the HFS redrew the boundaries according to another cluster of attributes—rural, agricultural, working class—adjacent to the American mainstream. It was this wider turn in the HFS that allowed it to play, in its second decade and beyond, a pivotal role in the civil rights movement and that assures its political legacy a measure of continuity unavailable to the Nashville Agrarians.

Where Is Progress?

In their own way, Don West and the authors of *I'll Take My Stand* are each working against what Marx and Engels call, perhaps dismissively, the "idiocy of rural life."[51] While Edward Soja explains the adjective's use with reference to its Greek root, *idios*, meaning "one's own, private, separate, set apart," it's clear that in *The Communist Manifesto* rural life is a zone of political disengagement and that its authors remain unconvinced of its revolutionary potential.[52] It's important here to acknowledge that Marx and Engels were likely operating under the widely held assumption that farming disallows the kind of extra time—leisure, in a word—necessary to foment economic and political revolution. For instance, Edward Berwick's fictional augmentation of Edward Bellamy's *Looking Backward*, "Farming in the Year 2000 A.D." (1890), presents late nineteenth-century farming as wholly incompatible with leisure: "as a rule, the farmer and his family were debarred from almost all social recreation, and precluded by excessive fatigue from mental culture at home."[53] Yet both West and the Agrarians operate under the contrary claim that in the industrial age a culture of agriculture actually creates greater opportunities for leisure. Examining their theories about the soil and the concept of "progress" will provide a better understanding of their distinct—though at times surprisingly complementary—ideas about the intersections of land, revolution, and the role of leisure in an ideal future.

Frank Owsley's assertion in *I'll Take My Stand* that "[t]houghts, words, ideas, concepts, life itself, grew from the soil" (69) is typical of the manifesto's "theory of agrarianism ... that the culture of the soil is the best and most sensitive of vocations, and that therefore it should have the economic preference and enlist the maximum number of workers" (xlvii), a particularly telling statement when you realize that the reference to "workers" is designed to occlude its authors.[54] This reading actually points more directly toward what we encounter in West's poems, where dirt is enriched by human sweat and where the ground is as likely to sprout crabgrass as it is usable crops: it is simultaneously a host to the noblest of professions and a problem to be overcome. Thus, while the latent power of the Agrarians' southern soil rises up to meet its inhabitants, the South of West's imagination needs attention, labor, reform. "I'll hammer you / into a beautiful song," the poet writes in the provocatively titled "My South" (135). His is not a narrative of restoration; it's about crafting a durable future from the physical matter of the present, hastening the southerner's "rendezvous with destiny." To sharpen this observation, it's important to consider how these texts conceptualize time and how such formulations shape their practical proposals. In both cases there exists a calculated struggle against what Martha Banta calls, in a nod to Frederick

Winslow Taylor's scientific approach to systems management, "Taylored time," wherein "time is both the greatest enemy of efficient work and the instrument with which to master effective production."[55] In this reading, industrialized approaches to time management ensure that time itself is met(er)ed out and measured as never before, through devices such as factory whistles and punch clocks. And yet it's precisely in such environments of overregulation that time constantly threatens to slip out of place. In an increasingly standardized world with an increasingly standardized sense of temporal distance and pacing, subjects who find themselves at odds with industrial time's flow feel their difference with new acuity.

In sum, people out of pace with the contemporary world lapse out of time; they become highlanders, yeoman farmers, country squires—agrarians. Bergson's configuration of time as an entity that exists beyond scientific measurements, in the flexible consciousness of its human subjects, bears repeating here as both groups seek to make time work for them rather than working for time.[56] The move in both the Highlander Project and among the Nashville Agrarians to emphasize the possibilities of leisure over and above economic production stands as a rejection of the ethos of early twentieth-century capitalism. In particular, the Agrarians sought to step off the track of industrialized time by actually moving backward—not, like West, forward-sideways. At the risk of simplifying their relative positions, it's fair to suggest that the Highlander Project exists in "progressive" time: it seeks to enter the stream of history by engaging time as it unfolds in the present and by nursing the inchoate beginnings of a wide-scale social-political realignment. The Agrarians, on the other hand, work to make the stream change its entire course, using notions of tradition and the mythos of a disappeared past to reenact a premodern, preindustrial society. They are obsessed, as West puts it in "They Take Their Stand," with the possibility of "turning the wheels of history back."

For the Nashville Agrarians, to be made over by modernity, to be industrialized, is to be stripped of a vital connection to one's own place and, by extension, one's sense of history; it is to become, in the words of Lyle Lanier, "unattached to that tremendous social anchor, land" (150). For Lanier, "progress," especially as exemplified by John Dewey–style pragmatism, is in some fundamental sense a catalyst for existential disconnection. This is not so far removed from West's notion of the South as a pocket of underdevelopment cut off from the American mainstream, except that Lanier's scenario represents a more fully formed retreat into the past, and one that requires a good deal of obfuscation and deliberate forgetting. It demands what Alfred Kazin, writing of Allen Tate, described as "the perfect manufactured traditionalism," for as Mark Lilla has recently observed of radical conservatism, it is "the militancy of his nostalgia [that] makes the reactionary a distinctly modern figure, not a traditional one."[57] So when Lanier pines for the "restoration of the balance of economic forces" that existed in antebellum America, he neglects to recall that given the instability of the global markets in which the planter class participated, such a balance likely never existed. It likewise ignores the fact that the vaunted balance was in large measure made possible by the availability of slave labor. "Progress is a comparatively modern idea" (125), Lanier assures us, as if that alone were enough to discredit it, and we realize that one problem with using the sign of the "modern" to draw up conflict is that it's a portable battle line, continually accommodating and reaccommodating itself to the needs of its philosophers. In his attempt to wrest "progress" out of a linear narrative, then, to replace one teleology with another, Lanier is himself participating in what we might recognize, alongside Lilla, as a complexly modern trick of assembling a potent compound of myth, history, and nostalgia, of grounding the ground ex nihilo. While Lanier may have been correct in arguing that "progress usually turns out to mean business" (123), in the analysis of W. J. Cash, a southern modernist of a different ideological cast, "Progress ... was the father of the forces" that precipitated the decline of southern horrors such as lynching.[58]

It's clear, then, that the two groups' different attitudes about the meanings of progress indicate a fundamental difference within their political and economic orientation. For the Twelve Southerners, the very specter of "progress" is inseparable from industrialism, which the South, as Andrew Lytle declaims, "should dread ... like a pizen snake" (234). It is the great hobgoblin of *I'll Take My Stand*, scrutinized directly in Lanier's "A Critique of the Philosophy of Progress" and indirectly everywhere else as the force pushing a geographically and culturally cohesive South, with its reservoirs of distinctive history and "heritage," toward the shapeless oblivion of industrial society— toward, at its outer edge in the South, communism.

Predictably enough, Don West took a different tack when it came to progress. In "Knotts County"—completed during the full flowering of Nashville Agrarianism and across campus at Vanderbilt—West described the Kentucky county as a community ringed by mountains that have "locked the people in and *pushed progress out*" (23, emphasis mine). West is careful with the term, however, qualifying its meaning here as "the so-called material progress, over which America has gone wild, but which I am not at all content to call such" (23). He isn't willing to abandon the idea of progress but wants a sharper sense of distinction between progress "so-called" and the real thing, between "progress" as an ever-churning tide of mechanization and commercialization, and the political advancements that would eliminate suffering in places like rural Kentucky. Elsewhere in the essay, West admits that Knotts County has undergone changes, lamenting that the "new blood will not carry on in the same old way." Sounding a little like the same Agrarians he seeks to disavow, West regrets the threat posed to cultural preservation by the industrial age: "Modern machinery and methods are coming in to replace many of the old customs which were really not so bad at all" (26). In the end, he is unprepared to endorse any version of progress that threatens regional distinctiveness.

It is ultimately a mutual concern about the effects of "industrial capitalism"—a phrase the Twelve Southerners share with Marx—that most tightly binds the Highlander Project to the Nashville Agrarians. In fact, the *Communist Manifesto*'s description of the effects of industrial capitalism is of a piece with what we find in both *I'll Take My Stand* and West's writings: "Modern industry has converted the little workshop of the patriarchal master into the great factory of the industrial capitalist. Masses of laborers, crowded into the factory, are organized like soldiers.... [T]hey are daily and hourly enslaved by the machine, by the foreman, and, above all, by the individual bourgeois manufacturer himself."[59] While the specific marker "bourgeois" is only deployed once, by Herman Nixon in "Whither Southern Economy?," the concept of enslaving machinery and concerns about industrial capitalism are central to both Nashville Agrarianism and the Highlander Project.[60] In his account of a year spent as Andrew Lytle's live-in assistant late in the author's life, essayist John Jeremiah Sullivan recalls Lytle's admonition to "beware the machinations of the enemy." Asked to identify the enemy, Lytle was quick to respond: "Why, boy . . . the *bourgeoisie!*"[61]

And yet the specific terms in which the Agrarians register their complaint about modern America sounds a distinctly bourgeois chime. If *I'll Take My Stand* worries about an absence of leisure, about the disappearance of tradition, and about the poverty of classically defined aesthetic and intellectual qualities in their region, it's important to remember that those values are very much the superstructural equivalent of a bourgeois division of labor that separates out mental and manual work, thereby facilitating the elevation of art as an autonomous realm of creative activity, a tendency that clashes loudly with West's image of the poet who rhymes the soil in expressions of labor-as-art. While the Twelve Southerners would likely dispute any characterization that tied their model to Veblen's formulations of leisure, the conspicuous pursuit of "non-productive consumption of time" is a major aspiration of Nashville Agrarianism and one that is, unconsciously perhaps, in constant competition with its celebrations of labor (43). The distinction between labor and leisure remains, in Theodor Adorno's estimation, just another contributing feature of a capitalist economy—"Free time is shackled to its opposite."[62] By this logic, then, the paradox of leisure-labor stands as further evidence of *I'll Take My Stand*'s status as, to again borrow Weaks-Baxter's phrase, "an enigma."

It is, however, an enigma that reveals the dense tangle of Nashville Agrarian politics. For instance, in "Not in Memoriam, But in Defense," Stark Young insists that the planter model's emphasis on leisure-class privilege promises to make labor the purest kind of abstraction by implying, against its own intentions, the bodily presence of tenant farmers or slaves. When Frank Owsley, by contrast, states that the "life of the South was leisurely and unhurried for the planter, the yeoman, or the landless tenant" (71), it's essential to recall that among the ranks of class experience to which Owsley refers we're dealing with fundamentally different modes and manners of leisure. In Richard Gray's assessment, the voices bound together in *I'll Take My Stand* occasionally make the mistake of assuming that the "values by which [the planter and the yeoman classes] live are somehow reconcilable or interchangeable," of assuming, in other words, that leisure for some isn't boredom or desperate unemployment for others.[63] In the final analysis, however, the two forms cannot ultimately be severed, and the Twelve Southerners vary in the degree to which they recognize the simultaneous difference and codependence of these classes.

For his part, W. J. Cash famously approaches Ransom's vision of a southern squireocracy with skepticism. Cash, sounding an awful lot like Don West, holds that "the squire's agrarianism was a highly formalized and artificial thing . . . a tradition with a great deal more of the salon than of the earth in it."[64] Moreover, the promotion of a planter-class squireocracy introduced a fatal fracture in *I'll Take My Stand*'s protests against the money economy since the planter, with his vast inventories and dependence on far-flung trade routes, had long been a key player in elaborate networks of transnational capital exchange.[65] For instance, the South's agricultural interests participated in, and continued to be influenced by, the world cotton market, which exploded in Japan and Brazil in the 1930s, making it practically impossible for the Agrarian fear of foreign influence on the regional markets and the realities of the planter class to share a common basis. To this point, Jack Temple Kirby explained that the "[e]xpansion of plantation production areas within [the South] . . . always amounted to an expansion of 'modernity' and the end of an isolated, 'premodern' rural life in southern subregions where the plantations and staple culture spread."[66] In short, the massive proportions and intricately spun webs of global interchange promoted by the planter system determine that agricultural projects of the Cotton Belt South were always already immersed in the methods and modes of capitalist modernity.

Historian Dewey Grantham acknowledged another untamed conflict in the anthology when he noted that Agrarian efforts to exalt the yeoman farmer were undercut by the inescapable realities of poor white farming in the South: "The agrarian myth that celebrated a rural America of sturdy and independent yeomen reached the limits of credibility when it came to the southern sharecropper."[67] Any story of agricultural labor that fails to account for the rural poverty and dispossession that prevailed throughout the sharecropping South is incomplete. And so despite the images that inform the projects of the Twelve Southerners—what Richard Pells called the "symposium's rural utopianism and its reactionary economics"—their visions fail to offer a workable solution to problems they perceived in agriculture's participation in the larger industrial economy.[68] Since this is a historical development that can't really be undone, the question becomes, What's to be done with it? Better, perhaps, is the Highlander approach, with its promotion of agri-cultures magnetized by a different political polarity, one that seeks to directly redress the challenges of rural southern poverty.

Politics and the Promise of Leisure

Whatever their differences, each author presented in this chapter was writing to push against a world that, in his own mind at least, was holding him at arm's length. The Twelve Southerners address this distance as a matter of psychic and cultural alienation that demands a coherent and impregnable "South." For the audience summoned by West's work, it's more immediately a material issue, wherein the threat of being left behind or actively persecuted because of racial or class difference poses a direct bodily threat. In "My South," West weighs these qualities against the "sad solemn beauty" of the place in order to probe the conflicts of his own regional background. His is a South burdened by "deep sorrow," "cruel chains of hunger," and "charred bones," the physical remains of a lynching (134–35).

Of course, just as the Great Depression exposed failures of early twentieth-century market capitalism, it also created room for the emergence of alternative political, economic, and social systems. And the chief appeal of agri-culture is its insistence that economic development root itself in the land and in agriculture—a system that is nominally more scrutable, and at the very least more familiar, than industrial capitalism. Skepticism about the increased abstraction of the modern economy persisted into the next decade and beyond, often asserting itself as a signal of regional identity, an attitude present in a 1945 comment by Harry Truman on Keynesian economics: "[N]obody can ever convince me that Government can spend a dollar that it's not got. I'm just a country boy."[69] In the cultural coding of this arrangement, distrust of the kind of logic used to pull the nation out of economic free fall in the Depression through deficit spending stands as a "country" virtue, even when, as with the Twelve Southerners, their own solutions to capitalist crisis are rife with abstractions of a different sort.

It's clear, however, that certain of the Agrarians were aware of the practical shortcomings of their original manifesto. As Martyn Bone reminds us, only in later publications—such as John Crowe Ransom's *Harper's* article "Land! A

Solution to the Unemployment Problem" (1932) and the group-authored *Who Owns America? A New Declaration of Independence* (1936)—did the Agrarians work out a "more stringent critique of monopoly- and finance-capitalism" by promoting specific policies and economic arrangements.[70] To that end, Ransom was the member of the original group who tried hardest to convert the spirit of Agrarianism into a feasible set of economic alternatives. Despite his sweeping proposals, however, Ransom never abandoned capitalism outright, as evidenced in his contribution to *Who Owns America?*, "What Does the South Want?" But in doing his best to pull off the trick of posting a radical critique of U.S. capitalism without sounding like one of its radical critics, Ransom reverts to a familiar strategy—he looks back at an orthodoxy that never existed. "Orthodox capitalism," as he calls it, sounds an awful lot like social capitalism, a philosophy and a practice that will reinforce the interests of the South through an "economy with a wide distribution of the tangible capital properties."[71] As a politico-economic system, of course, Ransom's never gained enough purchase to present an actual alternative to investment capital and industrialism, and since it fails on a pragmatic level, Nashville Agrarianism registers most profoundly as a kind of poetic exploration of the intersections of an idealized vision of southern history, the landscape itself, and the direction of the South to come. On the practical realities of achieving a vibrant class of independent yeoman farmers—or of making the privileges of the planter class more widely accessible—the text is, as I've suggested above, infamously fuzzy. The necessary thing was to make land more widely accessible, even if this meant embracing agrarianism's original political definition as "the theory, advocacy, or practice of equal division of land" (*OED*) and courting forms of distributism. "[T]hey have never got around to telling us precisely how the redistribution of the land is to be brought about," Cash wrote, "though that is not to be too much held against them, since the problem is obviously one of staggering difficulties."[72]

Further, alongside the force of rural southern conservatism, the existence of enthusiastic labor organizations such as the HFS and the Southern Tenant Farmers' Union, the subject of my next chapter, complicate any picture of the region as uniformly retrograde. According to Jim Bissett, socialist movements took root in the Southwest because of—not despite—a constellation of regional traditions that valued a "Jeffersonian emphasis on the common man, the dignity of labor, and the importance of the land" as well as a Depression-inspired "indictment of capitalism" and a virulent strain of evangelical Protestantism that took seriously the social consequences of the Gospels' moral imperatives.[73]

It is against this backdrop of southwestern agricultural socialism, which in Bissett's analysis had largely run its course by 1920, that the Twelve Southerners crafted a manifesto which made explicit its disapproval of "Cooperationists," "Socialists," "Sovietists," and "Communists" (xli).[74] Yet in its later phase the agropolitical solutions of the Agrarian project—what Cash correctly identifies as the "redistribution of land"—run perilously close to socialism. This is especially true in the more practically minded essays of *Who Owns America?* Consider John C. Rawe's contribution, "Agriculture and the Property State," which promotes the "widespread ownership and co-operation under a general freehold tenure of property" as an essential *"return to the Jeffersonian concept of the Constitution."*[75] As Agrarianism developed through the decade of the 1930s, it became clear that the problems of rural inequality could only be solved through a fundamental reordering of the structures of ownership and tenancy. It's also clear, though, that in attempting to triangulate their position in relation to American capitalism and Soviet communism, the Southern Agrarians relied on an overwrought sense of difference that continually edges toward collapse.

The importance of difference here becomes significant from another angle when one considers the degree to which white Agrarian paranoia about blackness flows into a more generalized fear of communism. In 1944 Donald Davidson—Agrarianism's most unrepentant racist—contributed a review of *What the Negro Wants*, a symposium of black writers, to *The Nashville Banner*, drawing close attention to what he perceived as the book's overwhelming "Marxist tendencies." Alarmingly for Davidson, even its more moderate contributors leveraged the conceptual vocabulary of communism: Charles H. Wesley, for instance, who "speaks of racial discrimination as 'fascist racism,' and calls for united action by white and black workers."[76] The extent to which blackness functioned as a proxy for communism underscores an important dynamic in Nashville Agrarianism; it also historicizes this geotemporal moment, given Nashville's close proximity to Birmingham, Alabama, a hotbed of Communist Party radicalism in the late 1920s and early 1930s.[77]

These links between communism and blackness present a line of inquiry that deserves investigation not simply as an example of Davidson's deplorable racial attitudes—he remained an active segregationist well into the 1960s—but also because it reveals connections between the racial, agricultural, and political subtexts of a collection of essays alternately titled "Tracts against Communism." There was, we know, reluctance on the part of Agrarians such as Tate to condemn the brands of socialism held by certain of their literary and academic friends. If, however, communism could be imprinted with the specter of blackness, then the results might resonate along two overlapping axes of abjection. However wrongheaded, Davidson's fearful rhetoric was at least partially founded in sociological fact: as Kelley explained, the Alabama arm of the Socialist Party of America was a "white man's party," leaving the Communist Party the last best option for black agricultural workers hoping to organize in that state.[78] James Lorence has recently considered efforts made by the Communist Party to recruit unemployed Atlantans during the Great Depression, a project that included a special emphasis on African American recruits. As evidence, he quotes former party activist R. C. Miller's testimony to a House Special Investigating Committee: "might near every colored man you met was a sympathizer when he read those [communist] pamphlets."[79] While the Communist Party found a tenuous foothold in Atlanta—and feinted toward racial integration—it's clear that conditions in southern cities, especially the New South paragon of Atlanta, are not the same as those in the country, where opportunities for transformative revolution appeared even greater: in the sharecropping districts, weary tenants outnumbered the wary landowners, a fact that helps explain the urgency of Davidson's insistence upon the construction of a defiantly white rural South. The region must defend itself against dangerous fusions of blackness and communism, against the very kind of activities West celebrated in his account of working as a "state organizer of Georgia for the Communist Party" (32).

The possibilities of such an alliance were certainly part of the global communist project. Historian Glenda Gilmore has expansively treated the relationship between radical politics and the civil rights movement in the United States, describing the Bolsheviks' recognition in the 1910s and 1920s that African Americans in the rural South presented one of communism's major untapped resources: "Because the South represented the least industrialized and least unionized part of the United States, the region weighed heavily on Communist minds. In 1920, 9 million African Americans lived within the confines of the Old Confederacy, the border states of Kentucky and Oklahoma, and the mid-Atlantic states of Maryland and Delaware. Only 1.5 million African Americans lived outside these bounds. If southern African Americans became Communists, they could lead the revolution in their region."[80]

In reconstructing Soviet efforts to catalyze a southern revolution, Gilmore tells the fascinating story of Lovett Fort-Whiteman, whose journey took him from rural Alabama and the Tuskegee Institute to the podium of 1924's Fifth World Congress of the Third International in Moscow, where his audience included Stalin and Ho Chi Minh. According to Gilmore, Fort-Whiteman "advised the Party to move into the South and 'exploit' rising dissatisfaction among sharecroppers."[81] With this declaration, the Soviet Communist Party essentially endorsed the "imperium in imperio" argument pursued decades earlier by black intellectuals such as Sutton Griggs and Martin R. Delany, formally recognizing black America as an oppressed nation.[82] That the powder was already in the keg must have been clear to advocates of a white southern future such as Davidson, and it helps explain the extent to which organized labor in the rural South was rhetorically bound to blackness, even when its participants were white.[83]

The rural South conjured by Don West's writings is under no such defensive strain. His own dream of a cooperative, consolidated South consistently arrives through the voice of a rural southern body united, across racial difference, by economic and social dispossession. Enter the eponymous "clodhopper" of this 1940 poem:

> I'm the Clodhopper—
> Have you heard about me—
> The lump that feeds the world.
> A lowland Georgia Cracker,
> Song singer from the mountains—
> A cotton-picking Brown Skin— (130)

From the lowlands to the mountains to the cotton fields, as "Georgia Cracker" and "Brown Skin," the "lump that feeds the world" moves at a similar rhythm, and at a similar distance from privilege. Hence West's drive to imagine a "South" that rises along class lines: "If they can ever be moved to see the advantages of cooperation—Socialism—they would form an irresistible force to hurl at the present inhuman system which is grinding out the blood of the people in every section" (27). Such force requires, of course, a high degree of commitment to common principles and a shared set of images and ideas.

A similar reliance on the practical necessity of unity is essential to the Twelve Southerners as well. Writing about the political theories undergirding the Agrarian movement, Christopher Duncan describes the importance of "communitism": a community such as the one imagined by the Agrarians requires "solidarity, fraternity, and fellowship within an expanded non-familial association of like-minded individuals."[84] Translating idealism into political reality demands the force of cohesion, of similarity. Yet in the Agrarians' South of the 1930s, a dubious set of criteria determined the parameters of similarity. No level of philosophical agreement can change the vital difference of "blackness" written on the body, differences that rigidly dictate each subject's fixed relationship to bodies and systems of power: it is by marginalizing blackness that the centripetal energies of whiteness gain momentum. This is another reason why blackness creates such a problem for the Twelve Southerners—to admit the aligning economic interests of the underprivileged white yeoman farmer and his African American counterpart is to take a truly radical stand at the side of Don West and the HFS.

Given their inability to generate functional action outside of literary society and academe, the Nashville Agrarian movement could only ever rise to the level of fantasia. And, as fantasies often do, this one makes its deepest impressions through images. Accordingly, the dangers of a rapidly modernizing

South are most vividly rendered in aesthetic terms. As *I'll Take My Stand*'s introduction explains, under the sway of industrial progress the region threatens to become an "undistinguished replica" of the country at large (xxxix), the literal opposite of which would be a distinguished original. For Rupert Vance, a member of the Chapel Hill Regionalist movement decried as "modernists" in Ransom's "What Does the South Want?," the Agrarian program of sociological reform misses the mark, failing to present a model of agricultural sustainability that can accommodate the demand of the region's population. Yet, tellingly, Vance's takedown of Agrarianism doesn't fault the Agrarians' aesthetic project; their "rightful task," he holds, is the "formulation of the culture and social values of an agricultural people."[85] The sociologist can't pass off on the numbers, but the regionalist can't disown the appeal of the cultural image.

West's work, on the other hand, is committed to an inextricable link between aesthetics and ethics, a sensibility conveyed in his stated desire to deliver "a poem with its roots in the earth; a poem that finds beauty in the lives of common people, and perhaps a poem that may sometimes show the reasons for the heartache and sorrow of the plain folks and sometimes point the way ahead" (3). If beauty is truth—an observation that seems a guiding principle for Agrarian aesthetes like Allen Tate—then West recognizes the need to magnify troublesome truths and to transform ethical obligations by reshaping common notions of beauty. And if an appreciation of beauty can, as Elaine Scarry has recently argued, refine our sense of fairness, then an expanded sense of what constitutes beauty seems in order.[86] For West's poetic project, to formalize new notions of beauty via the demotic is to write in the service of the democratic. As we've seen before, West's aesthetic sense is bound up in direct contact with the ground itself—even an obstinate patch of crabgrass-yielding dirt—and with pictures of southern poverty that *I'll Take My Stand* carefully elides. In Richard Dorman's analysis, twentieth-century regionalists like the Agrarians were "engaged in the modernist quest for a reconstructed, *integrated* culture, all of them seeking the alternative values and principles with which to heal the voids and dysfunctions of modern life."[87] The Highlander Project, however, called for something beyond the production of a coherent, stable sense of regional identity; it demanded *racial integration*. And the "alternative values and principles" it espoused were motivated by the goal—most fully realized in the middle of the century but present from the start—of undoing one particularly insidious product of southern modernization: segregation.

To return to this chapter's governing motif, the project of yoking the HFS and the Twelve Southerners as "leisure agrarians" forces a difficult question: what's the meaning of leisure within the nonleisure class, the population served by the Highlander Project? It may be squeezed, shrunk, overshadowed, but it can nevertheless exist. And as the life and work of Don West demonstrates, for persons outside of the leisure class, free time is necessarily directed toward gaining greater freedom. The profile of West's own class position hovers, in contemporary terminology, between the working class and the professional class, between the proletariat and the bourgeoisie: he was, variously, a schoolteacher and administrator, a minister, a faculty member at Oglethorpe University, and a cultivator of vegetables on his parents' farm. Yet for all their persistent engagement with the culture at large and for all their radicalism, West's writings act, under strict definition, as an expression of leisure.

It seems almost perverse to present the kind of social justice work done at Highlander as a leisure activity. But that's precisely the point: from its work educating and organizing textile laborers in the 1930s to the famous seminars in civil disobedience that trained Rosa Parks in the summer of 1955 on to its current role, as the Highlander Research and Education Centers, in promoting "grassroots organizing and movement building" among "people fighting for justice, equality, and sustainability," all the institution's efforts have relied on time "off the clock."[88] Extralabor activities such as the "adult education" of the folk school model take on new significance depending on your class position, proving that just as the Agrarians and Don West projected different models of the rural South, they also enacted competing visions of the possibilities of leisure.

Still, though their positions varied widely, each party found something worth preserving, the seed of a new society, in the practices and attitudes of a rural South presumed to be marching toward obsolescence. In this common tendency to locate models for an idealized society in the past, both the Agrarians and Don West realize the observations of Walter Benjamin, who explained in a 1935 entry from the *Arcades Project*: "The utopian images which accompany the emergence of the new always, at the same time, reach back to the primal past."[89] The Highlander Project does reach back but never, as the Agrarians seem to do, *only* toward the primal past. What a survey of the Twelve Southerners and Don West through the optic of leisure agrarianism most pointedly offers is a study in perspective. Regardless of political motivations, it becomes clear that when thinking about the distinct orientations of these figures to notions of time and history, aesthetics and ethics, the backward glance is an indulgence allowed only to those with the time and resources, with the leisure, to take it.

CHAPTER FOUR

Disinherited Speech Acts

The Body as Archive in Labor Agrarianism

In December 2015, 160 workers in skilled trades at the Volkswagen plant in Chattanooga, Tennessee, voted to join the United Auto Workers (UAW), a development hailed as a major victory for labor activists in the automotive assembly plants of the twenty-first-century South. Nissan in Canton, Mississippi; Honda in Lincoln, Alabama; Kia in West Point, Georgia; BMW in Greer, South Carolina—all have been cited as proof that global capital has a friend in the *new* New South, a region still marked by low wages, low taxes, and broad opposition to unionization. In April 2016 Volkswagen, operating under the pressure of a massive emissions scandal, pushed back, taking the case to a federal appeals court.[1] Although the particulars of this case expose old fault lines between skilled versus unskilled labor, they also reveal pressures between capital and labor that have indelibly shaped the region's history and culture.

It's too soon to tell whether Volkswagen might initiate a larger process of unionization in southern auto plants. The difficulty of planting a union in the South, however, is long-standing. In 2013, when the UAW tried to recruit at the Nissan factories in Canton, the labor force was split, powerfully enough at times that regional disputes of U.S. auto manufacturing spilled out onto the production floor: workers who opposed the union donned T-shirts advising, "If you want a union, move to Detroit."[2] The slogan underscores a larger philosophy supporting industrial installations in the South: southern labor is nonunion labor, and, from the perspective of capital, it stands prepared to collect the benefits that in earlier decades would have accrued to rust belt cities in the North, all without accumulating the costs. As the newsworthiness of the T-shirt proves, these messages are borne on the body itself. And such episodes stand as a reminder that unionization in the U.S. South proceeds gingerly, with short steps and a general wariness that ultimately imprints both capital and its laboring bodies.

The mechanization of agriculture, which more than any other single factor brought an end to the age of tenancy, may have also set the stage for a labor bargain in which cars replace cotton as the South's most symbolically significant economic output. A dispatch from one of the region's most prominent farming unions foretold change in the 1930s, warning that the rise of mechanization increased the need to organize: "The result of perfection of both the cotton picking machine and cotton chopping machine, along with the present trend in the use of tractors for cotton farming, may in the next few years completely change the southern farming scene making it more necessary than ever for unionization of cotton workers."[3] Throughout the decade, however, when the power of southern bodies remained essential to the industrial manufacture of agricultural products, the body itself functions as an effective archive of rural insurgent movements—a group I call, with conscious juxtaposition to the subjects of the previous chapter, "labor agrarians."

At the outset, to make any headway with this concept requires setting aside the pleasures and ethics of consumption—particularly the consumption of food—that seem to animate so many contemporary endorsements of agrarianism. This because such pleasures and ethics are often possible only for those privileged to inhabit a given place across time, a privilege most generally obtained—in the U.S. South and beyond—through racialized conquest or by accident of birth. "The agrarian insistence on place," Janet Fiskio has recently argued, "implicitly, and sometimes explicitly, devalues the experience, epistemology, and ethical agency of migrant and transnational communities."[4] The same has been true for people whose connections to the land are precarious, unhealthful, and forced—the tenants and sharecroppers studied in this chapter, for example, who worked on the front line of conflicts with ineluctably modern terms of engagement, and whose very lives and expressive artifacts render Agrarian-style southern exceptionalism absurd and even dangerous. How do such figures interact with what Fiskio identifies as an "agrarian" notion of "settlement and wholeness as fundamental to character and citizenship"?[5] "An agrarianism of the margins," she continues, "unsettles" such assumptions, "opening a space for multiple and transitory ways of creating food, community, and place."[6] To this particular trio I would add the production of cash crops, a difference that fundamentally alters the calculus—from subsistence to participation in what Edward Comentale provocatively calls the "rural factory" of postbellum cotton production.[7] What does labor agrarianism look like? What does it taste, smell, sound, and feel like? These are the questions that an expressive history of the category would seek to explore—a task I take up, in part, in this chapter.

While the Twelve Southerners created versions of the rural that turn agricultural labor and its environments into projections of their cultural and political idealism, expressions of labor agrarianism represent lived experience—a fact revealed in practices of meaning-making that highlight the body, either through uniquely embodied discourse or by presenting physical bodies themselves as texts of protest. Lauren Berlant has claimed that the "power to suppress the body, to cover its tracks and its traces, is the real sign of authority"; the cultural productions discussed below prove that an essential strategy for pressing against malignant forms of authority (i.e., the planter class) is to bring the tenant body to the foreground, to make it newly and vividly legible.[8] Such focus exposes the body as indexing modernity's "other agrarians" and its "other Souths," just as it highlights tensions between the individual and the collective, between the concrete and the abstract, that have both enabled and disabled labor movements in the agricultural South.[9] The result is a more fully modeled sense of the challenges agricultural laborers have faced in the past and continue to face in the present.

Bodies in the Mail

The roots of rural insurgency in the South of the late 1930s and early 1940s, the beginnings of an expressive strain of labor agrarianism, are most visible in the populist movement of the 1880s and 1890s, when rural subjects embraced their place on the margins in order to protest what they saw as a lack of representation in American political, economic, and cultural institutions. As Edward Ayers explains of the movement, "Farmers were not afraid of modern America, but they were angry that national progress seemed to be built on their backs."[10] An 1891 bulletin in the *Pontotoc Democrat* lapses into something like prosody to communicate its message:

> Primary on the 25th
> And the "rednecks" will be there.
> And the "Yaller-heels" will be there, also.
> And the "hayseeds" and the "gray-dillers," they'll be there, too.
> And the "subordinates" and "subalterns" will be there to rebuke their slanderers and traducers.[11]

Just as populists ironically embraced their subordinate status, they also intended to make their physical presence function as a means of dissent. It wasn't just a matter of casting a ballot but of *being there*, of affirming one's existence in the face of hostility such that the subaltern body itself becomes the most poignant text of protest possible. As the populist revolution foundered and economic opportunities for small-scale farmers further receded, the anger Ayers mentions didn't dissipate entirely but frequently found new channels in organized labor and radical politics, movements that could appear as varied responses to the *Communist Manifesto*'s call for the "establishment of industrial armies ... for agriculture."[12] And they took a number of forms in the 1930s: the Alabama-based Sharecroppers' Union, for instance, and the freshly revitalized Socialist Party of Oklahoma. Most prominent, perhaps, was the Southern Tenant Farmers' Union (STFU), a collective of tenant farmers and sharecroppers established in Arkansas in 1934 with branches stretching throughout the agricultural South.[13]

The STFU is most frequently remembered for its attempt to promote interracial cooperation against the "evils of the present sharecropping system," an alternative that would elevate the entire tenant class together.[14] And though the dream of a definitive rebuke never fully took shape, the movement does represent a coordinated effort to establish a more sustainable future for agricultural laborers in the industrial age. Nevertheless, the STFU's legacy of cultural production has been largely overlooked. For instance, the organization warrants just a single mention in *The Cultural Front*, Michael Denning's capacious study of the period, in a brief glance at STFU gospel-balladeer John Handcox that rounds out a sustained analysis of Woody Guthrie.[15] Given this relative dearth of critical attention, it's important to begin with one of the movement's most vibrant artifacts: a series of letters sent to STFU secretary H. L. Mitchell, collected as *The Disinherited Speak: Letters from Sharecroppers* and published by the Workers Defense League in 1937. To broaden the view of epistolary abjection in the period, I will also analyze selections from *Dear Mrs. Roosevelt: Letters from Children of the Great Depression*, a collection of letters sent to Eleanor Roosevelt compiled recently by Robert Cohen, paying special attention to writers originating in the rural South.

The alterity of southern tenant farmers and sharecroppers in the 1930s is a matter of public record: some of the period's most celebrated documentary projects, including the extensive photographic archives of the Farm Securities Administration, feature rural southern subjects. Yet the issue of self-representation in these texts remains unresolved, prompting a variation on Gayatri Spivak's famous question: Can the *rural* subaltern speak? The problem is arguably compounded by the medium of the photograph, where performance, unlike speech per se, can be crystallized as a single specific moment. Though the letters I analyze vary widely in both style and substance, they represent a concentrated effort to answer my version of Spivak's question in the affirmative. And, in contrast to the writerly efforts of the previous chapter's subjects, the manner of representation under analysis here draws upon the expressive possibilities of the very bodiness of the body. It's a subtle but essential distinction: where leisure agrarians emphasize the *earth* in contact with the body, labor agrarians highlight the *body* in contact with the earth. "Class," Nancy Isenberg reports, "has never been about income or financial worth alone. It has been fashioned in physical—and yes, bodily—terms."[16] And so the body acts as the rigging that holds these texts in place. Jay Watson has examined the extent to which artists and thinkers from the

South have shortsightedly sought to explore the "mind" of the South at the expense of the body, for "if southern ways of life have been built upon particular guiding ideas and visions, they have in an even more profound way been built upon, and by, southern bodies."[17] While these letters reveal the centrality of bodies in the southern economic and cultural landscape, they also present a fascinating form of embodied discourse—one that allows rural subjects a chance at *being there*, like the populist agitators referenced earlier, in writing. This is especially true of *Disinherited*, which was released with the unequivocal intent of drumming up support for the union. As an activist tool, the collection's primary technique is to render the world of the sharecropper legible to the outside by making the voices both *sound* and *look* like direct transcriptions, a quality the text reaches for by getting as close as it can to its subjects' somatic condition.

Such an effect is best achieved in these cases by using the personal to lend specific shape to abstraction. In the first place, then, the most direct topic of each letter is the individuated experience of the sender—we cannot understand anything about the state of the sharecropper or rural southern abjection without first confronting the cluster of concerns addressed in the letter itself. Fittingly, the worries that recur most frequently center on the state of the body itself. In the hardscrabble world conveyed by the writers' words, there's scant attention to intellectual or spiritual matters but an unceasing interest in food, clothing, shelter, and the opportunity to convert physical labor into these essential commodities.

Representations of the body in *Disinherited* must ultimately also come to terms with the threat of bodily violence. To write the body from the tenant position is to draw a world shadowed by the prospect of physical force that cannot safely be retaliated against. For example, Lester Robinson's letter from Proctor, Arkansas, tells of landowner Henry Croft's attempts to purge his tracts of the union through intimidation: "[Croft] raided the home of Nathan Peoples Negro here own this place, threaten to kill him and drew their guns own hom because of they thought he was and my sister was a union member" (13). There's no word on how Nathan Peoples reacted, but it goes without saying that resistance yields escalation and the physical consummation of verbal threats. The text's silence in this regard reinforces the extent to which both law and custom collude to render sharecropping bodies passive, particularly those belonging to African Americans and union members. Robinson's letter further uncovers the centrality of violence by signaling an awareness of the ways in which guns interact with sharecropping bodies, of how they function as ominous extensions of the landowning person. D. Gatewood relates an incident in which the local "Boss" and "Book Keeper" "Came down on the farm one night drunk and went in a widdow woman house and tried to make her tell something about this union and also cocked a Revolver in a man stomach" (15). The gun is cocked "in" the man's stomach; the language here envisions a puncture, an invasion, and an intimation of rape, all with the prodding pistol. And the sovereignty of the individual body, as I've mentioned before, is violated in a gesture that reveals the severity of the situation's stakes: in an economy of values that permanently links ground and body, to own one is to own the other, with all the control that ownership implies.

The letters' interests in the body proceed beyond content into form. One way that the physical corpus reveals itself in these written documents is by preserving their nonstandard orthographic features. Appearances of irregular grammar, spelling, and punctuation do more than indicate the literacy of the writer; they point toward a merger of text and voice, albeit a voice consciously reaching for the register of "writer." Textual irregularities likewise emphasize these letters' origins in the physical world. With the individual writer's unredacted tendencies intact, it's easier to appreciate the materiality of both the letter and the author as the recoupling of the written artifact to the bodily event of writing comes into focus. To a greater degree than writing matched to the standards of editorial style guides, these letters make it possible to espy the signing presence of the author's body lingering above the text. Michel de Certeau theorized some of the consequences of this dynamic when he considered the relationship between technologies of writing and the body itself: "Between the tool and the flesh, there is thus an interaction that shows itself . . . by the cry, which shrieks an inarticulable pain and constitutes the unthought part of the bodily difference."[18] It's not simply the text, then, but the production of the text—preserved in the letters' orthographic quirks—that represents an unconscious drive to overcome the fundamental divisions between incarnate persons, a drive consistently undermined by the limitations of expression via language. So while what Certeau calls "bodily difference" may be impossible to bridge definitively, its effects can be alleviated, in starts and stops, through language.

Of *Disinherited*'s authors' difficulties representing and theorizing their experiences, William Stott has suggested that "[m]any of them were so innocent, so inexperienced, that they did not really conceive the otherness of others."[19] It is impossible to know from these brief missives if or how they "conceived" the other, but the problem he describes isn't unique to this group of writers alone. And it's hard to understand, in Stott's mind at least, what qualifies as experience, hard to understand how the contributors to *Disinherited* could possibly appear as innocents. What we can determine is that if, as I've argued above, the presence of the physical body is among the most effective means of protest available to rural subalterns, then the editorial decision—made by both H. L. Mitchell and *Dear Mrs. Roosevelt*'s editor, Robert Cohen—to present these texts in their original orthographic form gives the letters a sharper political edge, a more refined message in self-representation made ready-to-hand.

In addition to their importance as signs of social conflict, I argue that these texts also present themselves, unwittingly perhaps, as participants in the period's outpouring of modernist expression. For instance, as *The Disinherited Speak* responds to the conditions of a modernizing region—greater presence of communication technologies and mechanization, increased influence of the nation-state, the abstractions of market capitalism and the alienation of labor it engenders—it becomes a resonant countertext to *I'll Take My Stand*. As I mentioned in the previous chapter, the Agrarians' messages often divided against themselves, producing a modernist effect of multiplicity and multivocality beneath a nominally unified front. Likewise, *The Disinherited Speak* stands as a collection of distinct voices loosely grouped according to a series of shared concerns. But the separate interests and histories of the individual letter writers frequently rise to the top. Most practically, the letters work to construct a viable union community through writing. Letter after letter speaks to and through Mitchell to write the group into existence while simultaneously highlighting the impossibilities of growing such an organization in a world carefully composed to thwart collectivity. To make a union out of language, to call up and conjoin the bodies and spaces such an organization must span, is not so different, perhaps, from Eliot's impulse to "shore up" the fragments of a fractured mythos. But unlike Eliot's highly intellectualized exercise in re-creating a centered sense of history and culture, the efforts of the writers of the *Disinherited* letters are tied to—and to some extent circumscribed by—the material necessities of the sharecropping South.

Of course, the most painful difference between *I'll Take My Stand* and *Disinherited* consists in the latter's ability to create specific pictures from the other side of the farming life. Against the Agrarians' essayistic musings, we get grainy details about spoiled hog meat and water snakes, cotton prices and rent negotiations. More pointedly, in fact, the STFU letters uncover a desperate and unrelenting interest in the material concerns of tenancy: goods, services, contracts; meals and dues and spare change—the nuts and bolts of rural survival. This is especially apparent in the voices of *Disinherited*'s female contributors. A letter from Marie Pierce, for instance, outlines the difficulties of securing basic sustenance for her family (6). We get the sense, from Pierce and from other women members of the STFU represented here, that they labor with a centripetal force which works to keep families intact, while juggling domestic realities that constantly threaten to spin their world apart. These are conditions so dire that only whisper-thin margins separate the living and the dead: in Pierce's letter, a $0.35 can of Eagle Brand milk is the last hope for a sick baby, and yet it is an expense that tips a family into insolvency. Whatever else this might mean, the beneficent presence here of a mass-produced commodity makes Lyle Lanier's ironic comment in *I'll Take My Stand* about the "liberatory" failures of the Detroit-made bag of potato chips sound like a bourgeois potshot (145). At the very least, the comparison reveals a differently calibrated system of values: aesthetics and reductive notions of authenticity on the part of Agrarians like Lanier; survival for writers like Pierce.

The competing values of these texts reveal themselves in a more fundamental way: concomitant with its commitment to biracial collaboration, *Disinherited* makes no clear editorial division between black and white voices. Yet the presence of distinctly African American concerns continually seeps through. For instance, an unsigned letter from Marked Tree, Arkansas, explains: "i am tired warking for nothin it is worser now than it was Slavery—thy woad give us close an foad but know thy just give us a hard way to go an till lies to keep enyone else from helping the poar" (7). While the STFU could never ultimately absorb or deflect the effects of Jim Crow, the movement does prove that correlated effort is possible, even when it remains shadowed by segregation and the legacies of slavery. Across the realities of difference, it accepts the impossibility, even undesirability, of uniformity just as it pursues a politics of unity. If racial difference manifests most readily as a bodily condition, then it's no surprise that a different set of concerns about the conflicts of sharecropping beset black bodies in *Disinherited*.

Fittingly, *Disinherited* reveals the degree to which women and people of color hold positions of power in the STFU. Indeed, by the measure of these letters, they appear as the union's most committed members. Lester Robinson discusses the issue: "We have most of the negroes but havent got any White labors in" (21). Luella McDonald, who identifies herself as a secretary, reveals her place in the organization: "Now I am a woman but as I understand we are to go on equal footing with the men" (17); while L— M—, a leader in Turrell, Arkansas, writes of Ellen Franch, explaining that "she will doo all She can to get members for our local" (23). Another letter, by member Lula Parchman, contains the following exhortation: "Regardless of color or creed . . . Pray to god for the continue growth and Strength of The Southern Tenant Farmers Union and want to do every Thing I can do to help make The union Strong" (27). The female authors of these letters are not only quick to identify themselves as women but to recognize their own importance in the organization and the relative shortcomings of the union's white male members. Thus the version of the STFU written by the *Disinherited* letters is one of provisional female—and black—autonomy, a fact that clashes harshly with the rationale of the white-controlled, masculinist world of the landowners (not to mention the Nashville Agrarians).

One of the most obvious signs of that control is space. As Robin D. G. Kelley tells it, the question of how much "private" space tenants could maintain on the land provided a flashpoint of conflict throughout the tenant-farming

South. In Kelley's account of the violent encounter between the Alabama Sharecroppers' Union and the white mob in Camp Hill, Alabama, for instance, we learn that one of the major issues precipitating the incident was a disagreement about whether or not tenants ought to have access to personal gardens on contracted lands.[20] The key question is one of stewardship: Is there any line distinguishing private space from space controlled by owners? How far does the landlord's authority extend? In an environment where occupying land and working land are indistinguishable parts of the same chain of production, the leverage of the landowner is immense, as is their fear of displacement through collective action. Populist demagogue Tom Watson identified this nerve in a private letter from 1910, arguing that socialism "would sweep the rural districts like a prairie fire if not opposed in time."[21] Closer, in both time and space, to the terrain of the STFU is the Elaine Massacre of 1919, a conflict that, according to NAACP agent Walter White, resulted in the death of over two hundred African Americans in Phillips County, Arkansas. The whole impetus for violence was an attempt by white landowners to break up the Progressive Farmers and Household Union of America, a black agricultural collective.[22]

It is in this charged climate that landowner Henry Croft, one letter reports, "Swares that a union man cant Stay on his place" (14), a poignant reminder of the stakes of union membership and the disadvantages of a scenario in which private ownership of the land remains, for all intents and purposes, untenable for tenants. A person's ability to survive depends on her ability to labor, which requires an opportunity to occupy a space, which itself depends on her willingness to appease the landowner. This concatenation of obligations and rewards, all determined from outside the self, reveals the union members' basic vulnerability. It's a condition the letters seek to redress, in part, *textually*, via voice and discourse, and it also provides a primary source for the overwhelming antagonism through which all the authors' words are strained.

L., from the Twist farm in Arkansas, offers a succinct summary of his complaint: "This country is suposed be owned By the people and Ruled By the People But instead of that it is owned by few Planters and Ruled by mr. Hood and mr. Preacher" (9). We don't get any further details on Mr. Preacher or Mr. Hood—is "Hood" a metonym for the Klan?—nor does L. elaborate on his theory of collectivity, but the letter reveals a deep-rooted disagreement about the configuration of landownership. It's possible, though, to allow L's "country" to stand at once for the rural landscape and for the nation at large, turning the letter against a country (both local and national) that has betrayed him: betrayed him, in the first case, with an inexplicable physical inhospitality and a willingness to submit to "mr. Hood and mr. Preacher"; betrayed him in the second case in the country's inability to realize Lincoln's promise of a nation crafted of the people, by the people, and for the people. The letter's rhetorical debts to the Gettysburg Address are clear enough, and despite the frustration it exudes, the egalitarian promises of both the landscape and nation of the Great Emancipator resonate loudly.

The letters further detail the practices of regulating space by unveiling the contours of resistance and the consequences of the landowners' tactics of control. Specifically, when landowners attempt to discourage collusion between croppers by locating tenant cabins at wide removes, the letter writers recognize that one way to undo distance is through the mail, making the postal routes and mailboxes important, and rare, spaces of federally protected rights to privacy. Understandably, breaches in that privacy become acutely painful, and *Disinherited* can occasionally feel like an anthology of letters about letters. One, from "F——" of Parkin, Arkansas, complains that his "Mail was tampered with," imploring Mitchell to make his communications as anonymous as possible: "So when you send me any thing have it fix that no one can see where it come from or where or who it is" (8). More, the suspicions raised by an active postal box come through loudly in a letter signed by L—— M—— and Ellen French: "When I get my mail here it open at the post office. I have been told to I get to much mail" (23). The mail's ability to create communities across space and time is not lost on either the union members or their enemies. Marx and Engels predicted just such a scenario when they argued that the "union is helped on by the improved means of communication that are created by modern industry and that place the workers of different localities in contact with one another."[23] Yet the STFU's use of the mail, a federal installment, indicates reliance on a resource associated with the *nation* rather than with centers of regional authority or power, and the union's aim is not to abandon the nation but to make its institutions do more for its most vulnerable citizens.

It's also true, however, that the possibility of subverting the sharecropping system is not simply restricted to postal communications between STFU headquarters and the union's outer branches. Language itself becomes the great uncontainable source of unrest, and one of the overriding messages of *Disinherited* is that these fluidly circulating texts and the nonstandard literacies they embody may be uniquely capable of sowing the seeds of transformative action. Not surprisingly, the letters of *Disinherited* touch time and again on issues of literacy and the functionality of texts. John Carlos Rowe's assessment of Muriel Rukeyser's sequence of poems *The Book of the Dead* (1938) feels appropriate. Rukeyser's work is roughly contemporaneous with *Disinherited* and emerges from a similar set of concerns about the physical and political disadvantages of rural southern workers—and although each occupies separate genres, both "call attention to the textualist conditions of everyday reality."[24] For Rukeyser, this means the direct incorporation of medical reports, stock profiles, and personal testimonies into her poems; for *Dis-*

inherited, it manifests as an awareness of—and occasional anxiety about—the work done by letters, ledger sheets, and magazines (*The Sharecroppers' Voice*, *The Black Man*, and *The Negro World* all figure prominently).[25] In order to critique the economic structures responsible for the suffering at the center of each, both *Disinherited* and *The Book of the Dead* depend on the exposure of submerged viewpoints via text, and both reveal a fundamental trust in the power of the written word to make and unmake the worlds we inhabit.

The models of expression on display in these texts, however, don't manifest in predictable ways: one of the most potentially provocative acts of signification performed in *Disinherited* involves the seemingly innocuous gesture of wearing a union button. "I want to wear my button," writes E. B. McKenney, "but my members kicked so and said That we was to week, and said That I would get beat up" (28). The combination of text and body carries a radical charge: one can be a union member and still pass as a benign worker, but the signs associated with the button mark the body in a way that definitively answers the question of the union ballad, Which side are you on? McKenney's button acts like the 2013 Nissan-plant T-shirt in reverse: language and body bound together *create* union membership and identity in a way that fuses abstraction and materiality. The result is a speech act with revolutionary consequences, one that crystallizes *Disinherited*'s larger investments in the word made flesh and the flesh made word.

Signal-to-Epistolary Noise

Rural southern bodies of protest interact with modern technologies in curious ways. Although they lack the organizing logic of unions, the Depression-era letters from children compiled by Robert Cohen in *Dear Mrs. Roosevelt* (2002) supply artifacts of a vivid epistolary embodiment achieved by young people reaching out to the first lady through the mail. While it acknowledges the extent to which Roosevelt's presence extended through other forms of mass media like the syndicated column and photographic reproductions, the collection also uncovers intriguing forms of wireless incarnation in its presentation of these messages as one half of a dialogue staged between an intricately imagined Roosevelt and a crowd of anxious, underrepresented listeners. As Jill Lepore has recently explained, the number of letters received by the Roosevelts far exceeded that of any previous presidency—and the profusion of mail was a distinct "product of radio."[26] If radio exists in evanescent interstices as "the dissipation of waves in space," it's no wonder that it has been "almost impossible to reconstitute that very radio *presence* that so fundamentally marked the decades of the 1920s and 1930s."[27] Yet the letters gathered by Cohen that mention Roosevelt's radio persona remediate, in part, such loss. In his discussion of radio's ability to produce newly wrought "intimate publics," Jason Loviglio correctly argues that, in contrast to her husband's Fireside Chats, Eleanor's "nearly forgotten radio career demonstrate[s] how radio could be used to negotiate women's tenuous access to public life and the power to define where public and private begin, end, and blur together."[28] If we broaden Loviglio's analysis to include a less-visible public—impoverished youth of all gender and racial positions, many from the rural South—we can read these young people's responses to Roosevelt's radio existence as attempts to assert themselves as citizens and as listening subjects in a world that controlled their basic mobility on nearly every front.

It's worth pausing briefly to unpack Eleanor Roosevelt's relation to the radio as well as the medium's interactions with modernity and modernism. Roosevelt had a long history as a broadcaster. She worked in radio in New York throughout the 1920s and continued to appear on the airwaves intermittently until the early 1950s; in her official capacity as first lady, Roosevelt was a voice for the administration from the pre-inaugural period until the sudden end of her husband's tenure in 1945. These were commercial jobs, sponsored by companies such as Pond's, Simmons Mattresses, Selby Shoes, and Sweetheart Soaps, and they paid well, a source of minor controversy for the Roosevelts' critics. They were also, in the main, designed to give listeners a carefully arbitrated taste of life in the White House and to discuss, as the announcer for *Mrs. Eleanor Roosevelt's Own Program* put it in the 1940 pilot broadcast, "topics of a special interest to American women."[29] Although at least one of the program's episodes was devoted to "Youth and Youth Organizations," Roosevelt's primary imagined audience in all her radio ventures was potential voters—adults, most particularly middle-class women who would have access to midday broadcasts.[30] Yet the radio functions as a strange disseminator of culture, one whose signifying capabilities are not circumscribed by any intended demographic target; it demonstrates, in Todd Avery's phrase, an "unwield[iness]," with a range that frequently swerves from its intended path.[31]

More broadly, as a medium of representation, radio offers new ways to recount and experience a world ordered by technology. It's tempting, in fact, to conceive of radio's expressive grammars through the contemporary classification "virtual reality," but since that phrase implies a visual interface these broadcasts lack, I offer an alternate term, "static reality," for its ability to capture a sense of the uncanny aural to which the Roosevelt letters respond. James A. Connor has surveyed a similar sonic terrain in his reading of radio as a source for *Finnegans Wake*, emphasizing the medium's untamed multivocality—a function of the early technology's unreliable transmissions and its lack of adjustable frequency stabilizers. To make his case, Connor outlines two related characteristics of static: it is both "generic radio interference, including words and unintelligible sounds," and "that hissing sibilant white noise, close to pure chaos."[32] Radio fills the void between sign and signified with shards and scraps of sound nearly palpable in their density. Yet their ephemerality is undeniable. The project of radio listening inevitably requires management of unexpected and unexplained intrusions that disrupt its notionally linear lines of discourse. Radio listeners, in other words, inevitably become modernist readers.

So the medium's potential to invoke a series of visual cues to complement its aural ones may be a function of its fundamental fuzziness—a fuzziness that provides the broad outlines of the speaker's body and allows listeners to supply the rest. In *Dear Mrs. Roosevelt*, letter after letter turns on the interpretation of Roosevelt's imagined corpus, with "corpus" acting as a key term here since it minds the gap between a subject's physical body and a body of writing, a body of words delivered either through the radio or through her widely printed columns. When conjured via an invisible signal, both bodies become manifestly intimate, and radio's sonic and discursive opacities provide a scaffold upon which to hang the letter writers' imaginative misreadings. These misreadings commonly mix both the comic and the tragic, as in the case of a Texas teenager who implores Roosevelt to send him the products of her "big machine [that] make[s] money" (28).

Of course, writing letters to the first lady is a standard practice, and it was especially common for working-class men and women to directly address this one—the central conceit of the Woody Guthrie ballad that gives Cohen's collection its title, "Dear Mrs. Roosevelt," is that a special relationship existed between Roosevelt and the working class. What's significant about these letters, though, is the demographic profile of the authors—children and teenagers of variable levels of literacy—and their interaction with modern technologies of communication. More specifically, these letters' very existence, and their diverse geographic origins, highlight the wide scope of the radio's discursive purview as well as its ability to make a distant figure of authority appear both familiar and accessible.[33] "After listening to you over the radio..." (204), begins one letter; "I've been reading a great deal of your activities on the radio and heard you on the radio," starts another (119).[34]

In fact, the characteristics and preoccupations of these letters, the strange paths that they traveled, engage Michael Warner's interest in publics and counterpublics, since a public created by the radio becomes an increasingly unchecked phenomenon, with radio transmissions reaching around the edges of its purportedly spherical shape to include, perhaps unintentionally, peripheral voices such as those belonging to poor rural children. Although they range broadly in locale and tone, the basic thematic unity of these letters attests to the creation of a sort of "unpublic" that takes shape in the cracks untended by radio-generated discourses. They also highlight the medium's ability to bridge distances—not just physical, spatial distances but also temporal, class, and cultural ones. Nancy Fraser's "subaltern counterpublics" feels like a close approximation, with its description of the "parallel discursive arenas where members of subordinated social groups invent and circulate counterdiscourses, which in turn permit them to formulate oppositional interpretations of their identities, interests, and needs."[35] But these letters are, by all appearances, discrete events; the "counterdiscourses" they "circulate" seem to go in one direction only, and to issue from uncoordinated points of departure: out of their varied locations in the rural provinces to the first lady's mailing address, they represent diffuse streams of communication converging on a single, central location.

More specifically, the letters unveil a segment of the national populace not fully addressed as members of a public, and not cohering as what Warner calls a "counterpublic," since there's no clear indication that these letter-sending children ever put pen to paper with knowledge of one another's actions. In short, this group of letters depends on a series of separate events, all moving in a common direction, and with many similarly catalyzed by the transmissive—and image-generating—power of the mass media. Following convention, Roosevelt's radio broadcasts typically began with the phrase "Ladies and gentlemen," and although Roosevelt repeatedly shows interest in the plight of children during her programs, the primary audience was unmistakably adult. That her radio broadcasts magnetized multiple demographics, simultaneously calling to action existing social worlds and helping construct new ones, points up the complex networks of communities both wittingly and unwittingly present in public addresses. As Warner theorizes,

> when people address publics, they engage in struggles—at varying levels of salience to consciousness, from calculated tactic to mute cognitive noise—over the conditions that bring them together as a public. The making of publics is the metapragmatic work newly taken up by every text at every reading. What kind of public is this? How is it being addressed? These questions and their answers are not always explicit—and cannot possibly be fully explicit, ever—but they have fateful consequences for the kind of social world to which we belong and for the kinds of actions and subjects that are possible in it.[36]

There is, Warner suggests, no way to control the consequences when one speaks into the void of a massively mediated public, especially if technologies as expansive as radio are involved. The function of these letters, addressed specifically to the first lady and making use of her ties to federal power, does ultimately pose some important questions, though: Can a person, particularly a person who comes in below the baseline requirements for active citizenship and hails from the nation's most abject region, force his or her way into the imagined community conjured by the media? Do textual performances in the form of letters make such a thing possible? Can you write a neglected body into a more prominent existence?

We are never allowed to forget that the letters' subjects emerge from matrices of space and time, concepts twisted into new shapes by communication technologies like the radio, the telegraph, and the newswire. While they're not self-consciously crafted as art objects, the letters do, to borrow Bakhtin's phrase, make time "artistically visible."[37] In calling for aid by relating the urgent needs of a particular moment in time, the letters both create and represent time-bound events, underscoring with distinctive heftiness their position in scaling temporal orbits. Miss M. C. of Epps, Louisiana, for example, asks Roosevelt to send winter clothes for herself and her five siblings: "We are just like orphans as our dad is sick all time and mother can't work and earn living for eight people. Although we farm we didn't make much cotton due to land acreage cut short." She ends with an echo of Marx's formulation of the coat as the paradigmatic commodity that multiplies use-value: "You can spare a little money for a coat for a poor girl who wants to finish school and look decent as the other girls. Maybe you have an old coat you could send me or some old clothes" (58–59).[38] Time is made visible here on several fronts: seasonal time (it's November; the weather is changing); historical time (the AAA's crop quotas have made it common for landowners to restrict production); the timeline of personal milestones (the author's mention of high school).[39] By plugging her letter into a national network of postal exchange, the author uncovers an awareness of the basic *timeliness* of the entire practice of letter-sending, with its sharply felt recognition of the temporal gap between sending and receiving: "Please try to please me by sending a package by Thanksgiving.... If you send me this you will be doing your deed for one *time*, I know" (59, emphasis mine). Time, the letters imply, is both a series of separate occurrences and a tightly woven tapestry of past, present, and future events lumpily knit together across space.

By contrast, the radio broadcasts were enmeshed directly within a capitalist communication structure, with the privately owned broadcast networks grudgingly donating airtime to the president and his administration in the 1930s. Writing of the radio's ability to provide women a larger stake in public culture, Michelle Hilmes explains, "Both radio's capacity to blur the basic distinctions of gender identity and its potential for allowing the private voices of women access to the public airwaves represented threats to established order that had to be contained."[40] With these letters as proof, it's possible to see something similar happening for disfranchised young people—the radio affords a rare chance at limited participation, across space and time, in public discourse.

It's not time alone then: the letters work to make space more "visible" as well. This is especially clear in those that make explicit reference to the writer's geographic coordinates. One dispatch, from E. B. of Double Springs, Alabama, reveals a highly fraught sense of place: "I live in Ala. on a farm, and it seem mighty hard for us. we have so much sickness in our home We have a farm. But it seems if there isn't something done we will lose it" (49). The author places herself on a farm twice within the space of two sentences. And what might be the redundancy of an unlettered writer may also reveal a combination of pride of ownership (the pronoun is tellingly capitalized in the statement "We have a farm") and sensitivity about perceptions of the rural: the author lives on a farm, her family seems to own a farm, she is, in a profoundly existential sense, *of* the farm; she is also keenly aware of the barriers that separate her from the letter's intended audience. According to a common rationale that associates rurality with abjection, to be of the farm is to be permanently bracketed as marginal. Yet it's the only thing to which the author can lay claim, and so to face the prospect of losing the farm lays open the possibility of physical, psychic, and cultural erasure.

While each letter writer locates herself or himself according to a specific geographic position, the most productive work these letters do is to write both the sender and the receiver into being, to work, much like the radio broadcast itself, to bring abstraction and materiality into a productive fusion. One of the most intriguing wrinkles in this configuration arises from the very fact of Eleanor Roosevelt's prominence, her physical inaccessibility matched to the saturating influence of her symbolic accessibility. Again and again, the letters' authors appeal to Roosevelt—the most visibly wealthy figure in their world—as if radio were still a two-way medium capable of transmission as well as reception, seeking something like compensation for radio's transition to a broadcast-only medium by the 1920s and 1930s. In his analysis of the discourse of early commercial broadcasting, John Durham Peters has argued that the medium "was quite self-conscious about overcoming the listener's sense of being stuck in a mass audience without mutual interaction or awareness." And so as radio communication developed, it "aim[ed] to restore lost presence."[41] Consequently, it's to be expected somehow that Roosevelt's presence would emerge from the disembodied space of the radio, operating as an open container to carry listeners'—particularly young listeners'—projections.

The voice without a body is a common occurrence in twentieth-century life: the radio, the phonograph, the telephone—each requires listeners to fill the void with images and other sensory information. And it's a phenomenon in which these letters participate fully. Like abstract modes of visual and literary representation, radio texts sign most powerfully through suggestion, outline, surface, and glance, however obscured. Charles Altieri's classic account of the relation between "painterly abstraction" and modernist poetry asserts that "abstraction is less a means of dissemination than an exemplary level of concentration, allowing one to compose livable orders out of... multiplicity."[42] The qualities of multiplicity that adhere to radio's representational grammar present it as an unsettled blend of the "abstract" and the material, particularly when it engages a person so prominently figured as Eleanor Roosevelt.

Thus, although photographic images of the first lady would be easy enough to come by, their stillness would need to meet the dynamics of a transmitted voice in order to be animated into what Steven Connor has called the "vocalic body." Connor explains, "Voices are produced by bodies but can also themselves produce bodies."[43] The radio serves as an ideal means of conjuring up vocalic bodies, and these letters to Mrs. Roosevelt provide insight into the particular version fleshed out by her broadcasts: her pinched northeastern accent and polished diction—presumably rare in the aural world of her young southern listeners—unveil a vocalic body dressed up by wealth and privilege.

It may be obvious enough at this point, but the dialogic qualities on display in the letters emerge as a single strand in a tangle of responses to a world in flux. They point out the difficulties of assigning ultimate meaning amid a dense fog of disparate voices present in fracture alone. Certeau is again useful here for his descriptions of a technology crisis wherein a "user" conscientiously interacts with the devices surrounding her. For instance, in Certeau's analysis, the television threatens to turn its viewers into "pure receiver[s]," just as radio, as I've indicated above, had already largely done when it ceased to be a two-way method of communication. Yet the child's penchant for illicitly drawing on schoolbooks offers a new expression of agency as "he has made a space for himself and signs his existence as an author on it."[44] It's clear that one cannot doodle atop the invisible transmissions of a radio broadcast, cannot "sign" it in any physical sense, but these letters, so often sent below the radar of parental or adult supervision, do represent an attempt to talk back to the radio. One missive includes a telling detail about its production: "I am writing this letter in school and have one eye on the teacher so I am not Writing as nice as I can . . ." (49), a description that doubles as an illustrative glimpse at a sensory profile of the modern subject-as-writer—an eye on the teacher, an ear ringing with the radio, and a hand full of writing instruments.

As with *Disinherited*, the editor carefully determines that the voice talking back both sounds and looks unmediated. While the letters don't completely undo categorical differences between written and spoken language, they frequently straddle the separation, featuring written voices that *sound* with the textures and rhythms of orality. Signs of the texts' embodied discourse likewise appear in their representations of, and overall interest in, bodies in duress. And the requests for clothing, shelter, and health care that characterize the Roosevelt letters highlight the unavoidable consequences of scarcity and material degradation on the body itself. Several letters, however, exhibit an unexpected double-movement in that they call attention to the author's bodily needs while simultaneously veiling the writer's identity. Take, for instance, W. S. from Stillmore, Georgia, who confesses to a deep antipathy toward her family and their condition while imploring Roosevelt, "please do not ever mention this to any one. I trusted that you wouldn't ever tell this, so please destroy this letter" (70). The difficulties of navigating the demands of the private and the public are especially apparent in letters addressing issues of food and clothing: anxieties about public manifestations of bodily needs crowd the private space of the letter, as evidenced by the multiple teens who write about the kind of social immobility created by a ragged wardrobe—"I can't go to Church or Sunday school any more for need of the clothes" (56). What Roosevelt can provide, they hope, are the material markers of middle-classness she is imagined to possess in excess—new shoes, a radio, a store-bought coat. "The main reason for my writing this letter," one child bluntly reports, "is to ask you what you do with your old clothes" (48).

The mutually reinforcing impulse to both enclose and disclose corresponds with the impulse to simultaneously ask for help and to decline it. Miss M. N. B. from Vinemont, Alabama, a thirteen-year-old girl suffering from an abscessing kidney with parents who have fallen behind on a twenty-five-acre mortgage, solicits assistance with this caveat: "Please, Mrs. Roosevelt, dont try to put us on relief for we dont like that" (63). The acceptability of a person-to-person form of aid rather than a faceless federal one points up the extent to which these letters seem to reject the abstract ("relief") while clinging to the concrete ("Mrs. Roosevelt"); it also reveals the ways in which acceptable levels of charity appear as personal largesse rather than the systemic change that would provide structural redistribution of wealth. In this sense, Roosevelt serves not only as a symbolic extension of federal power but also a bridge between the national government and the impervious corners of its constituency. Appropriately, the static reality that emerges around her radio broadcasts produces a politics that can't be mapped on a bipolar spectrum; it offers no stable sense of iconography, no hard division between the ethereal and the earthly.

In the opening of *Resisting Representation* (1994), Elaine Scarry notes a distinction between the "problematically abstract" and the "problematically concrete," positioning language's "immateriality" as insufficient to the task of communicating "truth and cognition," while holding the "materiality ... [of] phenomena such as physical pain and physical labor" outside the boundaries of language. This very tension has, in several key ways, been the subject of my analysis of *Dear Mrs. Roosevelt*: How can language's reliance on symbolization and abstraction ever be up to the task of telegraphing the urgencies of life as a young, unvoiced subaltern? The short answer, of course, is that it can't. But the particularized fusion of language and body, of abstraction and materiality, that recurs throughout these letters comes across as an effective means of speaking the unspeakable hardships of Depression-era poverty. According to Scarry, a "given subject resists representation," and so "[i]n order to overcome that resistance, the artist bends the sentence into a particular shape."[45] What, however, of the writer whose subject, whose text is, in fact, herself? Or whose message is, inversely, bent by language itself? Or, since this chapter contains so many rural abjects struggling to become active subjects, what of the artist who is preeminently the subject of representation? The documents comprising *Dear Mrs. Roosevelt* and *The Disinherited Speak* stand as proof that the most effective means of representation sometimes exist outside of artistry, in the simple act of being there—if only in a letter.

Pictures from Life's Other Side

Photography allows its subjects to present themselves through unique representational strategies. The exact range of this allowance, however, is a subject of considerable debate. Who speaks through photographs and how? When human figures appear, are they static or active participants? The answers are clearly contingent, as the abundance of rural images from the Depression prove. My purpose here is to evaluate these contingencies by considering how images of the labor agrarian in the rural South of the 1930s respond to the thinking of prominent theorists of photography, and how they allow—or disallow—their subjects to speak. In doing so, I'll uncover strategies for exploring perspectives that remain invisible in the literary ventures of the Twelve Southerners and the Highlander Project. These tactics, like those developed in the letters discussed above, draw on the signifying potential of the body and the graspable substance of the material world, a phenomenon that Roland Barthes recognizes as essential to the photographic medium writ large: "the Photograph always leads the corpus I need back to the body I see; it is the absolute Particular, the sovereign Contingency . . . in short, what Lacan calls the *Touché*, the Occasion, the Encounter, the Real, in its indefatigable expression."[46] In the elusive language of his late style, Barthes is after the work done by images designed to trouble viewers' sense of the world, theorizing a quality of somatic response in the viewer he labels "punctum": "A photograph's *punctum* is that accident which pricks me (but also bruises me, is poignant to me)."[47] Striking through boundaries between bodies, the punctum calls up a physical reaction that makes a version of the photographed subject's wounds felt by the viewer. It's an effect achieved variously but always with a language that is not strictly lingual. In this sense, Barthes's evocation of the Real becomes appropriate since, in his rendering, the photographic image makes possible body-to-body communication absent words and absent the physical presence of the other, recalling early fantasies of the photograph as a pure indexical sign. As Allan Sekula explains it, "Photography [comes] to establish and delimit the terrain of the *other*"; it opens up, in Sekula's phrase, a fresh and unexplored archive.[48]

Yet among other commentators, photography's ability to "delimit" this archive is precisely the cause for concern. Some things, it seems, are simply better left unseen. Susan Sontag, for one, famously worried about the link between the inescapable presence of photographic images in the twentieth century and photography's capabilities as a surveillance tool, since the medium "fragments continuities and feeds the pieces into an interminable dossier, thereby providing possibilities of control that could not even be dreamed of under the earlier system of recording information: writing."[49] The demarcation from writing is significant in that it gives a practical application to the commonplace notion that visual representations offer more direct access to their subjects; understood this way, photographs manifest as sheer "light-writing," with no human mediating the production of the image. At least nominally, they are easier to process and catalog than written accounts. Yet as readers of images, it behooves us to approach photography's documentary function with a degree of suspicion, since more conventional methods of reading aren't necessarily up to the task, a fact that is clear enough to Michael North, who describes photography as "neither linguistic nor pictorial but hovering in a kind of utopian space between, where the informational utility of writing meets the immediacy of sight."[50] A picture may be worth a thousand words—but from a poststructuralist view, that simply multiplies the likelihood of a misreading. And since these misreadings deal directly with actual human *subjects* made to operate as *objects* in the photographer's mise-en-scène, we must be especially careful.

When human figures are involved, then, the photographic subject's ineffable—and obscurable—subjectness is always central to the picture's capacities for meaning-making; its message collapses into the medium, as the body on display literally becomes the physical substance of the paper photograph itself. Tracing that phrase back to its origins, we see that in the technological determinism of Marshall McLuhan, the camera "tend[s] to turn people into things" as "the photograph extends and multiplies the human image to the proportions of mass-produced merchandise."[51] It's undoubtedly true that photography makes the human figure both more ubiquitous and more digestible. For the purposes of my argument, though, McLuhan's definition of "people" is too shapeless. A person is, after all, already a *thing* of a certain sort, and if the photograph serves to destabilize the human's position as, say, a Pascalian thinking reed, it might also work to emphasize and re-present the reediness of that reed. For better or worse, then, photographic presentations of the body contain the potential to shift our sense of what bodies outside of the self can be and should do. And it's not simply a matter of aesthetic defamiliarization: as a tool used to communicate the feel and form of the material world, the photograph occupies a special niche—and contains unique opportunities for mutual identification, for a glimpse of one's own body in the presentation of another's. Walter Benjamin famously theorized the benefits of photography's powers of representation, claiming that they lack the exclusionary "aura" of, say, a painted canvas.[52] However, its consequences of representation are uniquely calibrated: with an uncanny ability to promote strains of sympathy bound to the body itself, the photograph carries enormous potential as a text of protest, as decades of actual use as a political tool affirm. The major political difference in photography, then, is the parousia (second coming) of the human body. To this point, Judith Butler has recently argued for public assemblies as occasions where activists are "posing their challenge in corporeal terms, which means that when the body 'speaks' politically, it is not only in vocal or written language."[53] Photographs concentrate just such nonlingual political speech.

Yet when photographs of humans become texts of protest, texts whose content is the body itself, it's worth considering how—and by whom—its meaning is constructed. Again, who's the author? The simplest answer is the person operating the camera. But when the subjects of the images avail themselves of what I'll call a rhetoric of posture—when the presence, and the presentation, of their bodies contributes to the text's affective consequences—they become, at very least, coauthors, cocreators who participate in the construction of meaning. Photographic subjects practicing representational intentionality don't express the self through a shared set of linguistic signs, nor through any particular reference to the bodily self, as in the Lacanian imaginary, which reveals a basic consciousness of the self's physical form reflected back at itself. Here too Barthes's reference to the Lacanian Real is useful since it's clear that the camera's lens does not, in any simple sense, behave like a mirror. To create a signifying pose in the present moment—particularly a pose that attempts to prick viewers into reformative action—is to reproduce the shape one has seen in the mind's eye or in the bodies of others, to compose oneself as (if) emulated without the advantage of self-reflection vis-à-vis the mirrored glass. To the extent that such a thing is possible, self-fashioning via the photograph offers an attempt to recover the signifying tactics of the preverbal stage. And, for Barthes at least, this is the source of the medium's great power.

In the field of documentary photography, which often makes claims to direct, unnegotiated representation, the question of the subject's agency remains a knotty one. How does a documentarian strike a balance between her own vision and the visions of her subjects? One way to avoid the problem of competing subjectivities, of course, is to avoid other people altogether. An appropriate example here might be Dorothea Lange's 1937 series exploring the STFU's Delta and Providence cooperative farms at Hillhouse, Mississippi.

The poultry unit of the Delta cooperative farm, Hillhouse, Mississippi (1937), by Dorothea Lange (courtesy of the Library of Congress).

Though Lange's most iconic images involve human figures, and while the politics of her work were sympathetic to the union, the individuated human presence is dim in the Hillhouse photos. When the images do feature people, they are close portraits of children or anonymous farmworkers bearing the austere label "member." Far more prominent are pictures of the fields, the farming implements, houses, and outbuildings.

Lange's Hillhouse series offers an incisive glimpse into life at the farm, but it is only ever a glimpse; the photos make far greater use of the physical landscape than the human inhabitants, drawing viewers' attention to the exterior life of the farm's inhabitants while eliding the interior. It is Lange's vision that prevails, setting up the documentarian-as-auteur with the unfortunate result that the subject's agency dissolves in an atmosphere of authority created by the documentarian's camera. The subaltern gets a fine portrait in these images but never speaks.

An exaggerated version of this dynamic appears in 1937's *You Have Seen Their Faces*, a collection of Margaret Bourke-White photos that paired images of dispossessed rural southerners with captions by novelist Erskine Caldwell. It's a text that has drawn astute critical attention. William Stott, for instance, described it as an "overemotionalized" but ultimately well-intentioned attempt to force elite audiences to witness rural poverty.[54] More recently, Jeff Allred has sought to deconstruct this witness function of modernist photo documentary projects, *Faces* included, by exposing viewers to representa-

Member of the Delta cooperative farm at Hillhouse, Mississippi (1937), by Dorothea Lange (courtesy of the Library of Congress).

tions of Depression-era alterity that are too diffuse to cohere in a uniform statement.[55] What's at stake in this discussion is the relationship of subject, documentarian, and viewer, a cluster of connections to which Bourke-White and Caldwell pay special attention. Viewers might see "their" faces, but since all the information provided seems constructed to appeal to expectations—and, more luridly, the fascinations—of the viewer, we cannot escape the suspicion that these faces, bodies, and words have been manipulated to enhance the experience of spectatorship. One then recognizes the unintentional resonance of Bourke-White's title: a face already "seen," pre-viewed in such a way, both evokes a stereotype and panders to it, since you already effectively know what you are going to "have seen." By attempting to represent both the photographic subjects' external and internal worlds, the collection uses the lives, bodies, and environments of its human figures to foreground the concerns of its authors. In one startling image, Caldwell's statement is not attributed to a specific individual but to a pair of almost exaggeratedly haggard faces and the caption "Yazoo City, Mississippi," presumably placing the "I" in the mouth of one of the two figures: "I think it's only right that the government ought to be run with people like us in mind." Yet the "us" in this statement is at odds with the "their" of the project's title, severing the viewer and photographic subjects in a way that ultimately deepens the divide between us—the viewers—and them.

By way of loud and deliberate contrast, consider James Agee and Walker

"Yazoo City, Mississippi," by Margaret Bourke-White, in *You Have Seen Their Faces* (1937) (courtesy of the Special Collections Research Center, Syracuse University; © 2018 Estate of Margaret Bourke-White / Licensed by VAGA at Artists Rights Society [ARS], N.Y.).

Evans's monumental *Let Us Now Praise Famous Men* (1941). Unlike Lange's Hillhouse series and *You Have Seen Their Faces*, *Praise* assiduously tries to build its portraits of tenant farmers from the inside out by turning the genre upside down, working exhaustively to provide more fully modeled impressions while simultaneously unwriting the conventions of documentaries that flourished throughout the late 1930s and early 1940s, projects such as Lange and Paul Taylor's *American Exodus: A Record of Human Erosion* (1939), Archibald MacLeish's *Land of the Free* (1938), and Richard Wright's *12 Million Black Voices* (1941). With Agee narrating each turn, the text's formal attempts at total representation run up against the aporia of depicting the other. According to Susan Hegeman, the book "suggests that the project of detailing the lives of others for the purpose of cultural comparison, of knowing the details of how others negotiate the necessities of 'food, shelter, and clothing,' is the wrong project, is somehow obsolete."[56] In *Praise*, then, the presumption that a person can ever know a life other than one's own is fundamentally flawed. How can you ever be sure that your knowledge lines up with the experience of the documentary subject's? How does such a project announce its own limitations? For Agee, it is confession, and the creation of a hierarchy of artifacts that privileges the sensory-inducing "object" over "writing," a tendency captured in an oft-cited passage: "If I could do it, I'd do no writing at all here. It would be photographs; the rest would be fragments of cloth, bits of cotton, lumps of earth, records of speech, pieces of wood and iron, phials of odors, plates of food and of excrement."[57] In this provocation Agee expresses a desire to move beyond the flattened dimensions of printed text, to match images processed through the oracular to a more complete, multisensory experience, one that allows for immersive somatic contact—touch, taste, smell, and sound. And though Agee recognizes the limitations of his own print-bound project, he sticks to it, all while gesturing toward untapped possibilities of communicable understanding.

The book's readiness to compound its central tensions through a preoccupation with the very problem of looking at and explaining anything outside of the self can, Agee recognizes, amount to a conflicted level of political quietism, of leaving "them" alone out of principle while still grappling with the failures of inaction. It's a pressure that helps explain the contradictions, anxieties, and flashes of self-loathing that characterize Agee's voice in *Praise*: "It seems to me curious, not to say obscene and thoroughly terrifying, that it could occur to an association of human beings drawn together through need and chance and for profit into a company, an organ of journalism, to pry intimately into the lives of an undefended and appallingly damaged group of human beings, an ignorant and helpless rural family..."[58] And so on: the passage expands on that idea for some time. But these insecurities also threaten to render the text oddly apolitical. *Praise*, as critic Dwight Garner puts it, "isn't political; it's penitential."[59] Hegeman argues that when faced with "the impossibility and immorality of representing" the tenant-farming other, Agee reaches for a new "task, which is ultimately one of self-representation."[60] *Praise*'s most pressing questions, in fact, concern the role of language, the nature of representation, and the outer boundaries of sympathy.[61]

If the projects discussed above underscore the difficulties of allowing for the aesthetic and political agency of documentary subjects, and if this is especially true of photo-based documentaries, a compelling counterpoint arrives in the life and work of Arkansas STFU member Myrtle Lawrence. Lawrence, a sharecropper and union activist from central Arkansas, is largely invisible today, but she played a significant role in the STFU of the 1930s. For one thing, she was the most important subject—and participant—in an unpublished documentary project undertaken by two young women: journalist Priscilla Robertson and photographer Louise Boyle, classmates at Vassar who were spurred to action by what they had heard of the conditions of the sharecropping class in Arkansas. Robertson, who went on to author several histories of women and domestic life, and Boyle, who trained as a photographer at the New York Institute of Photography and had a long career working for Cornell University Press, were in many ways unlikely chroniclers of the agricultural underclass.⁶² But during the short time they spent with Lawrence and other STFU members ("a week or so in September at [Lawrence's] home outside of Wynne, Arkansas"), they compiled a repository of images and experiences that would reverberate throughout their lives.⁶³ (The pair continued to correspond about the experience until Robertson's death in 1989.⁶⁴) In the twenty-first century, Lawrence remains accessible through the efforts of historian Elizabeth Payne, whose work on Lawrence's life and its meanings in the history of labor, civil rights, and poor white identity provides the most complete point of entry into a captivating life.⁶⁵

Robertson's record of her Arkansas visit describes first meeting Lawrence at the Southern Labor School—"an institution intended by its founders to train organizers for the whole South"—in the summer of 1937.⁶⁶ "She was already used to publicity," Robertson explains, recalling how she and Boyle were eagerly invited to Lawrence's home in order to create the photographs: "I am sure she hoped our pictures and writing would aid in public understanding of what she and other union members were facing."⁶⁷ In notes from her account, Boyle agrees: "Myrtle was convinced that publicity would help sharecroppers."⁶⁸ As Katherine Henninger, in her astute analysis of southern womanhood and photography, has explained, "Women growing up in the South learn early: representations matter," a principle everywhere apparent in Lawrence's photographic performances.⁶⁹ No surprise, then, to find a 1937 letter from Lawrence to Boyle in which the author repeatedly approved of Boyle's photographs ("they are so goad") and offered continued assistance ("if ya make iny thang out of this and wat to make mare we will help ya all we cann").⁷⁰

Consequently, throughout Boyle's STFU photographs, Lawrence's own body and her interactions with the environment provide the stuff upon which both an act and a text of protest are crafted. They became, in Payne's words, an expression of "life as a human document."⁷¹ The signifying purposes of the images might drill down to something more elemental than "life," however, to the physical matter of the body itself. While Payne's biographical histories of Lawrence provide extensive accounts of her life and work, they contain little analysis of the meaning-making of the photographs as such, and my purpose here is to think through the significance of these images as expressive objects that, like the letters comprising *Disinherited*, present the sharecropping body as the clearest means of conveying the situation of early twentieth-century tenancy; they stand as deeply embodied speech acts.

Take, for instance, Lawrence's pose in the image reproduced here. With a baby in tow and straw hat drawn back on a tightly drawn face and furrowed brow, Lawrence squints into the horizon with an expression that combines foreboding, perseverance, and matronly responsibility. As a self-conscious posture, the image overlays an ordinary act with a heavily freighted one: this is another 1930s portrait of rural domesticity highlighting the gulf dividing

Myrtle Lawrence sits on her porch holding a sleeping baby (1937), by Louise Boyle (courtesy of the Kheel Center for Labor-Management Documentation and Archives, Cornell University).

the privileged and the disinherited, the expanse between living conditions on a sharecropper's tract and those of middle-class Americans; it is also a deliberate re-creation of that familiar scene, staged with an understanding of the power of images to generate sympathy. More pointedly, the vacant stare of a dispossessed rural woman is a riff in duet, played by Boyle and Lawrence, on a familiar theme. In Payne's reading, "Lawrence defied the mournful image in Dorothea Lange's photographs or the passive, blank faces of James Agee and Walker Evans's Alabama sharecroppers in *Let Us Now Praise Famous Men*."[72] It's important to add, though, that part of this defiance arrives through the scandal of particularity bound up in the presentation of Lawrence's given name, her actual identity: the sign—and the body—"Myrtle Lawrence" over against Lange's famed "Migrant Mother" (1936), whose name, Florence Owens Thompson, was famously obscured until the 1970s; or Evans's portrait of Allie Mae Burroughs, which appears at the Metropolitan Museum of Art as "Alabama Tenant Farmer Wife" and with no identifying caption at all in *Praise*. Lawrence is, in the title assigned this photo ("Myrtle Lawrence sits on her porch holding a sleeping baby"), both named and presented as the subject of a complete grammatical sentence. If, as Agee and Evans argue, the experience of the sharecropping other remains unknowable in any kind of linear, rational way, Lawrence trades upon this lacuna, filling the gap with a self-conscious demonstration of what tenancy looks and, just as importantly, feels like. As an embodied rhetorical tactic, then, her presentations' aims are clear: aid the collective by personalizing the individual.

In Payne's description, particularly in her account of Lawrence's attention-grabbing appearance as a snuff-dipping sharecropper at a New York City gala in 1937 (she brandished a pink "spit can"), the persona Lawrence developed acts as a tactful deployment of a series of tropes tied to rurality as commonly perceived in the early twentieth century: the hayseed adrift in the big city, the brash country wife, the weary and virtuous earth mother.[73] Under Joseph Roach's influential model, "Performance ... stands in for an elusive entity that it is not but that it must vainly aspire both to embody and to replace."[74] Yet Myrtle Lawrence both *is not* and *is* the selfsame person she portrays: the stage in these pictures is her home, her union rally, her field of labor; and the person she plays is, by all accounts, an adjacent version of herself or someone like her. And yet, to Roach's point, she fully inhabits these images in a way that troubles any firm differentiation between notions of reality and performance.

Boyle's images depicting Lawrence's domestic labor thus both draw upon and confront viewers' expectations. While Boyle's STFU series contains pictures that scan more immediately as "sharecropping"—one pair of photos offers a scene of Lawrence's sons weighing their cotton sacks and loading them in a wagon—they consistently underscore gendered divisions of labor. Boyle's larger project of showing the day-to-day existence of a woman activist in a sharecropping economy is achieved through images depicting the sideline labor necessary to the cultivation of cash crops: we see Lawrence shelling peas, surrounded by her children; see her churning butter on the front porch. Tellingly, in a moment when concern about mechanization was peaking, the farming tools are all hand-powered, and, as the title of the pea-shelling photo tells us, the practice of sharecropping labor bleeds into and shapes the domestic space ("the family dining room"). Gaston Bachelard's phenomenologist reading of the house theorizes its "chief benefits" as providing a place that "shelters daydreaming, the house protects the dreamer, the house allows one to dream in peace."[75] While the photographs only hint at the psychic realities of their subjects, they are pitched at an angle that suggests the degree to which sharecropping labor strips the home space of this "primitive" function. Peace, it seems, is precisely the promise extended by the union; its absence is the truth of the individualist status quo. All of which implies that, contra classical liberal ideology, peace cannot be attained individually but only through the efforts of the group.

The staggering difficulty of securing such stability on a tenant tract, especially for a woman, is the precise topic of Edith Summers Kelley's *Weeds* (1923), a novel that acts as a devastating fictional counterpart to Boyle's STFU photos. Detailing the slow slide of a spirited woman on a Kentucky tobacco farm, the novel describes Judith Pippinger's struggle against the unrelenting

Myrtle Lawrence churning butter on her front porch with Sylvia Lawrence, sixteen-year-old bride of Elvin "Doodle" Lawrence, in the background (1937), by Louise Boyle (courtesy of the Kheel Center for Labor-Management Documentation and Archives, Cornell University).

demands of the physical environment, stifling social conventions, and the destructive economies of tenancy. On its every edge the novel bears out the deadening effects of tenancy. Read against "Myrtle Lawrence churning butter," the following passage helps recast a nominally mundane chore as another burdensome layer in a never-ending series of tasks: "[Judith] grew more and more shiftless and slatternly about the house. More and more mechanically she dragged through the days. As she hung over the washtub or plunged the dasher up and down in the ancient oaken churn or stood by the stove frying three times a day the endlessly recurring corn cakes, her body moved with the dead automatic rhythm of old habit. Her face was habitually sullen and heavy, her eyes glazed and turned inward or looking out upon vacancy with an abstracted stare."[76] The "abstracted stare" of Kelley's fiction matches the blank expression on Lawrence's face: a stoic mask riven with weariness, this presentation of affect threads a line of discontent across an otherwise innocent scenario. The body, with its "dead automatic rhythm," becomes a synchronized machine in Kelley's description, revealing the imbrication of bodies in/and landscapes required by the exacting production methods of modern rural tenancy. Boyle's image may also comment on the deadening effects of labor on the body by drawing out the internal contradistinctions between labor and leisure. For instance, the rocking chair on the front porch is perhaps the strongest, most obvious evocation of rural leisure on display in the series, and in this image Lawrence's body transforms it, as her distant gaze points the viewer to some threatening offstage presence that may well be the land itself. Throughout Boyle's photographs of Lawrence, there seems little escape from the demands of the land. Or, perhaps more completely, there is no escape from demands placed on the land and its stewards by a turn in U.S. capitalism that exploits both the farmers and the environments on which they depend. These photos flatly undermine the theory, widely promoted by the Nashville Agrarians, that increased leisure is a natural byproduct of a society centered on agriculture. One needs only compare Boyle's images with descriptions of the Agrarians' activities at Allen Tate's Benfolly to understand how different experiences of the agricultural create different opportunities for leisure. One party's leisure, in fact, might be another party's labor.

Although other photos in the series suggest that cotton was the cash crop produced on the Lawrence tract, the object of the pea in the photo below is perhaps the truest symptom of their farm. In addition to its role as an unmanageable source of sustenance, the immensity of its presence in the photograph becomes a telling metaphor of the organic-turned-industrial effort of farming via tenancy; it's at once too much to treat by hand and too valuable to discard—labor at an industrial scale, processed manually. And although in a different context this scene might represent a gentle intergenerational harvest ritual, here it feels more like an ominous prediction of a repetition, as the participating children are folded into the tedium of a seemingly bottomless task, now and forevermore. And the photo creates an opening through which to view the absurdly proportioned conditions of domestic labor on a sharecropping tract. Indeed, the hint of grotesquerie permeating the photo ensures that it cannot be dismissed sentimentally or romantically as leisure. Instead, the image's excess helps metaphorize degrees to which surplus can alienate the worker, become her burden. Joseph Entin's configuration of "sensational modernism" proposes an "aesthetic of social extremity that pushes ... beyond the bounds of conventional modes and registers" in both fiction and photography. There is, I suggest, a similar brand of the sensational on display in the image, with its absurdly large harvest spilling out across the living room, suggesting that even abundance can, under the wrong conditions, oppress. All this was ultimately enacted by what Entin describes as "an effort to confront and convey the sharpening social inequality brought about by the Great Depression."[77]

Again, while pea-shelling on the front porch is precisely the sort of bucolic scene celebrated in *I'll Take My Stand*, what this image emphasizes is the point where leisure gives way to labor, where the extremity and urgency of the task transforms the activity into a new classification. As the pile reaches higher than any human figure and is uncontained by the photo's borders, the

Lucille Kimbrell, Icy Jewel Lawrence, Myrtle Lawrence, and Elroe Kimbrell shelling peas in the family dining room (1937), by Louise Boyle (courtesy of the Kheel Center for Labor-Management Documentation and Archives, Cornell University).

hint of surrealism haunting the edges of this scene calls up Walter Benjamin's conceptualization of the "optical unconscious" at work in early photography: to drown in a pile of peas, it seems, is the sublimated reality of the sharecropping mind;[78] it is, to return to Bachelard, a bad dream, devoid of "peace." The larger point here is that agricultural labor in the sharecropping system absorbs everything, fills every space and spare moment. In a bitter irony, however, it's better than the alternative: fewer opportunities to turn out crops and less income—a threatening specter made real by the passage of the Agricultural Adjustment Act in 1933.

In these photographic depictions of labor, Lawrence actively makes her private life an artifact for public consideration. By drawing out the contrast between herself and her audience and by highlighting her audience's complicity with her condition, she brings into view the invisible logic holding these individuals in place. The design of this dual purpose, of course, is to drum up support for her union, but it also represents a sophisticated signifying practice. If meaning-via-language adheres in the space between the sign and signified, its visual counterpoint depends on the space between object and viewer—and, again, when the object is actually a human *subject* suspended in a visual field that originates in precise spatial and temporal coordinates, distance dissolves and the shock of recognition takes on a sharpened cast. That is, the synchronic moment captured in the image—what Sontag calls "a neat slice of time"—flows into a more diachronic exploration of the relationships between labor, landscape, and the capitalist substructures that have, across time, created—and continue to create—those relationships.[79]

As a result, these photos, like their epistolary counterparts, make time "visible." Damian Sutton has provided a useful model by applying Deleuze's "crystal image"—a concept developed for the analysis of cinema—to describe photographic events in which "[t]ime splits ... not into the abstract notion of narrative ellipsis but into a pure image of time.... The past of the image is constituted simultaneously with the present, and each is launched into a time image."[80] One function of the "pure image of time" is to push viewers to engage with the material realities represented in the photo: in "Shelling Peas," which shows each of the photo's human subjects—from the adult on to the youngest child—handling the crops, the urgency of the task and the burden of the looming pile of peas is not sloughed off to a distant past, neither is it rerouted to the future, nor is it absorbed—and perhaps absolved—by some larger narrative. The burden is the photo's singular reality. To return to Barthes, it is the photo's punctum—the instrument that "bruises" and creates a somatic response in the viewer. The viewer who completes the half-circle formed by the human figures in this tableau is playing witness but also acting as an entangled contributor to the conditions of the sharecropping poor more broadly, for, as Peggy Phelan reminds us, the "relationship between the looker and the given to be seen ... is a version of the relation between self and other."[81] By looking at alterity, viewers help bring it into existence—just as by participating, however benignly, in an economy that depends on abusive labor practices like sharecropping, they unconsciously maintain it. Moreover, this image of overproducers, of producers-in-excess, also evokes anxieties about unproductive consumers such as us, the viewers. Inasmuch as these photos highlight the dialectical connection linking privilege to poverty under the sign of the single nation, they call up a dynamic that Slavoj Žižek calls the "proximity of the Neighbour."[82] Though he is specifically interested in psychologies of twenty-first-century torture, Žižek's phrase gets at the contradictions that crop up between a Judeo-Christian obligation to the sufferer and a person's unwitting benefit from that suffering, a dynamic compounded during the capitalist crisis of the Great Depression.

The reasons for the STFU's ultimate failure continue to generate debate. In a 2006 address, Payne argued that the union could never resolve the tensions between the collective and the individual, specifically as they revolve around questions of land ownership.[83] Making a complementary point from a slightly different angle, Donald Grubbs has described how southern officials in government and business used the palliative of personal property to manage the revolutionary potential of groups like the STFU: "[T]hey saw home ownership as a good American manner of meeting a problem that might otherwise be solved in very unsettling and un-American ways."[84] Boyle's STFU photographs convey this tension: the focus on Lawrence as a discrete subject in the photos points up a conflict between the individual and the collective that troubled not just the union's strategies of representation but its character as a whole. Much as the STFU flirted with the theoretical impulses of socialism, it could not shake the dreams of private ownership and individual accomplishment so central to the American middle class. In short, the STFU struggled to keep its feet amid a swirl of crosswise currents.

These conflicts registered widely. In 2013 the lost manuscript of a 1947 novel by Woody Guthrie was published as *House of Earth*. It tells of a couple in the hardscrabble Dust Bowl of the Texas Panhandle, and their struggle to carve out a space of their own in a desolate physical environment and against the suffocating interests of invasive corporations. In 1944 Guthrie finished his classic ballad of communal ownership "This Land Is Your Land," with its famous refrain and infamous—though less heralded—verse: "Sign was painted, it said 'Private Property' / But on the back side it didn't say nothing."

Three years later, he composed a book-length narrative extolling the virtues of self-determination via private land ownership. The inconsistencies here are perhaps less crushing than they might appear: in either case, the basis of the protest is tethered to a search for individual dignity and material survival in a world warped by rapid transformations. It may well be, in the final analysis, that Guthrie's description of his own political sensibilities could be adopted by each of this chapter's subjects: "Left wing, right wing, chicken wing—it's the same thing to me."[85]

In *On Photography*, Sontag's anxieties about the medium stem from a fear that the ubiquity of images depicting inexpressible horror might somehow strip away that horror, make it commonplace. The inverse, however, may be that photographs presenting more subtle modes of suffering can make commonplace horrors inhabitable: they allow viewers a chance to recognize the inequities and casualties stalking their own backyards. In this project, the territory in question becomes the rural South—specifically the vast network of tenant tracts stretching throughout the region—and images detailing the privations of such labor arrangements don't inure viewers to sufferings but instead enhance their urgency. Boyle's photos of Myrtle Lawrence, like *The Disinherited Speak* and the *Dear Mrs. Roosevelt* letters, point out the unfulfilled promises of Jeffersonian America by fusing the abstractions of theoretical agrarianism to the grit and grind of rural bodies and landscapes bound by tenancy.

One of the reasons the STFU, a multiracial organization with women in highly visible positions of authority, would present such problems for the Agrarians is that it confounds their theory of a unified course of southern history and destiny. And while the aesthetic preoccupations of the Twelve Southerners emerge from a decidedly classed, raced, and gendered position that leans hard on *gemeinschaft* abstractions like Tradition, Family, Community, and Religion, the labor agrarians discussed above foreground an aesthetic sensibility trained by the body's interactions with the landscape. Instead of turning inward and developing a self-conscious process of imaginative responses to the surroundings (as even sometimes-radical Don West did), they push outward, presenting pieces of their own lives—and their own bodies—as the text itself, allowing viewers and readers to assess the significance of those lives.

In 1939, working under the Institute for Research in Social Sciences associated with the Chapel Hill Regionalists, Margaret Jarman Hagood published *Mothers in the South*, a work of "portraiture" that surveyed the state of mothering in cotton and tobacco tenant-farming arrangements, making the case that the production scales of tenancy extend beyond the fields, into domestic spheres: at one point Hagood describes the tenant farming house as "the physical plant for homemaking."[86] Although her fieldwork was primarily done in the Piedmont region, Hagood understood her project as one that would forward the South as a bellwether for the nation at large: "[I]t is admitted that the South must play a major role in reproducing the Nation and that its obligation to translate its cultural and economic potentialities into a national contribution is great."[87] And in Hagood's account, the potential of the nation is emblematized most fully by the economic and cultural agents who fill "the triple role of mother, housekeeper, and field laborer."[88] To underscore her point, she reproduces the sentiment of one friend, an "enthusiast" on the topic, who argued that "as goes the rural mother in the South, so goes the Nation!"[89] Though it never explicitly announces itself with the same degree of grandiosity, the Boyle-Lawrence collaboration seems committed to presenting domestic spaces and practices as zones of national significance. Churning butter, shelling peas, comforting children—these forms of incarnate labor are all, in Myrtle Lawrence's world at least, coded female, and they bear weight as a "microhistory" of the class—and perhaps the nation—as a whole. Jill Lepore's definition of microhistory is helpful here. "[H]owever singular a person's life may be," Lepore argues, "the value of examining it lies not in its uniqueness, but in its exemplariness, in how that individual's life serves as an allegory for broader issues affecting the culture as a whole."[90] Benjamin put a nearly metaphysical twist on the issue when he theorized the power of "blasting a specific life out of the era or a specific work out of the lifework . . . in the lifework, the era; and in the era, the entire course of history."[91] By this description, even a single, seemingly insignificant life can function as a crossroads in the "entire course of history." Closer to the ground of my analysis, Priscilla Robertson offered a similar assessment of her own work with Myrtle Lawrence in a 1984 letter: "Louise and I witnessed a miniature reflection of many large scale events."⁹² This happens not just with Boyle's photographs of Lawrence but also with the STFU and the *Mrs. Roosevelt* letters: as examinations of the "issues affecting the culture as a whole," their versions of the sharecropping South sound with a tough plangency that frequently achieves the broad resonance, the punctum, of art.

"Other South" Revisited

In a contemporary moment when questions of labor, race, and activism remain unavoidable, the utopian impulses of the STFU—on display in *Disinherited* and worn on the body of Myrtle Lawrence—still invite attention: the union was never so narrowly tied to a particular formulation of history and culture, or to a single definition of the "South," as to become entirely obsolete, and the underutilized alliance between white and black members of the working class still offers opportunities for reformative action. If internal disagreements prevented agricultural activists from achieving their full revolutionary potential, their work—and the world they imagined—remains before us.

When succeeding generations have looked for models of alternative-culture agrarianism, however, they have been more readily affiliated with *I'll Take My Stand* than *The Disinherited Speak*.⁹³ This could be, in large measure, a question of exposure—*Disinherited* never gained a wide audience, and the photographic archives of the STFU remain largely unseen. Still, it's a testament to the slipperiness of the Agrarians' thinking, and to the mutability of twentieth-century political identities, that, as a self-consciously "conservative" movement, its residue still coats strains of countercultural localist thinking. Expressions of labor agrarianism, on the other hand, remain harder to come by. First-person accounts and fictional representations of conditions in industrial cotton outfits in the twenty-first-century Delta, for instance, rarely surface. This is, as activists such as Myrtle Lawrence and H. L. Mitchell surely understood, the result of structures designed to keep the faces of labor out of view. With apologies to Bourke-White and Caldwell, you simply haven't seen their faces. That's just one reason, it seems, that the demographic profile of U.S. agricultural labor—both within the South and beyond—is in a state of continual renewal, always ready to incorporate the next group that lacks the means of making its voices heard and bodies visible: from poor whites and African Americans in the early twentieth century to Latin American migrant workers in the present day. In the end, then, it's difficult to evaluate the meanings of insurgent rurality in the early twentieth century without recognizing the irony that proposals of popular liberalism in the contemporary United States are, like those of the Agrarians in the 1930s, frequently guided by investigations into the past that fail to recognize the full measure of suffering on active display within the country's borders.

If the Agrarians have, once again, played a seemingly outsized role in the construction of my argument over these past two chapters, that hasn't been because they alone belong at the center of the frame. Their high profile, the amount of critical attention they garnered in their own moment and beyond, was achieved through prominence in U.S. literary society and in academe, and it simply means that they left a much wider path than their peers in the STFU. My hope, in fact, is that the alternate modes of agri-cultural expression on display in the texts discussed above have not just nudged the Twelve Southerners out of the center but have showed that there was no center to begin with. As Jonathan Daniels explained in a widely repeated line from his 1938 travelogue, *A Southerner Discovers the South* (a book tellingly despised by Donald Davidson): "There are as many Souths, perhaps, as there are people living in it."[94]

Not long after Daniels, H. L. Mitchell sought to define one such South. In January 1946, a month after the STFU rebranded itself as the National Farm Labor Union, Mitchell submitted a dispatch to the American Press Associates entitled "The Other South." In Mitchell's account, the "other South" takes shape in spaces of racial integration such as those practiced by his union, for in addition to its touted white-black alliances, "the Union has had in its membership Mexicans, Cherokee and Choctaw Indians, Puerto Ricans and other minorities." And for Mitchell, the importance of bringing this South to the fore isn't just about reforming a backward region: "a nation's freedom rests on quicksand as long as agricultural exploitation continues and landowners maintain their power by pitting one group against another."[95] What Mitchell's union means is a question that supersedes its place and time in history; the success of pluralist democracy in the United States hangs in the balance, and so the union's projection of the "other South" retains both piquancy and great urgency. Recent moves in American studies have determined that the task of theorizing other Souths is designed to destabilize popular configurations of the region by uncovering the global or hemispheric dimensions of its complex identity. Yet there's a sense in which the deconstruction of the single South imagined by the Nashville Agrarians was inevitable, was already well underway in their own place and time: across the very landscape and labor practices they celebrated, a powerfully vibrant, and deeply disquieting, collection of voices still hovers, finding unity across difference while it strives to level the uneven ground of American life.

PART III

Migratory Modernism

CHAPTER FIVE

Station to Station

New York City and the Returns of the Rural

Though the rural South is routinely imagined as the fount of prewar vernacular music—old-time string band, country blues, gospel—there's a strong argument to be made for New York City as the music's true nexus. A staggering lineup of performers left their homes in the South of the 1920s and 1930s to translate performances into commodities via New York recording studios: Charley Patton, the Carter Family, Amédé Ardoin, Uncle Dave Macon, Fiddlin' John Carson among them.[1] And not surprisingly, perhaps, the recordings themselves frequently work to negotiate a cultural distance between manifestations of the country and the city in the early twentieth century, between the rural profile of their home region and the industrial and commercial advancements of the metropolis. In this sense, Joel Dinerstein's appraisal of the signifying power of prebop jazz artists might also apply to the work of other vernacular musicians from the period: "[T]hey created a genuine popular art that mediated the need for both accommodation and resistance to the technological society."[2] Accommodation and resistance, embrace and deflection: all inform the complex of responses that echoes throughout the discussion below.

If, as Edward Comentale and J. M. Mancini have recently argued, modernism is the best template by which to evaluate the commercial emergence of regional musics in the period, then it's possible to place the New York City experiences of these old-time musicians alongside the era's more widely canonized arts of migration. Comentale rightly encourages readers to "explore [the music's] inherent modernism," a move that allows for recognition of the "vast and varied aesthetic experience of modern life that ... sustained a vital forum of exchange and transformation for those otherwise excluded from traditional forms of power and prestige."[3] Instead of cordoning vernacular expression off from the canons of modernism, then, we ought to consider the ways that it addresses a common set of conditions, what Comentale calls "modern life." I survey a similar terrain by analyzing a group of short stories that each negotiates between and across a range of modern spaces. These readings provide the material through which to theorize forms of what I call "migratory modernism," a category that takes its place alongside previously theorized expressions of the modern from the period.[4]

In its broadest dimensions, then, this chapter seeks a connection between narratives of migration and theories of modernism, modernity, and modernization. Perhaps the most obvious way to uncover these links is to focus on the proliferation of works by Harlem Renaissance writers and artists that narrate the experience of the Great Migration. While both Farah Jasmine Griffin and Lawrence Rodgers have provided important insights into the cultural meanings of migration through wide-scoped analyses of African American narratives, I cover some of the same ground with different points of emphasis.[5] More specifically, this chapter brings the expansive models of new modernist studies to bear on less frequently studied texts—the sound recordings of Charlie Poole, a trio of migration stories by Rudolph Fisher ("City of Refuge" [1925], "The South Lingers On" [1925], and "The Promised Land" [1927]), as well as Zora Neale Hurston's "Story in Harlem Slang" (1941) and "Now You Cookin' with Gas" (an early version of "Harlem Slang," unpublished until 1995)—making them speak to a fresh and enlarged network of concerns. I also extend the conversation by reorienting it around both white and black subjects on the move, and by considering representations of terminal migrations from the South to the North alongside one with less straightforward linearity: the horseshoe-shaped migrations present in Ellen Glasgow's novel *Barren Ground* (1925). For all their focus on dislocation, alienation, and discontinuity, my readings also reveal the satisfactions of mobility and migration, exploring a broad spectrum of experience from figures who both epitomize and resist the tensions that arise between the urban and the rural, the North and the South. To this end, the chapter also uncovers means by which rusticity as an identity marker is manipulated and dodged, embraced and escaped.

It's important at the outset to define my keywords, particularly as they relate to heavily freighted discourses of the modern. Postcolonial critics have led the conversation about the kinds of alternative modernities that spring up along the edges of the dominant culture, often as a means of explaining the strange simultaneity of the modern and the antimodern, of the familiar and the foreign, along the colonial margins.[6] My configuration of "migratory modernism" continues in this direction: I look for ways in which the rural modern is already inside, and contributing to, expressions of the urban modern, and seek out confluences of content and form by examining narratives that take on movement as a subject at the same time as they offer representational strategies that mirror the jagged range of interior responses to relocation and displacement. Fredric Jameson's thinking about the psychology of modernism is especially useful in this regard: Jameson holds that modernist art depends on the pressure born of a "longing for ... monadic closure" and the modern world's inability to provide it.[7] Such is, to borrow from a passage of *Mrs. Dalloway*, a sensation common to individuals forever "feeling the impossibility of reaching the centre which, mystically, evaded them."[8] As both a sociological subject and as an embodied metaphor, then, the migrant is a useful figure since he or she navigates a newly uprooted world, often driven by paradoxical impulses toward connection via disconnection and guided by aesthetic tactics that make it possible to dramatize the intricate psychological effects of removal and adaptation.

Each of the texts analyzed below works to address a version of the modern that arrives and rearrives with the total saturation of capitalist modernity, one that prints itself on the minds of its participants—both willing and unwilling—through a cavalcade of sensations generated by new technologies, new commercial products, and landscapes moving at the speed and scale of industrialization. I also describe how the pace of the modern can create a sudden foreshortening—a chronological whiplash effect wherein the past's embeddedness in the present asserts itself with startling sharpness. In its ability to showcase sites where the boundaries between regions, cultural forms, and even temporal zones are crossed and where demarcations dissolve, migratory modernism makes visible the essential contradictions that give modernity in the Atlantic world its particular shapes.

This chapter's attention to New York as a locus of migratory modernism shouldn't be taken to reinforce the long-established tradition of reading the South as the urban North's rural foil. One doesn't have to look far beyond any canon of southern literature to find examples of literary representations of the movement in and out of the *urban* South. Faulkner's depictions of Memphis frequently create a chiaroscuro of permissiveness and transgression against a drapery of provincial country moralism, as rural characters come into contact with Popeye's hideout in *Sanctuary* (1931), the adultery hotels and baleful gangsters of *Light in August* (1932), the whiskey providers of *Go Down, Moses* (1942), the brothels of *The Reivers* (1962). Significantly for my purposes here, *Light in August* offers a depiction of Beale Street that doubles as a vigorous argument about capitals of black culture—urban North versus urban South—in its description of "that three or four Memphis city blocks in comparison with which Harlem is a movie set."[9] Faulkner's Memphis is also matched to images of New Orleans as a cosmopolitan crosscurrent swelling in the backwash of a circum-Atlantic contact zone, a characterization on display in *Mosquitoes* (1925), *Pylon* (1935), *Absalom, Absalom!* (1936), and the 1925 sketches he published in the *Times-Picayune* and the *Double Dealer*.

More, in Richard Wright's *Black Boy* (1945), the two years the author spent in Memphis act as a training ground for his experience in Chicago and beyond;

for Zora Neale Hurston, New Orleans—"the hoodoo capital of America"—provided materials for the novelistic ethnographies of 1935's *Mules and Men*.[10] Gabriel Briggs, investigating the years that immediately followed Reconstruction, has recently argued for the importance of Nashville as a major source in the development of a turn-of-the-century black intelligentsia.[11] Likewise, none of the public—and decidedly *rural*—self- and race-fashioning achieved in Booker T. Washington's appearance at the 1895 Cotton States and International Exposition would have been possible without the density of people and amenities of the southern metropolis—a reality captured in the shorthand for the posture Washington struck that day, the so-called "Atlanta compromise." My survey is admittedly incomplete, but it should reveal the urban South as a space of both social and cultural significance, and refute any tendency to reinscribe the rural South as the antithesis of the urban North. Still and all, this chapter focuses on literary accounts of migrations to and through New York City, a point of emphasis that draws out the formative role played by the commercial distribution of cotton, via financial and mercantile industries, that bind the material and cultural development of New York City modernity to southern agricultural districts.

Across time and space, migration is an ineluctably human fact. The recorded history of the North American continent alone is endlessly marked by movement: American Indians along ancient game and trade routes; the Mormon and Oregon Trails that took settlers into the Far West; the massive, forced relocation of the Trail of Tears; the African American "Exodusters" who went west to Kansas immediately following the end of Reconstruction; the waves of immigrants who arrived on both coasts and took up residence there or fanned out across the country; immigrants from Central and South America who continue across the southern border in our own days. What I hope to underscore, however, are the manifold ways that the emergent technologies and thought of the modernist period arbitrate the experience of mobility between the 1890s and the 1940s, and how the cultural products of collision enabled by these migrations intersect with material, aesthetic, and philosophical manifestations of the modern.

Prelude: Charlie Poole Sounds Out Migration

One example of migratory modernism's signifying possibilities arrives in the recorded work of Charlie Poole, a rambunctious banjo player from the Piedmont region of North Carolina. Poole began adulthood as a textile millworker but soon gained enough attention with his group, the North Carolina Ramblers, to secure a contract with Columbia Records. Hence his first trip to New York City, to make a recording, in 1925. He returned again the next year. Given New York's function as a center of North American cultural production, Poole's journey to the city is predictable enough, yet like many of his musical compatriots, Poole's public persona remained indelibly, even loudly, tied to his home region. And though Poole's work emerged from a milieu of industrial development (Piedmont mills and New York studios), Patrick Huber has shown that it was deliberately constructed to sound "anachronistic": Poole's recordings, and those of his peers in the old-time movement of the 1920s and 1930s, "offered comforting reassurances that authentic traditional music and joyous preindustrial pastimes could survive in a modern, urban-industrial America."[12] They were always already designed to act as an aural equivalent of lost time, of *old time*. Richard Middleton made a related point when discussing the popular music of the period: it draws upon a "nostalgia that is actually emblematic of modernity."[13] The modernity of these art objects, in other words, abides in the careful conjuration of an aesthetic seemingly threatened by modernity's tendency toward a world of standardized parts, mass media, and the expansion of urbanity.

Poole's instrument of choice, the banjo, bears directly on these phenomena. Banjos began to saturate his home region from the 1890s onward, aided by industrial processes that fitted the instrument with more durable, standardized parts—metal tone rings and tension hoops, steel frets and strings—and by ready access to instruction booklets and sound recordings.[14] The instrument's associations with African and African American vernacular culture, with minstrelsy, and, increasingly, with the middle-class parlor concretized an experience of the modern that is decidedly decentralized, a point recently underscored by Laurent Dubois: "The banjo, created in the midst of exile and upheaval, spoke easily to the realities of a new era of dispersal and motion, finding a place in a multiplicity of musical spaces and musical forms."[15] To augment Dubois's formulation of "musical spaces and ... forms," I want to notice the broader political and cultural significance of the banjo-in-motion in Poole's work, a move that makes it possible to hear the significance of a mostly forgotten recording—"A Trip to New York, Parts I, II, III, and IV."

Cut in 1929 with a one-off group called the Highlanders, this is, for my purposes here, Poole's most provocative recording. Although Poole's Ramblers featured a trio of guitar, banjo, and fiddle, he had toured with a five-piece outfit augmented by twin fiddles and a piano. When Columbia Records A&R representative Frank Walker balked at the idea of recording this larger group, Poole, somewhat surreptitiously, sought out a contract with Paramount/Brunswick Records as a member of the Highlanders/the Allegheny Highlanders, and the group made their only recordings at New York Recording Laboratories.[16] "A Trip to New York" is, strictly speaking, more skit than song, and its autobiographical resonances are unmistakable: stretching across four 78-rpm disc sides, the performance maps the moves of a band of rural musicians from their origins in the Appalachian village of Gobbler's Knob, North Carolina, all the way to New York City, plugging the gaps between songs with sound effects and narration belonging to a character who fills, with a knowing combination of wryness and urgency, the role of rural hayseed heading to the big town. The musical breaks, however, consciously conjure the sound of the past, with their incorporation of fiddle tunes ("Richmond," "New River Train") and songs associated with minstrel shows ("Turkey in the Straw"); the sound effects—which include aural approximations of mule hooves and train whistles—argue that the band's instruments and their expressive bodies carry all the power necessary to re-create and accommodate means of transportation both agricultural and industrial. Moreover, the paradox by which songs pointing toward the past are nevertheless named after cities ("Richmond") and modern technologies (the train) further invites listeners to recognize the deep investments of newness in expressions of the old-time and of oldness in expressions of the new.

The band begins its train tour of the upper Alleghenies with a pass through Washington, D.C., the account of which operates as a kind of audio postcard during a period when the ubiquity of the physical postcard was peaking. According to one account, in the early decades of the twentieth century "the postcard emerge[d] as a mediator of modernity, a means to identify and possess the totality of the city at a time when it was in fact fragmenting physically and socially."[17] Poole's reduction of the city to a single landmark, the Washington Monument, ventures to make the social and physical complexities of the urban landscape more easily comprehensible by offering subjects in—or from—rural outposts such as Gobbler's Knob a glimpse, however obscured, of what the city looks and sounds like from an appropriately safe distance. It also provides occasion for a hackneyed joke: spotting the monument, Poole explains, "[Washington] was the father of our country"; a bandmate's response: "I'll bet they had big families in those days." The exchange is indicative of a postcard vision of history: truncated, anecdotal, cropped and framed for consumption—all stuffed into a package tight enough to fit the casing of a train window or a 4" x 6" piece of pasteboard.

As the skit continues, it becomes clear that Poole is not just the narrator but also the navigator: modernity must be negotiated, and the singer stands ready to do it, a posture that makes his performance of rural naïveté all the more peculiar. For instance, when the band encounters the representative of an urban record company, the singer asks the city man how much he charges to make a record, expressing befuddlement to learn that the record company pays its performers: "Oh no, we don't want nothing out of it—no money, nothing. We never thought of that." Cash exchange, the predominant motivation of modern development, is deliberately denied purchase in the narrative. Padding out his position, the singer describes the group's existence outside of a cash economy: they were paid five dollars for a big wedding once, but mostly they just barter—"We usually get paid in corn, buckwheat flour, cane molasses. Just anything." This is not true, of course: the Highlanders' whole existence owes itself to a contract dispute. But Charlie Poole-the-businessman's relative savvy about contracts and compensation can't be allowed to interfere with Charlie Poole-the-character's enactment of rural rube.

Poole's performance opens wider as the singer marvels at the size of the city's train depot, making loud comparison to its diminutive counterpart in Gobbler's Knob. And when the band crosses Broadway, the singer signals the perils of modern technology, decrying the dangers of machined mobility in both the passenger car ("Better watch out for those automobiles. They don't slow down for ya") and the recording studio's elevator ("I hate to ride these things"). Upon arriving in the Brunswick studio, the song the group ultimately performs is "No Room for a Tramp," and it becomes difficult not to notice the parallels between our hapless train riders and the out-of-place tramp—an observation that raises an important question: why emphasize your out-of-placeness? If the nation's rush toward modernization determines that rurality is increasingly another mode of marginality, why court devaluation by embracing it?

The most obvious response might be that performances of regional distinction provide a backhanded way of emphasizing your relative autonomy against the standardization of modernization. It is also a means of appealing to two distinct audiences: curious urbanites and fellow country people, all while accruing "prestige from below" by wearing rusticity as a badge of honor.[18] This recital of rurality—the conscious adoption of a "poor white" mask—might also allow its participants a chance to control the terms by which they are apprehended in a new environment: to present oneself as a rustic in the city is to signal an awareness of the very cultural vocabulary responsible for descriptors such as "rustic" and "urbane." If Poole's strategy of representation is designed to mitigate the chaos that adheres to relocation and travel, it also provides a stable lens through which to recognize the self: you show who you are to those around you *and* to yourself by speaking, dressing, and gesticulating in an identifiable way. This dynamic is particularly acute when the contrasts are as dramatically pitched as they are in "A Trip to New York": Gobbler's Knob against New York City. And if the dominating space (New York) is emblematic of the future, the conflict signals a key tension undergirding the emergence of both modernization and modernism: the rural backwater signing in the shadow of the big city.

Moreover, the group's deliberate association with migrancy in "No Room for a Tramp" places them in the company of other prototypically modern figures who wander the city, Chaplin's Little Tramp, say, or the flâneur of Benjamin and Baudelaire. Their rurality, and the interregional arc of their wandering, is simply another thread in an already tangled web of wobbly identity markers. The recording never tells us whether Poole and his troupe ever made it back to Gobbler's Knob, but it doesn't seem to matter much since the most useful part of the story consists in those initial forays into a contact zone where, to adapt Mary Louise Pratt's famous model, distinct strands of the cultures of the rural South and the urban North "meet, clash, and grapple with each other."[19] That New York City is both the subject of the song and the launching pad for its circulation indicates the extent to which the "South" was already enmeshed in the city's culture industry of record labels and recording studios, from nineteenth-century minstrelsy to the race and hillbilly records of the 1920s and 1930s; in a roundabout way, it also highlights the part the metropolis plays in the production of "southern" literary texts—via publishing houses and periodicals—such as those discussed below. As I hope to demonstrate, what Griffin perceptively calls the "South in the City" is perhaps a stranger and more varied phenomenon than even she recognized, with roots and branches that spread out in all sorts of unpredictable ways.[20]

Away Up South: Harlem as Dixie in the Great Migration

Historians typically take the Great Migration of African Americans from the South to the industrial North to comprise two distinct waves: the first coincided with the outbreak of the First World War and a series of agricultural and ecological setbacks in the South, including a boll weevil infestation and the cratering of the cotton market of the 1920s, and continued until the Great Depression; the second stretched from the end of World War II until the early 1970s. Yet even within each distinct wave, migration proceeded in stages. Eric Arnesen offers this consensus of the first wave: "Most historians agree that roughly 450,000 to 500,000 black southerners relocated to the North between 1915 and 1918, and following a brief but severe economic depression shortly after the end of World War I, at least another 700,000 southern blacks made their way north during the 1920s."[21] Journalist Nicholas Lemann, who wrote a stirring account of postwar migrations from Mississippi to Chicago, quotes figures that estimate a movement of five million African Americans from 1940 to 1970. Other historians push the number up above six million.[22] Needless to say, the literary consequences of this demographic shift were profound, contributing to the singular rush of black writing associated with the Negro Renaissance.

Yet arts of black migration are not limited to literature. So-called race films such as Oscar Micheaux's *Birthright* (1939) and Spencer Williams's *The Blood of Jesus* (1941) prominently trope the country and the city, the South and the North, and the consequences of their mingling. In 1941 Jacob Lawrence completed his celebrated series *The Migration of the Negro*, a sixty-panel collection of small tempura paintings accompanied by brief, explanatory captions offering a broad visual interpretation, and narrative, of the Great Migration. Building on postimpressionist management of space, color, texture, and shape to create a category he called "dynamic cubism," Lawrence's two-dimensional figures show how the physical and psychic experience of dislocation defies realist conventions of representation. And the combination of formal innovation and sociological interest on display in the series provides a visual counterpoint to other forms of migratory modernism analyzed in this chapter.[23]

The fictions considered herein, however, predate postwar migrations; they concern themselves exclusively with the raft of issues affecting the first wave of northbound migrants. Circuitous migrations certainly informed black novels and stories of previous decades—*Iola Leroy* and *The Quest of the Silver Fleece* are two examples from this monograph—but the narratives I discuss below home in on an exploration of the terminal condition of African American lives in the Jim Crow era. And where Lemann and others see Chicago as the ultimate destination of midcentury black movement, the African American migration narratives I read all center on New York, Harlem specifically. While both Fisher and Hurston affiliate with the Harlem Renaissance, they all have, at very least, an equivocal relationship with the place. There are no simple celebrations of Harlem's great promise in these fictions, and they consistently remind readers of the difficulties facing African Americans from the rural South who seek to integrate the "city within a city" that was Harlem in the early decades of the twentieth century.

The marginality of rural southerners isn't just a feature of the era's fiction. See, for example, James Weldon Johnson's multigeneric study *Black Manhattan* (1930), which betrays a strong preference for Harlem-bound migrants from the West Indies and the "cities and towns of the Atlantic seaboard states" above those from the rural South. According to Johnson, it was the unfortunate cities of the industrial Midwest that "received migrants from the mills of the lower Mississippi Valley, from the rural, even backwoods, districts, Negroes who were unused to city life or anything bearing a resemblance to modern industry."[24] An African American déraciné from the rural South, it seems, can never shake the disadvantages of abject blackness—even in the training ground of the New Negro. In her recent work on black masculinity and southernness, Riché Richardson has noted a persistent coupling of the image of Uncle Tom and a cultural logic that codes black men from the rural South as "apolitical and counterinsurgent."[25] While this isn't Johnson's point exactly, it does seem like an unspoken current shaping his opinions: by accident of birth and by dint of association with long-standing exploitation, black people from the rural South have been deemed unfit to confront the economic and political demands that face the New Negro in the North, and they remain unprepared to capitalize on opportunities for advancement the period might provide.

Locke himself puts a slightly different, though perhaps no less troubling, spin on the issue in "Enter the New Negro," his essay in the famed 1925 issue of *Survey Graphic* ("Harlem: Mecca of the New Negro") that became the introduction to *The New Negro* (1925). The outmigration of black citizens from the South to the urban North is depicted in an oft-quoted passage as "a deliberate flight not only from countryside to city, but from mediaeval America to modern."[26] And this opportunity for relocation is colored in supernatural shades: "A railroad ticket and a suitcase, like a Baghdad carpet, transport the Negro peasant from the cotton-field and farm to the heart of the most complex urban civilization."[27] It's not just about jumping out of space but across time, across centuries even—and these aren't simply people from another part of the same nation but from a whole different epoch.[28] Charles S. Johnson's contribution to *The New Negro* takes a more measured stance, conceding that despite their "vagrant desires and impulses," southern migrants to northern industrial and cultural centers are "becoming a part of . . . the cities' life and growth." Still, it remains a matter of evolution from low forms to high, from country to "city Negro."[29] It's clear in each of these examples that the project of making the familiar foreign, of marking individuals according to their place of origin, runs dangerously close to the rationale of segregation. One of the most unsparing entries in Zora Neale Hurston's "Glossary of Harlem Slang" is "Russian," meaning "a Southern Negro up north. 'Rushed up here,' hence a Russian" (137). Consequently, southern migrants remain segmented—and held under a suspicious eye—as the most abject other in a population consistently othered by U.S. legal and cultural practices.

In the stories I focus on below, Harlem is imagined as a space in which black southern migrants bring the conflicts of the South up north. While these fictions may lack the hard data of a sociological survey, they provide a chance to examine the multiple, occasionally contradictory, angles of the issue, angles that create variegated portraits of the psychic responses to migration—alienation and freedom, confusion and clarity. To this end, both Fisher and Hurston ironize the Promised Land narrative of African American redemption in the North in a way that prompts reevaluations of the "South," the "rural," and the links between expressive culture and modern subjectivity. In a reversal of Mark Storey's fruitful scenario, these narratives disclose the interplay between urban fictions and rural realities.[30]

Moving Up: Rudolph Fisher's Migratory Modernism

Although Rudolph Fisher is not typically identified as a southerner—he was born and raised in that border space Washington, D.C.—in his contributions to *The New Negro* and in several less conspicuous writings, he displays a keen sense of how a black southern identity is inhabited and an awareness of its particular vulnerability in the early twentieth century. While "City of Refuge" is widely anthologized, and although enthusiasm for Fisher's fiction—particularly *The Conjure Man Dies*, his 1932 detective novel—seems to be on the upswing, he has attracted less scholarly attention than other of his Harlem Renaissance peers. One explanation for this odd blend of prominence and relative lack of commentary is that despite his presence in the anthology, Fisher's unflattering depictions of Harlem and its uneasy relationship with southern emigrants help throw *The New Negro* into conflict with itself. It's fair, I think, to classify him as a literary migrant, drifting somewhere between Locke's positions and those found in *Fire!!* (1926), the grittier attempt at a Harlem Renaissance manifesto engineered by artists like Wallace Thurman, Aaron Douglas, Langston Hughes, and Hurston herself.

The narrative shape of "City of Refuge" proceeds along a common contour—an African American leaves the rural South for Harlem, the center of black culture in the industrial North. Unlike most participants in the Great Migrations of the early twentieth century, however, when the story's chief protagonist, King Solomon Gillis, makes it from Penn Station to Harlem, he is escaping the law in North Carolina, having killed an antagonistic white man. The text signals Gillis's disorientation by developing distinct phenomenologies of place, methods of highlighting links between sharp sensory experiences and the psychological absorption of a particular space.[31] In a prominent example from Gillis's case, we read of his arrival at Penn Station: "There had been strange and terrible sounds.... Shuffle of a thousand heels, innumerable echoes. Cracking rifle shots—no, snapping turnstiles.... Distant thunder, nearing. The screeching onslaught of the fiery hosts of hell, headlong, breathtaking" (35).

Gillis's tendency to misread the landscape, his inability to distinguish, for instance, between gunfire and turnstiles, shades his entire experience in Harlem and predicts the story's ironic turns: when Gillis hears the subway, his sensorium calls up the signs of a lynching as the sights and sounds of the northern landscape intensify his "southern" memory. Above all else the city here registers as a series of disorienting, abrasive sounds that lead Gillis, roughly, from one compromising situation to another.

Further, in the story's opening paragraph, he is disturbed by, and ultimately forced into, the mechanized ethos of the urban landscape: "the railroad station, the long, white-walled corridor, the impassable slot-machine, the terrifying subway train he felt as if he had been caught up in the jaws of a steam-shovel, jammed together with other helpless lumps of dirt, swept blindly along for a time, and at last abruptly dumped" (35). Dumped, like the materials from which steam-powered machines carve out the modern world. In these opening paragraphs, descriptions of hell, rifle fire, and Jonah struggling in the belly of the whale combine to welcome Gillis to his new home.

The suggestion that, on levels both economic and material, Manhattan modernity is a by-product of southern-human raw material is a perceptive one: eighteenth- and nineteenth-century slavery played a large, direct, and intimate part in the city's rise to global prominence and prosperity. It's worth pausing here to note, then, that any discussion of interchange between the rural South and New York City, particularly a discussion that looks toward race and labor, should also explore the city's long entanglements with slavery and the antebellum cotton trade. Edward Baptist's recent work has demonstrated how relentlessly the industrial economy in the antebellum North, the national site most readily identified with capitalist modernity, "was built on the backs of enslaved people."[32] Baptist's larger point is that slavery's contributions are prototypical, even generative, of modern capitalism, not antithetical to it, as commentators across four centuries have often insisted.[33] In sum, within these northeastern sectors of nineteenth-century capitalist expansion, New York City played a special role. According to Edward Glaeser, the city's fabulous affluence arrived because of its geographic centrality (farther south than Boston and more easily accessed than Philadelphia), its large river (the Hudson), and the advantageous composition of its harbor (deep, and usually free from ice drifts).[34] These physical features allowed the space to become a key node in the "Cotton Triangle," a trade route that promoted the flow of resources from southern ports to European harbors in Liverpool and Le Havre and that, in turn, brought European imports and manufactured goods to the South. The triangulated structure of exchange created thereby became, in Glaeser's description, an exemplary "hub-and-spoke transportation network."[35] The smokestacks and mills of Manchester also figure: one way to understand Friedrich Engels's *The Conditions of the Working Class in England* (1844), a study completed while the author worked in his family's Manchester thread factory, is as a critique of the manufacturing stage in a multistep industrial process initiated in the cotton fields of the Mississippi River valley. Yet even before the cotton gin intensified the tempo of this fluid trade structure, New York served as an essential destination for incoming shipments of slaves. Present-day Wall Street, for instance, served as the site of a bustling slave market; Moses Taylor, a founder of the institution that would become Citibank, was a chief financial backer of the slave trade; and Lehman Brothers, an Alabama banking firm that moved to New York City in 1858, prospered via commodity trading in antebellum cotton.[36]

In fact, the city's merchant, shipping, and banking interests all gained by the cheap cotton made possible through southern slavery. So much so that in 1861 New York City mayor Fernando Wood infamously proposed that the city secede from the union with its southern partners in the cotton trade. (Wood's support for the Confederacy continued during his wartime term in the House of Representatives, where he was a loud and vigorous opponent to the passage of the Thirteenth Amendment.) According to Philip Foner, the city remained an active participant in the illegal slave trade well into the 1860s, and when the city moved to abolish the slave trade in 1799, it threatened to cut off a vital source of the city's wealth by disconnecting one of the spokes from its hub, Glaeser argues that the cotton industry conveniently "solved this problem,"[37] establishing a pattern of exchange in which, as Edwin Burrows and Mike Wallace point out, New York shipping and financial interests brokered the flow of goods, "ringing up, at every turn, substantial profits in sales, freight charges, and commissions."[38] In his history of the city's nineteenth-century economic elites, Sven Beckert noted that "[t]rade in cotton was their most important business"; it was a venture that yoked the stakes of the southern planter class to New York merchants and financiers.[39] Further, "The export of cotton also secured the nation's credit on the European money markets and thus kept the city's banks afloat."[40] A slavery-fueled cotton trade wasn't just a source for the material profile of New York City but, through the backing of its financial institutions, the fiduciary solidity of the nation at large since "the empire of cotton was at its heart an empire of credit."[41] And it's the wealth and authority created through credits and debts that translated the South's raw materials and its forced labor into the structural wealth of the modern metropolis: "Eventually, New York superintended so great a share of the South's output that forty cents of every dollar paid for southern cotton allegedly wound up in the pockets of city merchants."[42]

Although New York City's position as an "urban colossus" (to borrow Glaeser's term) was established through more than the cotton trade alone—the ability to transfer goods across the Great Lakes to the continental interior through the Erie Canal was another essential development—it's impossible to deny that the city's ascendancy as a global center of finance and industry was funded in large part through its connection with the rural South, a relationship that stretches from the twentieth-century moment of Fisher's stories back to the eighteenth century. In looking for manifestations of the "South in the City" in the 1920s and 1930s, then, it becomes clear that, in some deep-rooted and undeniable ways, the South has been in the city from the beginning, as an enriching—if often unseen—presence. This history sounds a variation on Eric Hobsbawm's famous contention that, in Britain, "Whoever says Industrial Revolution says cotton"[43]: it may be equally possible to claim that whoever says cotton says modernization, and—more pointedly perhaps—whoever says New York says cotton, says exploitative labor, says South.

As each of this chapter's stories circles around and across the specter of a rural southern presence in the urban North, they throw the shadows of the city's nineteenth-century investments and returns into harsh relief with the nominally progressive social and political commitments of the modern city. If, as Baptist, Beckert, and Johnson have all recently argued, the cotton trade and the slave labor that supported it gave rise to capitalist modernity in the early decades of the 1800s, it's possible to see a similar, if more characteristically oblique, pronouncement in the thinking of Walter Benjamin. As I mentioned in the introduction, in *The Arcades Project* Benjamin claims that Paris became the locus of *die Moderne* through a "boom in the textile trade," and, in turn, "At one blow, [the arcades] became the hollow mold from which the image of 'modernity' was cast."[44] Yet it's important to recognize that Paris modernity, achieved by way of the textile boom, has roots in antebellum slavery and its southern environments. In the years leading up to the Civil War, France was one of several European countries dependent on raw cotton produced by slave labor in the United States: in 1859, for instance, 90 percent of the 192 million pounds used in France was supplied by U.S. interests.[45] Where Benjamin follows Baudelaire in theorizing Paris of the 1840s and 1850s as the fullest expression of the modern, it becomes clear that his twentieth-century visions were permeated by the inescapable presence of an earlier age. A passage from *Arcades* explains these "inheritances": "The nineteenth century is ... the set of noises that invades our dream, and which we interpret on awakening."[46] Writing from a different continent but during roughly the same decades as the authors investigated in this chapter, Benjamin was both haunted and encouraged by the past's installment in his present moment, since such a view alone provides a means of critiquing oppressive beliefs in "historical progress ... through a homogeneous, empty time."[47]

What this means for the fictions discussed below is that their descriptions of the South's northern remainders, ghostly and oneiric though they sometimes are, arrive as "interpretations" of the inescapable inheritances of modernity's rise and its debts to rural southern agricultural tracts and slavery. If painful intrusions of the past, of nineteenth-century realities assumedly buried and abandoned, continue to appear in the twentieth-century New York City journeys of this chapter's protagonists, it's probably because the city itself is underwritten by enslaved southern bodies and the production of cotton. In 1860 editor Thomas P. Kettell's influential pamphlet *Southern Wealth and Northern Profits* made the case that the "history of the wealth and power of nations is but a record of slave products."[48] It's a statement that harmonizes, however distressingly, with Benjamin's oft-repeated claim that "[t]here is no document of civilization which is not at the same time a document of barbarism."[49] And, as we'll see in the analysis that follows, inasmuch as the southern residues in the modern city represent a space out of space, it's also possible to configure them as intrusions of time out of time, such that thoughts, actions, words, and objects become indices signaling both the pastness-of-the-now and the inescapable nowness-of-the-past. As Benjamin notes, "every image of the past that is not recognized by the present as one of its own concerns threatens to disappear irretrievably."[50]

That histories of antebellum exploitation and complicity reemerge, with a shuffled set of variables, in narratives of twentieth-century African American migration isn't so remarkable then. One example includes the attitudes toward blackness and labor staged in Rudolph Fisher's "City of Refuge." As he moves through the streets of Harlem, Gillis's rural southern blackness makes him an easy mark: early on, he sidles up to Mouse Uggam, a character who uses their shared southernness—they both come from North Carolina—to gain Gillis's trust and then cons him into unwittingly fulfilling the distribution end of a drug ring. Not surprisingly, the most "southern" body in this arrangement is saddled with the most dangerous, degraded task—a micro-iteration of the larger, older enterprise of exploitation that provides the story's invisible backdrop. When authorities break up the operation, Gillis ferociously resists arrest but is dumbfounded and stilled by the presence of a black detective. The narrative's brief, parting glance at Gillis's interior is telling: "Harlem. Land of plenty. City of refuge—city of refuge. If you live long enough—" (47). According to "City of Refuge," Harlem and the Jim Crow South stand toe-to-toe as exemplary modes of a sadly familiar form of American cynicism. Gillis may marvel at the possibilities of his new home, but, according to Uggam, he remains "a baby jess in from the land o cotton and so dumb he think antebellum's an old woman" (37). In Uggam's speech, the long arm of cotton reaches out of the South, and out of an ostensibly distant past, to sketch an infantilized man with a comically distorted sense of history. The reference here points up the deep ruts of the New York–South past, ruts that prove effective in tripping twentieth-century black southerners like Gillis. In Fisher's Harlem, it seems, the disadvantages of rural southern blackness either migrate along with the migrants or are discovered anew in a city that has long profited by them.

Walter White's essay "The Paradox of Color," a piece that appears alongside "City of Refuge" in *The New Negro*, explains that even though New York presents itself "as nearly ideal a place for colored people as exists in America," the city is still rife with "Southern whites who brought North with them their hatreds" and, even more pervasively, with oppressive attitudes about a "Negro who is either a buffoon or a degenerate beast or a subservient lackey."[51] In White's eyes, the result is a defensive mainstay—the "definitely bounded city within a city" that is Harlem.[52] But, according to Fisher, Harlem itself is not nearly impervious enough. As the narrator relates in a subtle shift into double-voiced discourse at the story's opening, "In Harlem, black was white" (36). Black may be white, but the experience of King Solomon Gillis suggests that somebody still needs to be black—a fact that the story's persistent interest in degrees of blackness makes clear: Uggam is described as a "little ... yellow man" whose blackness, and southernness, fades as his authority seems to rise (36); the West Indian whom Gillis replaces as a grocery worker is "nigger" and "monkey-chaser" (40). In this light, "City of Refuge" is primarily an account of intraracial competition, and one template for this combination of setting and conflict may belong to Paul Laurence Dunbar, whose 1902 novel, *The Sport of the Gods*, features remarkably similar narrative outlines: set downtown, on 27th Street rather than in Harlem, it nevertheless includes a series of parallel tropes—migration, deception, disillusionment, and (very nearly, in the case of *Sport of the Gods*) self-destruction. Begrudging though it may be, however, the readiness to allow for a sense of racial—and spatial—reconciliation in Dunbar's novel is altogether absent in "City of Refuge."[53]

Pointing out the impossibilities of arriving at a firm sense of what and how blackness signifies in this new urban/rural context, "City of Refuge" de-essentializes race in nearly Foucauldian terms by acknowledging connections between discourse and power, wherein "black" becomes another technology of violence. From this perspective, "City of Refuge" acts as an unsettling addition to the Harlem Renaissance canon: it's not a celebration of blackness; it's an evacuation of "blackness" as a unifying mechanism. The story's depiction of black identity as a "floating signifier" matches Stuart Hall's depiction of race as a category that operates like language: it is most often learned and deployed somewhere below consciousness and is easily slotted into hierarchical modes of thinking and difference making.[54] But while its meanings are always contestable, it is nevertheless capable of determining one's social reality. In this sense, beneath all the story's talk of "refuge" and all its images of black authority, swift currents of raw power ripple, political technologies waiting to be appropriated by the most resourceful subjects or groups.

As I mentioned before, Fisher's use of Harlem as a staging ground for the struggles of southern migrants isn't restricted to "City of Refuge" alone. Between 1925 and 1933, the author published a suite of stories devoted to the experience of the new migrant in Harlem: "Ringtail" (1925), "The South Lingers On" (1925), "The Promised Land" (1927), "Ezekiel" (1932), and "Ezekiel Learns" (1933). Of these, "The Promised Land" and "The South Lingers On" join "City of Refuge" to forge a loose triptych of narratives that directly confront the sense of disconnection and disenchantment that greeted many southern migrants upon their arrival in Harlem.

"The South Lingers On," a story altered slightly and retitled "Vestiges" for inclusion in *The New Negro*, offers subtle variations on the above-stated themes. The narrative depicts the disorientation of a rural southern preacher, Ezekiel Taylor, adrift in Harlem, where his charismatic religiosity becomes a substitute for the back-home South at large. Like his biblical namesake, Taylor is exiled from his homeland and wandering, "walk[ing] slowly along 133rd Street, conspicuously alien." Where "City of Refuge" makes use of Harlem's ability to impart prestige and authority to black subjects, like the traffic cop or the detectives that collar Gillis, "The South Lingers On" runs that same scenario backward: Taylor, a respected religious authority back home, is recast as a comic figure of scorn and embarrassment, "the colored Santa Claus." And the preacher himself refutes any typology that would present the urban North as Canaan: "The kingdom of Harlem. Children turned into mockers. Satan in the hearts of infants. Harlem—city of the devil—outpost of hell" (60). It would be easy to dismiss these as the musings of a fusty old man if the story didn't provide a fully modeled demon to populate Taylor's hell: Reverend Shackleton Ealey, who operates as this text's Mouse Uggam figure, the sharpie clergyman who fills his collection plate by camping out at Penn Station and ushering incoming migrants into his church.

For Ealey, Taylor represents "fertile soil" (62), and in order to thicken his own crop, he provides the preacher a pulpit. It's a scheme that seems to be working, as Taylor's revival pulls a swelling crowd to Ealey's church. But when Lucky, a self-styled cynic who is himself the son of a southern preacher, runs with a group of young men bent on upstaging Taylor's revival, he is startled at his response to the proceedings: "Dam' 'f I know what it is—maybe because it makes me think of the old folks or somethin'... it just sorter—gets me" (69). The South clearly does linger on, particularly in that most intimate of all "Souths," the individual consciousness. Yet, above all else, this is an argument based on phenomenological accounts of place—the South endures not simply in the consciousness, then, but more specifically in affect, in an emotional register that is, as Lucky describes it, just beyond the reach of reason. The region—and its associations with the people and places of the past—becomes intelligible to Lucky only by accessing a kind of memory of feelings, feelings he never knew he had.

Like "City of Refuge," "The Promised Land" works to ironize the notion of Harlem as a sanctuary for African Americans disfranchised in the Jim Crow South by highlighting the conflicts that greet three different kinds of southern migrants, all bound by a common lineage and a shared apartment: Mammy, the pious grandmother who is convinced of Harlem's essential sinfulness; her grandson Sam, an able mechanic who makes a steady living in Harlem; and her other grandson Wesley, Sam's less fortunate cousin who struggles to find work.[55] The two young men compete for the affections of a woman named Ellie, this story's hardened Mouse Uggam, and its major movement is catalyzed when, through her window, Mammy spies Wesley and Sam fighting over Ellie at a rent party. She intervenes by throwing her Bible through the neighboring porthole. In contrast to "City of Refuge," "The Promised Land" actualizes the latent psychic violence of migration, and Harlem itself arrives as the corrupting influence: "the city had done something to Wesley and Sam" (80), the text warns. If the character of the city itself is a corrupter, then Ellie is corruption's purest epitome. For instance, when Mammy urges Ellie to choose between Wesley and Sam, Ellie's response uncovers something of the rift that divides recent migrants and more established Harlemites: "D' you s'pose I'm chasin' after your farmer boys?... Pity you old handkerchief heads would n' stay down South where you belong" (84). Toward the end of the exchange, the narrator reveals Ellie's motivations: "Both the bumpkins spent on her. Why reduce her chances for a good time by making a betraying choice?" (83). This scene offers another variation on Fisher's common theme: for Harlem veterans like Ellie, newcomers from the South ("farmer boys") are only worthwhile to the extent that they are exploitable and capable of granting her access to the city's consumptive wonders.

The narrative succinctness of "The Promised Land" is matched by its thematic interest in limited opportunities as well as its tight geographic scope: the whole of the action occurs within the family's cramped apartment, and so every corner becomes an essential variable in the text's economy of action. Unsurprisingly, then, the most prominent feature of the apartment—an airshaft—ends up playing a major role at the story's climax when the cousins come to blows and Wesley is pushed across its threshold, down to his death. Given its portentous function in "The Promised Land," it's important to consider the multiple meanings bound up in the Harlem airshaft. According to Luc Sante's survey of life along the margins in early twentieth-century Manhattan, most airshafts ventilating the city's tenement apartments in the 1920s were barely adequate to their task, often posing more problems than they solved by blocking light and serving as convenient, and dangerous, dumping grounds.[56] Yet in Fisher's mind, the airshaft provided a sensory link to the sounds and smells of the larger community: it acts as a portal syncing the inhabitants of individual apartments to the pulse of the larger community; it's the stream that carries the sonic and olfactory detritus of the neighborhood, as we see in an undated speech by Fisher, "Harlem, the Negro Metropolis": "Come into one of the old apartment houses and you will observe all the hubbub of a Harlem airshaft—three player pianos and six radios out-crying each other, liver and onions sputtering, cabbage and chitterlings bubbling and smelling, a couple exchanging compliments, a neglected baby wailing, blues-hymns—a girl weeping heartbrokenly" (330). This dense weave of smells and sounds, the sensory survey of Harlem, highlights the free and open exchange of a patchwork collective of black subjects occupying their most celebrated environment. It serves as a metaphor of unity through diversity. In the sensoriums of its inhabitants, the vibrant phenomenology of this place is made indistinguishable from its social and cultural purposes.

Another Harlem modernist of major distinction, Duke Ellington, likewise extolled the airshaft in the aptly titled composition "Harlem Air Shaft" (1940). In 1944, as part of an extensive profile in the *New Yorker*, Ellington presents the song as a piece of program music designed to reveal the texture and tone of urban black life. In its focus on sights, sounds, and smells, his account of the airshaft's significance is strikingly similar to Fisher's: "So much goes on in a Harlem air shaft. You get the full essence of Harlem in an air shaft. You hear fights, you smell dinner, you hear people making love. You hear intimate gossip floating down. You hear the radio. An air shaft is one great big loudspeaker. You see your neighbor's laundry.... An air shaft has got every contrast.... You hear people praying, fighting, snoring."[57] What Fisher labels the community's "hubbub," Ellington calls the "full essence of Harlem."[58] But the account in "Harlem" hits so many of the same notes as Ellington's that we might use Ellington's language to reinscribe Wesley's fate, such that it's easy enough to see him as a country boy who is, quite literally, swallowed whole by the *essence* of Harlem.

In the story's final scene, the text completes its revision of the airshaft's function as community conduit with a parting vignette that wraps up the story where it began, with Mammy staring out the window holding a Bible in her lap, ruminating on her new world: "Out of the airshaft sounds came to her, sounds of the land of promise. Noise of a rent party somewhere below.... Noise of a money quarrel somewhere above, charges, taunts, disputes — fruit of a land where sudden wide differences in work and pay summoned disaster. Noise of sinful singing and dancing, pastime of Ellie's generation, breed of a city where children cursed and threatened the old and went free" (88). The airshaft may well be the most immediate gateway to the sounds and smells of the neighborhood, but in Mammy's Harlem all it brings is "charges, taunts, disputes," unwanted noise and painful reminders of the consequences of an arrangement that had "quickly estranged" her two grandsons "simply by paying the one twice as much as the other" (81). While Fisher's speech embraced the unfiltered environment provided by the airshaft, his fiction is decidedly more skeptical. The story's final chord lays a melancholy overtone atop Fisher's celebration of the airshaft and Harlem's potential as a closely quartered, tight-knit community. Intimacy has collapsed into claustrophobia; the smells and sounds of the neighborhood now signal suffocation, and the loudspeaker of Ellington's airshaft becomes an increasingly intrusive, nearly totalitarian, presence. The story thus concretizes a situation in which a character like Mammy can "move up" to the cultural center and still be left behind. Where the labor systems of the rural South were obviously perverse, Mammy's Harlem follows the hard line of U.S. capitalism by using compensation and reward as a subtler — if no less damaging — fulcrum for segregating its inhabitants. Patricia Yaeger's interest in the "throwaway bodies whose loss hovers in the margins of pre- and post–World War II American culture" provides useful language for describing the effects of a strictly market-oriented capitalist regime in which anyone who is underpaid becomes a "no-body," a disposable person who doesn't matter enough to carry a social or cultural charge.⁵⁹ This is an accurate description of Mammy, but it applies with special force to Wesley, who is literally thrown into the trash heap.

In each of these stories, Fisher's harsh portrait of Harlem offers an uncertain configuration of the meanings of the New Negro, since his sense of the new is indebted to the fundamental violence undergirding Joseph Tschumpeter's model of creative destruction: the process of creation requires that something already in existence must be irreversibly altered or destroyed.⁶⁰ In some sense, Fisher's work seeks to answer an existential question memorably posed in verse by Salman Rushdie's *The Satanic Verses*. Although Rushdie's work arrived more than half a century after Fisher's and is more specifically interested in the experience of transplanted Indians in England, its concern for the dislocation and violence of creation feels appropriate to Fisher's migration stories.

> How does newness come into the world? How is it born?
> Of what fusions, translations, conjoinings is it made?
> How does it survive, extreme and dangerous as it is?⁶¹

In representing the process by which the New Negro comes into being, Fisher highlights the turbulence, and the causalities, that accompany these New York "translations": Ezekiel, Wesley, Mammy, King Solomon Gillis—all undone, and recycled, by the forces that breed newness. Specifically, Wesley's transformation into waste, his fatal trip through the airshaft, seems to complete a circuit opened in "City of Refuge," when Gillis is "dumped" into Harlem along with the other raw materials from which the city is endlessly remade. Broadly posed, these tropes of dumping, salvage, and regeneration direct us to a human infrastructure of urban modernity in which the "City of Refuge" doubles as a city of refuse.

In an influential account of African American narratives of migration and travel, Toni Morrison writes convincingly of the image of the ancestor. These figures are, in Morrison's words, "sort of timeless people whose relationships to the characters are benevolent, instructive, and protective, and they provide a certain kind of wisdom."⁶² Farah Jasmine Griffin makes Morrison's ancestors a central feature of her analysis and expands the concept to include forms of expression associated with black vernacular culture like cooking, music, and dance. In these fictions of Fisher's, however, the support network that is supposed to extend out from the "ancestor" falters. The ancestors are obsolescents: they are mocked and manipulated, like Ezekiel; ignored and scorned, like Mammy. For Griffin, the ancestors work to "soften the impact of urbanization."⁶³ No such luck in Fisher. The New Negro in these stories must pass through a bumpy channel shaped by an unresolved series of tensions—urban, rural, northern, southern, traditional, modern, religious, impious. And his guide to the new environment and to a fully realized sense of blackness is more likely a con artist than a concerned compatriot.

In his reading of "City of Refuge," Lawrence Rodgers makes a similar point about the tragic absence of ancestors, but he is less interested in what their absent presence in the text means for Harlem or its role in the formation of the New Negro.[64] Rodgers's concern might be even better directed at "The Promised Land" and "The South Lingers On," where all evidence of the old is discarded and the characters that fail to adapt to the ethos of the city are simply overrun. Wesley of "The Promised Land" is just the most obvious example: the story makes clear that, unlike his cousin Sam, Wesley is not an efficient contributor to the networks of consumption and production essential to the urban experience. Where Sam is good with his hands, draws a salary, and cycles more capital back into the economy, Wesley skirts penury. It's not necessarily the case that Sam has more skillfully adopted the cultural codes of Harlem—both cousins seem well versed in the hip patois of their new neighborhood—it's that he has figured out a clearer path toward "productivity." Fisher's take on migration stands as a clear-eyed recognition of the consequences of the attitudes expressed in Johnson's *Black Manhattan*: the most desirable migrants are those who have made themselves amenable to wage labor and, in doing so, have created greater distance between themselves and slavery. In short, the satire of Fisher's stories is aimed at a series of structures that reserves its rewards for those who can contribute to the economy of capitalist modernity, an economy that exists as both the ethos and the logic of the city. That's not to say the rural South exists outside the realm of capitalism's influence; it's simply an acknowledgment that the freedoms Harlem extends are all conditional, and one of the chief conditions is the kind of labor one performs. Mammy's services as a caretaker are outmoded; Ezekiel's preaching provides the regional magnet for homesick migrants, but he is unknowingly aligned with a corrupt church; Gillis makes a good drug mule in Harlem and not much else; Wesley is clumsy with his hands and can't secure a permanent position.

Jolene Hubbs's thinking about the "rural modernism" of Faulkner's fiction offers a strategy for reading Fisher's characters' inability to adapt to their new urban environment. Writing of *As I Lay Dying*, Hubbs describes a state of "perennial obsolescence" wherein "poor whites are seen not in terms of certain practices and objects that might be outmoded but rather as uniformly and perpetually archaic."[65] Although her analysis focuses exclusively on the experience of poor white southerners, it's a short step to apply it to rural black migrants in the city as well. Mouse Uggam, for example, is also a southern transplant to New York, but his experience with Gillis suggests that the space itself grants provisional authority to the most thoroughly urbanized, the most fully assimilated to the attitudes and standards of capitalism-as-modernity. As a reflection of—and, perhaps, a contributor to—the effects of modernity, Fisher's take on a violently divisive Harlem uncovers the paradox whereby discourses of New Negro newness emerge as newly veiled versions of the same old story.

Speaking Up South: Zora Neale Hurston and the Language of the Urban Folk

True to its title, Zora Neale Hurston's "Story in Harlem Slang" is a story in, and about, a distinctive mode of language. The emphasis on language perhaps compels the arc of the story to remain fairly low as its explorations of dialect provide a flat surface for the examination of migratory modernism's frictions. The main character, Jelly, is a recent émigré from Alabama; he's drifting in Harlem, often hungry and lonely. After meeting up with a friend, Sweet Back, he plays a round of the dozens before trying to pick up a woman. Rejected and dejected, the story ends by taking us into Jelly's head for a nostalgic reverie: "Jelly's thoughts were far away. He was remembering those full, hot meals he had left back in Alabama to seek wealth and splendor in Harlem without working" (133). Somehow in this performance the medium drives the message, as the story's representations of the black vernacular's intricacies become another way of highlighting both language's slipperiness and its essential role in the formation of identity.

It's difficult not to see Hurston's training as an anthropologist in the story's ethnographic scope: there's a sense in which these performances of dialect, appearing in the high-minded *American Mercury* of the early 1940s, are designed as an insider's portrait of an African American subculture. More specifically, the story stages experiments in Harlem jive—an argot invented by Harlem's zoot-suiters and beboppers—at the same time as its glossary participates in an impulse to establish a meaningful, even legitimizing, lexicography for the idiom. (This same drive produced a pair of prominent contemporaneous texts: Cab Calloway's *Hepster's Dictionary: Language of Jive* [1939] and Dan Burley's *Original Handbook of Harlem Jive* [1944].)

The story is about language, but its language also acts as a lever that widens Hurston's status as a major American writer, one whose actual interests exceed her reputation. In 2011 Glenda Carpio and Werner Sollors called for greater scholarly attention to Hurston's "urban stories," claiming that these largely neglected narratives provide a more complete picture of Hurston's imaginative, social, and political concerns.[66] I seek to respond below by making the more granular argument that "Story in Harlem Slang's" narrative of South–North migration uses several specific traits of black English in the urban North to dramatize the emotional and psychological effects of relocation and to trouble the instant correlation of the rural South and the "folk." In the story, jive provides an appropriate reflection of the divided interiors of the story's characters, often by underlining the presence of rurality in their highly stylized "urban" modes of expression. As if to emphasize the divisiveness of these internal splits, "Harlem Slang" never offers any substantive example of successful communication-via-language: language, even when celebrated as a ritual of African American sovereignty, serves as an expressive resource but not an effectively communicative one; it does little to alleviate the overwhelming mood of alienation that pervades the narrative. And yet, when considering ways that the story models larger patterns of rural–urban/South–North migration, it's clear that language is the current which carries the two opposing charges (urban and rural), that it creates a venue for collision, dialogue, and synthesis. Upon investigation, Hurston shows, it turns out that Harlem slang has always been infused with the sounds of the South and, inevitably, the sounds of the country.

Never published commercially until the release of Hurston's *Complete Stories* in 1995, "Now You Cookin' with Gas" is essentially identical to "Story in Harlem Slang" save for a few minor, though telling, differences. For one thing, "Harlem Slang" suggests that Jelly migrated out of ambition, to style himself as a New Negro and to find a new line of work. According to Jelly, he also migrated to get away from the wiles of southern white women: "I had to leave from down south 'cause Miss Anne used to worry me so bad" (130). "Now You Cookin' with Gas," however, sharpens the critique by making plain a link between the attention of white women and the violence only hinted at in "Harlem Slang": "Mister Charlie down there plays too rough to suit me," Jelly explains. "I ain't none of them cowards like them shines down in Bam. I'm mean!... I just come on off to keep from killing somebody" (238). To emphasize the point, we learn in "Cookin'" that Jelly's counterpart Sweet Back actually has killed somebody, a white police officer in Georgia. In "Story in Harlem Slang," the threat of black-on-white violence is less pronounced, eliding an idea that both Fisher's "City of Refuge" and "Now You Cookin' with Gas" rely on: the creation of a sovereign identity depends on a violent encounter that upends the dominating force. And as in Fisher, the creation of something new is only accomplished through the destruction of something already extant, a form of murder as ontogenesis. But the story is also deeply concerned with what happens when the residue of the destroyed element—in this case, the trappings and shadings of Jelly's rural past—can't be scrubbed out, when newness is made old again or when oldness is revealed to be intrinsic and internal to the new.

In contrast to "City of Refuge," "Cookin'" relays the information about Sweet Back's violence through the mouth of its characters, not the voice of the narrator. Sweet Back receives no corroboration from either the narrator or from any of the story's other characters. This is not to question his account, exactly, but it does present a picture of the essential role that language plays in the construction of a public self and a public history, especially in a social milieu characterized by mobility. Lacking *author*itative confirmation from a narrator, it seems as if language's most important function is to establish identity, to write into existence one's own history and to perform a newly created self.

Of course, these new selves are never simply formed. Practices of self-fashioning in Hurston's Harlem stories intersect in intriguing ways with their evocations of the folk and with the stories' larger attempts to locate the expressive grammar of a kind of urban folklore. At the outset here, it's necessary to recognize that, as I suggested in chapter 4, "folk" can be a categorical imposition, foisted on subjects, situations, and performances from the outside. As Kenneth Warren and Adolph Reed remind us, the whole concept of the "folk" and its relation to the experiences of black subjects "emerged within the patterns of elite discourse that evolved between the second half of the nineteenth century and the middle of the twentieth."[67] It is also routinely associated with rurality. When discussing African Americans from the rural South during the New Negro period, it's obvious that "folk" effectively indicates a subject's orientation to modern projects of standardization and classification. Yet to the anthropological mind at least, once something is self-consciously presented as "folk" it is no longer authentic. The result is a peculiar double-bind for African Americans: there's no simple way to embrace the folk, but neither can you avoid its force, a force that is, not surprisingly, exercised most enthusiastically by arbiters of cultural capital. Walter Benn Michaels gets at precisely this problem in his discussion of the nativist/pluralist paradox: when speaking of national identity, it's clear that there is a "disconnection of one's culture from one's actual beliefs and practices. Pluralism makes this disconnection possible by *deriving* one's beliefs and practices *from* one's cultural identity instead of *equating* one's beliefs and practices *with* one's cultural identity."[68] This issue of the folk highlights the need to aspire to possess a culture that is already supposed to be a fundamental element of your ethnic identity. And intentionally or not, the restricting power that the category of the folk can create provides a mechanism for limiting mobility, for circumscribing the parameters of acceptable expression.

Hurston seems to understand precisely how complicated these issues of insider/outsider can be. As someone who operated in influential spheres of U.S. literary and anthropological culture and as an African American who migrated to Harlem from rural Florida, Hurston positions herself carefully both *as* a writer and *through* her writing, using fiction as an opportunity to explore her insider status. These dynamics offer one explanation as to why "Harlem Slang" aims for complete fusion of the written and oral, refusing to bracket off its transcriptions of slang's nonstandard English to the characters alone: the story's narrator also speaks jive—"Wait till I light up my coalpot and *I'll tell* you about this Zigaboo called Jelly" (127, emphasis mine). It's a situation of total saturation, as every textual utterance—those of the narrator and of each individual character—is made in Harlem slang. While the exact terms of their dissent are mostly unstated, all the voices present in "Harlem Slang" seek to verbally distinguish themselves from the world outside of Harlem, a world that includes not just governing forces of whiteness but also versions of rural southern blackness. Eric Lott once argued that bebop jargon "bucked the regulations of accepted articulateness," and it's clear from Hurston's fictions that the speakers of Harlem slang were working to "make it new" at the level of diction, syntax, and grammar—they inhabit the sound of their new environment as an essential opportunity to self-consciously perform the urban modern.[69]

Both iterations of the story, then, emphasize the role that language plays in strategies of selfhood utilized by rural migrants working to establish themselves in the new environments of the urban North. If language serves as the most prominent means of lining up a subject's interior world with the world outside the self, it also promises access to the slippage between outward selves and inward ones. Although both stories are related through an omniscient, third-person narrator, the sustained exploration of free-indirect discourse in "Cookin'" provides deeper penetration into the mind of the story's subject and underscores the ways in which the text's spoken language engages Jelly's internal dialogue. The presence of free-indirect discourse in both stories matches a series of observations made by Henry Louis Gates Jr. about Hurston's narrative strategies in *Their Eyes Were Watching God*. For Gates, Hurston's narration becomes a "third or mediating term between narrative commentary and direct discourse," a move that renders the novel capable of "resolv[ing] that implicit tension between standard English and black dialect."[70] In much the same way, these stories' ability to foreground the psychological turbulence of the recently arrived migrant underscores the unsteady relationship between the narrator's language and the internal divide of Jelly's public voice over against his private one. For instance, the narrator's evocation of rustic images such as "branch water" and "[g]ood Southern cornbread" move in opposition to Jelly's continual efforts to distance himself from his regional roots (128, 129). And it's not just the narrator: "Oh, don't try to make out youse no northerner, you! Youse from right down in 'Bam your ownself" (132), the unnamed woman tells Jelly when he seems to be putting on urban airs. In a similar way, Sweet Back's final shot directly alludes to familiar figures and forms of rurality: "I'll tell you like the farmer told the potato—plant you now and dig you later" (133).

In the glossary of "Harlem Slang," we find further examples of how different phrases and words create new meanings when read, misread, or translated across regions: "*Boogie-woogie*," for example, is defined as "a type of dancing and rhythm," but "[f]or years, in the South," the glossary explains, "it meant secondary syphilis" (134). The "South" here acts as the sign of a more conservative temperament that draws out perceived ties between lasciviousness and dancing, and those meanings provide an essential entry in the word's semantic genealogy. Consciously or not, then, at some level you can't boogie-woogie without calling up the nimbus of secondary syphilis. Similarly, the glossary explains *"Sugar Hill"* as a reference to the high-toned "northwest sector of Harlem" but also notes that the "expression has been distorted in the South to mean a Negro red light district" (137). Regionalized connotations work their way into urban semantic fields, as distortions and deferred meanings become a key feature of "Harlem Slang's" archaeology of Harlem slang.

Although this technique of unintentionally signing the rural South pulls some attention away from the expressive distinctiveness of Harlem slang, it does profitably highlight the psychic dimensions of the migrant's experience in crafting a new identity. Again, readers are allowed to test the correspondence between the voice inside and the voice outside, uncovering a paradox whereby language is at once an immediate yet unreliable means of constructing the self. Just like projections of identity made through clothing or physical gesture, language is frequently intractable: a speaker is always in danger of unintentionally betraying herself, of pushing up against boundaries of selfhood imposed both from within and without. As Jelly provocatively warns Sweet Back, "You fixing to *talk out of place*" (130, emphasis mine).

Yet what is this story, finally, if not an exploration of the thrills and threats that accompany "talking out of place"? Jelly and Sweet Back's whole experiment with language is an attempt to "talk" themselves out of the rural South, using language as a protean tool for becoming someone, and inhabiting someplace, new. As William Labov's study of black English vernacular (BEV) (now more commonly known as African American vernacular English [AAVE]) in the inner cities shows, however, these new language-formed personae will inevitably stand as strange blends of the familiar and the unfamiliar: "Almost every feature of BEV can be found among white speakers in the South."[71] Not only residues of the South or of the rural but also whiteness characterize the speech of the New Negro, providing an elaboration on W. J. Cash's famous statement, made a year after the publication of "Harlem Slang," on the interdependence of an (often unconsciously) shared expressive culture: "Negro entered white man as profoundly as white man entered into Negro—subtly influencing every gesture, every word, every emotion and idea, every attitude."[72] In Hurston's stories, instances of cross-regional, cross-racial contact remain as immediate—and as intimate—as the sounds formed in a person's mouth.

The jive argot bears a halo of transgression in the 1940s, and yet, in "Harlem Slang" at least, its innovations never equal transformation. Still, it's worth a try. For instance, language's role in the (re)creation of personal identity is made obvious in the story's description of Jelly's name-changing episode: "His mama named him Marvel, but after a month on Lennox Avenue, he changed all that to Jelly" (127). Changed "all that"? The story strains to show how inconsequential Jelly's changes have been: he has picked up some new patterns of speech, some new clothes, and a new vocabulary of gestures (the "pimps' salute" [241]), but the linguistic sign of his proper name is only a "serviceable 'metonymic contraction,'" to cite Gayatri Spivak's gloss of Derrida.[73] Where his former name, Marvel, pointed toward something reverent and vaguely spiritual, his new name is intentionally impolite: Hurston's glossary presents "jelly" as a common euphemism for sex. Jelly's act of adopting another name offers a glimpse of the creative destruction of newness, as the new name is simply inscribed over an erasure of the old one. And it's a decidedly incomplete exercise in destruction: Jelly can change his name, and by doing so he can make minor adjustments to the terms by which he is perceived, but the language in his mind shows us that he has simply discovered a new way to talk about familiar conditions—loneliness, isolation, material deprivation.

When Jelly's thoughts drift south at the story's conclusion, with a homesick reminiscence of "those full, hot meals he had left back in Alabama," the narrator points out a crack in the composition of his carefully groomed identity, a disparity between his public performance and some inner connection to the spaces and histories he came north to escape: "He had even forgotten to *look* cocky and rich" (133, emphasis mine). The importance of looking cocky and rich stands astride sounding cocky and rich as a key component in Jelly's assumption of a new northern self, and the disruptive trace of a suppressed history always lingers just beneath the surface.

Intentionally or not, Jelly's reverie takes him out of the temporality of the city, back in both place and time, drawing attention to what Leigh Anne Duck, writing of Hurston, calls the "paradoxical nature of modern time," wherein time "may be understood to be uniform across space, [though] not all subjects in all spaces are understood to participate in it uniformly."[74] Duck's larger point relates to ways in which the South of the New Negro period is often presented as a "different developmental era and a different experience of time."[75] In the context of these stories, it's also important to consider how these alternate, seemingly antimodern temporalities stand as internal to modern time's structure and functioning: the intrusions of a tamped-down past can never be escaped for Hurston's characters, and it also acts as a partial explanation for the uneven developments of modernity more broadly.

While "Harlem Slang" ends with the line about forgetting to look "cocky and rich," "Cookin'" pushes further into Jelly's mind, representing a second sound to Jelly's voice. In response, the dialogue flutters between the narrator's observations and direct access to Jelly's thoughts: "[T]hese Harlem landladies! They didn't want a thing out of you but your rent" (241), Jelly grumbles in a string of complaints that references the strictness of northern whites and the coldness of northern women. Although there's no indication that Jelly would actually trade his current position for his former one, the story's stubborn obliquity in regard to both Harlem and the South presents a more resonant representation of the deeply planted problems of black migration in the modern era. While Michael North's reading of Hurston scrutinizes the tensions between "folk" language and discourses of modernism, his analysis applies with equal force to the "divisions" between urbanity and rurality that manifest in these stories' language: "Hurston does not reconcile or celebrate the divisions within her text or within the African American folk texts she found in her travels. Instead, she utterly redefines the dichotomies that seem to produce these divisions."[76] In both "Cookin'" and "Harlem Slang," the divisions Hurston redefines are posed between southern African Americans and those from the North by showing the extent to which the dialogue between the rural South and the urban North plays out in a common vernacular, the insider's jargon of urban jive. And, tellingly, this is a dialogue that is internal to, and constitutive of, both the migrant subject and the modern urban world itself.

In response to the enthusiasm Hurston's work garners in the academy, Hazel Carby has made the case that scholarly interest in Hurston's representations of black rurality threatens to construe expressions of the "folk" as the single most representative form of blackness. According to Carby, prevailing wisdom about the Harlem Renaissance tells of how "black intellectuals assertively established a folk heritage as the source of, and inspiration for, authentic African American art forms."[77] A problem arises, however, when the centering of rural-based epistemologies offers critics an opportunity to sidestep challenges of black urban life in the present. With its New York City setting and its commitment to investigating the material conflicts of that space, "Story in Harlem Slang" answers Carby's analysis by resituating folk tropes in an urban environment. And, seen through the prism of "Harlem Slang" and "Cookin'," Hurston's evocations of the folk seem more pliant, more flexibly planted in southern regionalisms than many critics have recognized. For in addition to her interest in the cultures of the rural South, Hurston is also committed to documenting variations of the *urban folk*, suggesting that the urban is always in part enacted by the rural: rural subject, signifiers, affects, intensities, and histories are all on display in the bodies and words of the stories' migrants. Hurston thus provides an uneasy fusion that troubles the automatic and ironclad associations of "South" and "folk." While "Harlem Slang" and "Cookin'" are at odds with the suggestion that the simplest way to signal one's identity as a New Negro is to adopt the patterns of its "official" language, they both understand that the interdependence of signifiers promoted by South–North migration also creates a dialogue that echoes with uncanny resonance in the minds of its participants.

To say that these stories simply celebrate the persistence of the rural South at their conclusions is to miss how plainly they evoke the region's violence and oppression. Hurston's oft-vaunted optimism, on display both here and elsewhere in her oeuvre, is duly noted. But beneath this story's slightly whimsical tone stirs a nagging problem: Jelly is hungry, and there's no clear path toward a lasting solution. In its attention to the intergenerational effects of the Great Migration, James Baldwin's *Go Tell It on the Mountain* (1953) includes an observation that nicely punctuates the phenomenon analyzed here: "There was not, after all, a great difference between the world of the North and that of the South ... there was only this difference: the North promised more."[78] These migration stories' willingness to implicate both North and South within patterns of oppression pushes the story out beyond any regional frame; they sign most prominently as a condemnation of a national paradox: if you're black in modern America, you can't go home again, but neither can you go away. You're always "home," perhaps, but home is a site of hostility rather than nurture. Or, as Baldwin put it elsewhere, in a description of the disillusionment experienced by many black American soldiers returning to the United States from environments of relative tolerance in World War II–era Europe: "*Home!* The very word begins to have a despairing and diabolical ring."[79] Michel de Certeau, commenting on the importance of the "return of the repressed" in Freud, offers a description that captures this dynamic: "It resurfaces, it troubles, it turns the present's feeling of being 'at home' into an illusion."[80] The return of the (repressed) rural scatters its unwanted debris throughout the minds and bodies of this chapter's subjects, estranging them at every destination.

My model of migratory modernism suggests that acts of dislocation and relocation, and the figures that engage in these acts, serve as useful metaphors for the modern more broadly since they give body to the modernist notion of the self out of place (and time). Ultimately, when migratory modernism's patterns of representation cross paths with historical realities of the Great Migration, we're led to consider how African American migrants in the period balanced the meanings and associations of opposing spaces and opposing identities, in particular the rural South alongside the urban North. To be perceived as black in America is to struggle with—or against—an inheritance of rural southern blackness. While there's no escaping the southern cadences lining the edges of Hurston's Harlem slang, the region's influence is felt even in the lives of black subjects lacking any firm connection to the U.S. South, since one outcome of the cultural project of displacing national racism on "the South" has been to force all "black" people in the United States to answer to the call of southern histories of racial violence and oppression. If migration to the North is at once a symbolic and an embodied rejection of the southern horrors of Jim Crow apartheid and slavery, it's understandable that African Americans in the North might exhibit an aversion to things southern and rural. Yet, as each of these stories displays, what amounts to a rejection of a national history of racial horror often results in further marginalization of black persons born in the South.

In the end, to consider figurations of the rural modern via migratory modernism is to confront ways of formulating African American mobility, which turns out to be an essential problem in the Jim Crow era and beyond. In 1920's *Darkwater*, for instance, Du Bois includes the "freedom . . . to ride on the railroads uncursed by color" as one in a relatively short list of essential freedoms that would signal "Liberty for all men."[81] The centrality of mobility in the long civil rights movement is plain: from Homer Plessy's 1892 trip in the whites-only passenger car of the East Louisiana Railroad to Rosa Parks's efforts against Montgomery's segregated buses on to present practices of racial profiling, redlining, and mandatory minimum sentencing; it's also important to remember that the whole incident of the Scottsboro Boys occurred on a train hitched by a group of teenagers traveling between Memphis and Chattanooga.[82] (Perhaps it's no coincidence that two of these events—Plessy's 1892 trip and Parks's 1943 attempt at integration—correspond closely to *The Whole Machinery*'s chronological parameters.) Regardless, for African Americans in the Jim Crow South, mobility and the ability to search out a world elsewhere is often elusive, as familiar white discourse about keeping African Americans "in their place" reveals the dominant culture's anxieties over losing a cheap, often disposable, labor source—and an easily identifiable segment of the population whose mass suppression contributes to broad-based feelings of white superiority.

David Harvey's thinking about the effects of immobility offers insight into what's at stake in the transformative movements of the migrant: "Once intergenerational mobility is limited, social distinctions become relatively fixed features of the social landscape and provide the possibility for the crystallization of social differentiation within the population as a whole."[83] While it's easy to simplistically associate the folk with immobility ("rootedness"), as with an authentic linguistic/vernacular stability, fluidity in each domain (spatial mobility and linguistic slipperiness, for example) actually functions as a modern asset that the folk already possess. So both mobility *and* the comprehensive attempt to fix mobility function as modern phenomena, contributing to the same tangle of contradictions and mixtures that characterize the experiences, and the innovative language, of Hurston's migrants.

New Again: *Barren Ground*, New York, New South

Examining literary representations of the Great Migration, it's possible to wonder how and why only black migrants come under scrutiny. A relative shortage in documentation of the experience of whites leaving the South promotes the mistaken belief that African Americans were the only ones making their way north in significant numbers. James Gregory's recent work, however, presents a more intricate story: white migration in the period poses a wide—and widely underrepresented—band in a broad movement he calls the "southern diaspora." According to Gregory, even during "the Great Migration era of the early twentieth century, when African Americans moved North for the first time in large numbers and established much-noticed communities in the major cities, less-noticed white southerners actually outnumbered them roughly two to one."[84] Yet the trails are harder to follow and the precise dimensions opaque. As Jack Temple Kirby has declared, "The ideal history of the great southern exodus—especially of the whites—may not be possible."[85]

People did move though. And one question this chapter poses is why the uneven proportion of fictions addressing these migrations? If a conventional "history" is unwritable, what of the imaginative histories? African American literature is filled with accounts of southern migrants moving to the industrial North, but a larger survey of the period's literature reveals relatively few texts describing white experiences of relocation. One obvious reason is that black migrants leaving the South were cutting themselves loose from the homeland of slavery and Jim Crow, experiences that infinitely heighten the dramatic stakes. Poor whites from the rural South undoubtedly had hardships and prejudices to flee, but the crushing networks of discrimination and exploitation simply weren't as severe. A related possibility is that there's no white analogue for the formation of a liberated black intelligentsia seeking to represent the saga of a race's urban transformation. In Appalachian contexts in particular, consider the host of cultural productions presenting comic examples of country figures—the stereotypical hillbilly usually—trying to navigate the city across a variety of media throughout the twentieth century: from the hapless hayseeds of old-time songs such as the Charlie Poole recording referenced at the beginning of the chapter to the occasional urban adventures of the Li'l Abner clan in the comic strip to, in the 1960s and early 1970s, *The Beverly Hillbillies* on TV. Self-consciously "literary" works on postwar migrations of the so-called hillbilly highway—such as Harriette Arnow's *The Dollmaker* (1954) or Bobbie Ann Mason's "Detroit Skyline, 1949" (1981)—depict a slightly later moment, not the 1920s and 1930s. Bluntly, there was no white Harlem Renaissance in the first half of the twentieth century. Still another possible explanation for a paucity of representations of white migrations: African American subjects arriving in northern cities—even cities featuring greater diversity than those in the South—would make a more conspicuous presence than white migrants. Their communities would become, as Gregory put it, "much-noticed" amid the swelling ranks of European immigrants and Anglo inhabitants.[86]

Yet if the story of white folks moving out of the South lacks the dramatic intensity of Great Migration narratives, it may also be true that their relative absence in literary histories exists because, unlike their black counterparts, whites more rarely stayed put. Even when poor whites shared a social and economic station with black migrants, they were less likely to permanently relocate in the North. As Gregory demonstrates, "Fewer than half of the nearly 20 million whites who left the South [during the twentieth century] actually left for good," so that the "white diaspora is best understood as a circulation, not as a one-way population transfer."[87] Southern employers certainly missed the cheap labor that black—and poor white—bodies provided, and contemporary newspapers were full of ads designed to scare would-be migrants and to lure their predecessors back south. But it's safe to assume that the great majority of these ads went unanswered by relocated African Americans. White migrants, it seems, were more easily drawn back south—by work, by family, by cultural attachments—just as they were more easily drawn westward. Whereas Langston Hughes memorialized the "one-way ticket" out of Dixie in a 1949 poem of the same name, the white protagonist of the novel discussed below holds a different, more discretionary kind of authorization. This section, then, investigates how the horseshoe-shaped migration of Ellen Glasgow's novel *Barren Ground* (1925) uncovers the consequences and dilemmas of white migrations and, in so doing, highlights ways in which modern mobility is often configured along racial lines. While accounts of white movement from south to north during the period of the Great Migration are ostensibly harder to plug into a larger story about exodus and redemption, they offer important, and underexplored, messages about the relationships between the people, places, and politics of migration.[88] Like other texts referenced above, *Barren Ground* narrates the Proustian complications of such migrations by probing the sensorium's ability to launch time and space travel—between the country and the city; between the past and the present—across the "vast structure of recollection" hosted by involuntary memory.[89] And just as it shows how the period's spatial differentiations might be "leveled out" and leveraged by a newly empowered capitalist agent, the novel also addresses the archival gap mentioned above by using the movements and actions of its protagonist, Dorinda Oakley, to depict white migration as a step toward the expansion of capitalist modernity that remunerates its participants at the same time as it exacts particular psychological costs: isolation and deracination, "the end of expectancy" and an incurable case of homesickness (521).

For its portrayal of an independent, industrious woman who bucks the patriarchal governance of the agricultural South, Glasgow considered *Barren Ground* her greatest personal achievement. It is a sweeping novel that employs the conventions of early twentieth-century romance: Dorinda, *Barren Ground*'s hero, begins the narrative as the child of a poor dirt farmer in southern Virginia whose land—"Old Farm"—is choked by an untrammeled growth of broomsedge grass. Teenage Dorinda, dissatisfied with her life and prospects, is swept up in the attentions of Jason Greylock, the son of the local doctor, who seduces and abandons her. Upon learning she is pregnant, Dorinda takes the train to New York, where she passes out in the street, is struck by a streetcar, and loses the baby. Recuperating in the hospital, she comes under the care of Dr. Faraday, who nurses her back to health, provides employment, and introduces her to a new world of ideas and metropolitan comforts. It's here, among all the lectures and books to which she is exposed, that Dorinda encounters fresh theories of land cultivation and scientific approaches to agriculture that change both the course of her life and that of her homeland. Just before her father dies, Dorinda returns home to take over the operation of the farm, applying newly theorized methods of fertilization and crop rotation to revitalize its sterile soil. She also starts an industrialized dairy that uses the railways to supply butter to hotels and restaurants in Washington, D.C.[90] While Dorinda never finds the romantic fulfillment she seeks at the novel's beginning, her operation becomes the most admired in the region, a stark revision of turn-of-the-century tropes of self-effacing southern womanhood as well as a bold endorsement of "modern" farming techniques. Addressing this last point, William Conlogue convincingly argues that, contrary to past critics' interpretations, *Barren Ground*'s "promot[ion of] a farm economy built on market speculation, rapid technological change, strict divisions of labor, and dependence on university experts" marks a pivot from the pastoral, toward a celebration of rural industrialization.[91] It's a story, in short, of farming going "big," going modern.[92]

While, on one hand, *Barren Ground* appears as a conventional narrative about a transplanted southerner following the tug of blood and native soil, it also contains a more disruptive story about capitalist modernity's relationships to both the city and the country. Specifically, it highlights the modern's far-reaching associations with science and technological innovation: the "country" Dorinda revitalizes is actually an urban construction that depends on market capitalism's powers to transform people, their practices, and their environments. In addition to all this, the novel contains a forceful migration narrative. Although less than 10 percent of the text is devoted to Dorinda's time in New York, it acts as the novel's thematic hinge: the experiences and information she collects in the city inform all her succeeding actions, and Dorinda's movements—from Virginia to New York and then back again—offer the text's most revealing encounters with the signifying powers of migratory modernism.

In the novel's larger economy, the New York scenes set the stage for Dorinda's transition from young woman of longing and enchantment to hardened entrepreneur and accomplished agricultural innovator, and they achieve this shift by tracing an evolution that proceeds with concomitant emotional and perceptual signals. All of which is to say that the text represents Dorinda's development by recording her sensory responses to the world around her: when she loses consciousness in the street and falls beneath the wheels of a car, Dorinda is literally stripped of both feeling and language (she is twice described as "stone" [201, 222]; once as "wood" [222]; once as "dead" [222]), and the remainder of her time in New York is devoted to recuperating her emotional, physical, and mental capabilities. The modern city, from Georg Simmel forward, has been associated with the destabilizing effects of sensory overload, but in Dorinda's case it seems to provide a necessary correction to the sensory barrenness she brings up from the country.[93] Throughout her time in the city, Dorinda is reassembled and re-created as a human subject, in an environment and by institutions that are, to all appearances, diametrically opposed to those of her home at Pedlar's Mill. She becomes, in some strange sense, the very product of creative destruction, rebuilt with a sensibility and system of values best suited to the demands of the marketplace.

In a startling turn, however, the shock of the new that stuns Dorinda isn't an urban phenomenon at all but the result of a relatively underdeveloped geography and a series of rural, small-town relations, a quality at odds with Benjamin's Baudelaire, who repeatedly articulated "the figure of shock and contact with the metropolitan masses."[94] That the novel locates this symptom of modernity in Pedlar's Mill, not New York City, provides a sense of the complex geography wherein the modern is never a wholly urban modality and neither is the rural a reliably antimodern one. While the emotional numbness that has allowed Dorinda to endure the trauma of her experience with Jason also translates into a physical numbness, her senses are often erratically acute. So much so, in fact, that Dorinda's time in New York might be nothing so much as a catalog of sensations, a move that returns us to the phenomenology of place—the strategy of meaning-making that takes the measure of a person's experience of a place by processing her individual somatic reactions to it. And it's clear that her senses have been socialized to associate the signs of nature with the "natural" place of her youth—a logic severely disordered by the city's omnipresent mixtures of the organic and the industrial, hence Dorinda's inability to elude ties to her past and her home on the farm in Virginia. For example, although she dismisses Central Park as "merely an imitation of the country" (201), its imitative qualities behave in unpredictable ways, and the novel closely anticipates Gilles Deleuze's contention, contra Baudrillard, that "by simulacrum we should not understand a simple imitation but rather the act by which the very idea of a model or privileged position is challenged and overturned," so much so that "all resemblance [is] abolished so that one can no longer point to the existence of an original and a copy."[95] As Dorinda navigates the built environment of New York, she continually bumps up against expressions of the "natural world," encasements of organic life scattered amid the industrialized landscape that thrust her mind back to the rural South and revise imaginary distinctions between the "built" and the "natural" environments. Benjamin, in a cryptic collection of responses to Baudelaire evocatively titled "Central Park," probes *Les Fleurs du mal*'s renditions of newness and the modern via the city and the commodity, by noting the extent to which "[s]hock as poetic principle" governs his readers' visions of Paris: "It is a showplace and quite foreign."[96] *Barren Ground*'s Manhattan acts as both a showcase for a seemingly endless string of commodities and experiences *and* a showplace that houses unanticipated incursions of the pastness-of-the-now since, for Dorinda at least, the city's foreignness registers with startling somatic familiarity.

These bleary distinctions constitute the firmest element of Dorinda's encounters with the nonhuman in the novel. As Roy Rosenzweig and Elizabeth Blackmar explain in their history of Central Park, the early twentieth century of Glasgow's narrative represented an especially fraught period in which a strong development ethos threatened the park's role as a "designed natural landscape" created for purposes of "pure preservation."[97] Yet while the park is an industrial-scale installment that required an industrial-strength realignment of the city's topography, it still reliably performs the "nature" function. "There were moments," the narrator explains, "when [Dorinda] missed Old Farm, vivid moments when she smelt growing things in the Park, when she longed with all her heart for a sight of the April fields and the pear orchard in bloom and the big pine where birds were singing" (232). Later, when walking toward the park, she notes, "This smells like November at Old Farm.... Whenever I smell the country, I want to go home" (241). As she actually smells the country in the city, Dorinda's senses lead her out of place.

Elsewhere, as Dorinda passes a man preparing window decorations, the novel offers the following: "a whiff of wet earth penetrated her thoughts, and immediately, in a miracle of recollection, she was back at Five Oaks.... She had been dragged back by the wind, by an odour, into the suffocating atmosphere of the past" (211). Dorinda could never mistake Central Park for Old Farm or the window boxes filled with evergreens for the pines of Five Oaks, but, in the Proustian reflex of her sensory mind, she cannot make the separation. In other words, what seem like imitations of the country marooned in the city only sharpen Dorinda's involuntary sense of "country" realities, of their role in shaping her image of herself and the (re)construction of her personal history. The copy, with its obvious differences, can both defamiliarize and enhance the original; it folds the cognitive map upon itself and erases the distance between the two spaces. This stroke of recognition stirred by the senses appears throughout *Barren Ground*'s New York section. For example, when Dorinda determines to improve Old Farm through new understanding of the "chemistry of agriculture" (242), she has a vivid dream of plowing one of the family's old fields—and the first association she makes is with the smell of her surroundings: "the ghostly scent of the life-everlasting reminded her of the smell of her mother's flowered bandbox when she took it out of the closet on Sunday mornings" (244). The shadow of a smell, conjured in a dream, allows Dorinda to peel back the layers separating her from her past, her former home, and her family.

These are the sorts of ephemeral foundations upon which Dorinda builds her new life: it's not thought exactly, and not even emotion, but an asymmetrical bundle of the two, directed by the senses, that leads Dorinda through her period of numbness. Blankness gives way to sensation, which itself gives way to language and ideas. The diction used to describe the final stage in this process—when Dorinda diligently attends lectures and studies the "modern ways of getting the best out of the soil" (242)—makes pointed allusions to agricultural labor: "gleaning, winnowing, storing away in her memory the facts which she thought might someday be useful" (246). In the end it is the "*idea* of the country" that "worked like leaven in Dorinda's imagination," as an active, organic force that creates steady, irreversible change (249, emphasis mine). In a quintessentially modern gesture, agricultural labor has been theorized, standardized, and reconceptualized with an eye toward efficiency, scientific research, and the unbending demands of the marketplace. Or, to borrow Dorinda's own optimistic phrase, "Enterprise, industry, and a little capital with which to begin!" (246). She becomes, in this light, an unwitting avatar of the federally supported Country Life movement, which codified, through 1914's Smith-Lever Act, a "national system of agricultural extension services to help farmers apply scientific and business methods."[98] And following Raymond Williams's model, the ideological function of the "country"—Dorinda's own "idea of the country"—is achieved as the image of the pastoral arrives to abstract and mask inequitable labor arrangements and ecological instrumentalism.[99]

Dorinda's psychological recovery, such as it is, ends with a "shock of joy" as she realizes that "she was no longer benumbed, that she had come to life again. She had come to life again, but how differently!" (244). In the opening description of the New York section, when Dorinda is wandering without purpose, the text figures her as a "machine," and we're to understand that her time in the city animates a process by which she sheds the characteristics of machinery and reacquires humanity (203). Oddly enough, she becomes a machine in rural Virginia and a human being in an aggressively industrialized metropolis. It's worth noting the paradox: Dorinda's former lover Jason mechanized her by exploiting her biological fertility, and yet in the novel's decision to rebuild Dorinda as a capitalist par excellence, it's as if barren ground, in human form, is precisely the condition needed to grow a newly constituted producer.

We should also recognize that this reconstitution of the human is staged in spaces of clinical and scientific authority that didn't exist in Pedlar's Mill: the hospital and the physician's office, the university, the upper Manhattan parlor. More pointedly, following Foucault's lead in *The Birth of the Clinic*, it's surely significant that Dorinda's guide through all this is the ultimate figure of biopolitical authority in the modern episteme, the physician.[100] Dr. Farady and his wife enthusiastically endorse Dorinda's plan to revitalize Old Farm, and they provide both the training and the financial backing necessary to actualize it. Given all that, it's possible to see the novel presenting Dorinda herself as a kind of agricultural project, an empty plot of land cultivated and ushered into productivity by an attentive caregiver. Dorinda "had picked up more or less of the patter of science" (233), but there's a sense that, while she can vaguely comprehend the path forward and the methods at her disposal, she's been brought to those conclusions by powers beyond logical reckoning. And power, as configured in this text, is nicely captured by a phrase of David Harvey's—it is the "urbanization of capital."[101] Not the urbanization of bodies or of spaces directly, but capital itself, with all its flows and pressures. Such a configuration of power is not so much about the spread of urbanization-as-urbanity but the dispersal of capitalism's development function, which transforms barren ground into productive ground and idle workers into efficient ones. Agriculture, "the land" itself, acts as a vector of capitalist expansion through its incorporation into the larger modern/global market. Not for any benevolent purpose—indeed, the novel's conclusion makes it hard to tell whether Dorinda, or any other person in Pedlar's Mill, is better off for all her innovation—but to grow its sphere of influence. That Dorinda becomes the emissary of modern capital is predictable enough since she alone has been vaccinated against the threat of economic and cultural obsolescence that is presumed to adhere to rural southernness. It is also fitting, then, that upon arriving back in Virginia, Dorinda's brother Rufus tells her, with awe, "You've come back looking as if you could run the world" (258). Indeed she has.

But what of the differences between the country and the city? While the text performs an enlarged notion of spatial difference—Pedlar's Mill and New York are presented as oppositional entities—it also works in a contrary motion to show how interpenetrated each space is within the other. As I've discussed above, New York City is always shot through with signifiers of the country, while the future of Pedlar's Mill—its landscapes, its labor practices, its fashions—is shaped by the version of New York City that Dorinda brings to Virginia. Such a move produces, in Deleuze and Guattari's terms, a landscape made smooth by modernizing forces, with the whole country/city distinction effectively deterritorialized in favor of a monolithic space ruled by market forces.[102]

One curious episode from the opening of the New York section shows some of the subtlety with which the South lingers on in the novel. As she wanders the city, Dorinda finds herself drifting into "the only old-fashioned neighbourhood in New York" (205). Following Leigh Anne Duck again, we recognize this as a zone of temporal otherness, littered with "old stuff," much of it familiar. (Dorinda notices, for instance, "a wardrobe exactly like the one great-grandfather left" [206].) Her escort here is a woman named Garvey, who feeds her tea and listens to Dorinda's concerns, adding a few of her own: "[W]e are old-fashioned folks, and my husband sometimes says that we haven't got any business in the progressive 'nineties. Everything's too advanced for us now.... I guess it's living so much with old furniture and things that were made in the last century" (208).

It's an association with outdated *things* that identifies these people as old, as if what Bill Brown calls the "material unconscious" is rubbing off, burdening them with an unshakable air of anachronism. For Brown, the material unconscious is a means of using objects to delve into "history as the unconscious" so that the "necessarily repressed can be rendered visible in sites of contradiction or incomplete elision."[103] On Brown's model, the dominant narratives of progress that carried the 1890s require a sublimation of nonparticipants, figures such as Garvey and the residents of Pedlar's Mill. They sink out of view, occupying side streets and back alleys like the one Dorinda stumbles upon, but they remain an elemental component of the modern tableau, and their stuff remains stubborn evidence, like mass-produced memento mori for the not-yet-dead. It is this bracketed past—and Dorinda's instant recognition of it—that casts the "old-fashioned" street as a kind of South in miniature.

The link between an air of obsolescence and the South is further established when Dorinda walks the city streets, seeing herself through the eyes of Fifth Avenue: her dresses become "absurd and countrified" (228), and for the first time since she left Pedlar's Mill, she perceives herself as "old-fashioned and provincial" (210). In this scene, the text proposes a brand of accidental rusticity, a quality of "absurd[ity]" and "countrifi[cation]" that needs to be shaken as quickly as possible. But, as the New York episode concludes, it's plain that associations with her homeland are not so easily left behind, as the novel rewrites the standard story of a southerner's homecoming with an enigmatic twist: "She realized that the Pedlar's Mill of her mind and the Pedlar's Mill of actuality were two different places.... [S]he felt as strange as she had felt in New York" (256). Tellingly, this observation is not so far removed from an attitude expressed in the depths of her period of numbness: "Pedlar's Mill or New York, what did it matter? The city might have been built of straw, so little difference did it make" (204).

Despite her successful traversal of U.S. cultural and economic geography—South–North–South again—Dorinda, like a true modern, remains estranged anywhere and everywhere, at all places *and* times. Indeed, after resettling at Old Farm, the tendency toward melancholic reverie runs backward, up to the North. Seeing a sunset the "colour of autumn fruits," Dorinda reels back to "the heart of a pomegranate that she had seen in a window in New York; and immediately she was swept by a longing for the sights and sounds of the city" (314). The modernity of the metropolis—as represented in Benjamin's elaborations of the seemingly endless stalls of the Paris arcades—is fundamentally formed through the marketplace, by the imported pomegranate of the window display. And for Dorinda, the force of that marketplace carries across temporal and spatial boundaries. In this sense, Dorinda's reactions track Judith Butler's descriptions of a method of mourning compounded by "the sedimentation of objects loved and lost, the archaeological remainder, as it were, of unresolved grief":[104] this scene likewise displays as a sensory experience facilitated by "objects," but it is framed by commodification, a reminder that the central means by which the "country" becomes resituated in the "city" is through commercialization and the rule of the market. It's not just that shards of the periphery penetrate the cultural core; it's that the periphery can often dictate the core's very lines of definition.

Just as the novel unseats ideas of bounded country and city spaces, it likewise complicates related notions of regional difference. If the natural world of Virginia conjures the urban North, and if the very aura of the southern soil is accessible—is, in fact, inescapable—in New York City, then how much trust can we invest in narratives of regional exclusivity? In the passages depicting Dorinda's sensations and extralinguistic impressions, it's difficult—if not impossible—to make one thing stand for her Virginia roots and something else her New York City present without imposing a deeply subjective, and potentially reductive, order on the surroundings. This may all seem obvious enough, but it has important implications for a text so seemingly committed to the experiential differences between the country and the city. (So much so, in fact, that it has often been cast as a forerunner to southern exclusivist Nashville Agrarianism.) Like the black migrants in Fisher's stories, Dorinda hopes to flee her home for a new life in the city, only to reencounter alarming fragments of her old one. Yet the novel keeps with the larger sociological realities of white migration in that, unlike the African American figures in those stories, she's inclined—and allowed—to return and, most provocatively of all, to prosper.

Terminals and Depots

Throughout this chapter, I've tried to expose certain patterns of migration while noting that one of its major features as an aesthetic and philosophical disposition is that it creates new possibilities, that it runs patterns back on themselves. Bluntly, I acknowledge that migration can resist certain cultural and physical maps at the same time as it redraws other ones. A richly suggestive example, and one that would make a fine subject for subsequent studies in this vein, is the course of movement in Nella Larsen's *Quicksand* (1928). The formulations of migration I've presented throughout the chapter fit basically two molds: the terminal migrations of African Americans moving from the South to New York, and the horseshoe-shaped migrations of whites moving back and forth between the two spaces. But while Larsen's novel depends heavily on the energies and obstacles of movement, it scrambles any bipolar or triangulated account of migration, as Helga Crane—the mixed-race protagonist—goes from the rural South to Chicago to Harlem to Copenhagen, Harlem again, and then finally back to the rural South. George S. Schuyler's *Black No More* (1931) presents fascinating wrinkles as well. The novel is a satirical piece of speculative fiction that follows the unsavory career of Max Disher, an Atlanta-born Harlemite who is one of the first subjects of a radical medical procedure that can change pigmentation from dark to light, undermining established meanings of whiteness and blackness. When Disher first learns of the possibility of racial makeover, he is possessed by two goals: "To get white and to Atlanta."[105] And Disher's cynical transformation reaches its zenith when he assumes a role at the head of a Klan-style white-nationalist organization, a group that comes undone when its figurehead and its allies in the leadership of the Democratic Party are shown to have "black blood" in their ancestry. Like Helga Crane, Disher can cross regional and even national demarcations—his final appearance in the novel is on a beach at Cannes—but only under the cover of whiteness.

The southern turns in these texts can be grim, but their basic shape predicts a trend of reverse migration that has taken significant numbers of African Americans back south since the second half of the twentieth century. The same economic forces that drew workers north have drawn them south again, as the urban North has deindustrialized and middle-class opportunities have disappeared in places like New York City. Within that overall pattern, thinkers such as bell hooks and Carol B. Stack have productively demonstrated how and why it's not just the South's urban centers that receive southbound migrants.[106] If, however, the phenomenon is primarily driven by economic opportunities, then its influence would spread beyond any one racial group, presumably. And indeed it has: the population boom in the Sun Belt is one of the major U.S. demographic shifts of the past several decades. Furthermore, as postmodern technologies of connectivity enact a provisional erasure of regional differences, it has never been easier to evoke—and inhabit—a virtual region. The result is not a disappearance of the rural South or New York City, exactly, but a less geographically determined method for occupying regional or spatial identities. As Scott Romine has recently shown, in the twenty-first century there are always new ways of putting on a southern costume.[107] There is also, it must be noted, a dark side to the digital domain of southernness. Neo-Confederacy stretches comfortably beyond the southern states on the internet and occasionally makes horrific intrusions into the nondigital world, as Dylann Roof's assassination of nine black worshippers in Charleston's Emanuel AME Church in June 2015 proved. Not surprisingly, the Confederacy, and the Confederate battle flag in particular, played a major role in Roof's online persona.

If postmodernism-as-an-intensification-of-modernism reaches for maximum fluidity of identity, a smoothing away of the bumps on the paths that brought Charlie Poole on his trip to New York, what might this tell us about modernism's associations with migration? For starters, migration is cultural fragmentation in material and spatial form: it is a means of scattering the self and one's sense of rootedness. And as such, it might be subject to suspicion for all the reasons that high modernists like Eliot feared modernity's breaches: disconnection from one's originating culture, a foreshortened historical sense, a fractured interior, and a fissured sense of self. It is, in short, the lack of "monadic closure," to call up Jameson's phrase again. Eliot himself took a metaphysical approach to the issue, but the substance of his complaint is much the same: "The soul is so far from being a monad that we have not only to interpret other souls to ourself but to interpret ourself to ourself."[108] The migrants we've encountered in the fictions above find it necessary to shuffle multiple selves and contending histories, to make improvisation and adaptation a personal ontology. But since migration can't be pinned down as a strictly modern phenomenon, it's worth asking what, in addition to its immediate ability to provide greater economic or physical security, is the upside of migration? To put a finer point on it, what are the possible benefits of modern migration's fragmentation function?

For one thing, it creates slippery human figures that are harder to classify and coerce, harder to fit into a matrix of standardization. Fragmentation-as-a-product-of-migration offers new proof that identities are always multiple: as the migrants in the stories above demonstrate, to be at once North and South is a problem, but it's a potentially productive one since participation in a modern world requires the ability to match one's own multiple selves against the multiple selves of others. Believing, as someone like Ellie of "The Promised Land" apparently does, that any one person naturally belongs in any one place is a dangerous misreading: she is effectively the flipside of Mammy, and they are each, in their own way, disadvantaged by the undeniable permeability that attends to the emergence of the modern. Because just as capitalist modernity seeks out a grid of practices and theories that would create a newly standardized world, it unravels that same world by dispersing images, products, and people out beyond their place of origin.

As characters in all these narratives navigate displaced versions of the rural South, they are consistently reminded of the historical scaffolding of their environment and of the effects that landscape can have on the creation, recreation, and decreation of identities. Each story can, in turn, be read as an examination of the portability—and durability—of the "South." Ultimately, we must be willing to concede that any final conclusions are hemmed in by the limitations of language and labels: tropes of migration go beyond the experience of the migrant alone in the same way that images of the South "outside" the South are mostly visible through suggestion, memory, and emotion. Still, each of these narratives works to prove that, especially in the urban landscapes of the modern North, the South is not emptied of meaning but rerouted and reanimated in provocative ways.

CODA

Uneven Ground

One weekend in late April 2014, *New York Times* critic Dwight Garner published a column pressing for the oral history *All God's Dangers: The Life of Nate Shaw* as a major contribution to American literature. "[I]t is superb," Garner wrote, with characteristic verve, "both serious history and a serious pleasure, a story that reads as if Huddie Ledbetter spoke it while W. E. B. Du Bois took notation."[1] Assembled by historian Theodore Rosengarten and published in 1974, the book narrates, in the rough-hewn eloquence of its subject's own voice, the life and turbulent times of Nate Shaw—disguised name of Ned Cobb, a hardnosed sharecropper from Tallapoosa County, Alabama. Shaw raised cotton on shares from the age of nineteen, achieving, through unbending determination, an unusual degree of material success. He was the rare African American in his county, for instance, who could boast of owning an automobile. Along with the rest of his fellow croppers, though, the landlords set the outer limits of Shaw's opportunity; they controlled the price of cotton, rent, and supplies (the cost of "fertilize" is a frequent subject [75–76]), always with the backing of law and local custom. Proudly intractable, Shaw took up with the Alabama Sharecroppers' Union in 1931, an association that brought him into repeated clashes with the area's white authorities. For all the book's winding and searching, the shape of Shaw's life hinges on one particular flash of conflict, an event that provides *All God's Dangers* its dramatic climax: in December 1932 Shaw helped a friend resist the efforts of the deputy sheriff to confiscate his property; he traded fire with one Deputy Platt (Platt fired first) and served thirteen years in prison camps as a result.

In addition to investigating the tightest corners of Shaw's life, the book offers an up-close examination of the vagaries of race and class in the Black Belt during the sharecropping era, limning the ins and outs of guano, mules, and the boll weevil, of techniques in cotton chopping and crosstie cutting, of the unrelenting pressures of white supremacy. And although *All God's Dangers* won the National Book Award in 1975 and has, according to James C. Giesen, "come to dominate historians' thinking about sharecropping and sharecroppers," it has largely slipped out of the broader reading public's view.²

Garner's article, however, sparked a minor renaissance. It was pronounced enough, in fact, to briefly nudge the season's nonfiction best seller, Thomas Piketty's economic treatise *Capital in the Twenty-First Century*, to the number-two spot on Amazon's nonfiction list. Unlikely as *All God's Dangers'* position on the list may have been, the Piketty phenomenon was even more surprising. A nearly 700-page analysis of economic inequality, the book sifts through large, previously unexamined stores of data to theorize the causes and consequences of inequity in the United States and Europe. If the book has a single thesis, it's this: the "central contradiction of capitalism" is that returns on capital will inevitably, and consistently, outpace growth in income (a dynamic expressed in the simple equation $r>g$) (571–73). Consequently, capital, or "wealth" as it is alternately labeled, will forever have an edge on labor. And democracy, with its vital emphases on egalitarianism and meritocracy, is thrown out of balance, perhaps fatally, by the weight of outsized caches of capital. In Piketty's argument, only a fundamental restructuring, achieved primarily through comprehensive, global taxation on wealth, can prevent the slide into an ossified state of inequality, a repetition of the "patrimonial societies of the past" (241).

One uncommon feature of *Capital*'s economic analysis is its liberal use of literary fiction to explore these past conditions, with examples from Balzac, Austen, and, for good measure, *Gone with the Wind*, where inherited wealth acts as the major criterion for gauging the worthiness of Scarlett O'Hara's suitors (241). Piketty's wide-ranging data sets, his willingness to look beyond the quantitative alone, establishes a precedent that allows us to thread *All God's Dangers* through the eye of *Capital*, to use the occasion of their mutual appearance in the spring of 2014 to make some summary comments about *The Whole Machinery*'s subjects and their continued relevance in the twenty-first century. My purpose in this coda, then, is not to evaluate the validity of Piketty's economic analysis as such, nor is it to provide a comprehensive reading of *All God's Dangers*. I'm more interested in ways that these books' unpredictable popularity in 2014 surveys the terrain of the rural modern in our own moment.

How does the sharecropping of *All God's Dangers* exemplify, even ramify, Piketty's critiques in *Capital in the Twenty-First Century*? It's possible to read *All God's Dangers* as an extreme case of the very principle centralized in Piketty's argument. Specifically, in the agricultural economy of Tallapoosa County, the person holding the land will ever retain an advantage. And perhaps the ultimate way of maximizing profits on wealth—real estate, in this case—is to use it as a landowner does in tenancy: collecting rent, creating a captive customer base ("Weren't no use to kick against [the landlord's] orders, we, all of us on his places, was forced to trade where he sent us" [148]), and compelling a cut-rate labor source to produce a marketable good (cotton). Sharecropping, at root, depends on the acute stickiness of capital; it revolves around questions about who owns what and how the spoils are divided. *All God's Dangers* takes on this subject by positioning the unscrupulous landlord Mr. Tucker (representing growth via wealth) alongside Shaw (growth via income). As Shaw himself asks in a particularly interrogatory passage: "Now it's right for me to pay you for usin what's yours—your land, stock, plow tools, fertilize. But how much should I pay? The answer ought to be closely seeked. How much is a man due to pay out? Half his crop? A third part of his crop? And how much is he due to keep for hisself? You got a right to your part—rent; and I got a right to mine. But who's the man ought to decide how much? The one that owns the property or the one that works it?" (108). Shaw is describing an extreme version of Piketty's $r>g$ scenario wherein wealth never trickles down, never reconstitutes itself to the laborer's advantage; the tenant's economic actions become another tributary feeding the backed-up pool of capital. And for Shaw, these positions are distinctly racialized: "[T]he colored man's labor," he explains, "was worth more to the white man than the labor of his own color because it cost him less and he got just as much for his money" (190). It's no surprise that labor acts as an investment on the part of the landowner ("the white man" in Shaw's formulation), but it's the imbalance in benefits of that labor that Shaw decries, recognizing, alongside Piketty, that the only way to correct the imbalance is a more equitable distribution of wealth (e.g., property): "[Y]ou couldn't make a livin with common sense only—you had to have land" (112).[3] Ironically, in the book's final movement Shaw has a chance to comment on his own capital acquisition. At the end of his career, a newly minted landowner, Shaw pulls off a racial inversion of the labor-power structure, much to the chagrin of some of the locals: "Since I come out of prison, I had a white gentleman or two and their wives, would work in the field for me. White folks around here didn't like that" (424). But Shaw's take on the problem never dissolved. He tells of a time late in life when he came across a large hay farm ("twenty-seven hundred acres"), the smallest piece of a conglomerate held by a single owner: "Well, what man got any business ownin that much land and can't work it hisself? God don't give natural to one man more than to another" (484).

The stubborn immobility of capital's circulation as "wealth" is Piketty's great subject in *Capital*, and the production of cotton on sharecropping tracts provides a rich illustration. One noteworthy feature of Piketty's analysis is that the course of economic exploitation contained in Shaw's story neatly coincides with the chronology of what Piketty identifies as the "fairy tale" of decreasing inequality, a notion promoted by economist Simon Kuznets in his analysis of growth between 1913 and 1948 (11). In Piketty's longue durée of capitalist modernity's resource distribution, the positive trend lines created during these decades stand as exception rather than rule, since this was an era of heightened federal investment in waging world war and the economic stimuli of the New Deal. Piketty also underlines the irony whereby the "dizzying fall in the capital/income ratio" during the period celebrated by Kuznets was in large part due to the wanton destruction of wealth: the "budgetary and political shocks" of the two wars that resulted in devastating losses in European portfolios, precipitous drops in savings rates, and low asset prices as well as the ravaging of physical property in combat (148). Against Kuznets's assessment, Shaw's account shows that even during the period when income temporarily overtook growth and promised to ameliorate structural inequality, the sharecropping class stood as an example of debt slavery-as-capitalism in extremis; it also presents the armed conflict in Tallapoosa County as a microcosm of the violence—both physical and economic—that roiled the wider world.

For all his critique of economic inequality, however, Piketty's vision is informed less by revolution than by drastic reform, a position captured in the title of an important section of chapter 13: "Modernizing Rather Than Dismantling the Social State" (481). Piketty's diction is provocative here: imagining a more equitable future, he reaches for the overdetermined sign "modernization." Having paid special attention to the connections between modernization, modernity, and modernism throughout *The Whole Machinery*, this move takes on additional resonance within my argument. Pointedly, Jonathan Flately's configuration of these relationships makes the concepts reverberate in Piketty's argument: "[T]he situation in modernism is one in which modernization is felt to be incomplete, still in progress, and thus potentially redirected. It also means that the promises of modernity are still felt to be relevant, vital, and achievable."[4] Modernism, under this definition, is less about aesthetic agency and innovation than the process of distributing the gains that modernization is presumed to create. To "modernize," in Piketty's usage, is not to pursue newness but to address, and work to solve, the asymmetrical benefit distribution of capitalist modernity. This reflex to look forward as you look backward encapsulates both the form of *The Whole Machinery* and the preoccupations of many of its subjects.

Cue the question: Is late capitalism of the kind analyzed by Piketty inevitably postmodern? Or, perhaps, did Anthony Giddens have it right over twenty-five years ago? In *The Consequences of Modernity*, Giddens argued against the ascendancy of "postmodern" as a political and cultural designation, explaining that there is nothing "post" about a modern economy still riven by a broadly asymmetrical apportioning of resources. Like other examples from this study, *All God's Dangers*—with its depictions of radical political action, technological change, and the unnerving confluence of the local within the global via market capitalism—complicates a common calculus that codes the rural both material manifestation and metaphor of tradition, of the old and the obsolete. On the other hand, the modern functions as a nearly perfect inversion of the country: au courant, nominally urban, always informed of and promoting its own relevance. It's here that Giddens's theory about the link between "reflexivity" and modernity might help distill the question: "It is often said that modernity is marked by an appetite for the new, but this is not perhaps completely accurate. What is characteristic of modernity is not an embracing of the new for its own sake, but the presumption of wholesale reflexivity—which of course includes reflection upon the nature of reflection itself."[5] Thus the sharp distinction so commonly drawn between the modern and the rural, with no satisfactory account of the dyad's teleology. Is the modern the cause of the country or its effect? Could it somehow be both at once?

Rather than entertain a potential tautology, I want to propose the significance of two frameworks that can lend further definition to *The Whole Machinery*'s readings: the *rural-in-the-modern* and the *modern-in-the-rural*. To arrive here, I turn again to Walter Benjamin, whose explorations of the modern, space, and history have been a touchstone throughout my project. It's clear that for Benjamin the fullest expression of *die Moderne* was decidedly urban. And I find little to argue with in Benjamin's endlessly evocative descriptions of the modern-in-the-urban, yet I return to a question I've asked repeatedly: if the modern appears as an essential consequence of capitalist consumption, appears in the fungible objects that circulate fluidly throughout the city, what of the rural sources of the raw materials? I'd like to repeat an obvious adaptation of this equation, one that includes the commercial output of any network of production and exchange that relies on the mutual exploitation of rural bodies and rural landscapes.

Benjamin confidently implies that the notion of a distinctly urban space demands some kind of contrastive element, the darkness that creates the light. In "One-Way Street," for example, he bemoans the corrosive creep of the rural: "Just as all things, in a perpetual process of mingling, and contamination, are losing their intrinsic character while ambiguity displaces authenticity, so is the city. Great cities ... are seen to be breached at all points by the invading countryside."[6] It's easy enough to grant Benjamin's point here about the increased visual presence of an "invading countryside," but his vision of a "great city," uncontaminated and unmingled with the rural, feels uncharacteristically incomplete. There's no great city without its rural shadow, a shadow that feeds its need for resources. My larger point here is that if capitalism's arrival in the metropolis serves as a measure of the modern, we can gain a sense of its deeper dimensions by tracing its activities in the hinterland and by exploring the periphery's influence on the cultural core. By finding, in effect, the *rural-in-the-modern*.

Returning to *All God's Dangers*, consider the work Shaw does in constructing the railroad. "Cuttin cross-ties is nasty for a man to do," he explains, in an episode that stresses both the stringency of the labor and the beating he gets from Mr. Joe Grimes. Grimes, we learn, is the outfit's operator and the one who collects the crossties, "sellin em to the railroad and pocketin whatever money come of it" (21). Although there's not much in it for him financially, Shaw can claim his place among the laborers responsible for his country's industrial infrastructure, and if the railroad functions, in Marian Aguiar's description, as a familiar "symbol of modernity," then it's clear that Shaw is a direct and intimate participant in the production—both symbolic and actual—of modernity in the U.S. South.[7] Railroads, of course, traverse space, acting as supply lines that rush rural products and people into the metropolis, establishing a connection that, unlike in Benjamin, doesn't signal an unsavory phenomenon of "contamination" but perhaps the kind of cosmopolitan contamination celebrated by Kwame Anthony Appiah as a "counter-ideal" to reductive and potentially dangerous "ideal[s] of cultural purity."[8] Following Appiah, I suggest that the essential function of the railroad gives lie to claims about the purely urban and the purely modern.

Elsewhere, Shaw's description of working in a timber mill italicizes the overlapping planes of exploitation that bear down upon him as a rural subject in a modern world: "I hauled lumber until the mill shut down. They just cut this country out of wood, cut this country out of wood" (238). It's a common story: a resource reliably linked to the country (timber) is sacrificed to produce the industrial infrastructure. And the ecological consequences of industrial production come to the front of Shaw's mind repeatedly in *All God's Dangers*, as when he recalls the effects of a "cotton mill up there at Opelika": "they just poured dye in the creek, poison, and killed out the catfish in Sitimachas. You could see the signs of it way down in here, the color of the water—killed them catfish a goin and a comin. It's a pity to kill what people love, it's pity to kill it out" (474). What we might usefully identify as Shaw's environmental sensibility aligns with Rob Nixon's recent claim that "[i]n the global resource wars, the environmentalism of the poor is frequently triggered when an official landscape is forcibly imposed on a vernacular one." The map of the "official landscape," according to Nixon, "writes the land in a bureaucratic, externalizing, and extraction-driven manner that is often piteously instrumental." This in violation of the "vernacular landscape," which is "shaped by the affective, historically textured maps that communities have devised over generations ... maps alive to significant ecological and surface geological features."[9] It follows, then, that Shaw's voice—as powerful a tool of vernacular expression as one is likely to find in American writing—doubles as the voice of the vernacular landscape itself, celebrating its virtues, the form and function of its many surfaces, and mourning its destruction. Nixon also helps make sense of the frontispiece map, a thorough rendering of Shaw's "Lower Half of Tukabahchee County, Alabama," that roughly correlates to the landmarks of Ned Cobb's native Tallapoosa County. Yet the map further inscribes the "official landscape" with an alternate history. Minor variations in spelling can't disguise the fact that the map points toward the reinstallation of Tukabatchee—an ancient hub for the Muscogee Creek confederacy—as a cultural and political capital.

Unsurprisingly, Shaw's role as a participant in, if not consistent beneficiary of, industrialization pushes his recollections of the landscape toward the elegiac. *All God's Dangers* shows how Shaw earns his skepticism toward capitalist progress, a trait that comes into high relief as the narrative unspools and the narrator asserts an agricultural sensibility that befits *Go Down, Moses*'s Lucas Beauchamp, the black patriarch and McCaslin family heir who "refus[es] to let a tractor so much as cross [his] land."[10] Despite living in a tractor-powered world spun by technological gyrations, Shaw remains, like Lucas, a "mule farmin man to the last" (466).

"[W]ho is the backbone of the world?" Shaw asks. "It's the laborin man, it's the laborin man" (545). As Shaw well recognizes, wealth and the world it calls into being remain uncreated without labor, without the "laborin man." If we match the book's focus on the private realities of rural labor to a decidedly wider, more global perspective, *All God's Dangers* contains multiple examples of how exactly such a thing is true. Though alternately advantaged and disadvantaged by his efforts, Nate Shaw, a rural subject of very little world-historical consequence, worked to make the modern.

Inversely, it's also essential to note that Nate Shaw, a rural subject of very little world-historical consequence, made the modern work for him. To that end, I wish to underline the inescapable, if widely unremarked, existence of the *modern-in-the-rural*. *The Whole Machinery*'s central conceit is that the fragmentation of both rural labor and rural landscapes under capitalist modernity of the late nineteenth and early twentieth centuries creates a milieu of estrangement and uncertainty as profound as anything else in the modernist canon. Under this light, the differently stylized account contained in *All God's Dangers* joins *Let Us Now Praise Famous Men* as a high-water mark of modernist documentary, as both represent the vertiginous, inequitable, and unstable experience of life on a tenant tract linked to relentless flows of goods and capital in the global economy of the early twentieth century.

Nate Shaw, then, is not some rustic outlier left behind by distant processes of modernization but an exemplary figure, variously pushing with/in and against forces of modernization to create a rendition of the modern that turns to his advantage. Shaw's resilience is both the content and the form of his narrative: in the face of all his trials, he is never strictly a victim and never entirely stripped of power by the white-supremacist powers that surround

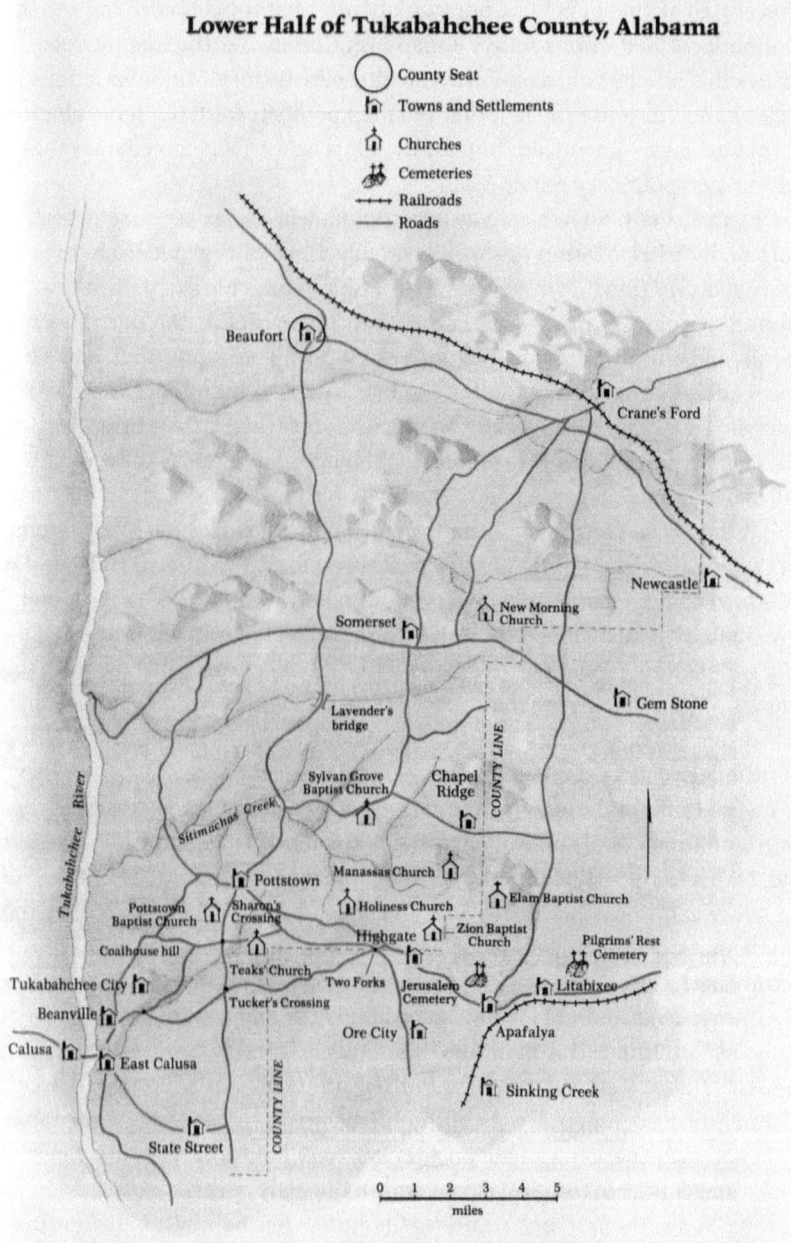

Lower Half of Tukabahchee County, Alabama, from *All God's Dangers*, by Theodore Rosengarten (copyright © 1974 by Theodore Rosengarten and the Estate of Ned Cobb; used by permission of Alfred A. Knopf, an imprint of the Knopf Doubleday Publishing Group, a division of Penguin Random House LLC; all rights reserved).

him. Shaw refuses to allow his identity to be reduced to the shape of white persecution: "All God's dangers aint a white man" (223), the narrator reminds us in a passage about the perils of the boll weevil that also serves as a broader statement of his own philosophy. Given this, his attitude appears to conform to Dilip Gaonkar's postcolonialist vision of an alternative modernity that endorses "creative adaptation," responses that generate "site[s] where a people 'make' themselves modern, as opposed to being 'made' modern by alien and impersonal forces, and where they give themselves an identity and destiny."[11]

One manifestation of this dynamic in *All God's Dangers* is Shaw's meticulously delineated strategies of consumption and production. In addition to its exploration of his role as producer, the text also carefully recalls Shaw's interactions with different brands of commercial products. In a thickly descriptive paragraph that sets up the showdown with Sheriff Beall and his deputies, Shaw notes his outfit: "Big 8 overalls," "Red Wing boots about knee high," and a .32 Smith and Wesson pistol (311); elsewhere, in a series of meditations on the automobile, he enters the long-standing debate about the merits of Ford versus Chevrolet (254–56). Shaw establishes sovereignty as a modern subject in his willingness to embrace certain technological innovations while rejecting others. Again, the tractor: "never did make a crop with a tractor. I did manage to own as much as two cars once" (466). And as a sign of his story's wide chronological arc and as a comment on the cycles of creative destruction built into the commodity-object itself, Shaw is fascinated to learn that the household goods he used as a sharecropper decades earlier have achieved second life as high-priced antiques (524).

In such a way, Shaw takes great pains to make clear his role in creating his own identity, a quality that draws out one of the text's most poignant motifs—the need for mutual recognition. Slavery's great evil, the narrator asserts, consists in the fact that the enslaved were not "recognized as people" (300). Mr. Black, for instance, gains Shaw's respect because he was a "different type of man ... a white man that recognized *all* men" (157, italics in original); the most impressive thing Shaw notices on a visit to Philadelphia is that "black and white both is recognized as people" (498). *All God's Dangers* magnifies this impulse, building an encyclopedic memoir out of a series of unflinching statements on personal identity and history, both marked by Shaw's own recalcitrant rurality: "I'm a country-raised fellow, all of my born days, and I love the country" (499).

Shaw's interest in the politics of recognition informs his very diction, which achieves its poignancy through irregular constructions. For example, he frequently deploys the prefix *dis-* to produce uncommon compound words such as "disremember" (324), "disencouraged" (36), and "disrecognized" (55). If, in accordance with the *OED*'s definition, the prefix *dis-* "impl[ies] removal, aversion, negation, reversal of action," then what does it mean to supplant "mis-recognized" with "disrecognized," as the author does repeatedly? In a passage that trenchantly retells African American history via slavery, Shaw writes, "The old boss man, the old marster, disregarded the nigger, disrecognized him in everything" (302). It wasn't incidental or mistaken, Shaw contends, not a quirk of *mis*recognition; the slave's lack of recognition—legally, morally, philosophically—was coordinated, purposeful, and thoroughly codified. It was an aggressive act of "removal," of "negation"; and it pervaded, to use Shaw's formulation, "everything." So when he describes a conflict with his landlord, Mr. Curtis, about the proper use of a mule, the sign "disrecognized" sounds with particular sharpness: "That was his mule, it weren't mine, but he just disrecognized me, considered me not to know nothing" (109). In the narrative's climactic scene, Shaw seizes white recognition via violence—a motif picked up in several prominent literary representations of African American masculinity, from Frederick Douglass's battle with Mr. Covey to Bigger Thomas to the prologue of *Invisible Man*—because within these relationships of power, there is no other way to assert skill, knowledge, autonomy. "The nigger was disrecognized; the white man in this country had everything fixed and mapped out" (340), Shaw insists when comparing his own trial to that of the Scottsboro Boys. In this picture of "everything fixed," Shaw presses against the map of Nixon's "official landscape," with its values assigned along a reliable set of coordinates that leave signing black subjects the burden of accepting life in their place.

"What is labor?" (537), Shaw asks toward his narrative's conclusion, sealing that question to a related one: "what'll become of the land?" (550). In the *Communist Manifesto*, Marx and Engels call for the "[c]ombination of agriculture with manufacturing industries," for the "gradual abolition of all distinction between town and country by a more equitable distribution of the population over the country."[12] In the *Manifesto*, it's plain that the program for a communist society includes a disintegration of both rural and urban distinctiveness achieved through the creation of an evenly peopled landscape, a landscape made smooth, to once again call upon a concept from Deleuze and Guattari.[13] Such a state, it appears, actualizes a dialectical view of history that proceeds with steady, uncompromising linearity: the rural-urban division undone by the forward momentum of urbanization. "Progress" is reliably unidirectional, and it carries predictable spatial properties. Yet as Benjamin himself reminds us, "Even though chronology places regularity above permanence, it cannot prevent heterogeneous, conspicuous fragments from remaining within it."[14] There are residual tracks that can't be smoothed away: a description that matches Baudelaire's Paris even as it applies with equal, if different, force to the southern milieu of Faulkner's Mississippi, Hurston's Florida, Jean Toomer's Georgia, even Mary Austin's Southwest. Given all this, I maintain that the braiding of the rural and the urban that accompanies modernity's imbalanced appearances is an essential segment in the long and increasingly knotty conversation about what—and how—the modern means.

In the early twenty-first century, these dynamics ride on. The issue of urban-rural divisions became unavoidable in the wake of the 2016 presidential election. Along with all the racial, religious, and gender animus unleashed by Trumpism, one of its animating energies was a pronounced sense of rural identity: among the most reliable predictors of the Trump voter turned out to be distance from a major metropolitan area. In the weeks leading up to the election, with most media outlets predicting a safe victory for Hilary Clinton, there was real speculation that Georgia, North Carolina, Florida, and Virginia could all turn blue. With Virginia as the exception, however, Trump and his party ran the table in the South and scored unexpected victories in Michigan, Wisconsin, Pennsylvania, and Ohio, rust belt states that had served as destinations in the southern diaspora of the twentieth century. Why did pollsters miscalculate so dramatically, and how did Democrats lose so much territory? Where and what did the cognoscenti fail to see? In the aftermath of Trump's victory, a passage from Richard Rorty's *Achieving Our Country* (1998) circulated widely, hailed for what felt like prophetic foresight. Imagining a thoroughly neoliberal society of the near future, where union laborers and "unorganized unskilled laborers" have been abandoned by the ruling class, Rorty predicted, "At that point, something will crack. The nonsuburban electorate will decide that the system has failed and start looking for a strongman to vote for."[15] For me, it's Rorty's attention to the "nonsuburban"—the rural, in a word—that rattles most loudly. In the wake of the 2016 election, it's plain that the often oppositional, always intertwined exchanges of the country and the city that created so much unrest in the period covered by *The Whole Machinery* motivate anxieties in the early twenty-first century as well, as a handful of U.S. cities thrive while great swaths of the country feel left behind. Sven Beckert has recently shown that although the establishment of the nation-state was essential to the development of industrial capitalism in the late nineteenth and early twentieth centuries, the rapid decoupling of the state from capital has shuffled the positions of "centers of growing ... and manufacturing," making some spaces obsolete and others newly essential.[16] There are, to be sure, both winners and losers in this restructure, but, in so many essential ways, the fundamental relationships between capital and labor remain intact. That rural districts—particularly in the South—overwhelmingly voted for a candidate who promoted upheaval of the economic and political status quo (#draintheswamp) may appear as a deliberate "dismantling," to use Piketty's language; at very least it is a symptom of the conditions of contemporary inequality since so many rural, Trump-voting counties have been bypassed by twenty-first-century economic growth. The Trumpist reality, though, has been an ungainly blend of anti-institutional anger, protectionism, and conservative economic policy that does little to change the basic relations and proportions of the U.S. economy.

Moreover, the state of racial unrest in the 2010s has a disconcerting feel of familiarity. The major point of twenty-first-century contrast may, as Isabel Wilkerson has suggested, simply be a matter of geographic dissemination. In 2014, when protests erupted around the police killings of black men and children—most prominently Michael Brown, Tamir Rice, and Eric Garner—Wilkerson noted an unsettling fact: to chart the location of the majority of these incidents is to call up "a map of the Great Migration: New York, Chicago, Cleveland, St. Louis, Philadelphia, Washington, Los Angeles, Oakland, all of them the major receiving stations of the movement."[17] In a separate article, in fact, Wilkerson argued that the best way to understand the turmoil of the 2010s is as an extension of the conflicts underwriting the Great Migration and the decades that preceded it: "Our current era," she writes, "seems oddly aligned with that moment." Citing a common set of figures that define the nadir as the period when the lynching of a black person occurred, on average, every four days, in 2016 Wilkerson made a staggering connection: "Today, in the era of the Charleston massacre, when, according to one analysis of F.B.I. statistics, an African American is killed by a white police officer roughly every three and a half days, has the makings of a second Nadir."[18] The circumference of terror may be geographically wider, but it's still ringed by the undeniable stain of America's great sin.

In June 2014—the summer of the Brown-Garner killings and just two months after the *All God's Dangers* revival—Ta-Nehisi Coates gained a wide audience by making a case for reparations that drew on the nexus of property, labor, and race, all in terms that Piketty would undoubtedly recognize. There are systemic reasons, stretching from slavery to contemporary forms of housing discrimination, that explain why the wealth gap between blacks and whites in the United States cannot be closed by income alone. And the intergenerational transmission of capital, largely tied to the ownership of property, generates a momentum that too frequently keeps wealth—even, or perhaps especially, wealth generated by black labor—in the hands of (largely white) property owners.[19] Read alongside Piketty and *All God's Dangers*, Coates's argument encapsulates one of the parting observations of this book: as much as capitalist modernity is driven, some might say haunted, by the need to endlessly innovate, the uneven ground it requires us to walk remains deeply ruptured by race-based inequality.

As I bring this study to a close with a peek into the twenty-first century, I acknowledge the narrowness of my viewfinder and the unavoidably circumscribed picture it allows. But I do want to stress the validity of the exercise. Shortly before his death, Raymond Williams argued that postmodernism represented little more than the trailing murmur of an incomplete conversation, and one that called for a bracing rejoinder. "If we are to break out of the non-historical fixity of *post*-modernism," Williams wrote, "then we must search out and counterpose an alternative tradition taken from the neglected works left in the wide margin of the century."[20] I contend that these works include cultural products from several undersung figures studied in *The Whole Machinery*—Don West, Myrtle Lawrence, the anonymous contributors to *The Disinherited Speak*, Ned Cobb—and that one possible "alternative tradition" becomes visible by reading the South through the optic of the rural modern. In Williams's mind, it is only the marginalia of modernism that can give rise to "a tradition which may address itself not to this by now exploitable because quite inhuman rewriting of the past but, for all our sakes, to a modern *future* in which community may be imagined again."[21] A searching investigation of the past is required to complete the vision of an equitable future.

At this study's conclusion, then, I want to take stock of a few questions prompted by my decision to use the agricultural South to trope the rural modern: should regional stories necessarily be resituated as national ones? Is the regional narrative simply a grace note in a longer, more complicated national history of flows and disruptions? Or does a national frame ultimately re-create the limitations of the regional one on a larger scale? What does this conversation gain—or possibly lose—by more deeply engaging global turns in new modernist, new southern, and new American studies? These are questions that prospective work in this direction must consider. But even more broadly, the basic parameters of the problem deserve a second look: popular thinking about the cities has too often taken for granted that they alone function as spaces of diffusion and contact, while the country is mired in stasis and tradition. Yet the fluidity—of bodies, material culture, ideas—demonstrated by *The Whole Machinery*'s protagonists highlights the dialogic encounters of, and within, the country and the city, suggesting that the dynamism of the southern rural districts, their inhabitants, and their variegated responses to modernity—these diverse and mobile figurations of the rural modern—deserve increased critical attention.

NOTES

Introduction. Limning the Land

1. Joseph Mitchell, *Up in the Old Hotel*, 690–91.
2. Joseph Mitchell, Author's Note, xii; Kunkel, *Man in Profile*, 10.
3. See Joseph Mitchell, "Brewers" and "Cool Swamp and Field Woman." I'm indebted here to Kunkel, *Man in Profile*, 45.
4. Cowley, "Grammar of Facts," 113.
5. Kunkel, *Man in Profile*, 107–8.
6. Joseph Mitchell, "Days in the Branch," 40.
7. Joseph Mitchell, *Up in the Old Hotel*, 71, 72.
8. Ibid., 83. See Osborne, *Politics of Time*, 1–29. See also Duck, *Nation's Region*, in particular her discussions of Erskine Caldwell and Hurston, 85–145.
9. Joseph Mitchell, *Up in the Old Hotel*, 41.
10. David A. Davis's recent configuration of "southern modernism" is typical of this reflex. Whatever modernity might be in Davis's *World War I*, it "developed in Europe before the war" (145). Subsequently, the South "encountered modernity as an onrush of disruption during World War I" (6).
11. Mao and Walkowitz, "New Modernist Studies," 738.
12. See Baptist, *Half Has Never Been Told*; Beckert, *Empire of Cotton*; Walter Johnson, *River of Dark Dreams*; Rothman, "The Contours of Cotton Capitalism"; Rosenthal, *Accounting for Slavery*. See also various entries in the edited collection *Slavery's Capitalism*, edited by Beckert and Rockman.
13. Beckert, *Empire of Cotton*, 441.
14. Woods, *Development Arrested*, 48.
15. Cedric Robinson, *Black Marxism*, 4.
16. Eric Williams, *Capitalism and Slavery*, 5. Without naming capitalism explicitly, W. E. B. Du Bois's *Black Reconstruction in America* (1935) places "black labor" at the base of North Atlantic capitalist expansion: "Black labor became the foundation stone not only of the Southern social structure, but of Northern manufacture and commerce, of the English factory system, of European commerce, of buying and selling on a world-wide scale" (5).
17. Woods's *Development Arrested* might complicate this claim since his focus is on the rise of blues culture within the plantation regime of the Mississippi Delta, but his methods are heavily sociological and unconcerned with modernism as such.
18. Casey, *New Heartland*, 4.
19. "In Southern modernism," David A. Davis has pithily explained, "the culture of cotton is just as important as the culture of cubism." Davis, "Southern Modernists and Modernity," 102.
20. See Allred, *American Modernism and Depression Documentary*; Child, "Aston-

ishing Byblows" and "Magical Real and the Rural Modern"; Duvall, "Regionalism in American Modernism"; Hubbs, "William Faulkner's Rural Modernism"; Moffitt, "Reviving the Rural"; Parrish, *Flood Year 1927*; Zandria Robinson, "Listening for the Country" and *Ain't No Chicago*; Watson, *William Faulkner and the Faces of Modernity*. Dore's "Modernism of Southern Literature" contains several essential insights, yet there is little about her analysis that engages the rural qua rural. Cronon's *Nature's Metropolis* aims to "eras[e] the false boundary" separating the country and the city in the early twentieth century (19). For an examination of this dynamic in British literature and culture, see *Rural Modernity in Britain: A Critical Intervention*, ed. Bluemel and McCluskey.

21. See also Duck, "Peripatetic Modernism."
22. Storey, *Rural Fictions, Urban Realities*, 2.
23. Farland, "Modernist Versions of Pastoral," 930.
24. Walkowitz's *Cosmopolitan Style* uses experiences and aesthetics of the urban to synthesize current conversations about modernism and transnationalism. Her argument, however necessary, makes little room for the rural. See also Harding's *Writing the City*, which presents the city as the locus of literary modernism.
25. Gaonkar, "On Alternative Modernities," 15.
26. Pratt, "Arts of the Contact Zone," 36. Emphasis mine.
27. Benjamin, *Arcades Project*, 3.
28. Perry Anderson, "Modernity and Revolution," 318. Italics in original.
29. See Gaonkar, "On Alternative Modernities"; Chakrabarty, *Provincializing Europe*. For more recent work on mapping modernism, see also Brooker and Thacker, *Geographies of Modernism*; Doyle and Winkiel, *Geomodernisms*. In *Death of a Discipline*, Spivak reads José Martí's "ruralist left-humanism" as a means of opening up "an internationalism that can ... shelter planetarity"—her alternative to the designations "post-colonial" and "global" (92). Hickman, in *Black Prometheus*, has recently worried that the formulation of "modern/differently modern" "merely remaps the racialized territories of the 'modern' and the 'primitive'" (3). I share his concern, but one of *The Whole Machinery*'s major points is that figurations of rurality which appear as "differently modern" are in fact internal to and constitutive of more widely recognizable (read *cosmopolitan*) forms of the modern.
30. Harvey, *Urban Experience*, 264. It's telling in this regard that my earliest published attempt to theorize the rural modern was in an analysis of the Cinema Novo movement in Brazil of the early 1960s ("Magical Real and the Rural Modern"). Several of the thinkers and concepts I incorporated in that essay—Berman's antidevelopment modernism, Bloch's unfinished world, Gaonkar's alternative modernities, Handley's poetics of oblivion—have been indispensable to this book's formulations of the rural modern in the U.S. South.
31. Harvey, *Urban Experience*, 264.
32. Braidotti, *Nomadic Subjects*, 1.
33. Jon Smith, *Finding Purple America*, 7–16.
34. The "metronormative" is a guiding trope in Herring's *Another Country*.
35. Raymond Williams, *The Country and the City*, 297.
36. Ching and Creed, "Recognizing Rusticity," 13.

37. Morton, *Ecology Without Nature*, 13.

38. For thorough discussions of the elements as objects of critical inquiry, see Cohen and Duckert, *Elemental Ecocriticism*.

39. Buell, *Environmental Imagination*, 8.

40. Chu, *Race, Nationalism, and the State*, 16.

41. Ibid., 17.

42. Mao and Walkowitz, "New Modernist Studies," 738.

43. Grant, *Personal Memoirs*, 639.

44. Max Weber, who perhaps most influentially theorized standardization as an outcome of modernization, explored "bureaucracy" as a product of modernity that creates uniform modes of behavior and communication that are both essential to the successful navigation of the modern world and debilitating to personal freedoms. Weber's fullest discussion of bureaucracy is found in *Economy and Society*. In mounting a critique of the Enlightenment's contributions to totalitarianism in the twentieth century, Adorno and Horkheimer adapt Weber's notion of "rationalization" and its tendency to create bureaucracy. See *Dialectic of Enlightenment*, 63–136.

45. The "modern" is clearly a slippery concept, with each period claiming its own iteration. At the outer edge, for instance, Greenblatt has made a case for Lucretius's epic *The Order of Things* (50 BCE) as ground zero; see *The Swerve*. Hickman's globalist reevaluation of modernity situates the start line at 1492, with the cosmological collision of Columbus's arrival in the Americas. See *Black Prometheus*, 33–73. It would obviously be irresponsible to conflate the attributes of twentieth-century modernity with the word's connotations in the eighteenth century. What interests me about Crèvecoeur's account is its ability to provide a brief sketch of the concept's genealogy, particularly as it relates to rurality and the agricultural countryside.

46. Crèvecoeur, *Letters*, 67.

47. Ibid., 72.

48. Gilman, *Women and Economics*, 32.

49. The modernization of the regional economy is covered in Woodward's classic *Origins of the New South*. See also Wright, *Old South, New South*. The modernization of the rural South in particular is covered in Daniel, *Breaking the Land*; Kirby, *Rural Worlds Lost*. Ingram's *Dixie Highway* provides a picture of the essential role that roadways played in the creation of the New South. For a brief, effective overview of the nexus of industrialization and labor in the post-Reconstruction South, see Letwin, "Labor Relations." The urbanization of the South is the subject of Cobb, *Industrialization*. For more on patterns of intellectual modernization in the South, see Cobb, *Away Down South*; Singal, *War Within*; and Hobson, *Tell about the South*. Grantham's *South in Modern America* aims at the totality of modernization in the South, with a special focus on electoral politics.

50. The core-periphery relationship is essential to Wallerstein's models of globalized economic dependency and a common feature in his prodigious output. For a succinct overview, see Wallerstein, *World-Systems Analysis*, 11–12, 28–29.

51. Quijano and Wallerstein, "Americanity," 449.

52. Clukey, "Plantation Modernity," 507. Cohn and Smith make a similar point when they situate the U.S. South "in a space unique within modernity: a space simulta-

neously (or alternately) center and margin, victor and defeated, empire and colony." Introduction, 9.

53. It may be superfluous at this point to call up Williams's famous claim that "culture" is "one of the two or three most complicated words in the English language," but his analysis of its lineage, from a "noun of process: the tending of something, basically crops or animals" to a sign pointing out the "relations between general human development and a particular way of life," in particular the "works and practices of art and intelligence," seems relevant to this discussion of agricultural labor and its connections to aesthetics and the politics of representation. Not incidentally, to either Williams's analysis or my own, "nature" is another of the "most complicated" words. *Keywords*, 97, 91.

54. Examples abound: Jones and Monteith, *South to a New Place*; Smith and Cohn, *Look Away!*; Cartwright, *Sacral Grooves*.

55. Stecopoulos, *Reconstructing the World*, 7.

56. I'm indebted here to Romine's concept of the "microSouth." *Real South*, 9–17.

57. Lillian Smith, *Killers of the Dream*, n.p.

58. Ibid., 10.

59. The Euro-American urge to establish modern racial orders extended beyond African Americans. Writing of America's indigenous peoples in *Everything You Know*, Smith makes a case for the category "Indian" as a product of the modernist era: "we only became Indians after the armed struggle was over in 1890. Before that we were Shoshone or Mohawk or Crow" (4).

60. Hale, *Making Whiteness*, 6. *Making Whiteness* shares chronological brackets with my study—and I follow Hale in thinking about how the social and cultural dynamics of segregation are inseparable from more widely recognized expressions of the modern.

61. In addition to Wells's antilynching journalism, accounts of Jim Crow segregation contemporaneous to this study's chronology include Dollard, *Caste and Class*; Powdermaker, *After Freedom*; Myrdal, *An American Dilemma*. Tellingly, Wells is the sole African American in this group, suggesting that the project of telling about the segregated South in print was considerably more challenging for black writers.

62. Wells, "Southern Horrors," 62.

63. Ibid., 56.

64. Outka's *Race and Nature* provides a rich overview of realities and representations of race and nature intertwining across different periods. See also Ruffin, *Black on Earth*. Glave's *Rooted in the Earth* offers a historical overview of black engagement with environmental issues. For a deft anthology highlighting African American writers' long-standing interest in nature and ecology, see Dungy, *Black Nature*.

65. Ronda, "Work and Wait."

66. See hooks, *Belonging*.

67. See Kreyling, *Inventing Southern Literature*.

68. See Payne, "Lady Was a Sharecropper."

69. I'm indebted to historian James Gregory for the term "southern diaspora." See Gregory, *Southern Diaspora*.

70. Garner, "Lost in Literary History," C1.

Chapter 1. "The True Reconstruction of the Country" in *Iola Leroy* and the Plantation Poems of Paul Laurence Dunbar

1. Hollis Street Theater in aid of Tuskegee Institute, Alabama, ca. 1899. W. E. B. Du Bois Papers (MS 312), Special Collections and University Archives, University of Massachusetts Amherst Libraries.

2. See Ali, *In the Lion's Mouth*; Gaither, *Blacks and the Populist Movement*. My thanks to John Connor for help with the term "agropolitics."

3. Richardson's *Black Masculinity* provides an essential overview of rural southern inflections of black masculinity, but she is less specifically concerned with intersections of agriculture and subjecthood.

4. Latour, *We Have Never Been Modern*, 10.

5. Ibid., 10–11.

6. Jameson, *Postmodernism*, ix.

7. Purdy, *After Nature*, 287.

8. I follow historians of the twentieth century in using "nadir"—short for "nadir of American race relations"—to refer to the period from the end of Reconstruction (1877) through the 1920s. This usage originates in Logan's *The Negro in American Life and Thought*.

9. Buell, *Environmental Imagination*, 439.

10. For Raymond Williams, the difference between pastoral and what he calls the "counter-pastoral" was the difference between "true and false ways of writing," between methods of representation that obscure the past and those that seek to confront and engage it. Williams, *Country and the City*, 13. Farland, arguing for a "modernist pastoral," seeks to correct the mode's "characteristic elision of class differences and conflicts." "Modernist Versions of Pastoral," 930. See also Conlogue, *Working the Garden*; MacKethan, *Dream of Arcady*; Simpson, *Dispossessed Garden*. More recently, in a perceptive synthesis of critical race studies and ecocriticism, Outka theorizes a variety of pastorals, including the "degraded pastoral of slavery." See Outka, *Race and Nature*, 27–49.

11. McCarthy, *Green Modernism*, 178.

12. Kimberly Johnson, Introduction, *Georgics*, xv.

13. For more on the distinctions between pastoral and georgic, see Sweet, *American Georgics*, 1–6.

14. Raymond Williams, *Country and the City*, 17.

15. Ibid., 17.

16. Ronda, "Work and Wait," 865.

17. Wagner-McCoy, "Virgilian Chesnutt," 200.

18. Commenting on the debate about whether the *Georgics* proposes a fundamentally positive or negative attitude toward its subjects, Perkell proposes "a more balanced, inclusive view of the poem, not because balance is inherently admirable or virtuous but because, as I believe, it is truer to the poem and, not incidentally, to life. As life has joy and grief, so this poem reflects the real tensions of most human experience." See *Poet's Truth*, 16.

19. Zakiyyah Iman Jackson, "Outer Worlds," 215.

20. Weheliye, *Habeas Viscus*, 4.

21. Jacques, *Change in the Weather*, 23. Baker's *Modernism* includes an extended case for the modernism of Washington's performance in *Up from Slavery* (1989). He reversed his position in *Turning South Again* (2001).

22. Smethurst, *African American Roots*, 26. For a prominent reading of Du Bois as modernist, see Gilroy, *Black Atlantic*, 111–45.

23. Friedman, "Definitional Excursions," 501.

24. Gaonkar, "On Alternative Modernities," 23. Italics removed.

25. Quoted in Stewart, *New Negro*, 88.

26. Ibid., 88. Quotation marks removed.

27. *New Negro*, ed. Locke, 7. Given the long history of Irish persecution of black New Yorkers on Manhattan island, it's important to note that in Locke's estimation Harlem belongs to the New Negro while the capital of New Ireland is in the Old World.

28. J. W. Johnson, Preface, xl–xli.

29. Keats, "To George and Tom Keats," 60.

30. Benjamin, "Theses," 257.

31. Blight, *Race and Reunion*, 300. Italics removed.

32. Benjamin, "Theses," 255.

33. Handley, "New World Poetics," 28. Dunbar's explorations of the plantation aren't restricted to poetry alone. For example, *Folks from Dixie* (1898) and *In Old Plantation Days* (1903) are story collections with plantation settings.

34. A similar sort of dynamic informs multiple entries from Chesnutt's *The Conjure Woman* (1899): "The Goophered Grapevine," for instance, in which Henry, the most highly commoditized of the story's enslaved characters, becomes a hybridized grapevine-human; or "Po Sandy," wherein the title character is transformed into a tree by his conjure-woman wife to stave off the forced movements imposed by his master. Decades later, the central metaphor of Billie Holiday's monumental "Strange Fruit" (1939) offers a grim turn on the convention when the fruit of "southern trees" becomes the dead and broken bodies of lynching victims.

35. For a trenchant critique of the convict-lease system, see Blackmon, *Slavery by Another Name*.

36. Timrod, *Poems*, 210.

37. See Slotkin, *Regeneration through Violence*. It's worth noting here that the georgic revival of post-Restoration England ushered in by Dryden's translation of the *Georgics* in 1697 offers another instance in which the literary mode both reflected and shaped a culture coming to terms with the turmoil of extended civil war (the Wars of the Three Kingdoms), political uncertainty (the Interregnum), and the reestablishment of a strong central governing body (Charles II). Recently, de Bruyn shows how Virgil's agricultural manual became a broader template for husbandry in Restoration England. See de Bruyn, "From Georgic Poetry," 107–39.

38. Ronda submits, "Dunbar's georgics offer portraits in negative of Washington's industrial-agricultural training regime with its capitalist model of progress-oriented labor" ("'Work and Wait Unwearying,'" 869). This may be true, but I don't think it's the whole truth: Washington's industrial-agricultural regime did indeed align itself with "progress-oriented labor," yet, as I argue in chapter 2, it also often represented a

defensive tactic for self-preservation in an environment of deadly racialized hostility. "Tuskegee Song," as well as "To Booker T. Washington," suggests that Dunbar recognized the value of such tactics.

39. Gates, *Signifying Monkey*, 176. For a suggestive, if brief, examination of Dunbar's relation to the signifying practices of the minstrel stage, see Carr, "Minstrelsy," 49–58. In addition to his perceptive readings of Dunbar's black dialect poems, Jones's *Strange Talk* features analyses of the poet's "vaudeville dialects," including attempts at Irish dialect writing: "Like that of many of his contemporary black vaudevillians, Dunbar's dialect work trod a fine line between racial representation and the perpetuation of racist conventions. The space where these African American artists could perform was narrow, making their subtle subversions more remarkable still" (181). A recent overview of Dunbar's dialect poetry is in Nurhussein, *Rhetorics of Literacy*, 90–142.

40. The politics of Foster's dialect lyrics have been subject to several revisions. Emerson's generous biography of Foster argued that "the kernel of social philosophy that . . . gave popular voice to a growing segment of Northerners uncomfortable with slavery," a claim complicated by Saunders's recent contention that "Foster's plantation melodies embody his own conventional, Democratic, middle-class values more than any progressive, utopian views about the politics of race." Emerson, *Doo-Dah*, 146–57; Saunders, "Social Agenda," 286. For an earlier set of black revisions of plantation idylls such as Foster's, see Martin Delany's unfinished novel *Blake; or the Huts of America*.

41. Foster, "My Old Kentucky Home," 18.

42. Lott, *Love and Theft*, 189.

43. Ronda, "Work and Wait," 870–71. I follow Saunders here in using the term "plantation melodies" since it points to pieces, such as "My Old Kentucky Home," that "straddle the line between parlor song and minstrel song." Saunders, "Social Agenda," 282.

44. Pellicer, "Pastoral and Georgic," 293.

45. A comprehensive survey of the banjo's New World histories is contained in Dubois, *The Banjo*. According to Dubois, the "instrument came to the [minstrel] stage in the hands of Virginian Joel Walker Sweeney," who first appeared with the banjo at the Old Italian Opera House, near Broadway, in 1839 (194). An assessment offered by a character named Goosey in Claude McKay's 1929 novel, *Banjo*, uncovers the instrument's tangled legacies: "Banjo is bondage. It's the instrument of slavery. The Dixie of the land of cotton and massa and missus and black mammy." The title character—a black banjo player from the U.S. South—loudly disagrees: "Nuts on that black-face. Tha's time-past stuff." McKay, *Banjo*, 90–91.

46. Douglass, *Narrative*, 48–49.

47. Handley, *Postslavery Literatures*, 101.

48. Robbins, Introduction, xxix.

49. Walter Johnson, *River of Dark Dreams*, 224.

50. In a celebrated article that includes readings of *Iola Leroy*, Berlant argues that the novel "seizes the scene of citizenship from white America and rebuilds it, in the classic sense, imagining a liberal public sphere located within the black community," noting how the "originary form for African American community building derives from the subversive vernacular practices of slave life." These practices are exemplified in the code-speaking scene that opens the novel. Berlant, "Queen of America," 561–62.

51. Levine, *Black Culture and Black Consciousness*, 80.

52. Baker, *Workings of the Spirit*, 31. It's also important to note that this sort of land reform is precisely what the white hero of Albion W. Tourgée's 1879 novel, *A Fool's Errand*, tried to enact. Unlike Robert, he failed, and the difference in outcome may tell us something essential about how differently raced imaginations conceive reconstructed spaces.

53. Castronovo, *Necro Citizenship*, 221, 243.

54. This connection might also inform discussions of Washington and Du Bois, wherein Washington's affinity for the country contrasts with the lighter-skinned Du Bois's combination of skepticism and urbanity.

55. Schmidt, *Sitting in Darkness*, 65.

56. Carby, *Reconstructing Womanhood*, 93.

57. Foucault, *Birth of Biopolitics*, 293.

58. Ayers, *Promise*, 436.

59. Gilroy, *Black Atlantic*, 115.

60. Ammons, *Conflicting Stories*, 27.

61. Smethurst, *African American Roots*.

62. Silber, *Romance of Reunion*, 2.

63. Eric Foner, *Reconstruction*, 82.

64. Marx, *Economic and Philosophical Manuscripts*, 53.

65. I'm indebted here to Porter's pairing of these texts in "*Gone with the Wind* and *Absalom, Absalom!*" 705–10.

66. Faulkner, *Light in August*, 424–25.

67. Margaret Mitchell, *Gone with the Wind*, 1357.

68. Outka, *Race and Nature*, 33.

69. Simpson, *Dispossessed Garden*, 61.

70. Bennett, "Anti-Pastoralism," 208.

71. Richardson, *Black Masculinity*, 127.

72. hooks, *Belonging*, 40.

73. Ibid., 36.

74. *Pigford* Cases, Congressional Research Service.

75. Breselor, "The Pigford Case."

76. Pickert, "When Shirley Sherrod." For more regarding the controversy about the payment of claims, see LaFraniere, "U.S. Opens Spigot." A blend of politics, race, and agriculture also shaped the conversations leading up to the passage of the Social Security Act in 1935, when southern Democrats persuaded President Roosevelt to disallow inclusion of "domestic" and agricultural workers, essentially barring large segments of the black citizenry from claiming the program's full benefits.

77. Bloch, *Principle of Hope*, 223.

Chapter 2. "Strange Vicissitudes"

1. Smethurst, *African American Roots*, 41. Du Bois was by no means Washington's only antagonist in this period. For instance, William Monroe Trotter, through his newspaper work at the *Boston Guardian* and his involvement in the Niagara Move-

ment, was an influential and highly visible member of the "anti-Bookerites." His activities are covered in Norrell, *Up from History*, 263–338.

2. In the address (reproduced in *Up from Slavery*), Washington infamously made the case to his white audience, "In all things social we can be as separate as the fingers, yet one as the hand in all things essential to mutual progress" (100). Washington denied the simile's application to segregationist agendas, however, in a letter sent less than a month after the speech: "If anybody understands me as meaning that riding in the same railroad car or sitting in the same room at a railroad station is social intercourse they certainly got the wrong idea of my position." See Washington to Edna Dow Littlehale Cheney, 56–57.

3. West has a term for this posture, "Washingtonianism." *Education of Booker T. Washington*, 14–16.

4. For more on plantation agriculture's responses to an industrializing New South, see Cobb, *Most Southern Place*, 98–124.

5. Williamson, *Rage for Order*, 63.

6. Zimmerman, *Alabama in Africa*, 22.

7. Norrell, *Up from History*, 48–49.

8. Fanon, *Wretched*, 9.

9. Despite their similarities, *Up from Slavery*'s deflective attitude toward violence is its most obvious point of contrast with Fanon's work, particularly in *Wretched of the Earth*. Fanon's belief that, "[f]or the colonized, life can only materialize from the rotting cadaver of the colonist" (50) rests uneasily against Washington's incessant—perhaps disingenuous—claims that African Americans harbor no "bitterness" toward their former oppressors. In a further illustration of Washington's postcolonial resonance, look to Spivak's discussion of José Martí as a "planetary" artist, which makes direct comparison between "[h]is ideas of the education of the rural population" and those of Washington. Spivak, *Death of a Discipline*, 94.

10. Ibid., 37. Washington elaborates on his theories regarding the natural alliance between farming and former slaves in *My Larger Education*. Citing one man's story of local uplift via agriculture, Washington claims boldly, and without exposition, that he "had solved the race problem" (72).

11. Fanon, *Wretched*, 129.

12. Washington, *Farthest Man Down*, 6.

13. Fanon, *Wretched*, 128.

14. Norrell, *Up from History*, 60.

15. For Baker's explanation of the *sound* of the minstrel mask, see *Modernism*, 22.

16. Although we read the song at adjacent angles, I'm indebted to musician Flemons's excellent unpacking of "Can You Blame the Colored Man?" See Flemons, "Can You Blame Gus Cannon?" 128–37. It's also important to note that the song's interest in food—"they're eating lamb, ham, veal, and goat / chicken, turkey, bread, and toast"—aligns with a similar preoccupation in *Up from Slavery*.

17. Washington, *Working with the Hands*, 156.

18. See Gottlieb and Joshi, *Food Justice*.

19. Washington to Beno von Herman auf Wain. Quoted in Beckert's discussion of the Togo colony in *Empire of Cotton*, 364. See also Zimmerman, *Alabama in Africa*.

20. Edge discusses the importance of food sovereignty as a civil rights issue in the 1960s South for activists like Unita Blackwell, Marian Wright, and especially Fannie Lou Hamer, who established Freedom Farm in Sunflower County, Mississippi, in 1969. *Potlikker Papers*, 49–66.

21. Nicholls, *Conjuring the Folk*, 11.

22. Hersey, *My Work*, 2.

23. Hicks, "W. E. B. Du Bois, Booker T. Washington, and Richard Wright," 205.

24. Washington, *Working*, 168.

25. Washington, "Speech," 503–4.

26. U.S. Census Reports 1900, 6:409.

27. For more on mass consumption from the period and white anxieties about its ability to erase the color line, see Hale, *Making Whiteness*, 121–97. See also Ownby, *American Dreams*.

28. Baucom, "Township Modernism," 234.

29. Baker, *Modernism*, 93.

30. Ibid., 5. Italics in original. Notwithstanding my great admiration and indebtedness to Baker's work, I depart from the model of modernism developed in his Washington reversal, *Turning South Again*. For Baker (circa 2002), *black modernism* is distinguishable from *mulatto modernism* in that it is bound to the prospect of "black citizenship that entails documented mobility (driver's license, passport, green card, social security card) and access to a decent job at a decent rate of pay." All this in place of the "gospel and dynamics of *uplift*" (33). In the project of "black male subject formation," black modernism—Martin Luther King Jr. is presented as an exemplary proponent—deserves encouragement over the types of mulatto modernism practiced by Washington. My own interest in figurations of the rural modern is predicated on multidirectional reflexes rather than any single response. In other words, I argue that what appears as a retreat to Baker can actually stand as a modern impulse, even as it drives its adherents farther from a white-dominated public sphere.

31. Berman, *All That Is Solid*, 235.

32. Leopold, *Sand County Almanac*, 178.

33. Fortune, *Black and White*, 137. In West's description, Fortune was Washington's "friend, sometimes opponent, and later lackey." Michael R. West, *Education*, 71. Fortune's role in Washington's public persona and policy is also explored in Norrell, *Up from History*, 7, 132–33, 305.

34. Jabavu, "My Tuskegee Pilgrimage," 29.

35. Baker, *Turning South Again*, 81.

36. Grandison, "Landscapes of Terror," 362.

37. Coclanis, "The Wizard of Tuskegee," 89.

38. Washington, *Working*, 162. Emphasis mine.

39. Washington, *Working*, 137. In *Beloved*, Toni Morrison uses the same phrase ("educated hands") to describe the character Paul D., a move that recognizes the ingenuity, intelligence, and value of physical labor (116).

40. Gilroy, *Black Atlantic*, 133.

41. Raine, "Du Bois's Ambient Poetics"; Belifuss, "Ironic Landscapes."

42. Du Bois, *Dusk of Dawn*, 16.

43. For Nixon's most succinct explanation of "slow violence," see *Slow Violence*, 6–10.

44. Cimbala, *Under the Guardianship*, 169. Originally issued in 1978, Oubre's *Forty Acres* is a comprehensive assessment of the bureau's successes and failures. Foner's standard *Reconstruction* expertly contextualizes the bureau alongside other features of the Reconstruction. More recently, Farmer-Kaiser's *Freewomen* offers a corrective to histories of the bureau that exclude the experience of women.

45. In *Souls*, Du Bois calls Howard "[a]n honest man, with too much faith in human nature, little aptitude for business and intricate detail"—an evaluation that might summarize his appraisal of the Freedmen's Bureau more generally (23).

46. Quoted in Du Bois, *Black Reconstruction*, 224.

47. Eric Foner, *Reconstruction*, 170.

48. Theodore R. Mitchell, *Political Education*, 76.

49. Williamson, *Crucible of Race*, 82.

50. Ibid., 81.

51. Cobb, *Away Down South*, 84.

52. Dougherty County, the town of Albany in particular, has particular resonance in the civil rights movement, from the desegregation push of 1961–62—the so-called Albany Movement—to the establishment of New Communities in 1969, an African American farm collective that pioneered forms of community land trust in the U.S. Shirley Sherrod—veteran of the civil rights movement, advocate for black farmers, and Obama-era USDA official fired in 2010 because of false controversy drummed up by the right-wing media—is a longtime resident of Albany and cofounder of New Communities. The collective failed in large part because it couldn't secure agricultural loans from the Reagan-era USDA; Sherrod and her husband, Charles, were major claimants in *Pigford v. Glickman*. For more on New Communities, see Witt and Swann, "Land," 244–53; on Sherrod's troubles in the Obama administration, see Coates, *We Were Eight Years*, 141–45, and Sherrod, *Courage to Hope*.

53. 1900 Census of Agriculture, 406.

54. *Soils and Men*, 151.

55. Ibid., 153.

56. For a thorough account of southern cotton's participation in antebellum global networks of trade and industrial manufacturing, see Schoen, *Fragile Fabric*. See also Walter Johnson, *River of Dark Dreams*.

57. Briggs, *New Negro*, 72.

58. Scheiber, "The Folk," 253.

59. Spivak, *Death of a Discipline*, 97.

60. Brodwin, "Veil Transcended," 306.

61. *Up from Slavery* also features a variation on the title of Tourgée's novel: chapter 10, which includes the brickmaking passages, is titled "A Harder Task Than Making Bricks Without Straw." By 1905, according to Harold Cruse, the "economic nationalism" promoted by Washington through the National Negro Business League had "become aggressive and assertive in economics but conservative in civil rights politics, hence the clash over 'program' between Washington and Du Bois's new civil rights 'radicalism'" (*Crisis*, 19).

62. Gilroy, *Black Atlantic*, 115.

63. Goodman, *Georgic Modernity*, 4.

64. Yaeger, *Dirt and Desire*, 18.

65. Belifuss, "Ironic Landscapes," 504.

66. Du Bois, *Dusk of Dawn*, 88.

67. Baker, *Turning South Again*, 33–34.

68. See, for instance, Du Bois, "Negroes of Farmville"; "Negro in the Black Belt"; "Negro Landholder of Georgia"; "Negro Farmer." The reason for Du Bois's interest in the issue is plain in the opening line of "Negro Landholder": "One of the greatest problems of emancipation in the United States was the relation of the freedman to the land" (647).

69. Du Bois, "Rural South," 80.

70. Du Bois, "Talented Tenth," in *The Negro Problem*, 33–34.

71. Du Bois, *Dusk of Dawn*, 134. Among the small but robust body of *Quest* criticism, McInnis's wonderful contribution, "Behold the Land"—which I didn't encounter until after having completed this manuscript—deserves special mention here. McInnis is also interested in the novel as an economic study, but he is primarily concerned with analyzing *Quest*'s "aesthetics" so as "to leverage a moral and economic critique of the plantation romance and plantation modernity" (74) and, to a lesser extent, with connecting the novel's "economic study" to Du Bois's unfinished fiction project of the 1950s, "The Cotton Slave / The Slave and the Cotton" ("Behold the Land," 94). See also Oliver, "W. E. B. Du Bois," 63–64.

72. According to Farland's perceptive reading of the novel, *Quest* provides a "reconstruction of the forgotten links between Du Bois's literary and scientific writings" by using the conventions of domestic fiction to make arguments against scientific notions of African American physical and mental inferiority. "W. E. B. Du Bois," 1019.

73. Greene, Introduction, xii.

74. Aptheker, Introduction, x–xi; Farland, "W. E. B. Du Bois," 1017–19; McInnis, "Behold the Land," 91.

75. For more on Washington's involvement with the Calhoun School, see Ellis, "Calhoun School."

76. Farland, for instance, notes that the novel "marked [Du Bois's] surprising affinities with the industrial and manual training association with Booker T. Washington" but says nothing further on the topic ("W. E. B. Du Bois," 1036). Elsewhere in the article, she offers an excellent overview of Du Bois's Lowndes County study (1017–19).

77. Sundquist, *To Wake the Nations*, 466.

78. Flately, *Affective Mapping*, 147.

79. Interview with Ben Cotton, *New York Mirror*, July 3, 1897. Quoted in Toll, *Blacking Up*, 46. Emphasis mine.

80. Ellison, "Change the Joke," 53.

81. Harper, *Iola Leroy*, 68. Emphasis mine.

82. Handy, *Father of the Blues*, 74. Emphasis mine.

83. In 1871 famed columnist Lafcadio Hearn used the same sign ("weird") in a dispatch from the Bucktown section of Cincinnati. At a nightclub on the banks of the Mississippi, Hearn noted a group consisting of mostly African American dancers and musicians—banjo pickers, fiddlers, a "bass viol" player—who emerged from and

around a steamboat in from New Orleans: "The musicians struck up that *weird*, wild, lively air, known perhaps to many of our readers as the 'Devil's Dream'" (emphasis mine). Hearn, *Lafcadio Hearn's America*, 49. Quoted in Dubois, *Banjo*, 211.

84. Emmons, *Agriculture*, v. Italics in original.

85. Belifuss examines Du Bois's interested in the "historical significance" of swampland "as a location of resistance to the oppressive, dominant culture," but his analysis contains no mention of *Quest*. "Ironic Pastorals," 497–98.

86. Allewaert, "Swamp Sublime," 341.

87. Latour, *We Have Never Been Modern*, 10.

88. The swamp's function as a zone of black autonomy echoes the account contained in Harriet Beecher Stowe's *Dred: A Tale of the Great Dismal Swamp* (1856), wherein the Nat Turner–style title character leads an insurrection with a group of Great Dismal Swamp Maroons. As in *Quest*, the swamp's potential for its black occupants derives from its undesirability and general inaccessibility.

89. Purdy, *After Nature*, 164.

90. *Report of the Commission on Country Life*, 19.

91. Letter to Liberty Hyde Bailey, Nov. 23, 1908.

92. *Report of the Commission on Country Life*, 62–64. None of the so-called Black Belt states were included in the commission's 1908 public hearings (56–57).

93. Schmidt, *Sitting in Darkness*, 196.

94. Gorky, "Comrade," 509.

95. Cooper, *Voice from the South*, 28. Italics in original.

96. Du Bois, "Criteria of Negro Art," 42.

97. Du Bois, "Negro Landholder," 666.

98. For more on the novel as a tabulation of Du Bois's 1910s socialism, see Van Wienan and Kraft, "How the Socialism."

99. Washington's *Working* includes a transcript from a declaration of principles adopted by the Farmers' Conference. It encapsulates exactly his antipathy to croplien: "To abolish and do away with the mortgage system just as rapidly as possible" (139).

100. McInnis emphasizes Zora's "rejection of European notions of labor, property ownership, and capital accumulation" (74; see also 90–91). It's an important observation, but I would add that the composition of her ideal community proposes a complex admixture of private property and public commons: one hundred acres of the two-hundred-acre parcel are retained for the "model farm," with the remaining land sold, in twenty-acre plots, to individual farmers (*Quest*, 221).

101. Rampersad, *Art and Imagination*, 129.

102. Beckert, *Empire of Cotton*, 70 (common variations throughout).

103. McInnis, "Behold the Land," 74

104. Aptheker makes a similar observation in his introduction (iv). See also Rosetti, "Turning the Corner."

105. As Du Bois observes in *Souls*: "[T]he negro forms today one of the chief figures in a great world industry" (90).

106. Morton, *Hyperobjects*, 1.

107. Cloud, *American Cotton Planter*, 11. Quoted in Beckert, *Empire of Cotton*, 119.

108. Compare McInnis, "Behold the Land," 80.

109. Denning, *Noise Uprising*, 7, 11. For an imaginative take on the phonographic effect of "Afro-Modernity" in Du Bois's *Souls*, see Weheliye, *Phonographies*, 73–105.

110. *Value of Swamp Lands*, 3.

111. See, for instance, Byerman on the "Southern romantic novel" ("Race and Romance," 59); Farland on "plantation fiction" ("Modernist Versions of Pastoral," 1028–32); Lee on "romance" ("Du Bois the Novelist," 383–89); McInnis on the "anti-plantation romance" ("Behold the Land," 74–76).

112. Lee, "Du Bois the Novelist," 391–92; Silber, *Romance of Reunion*, 112–23.

113. "[A]rguing with Mr. Thomas Nelson Page," Du Bois famously claims in *Souls*, is an "imperative duty of thinking black men" (44).

114. See Jane Campbell's discussion of the importance of white capital to Zora's settlement in *Mythic Black Fiction*, 69.

115. Morrison interview by Jana Wendt, *Toni Morrison Uncensored*.

116. Raine, "Du Bois's Ambient Poetics," 324.

117. Braidotti, *Posthuman*, 98.

118. Baker, *Turning South*, 83.

119. Ibid., 84.

Chapter 3. Making It Old in the New South

1. Sanneh, "Out of the Office," 85. See Pollan, *Omnivore's Dilemma*; McKibben, *Deep Economy*; Kingsolver, *Animal, Vegetable, Miracle*; Gussow, *This Organic Life*. See also *Modern Farmer*, an upmarket magazine founded in Hudson, New York, in 2015 and guided by the tagline "Farm. Food. Life." The political ambiguities of localism extend to the related New Domesticity movement, which embraces a set of values that at once protest contemporary culture and restage practices consistent with an earlier era of rigid gender roles. Commentators are at odds about whether this is an inevitable step in the evolution of third-wave feminism or a retreat. Throughout *The Whole Machinery*, "Agrarian" in the uppercase will specifically refer to the thought and actions of the Nashville Agrarians; "agrarian" in the lowercase carries larger associations with agricultural life and conflict.

2. Kreyling, *Inventing*, 6.

3. Kreyling's take on the Agrarians is a touchstone in southern literary studies, setting the stage for "postsouthern" readings of the region's literature and culture. For more in this direction, see Bone, *Postsouthern*. Bone effectively reframes readings of the Agrarians by deconstructing one of southern literature's most durable tropes: the sense of place. For a historical profile of the Agrarians, see Conkin's *Southern Agrarians*, a breezy account of the movement most useful for its proximity to the action—Conkin was a Vanderbilt history professor whose tenure closely followed that of Donald Davidson—but its sympathetic treatment of the material occasionally flirts with apologia. Murphy's *Rebuke of History* offers an ambitious reassessment of the Agrarian movement, emphasizing its critiques of American capitalism as well as its enduring influence on the development of twentieth-century conservatism. Murphy traces the Agrarian impulses up to the end of the century, unsorting the political positions of

neo-agrarian thinkers such as Wendell Berry and Eugene Genovese. Genovese's own *Southern Tradition* includes a generous treatment of southern history that also tracks the author's transition from Marxist to conservative in the Agrarian mode. The basis of Genovese's analysis is that socialism's failures in the twentieth century make "southern" conservatism's emphasis on the individual's role within a community preferable to the alienating effects of the kind of unrestrained capitalism protested in *I'll Take My Stand*. One doesn't have to agree with Genovese's position to recognize the ways in which his own intellectual ramblings underscore the movement's points of contact with twentieth-century socialist protest. None of these sources dwell on the coexistent realities of tenancy in the Agrarians' own historical moment.

4. Vernon, "Problematic History," 349.

5. Jon Smith, review of *Postsouthern*, 372.

6. The stubborn, even frustrating, persistence of "agrarian" as a descriptor in southern studies deserves a note. An instructive parallel to this phenomenon might be found in the function of the "frontier" in scholarship on the American West. Though the version espoused most prominently by Frederick Jackson Turner in 1893 has been thoroughly dismantled for its Eurocentrism and incomplete premises, the concept has continued to make and remake itself in discourses on the West. For instance, even Patricia Limerick's iconoclastic, field-shifting study, *Legacy of Conquest* (1989), which includes bracing critiques of Turner's frontier thesis, aims to "deemphasize" and redefine the concept rather than eliminate it altogether (26). Like "agrarian," the common point of reference provided by "frontier" remains, even as its earlier meanings are evacuated and replaced.

7. Murphy describes the "radical conservatism" of the Agrarians at length in *Rebuke of History*. See also Vernon, "Problematic History," 13.

8. Glen, *Highlander*, 19.

9. Ransom, "The South," 141.

10. Ibid., 139.

11. Veblen, *Theory of the Leisure Class*, 43.

12. May and Petgen, *Leisure and Its Use*, 3.

13. Gaonkar, "On Alternative Modernities," 23; Chu, *Race, Nationalism, and the State*, 117.

14. Moglen, *Mourning Modernity*, 28, 46. In an extended case study, Moglen explores the dialogue between the "two modernisms" that runs throughout John Dos Passos's *U.S.A. Trilogy*.

15. Berman, *Modernist Commitments*, 23–33.

16. Moglen, *Mourning Modernity*, 25.

17. Weaks-Baxter, *Reclaiming*, 40.

18. Friedman, "Definitional Excursions," 510.

19. Perry Anderson, "Modernity and Revolution," 105.

20. Ransom, "The South," 139.

21. Brinkmeyer, *Fourth Ghost*, 24.

22. William Carlos Williams, a canonical modernist who worked under the aegis of Pound in the early part of his career, explored similar kinds of voices and subject matter—albeit in a more forcefully stylized register; he also often found himself at

odds with prominent high modernists, particularly Eliot. For one example, see Mariani, *William Carlos Williams*, 215–25.

23. Kazin, *On Native Ground*, 441.

24. For an overview of the reception and circulation of West's work, see Biggers's introduction to *No Lonesome Road*, xiii–xlviii.

25. The status of "the fathers" remained on the track of Tate's imagination: his only novel, 1938's *The Fathers*, is also a meditation on southern ancestry and the threat of new national order represented by the Civil War.

26. Underwood, *Allen Tate*, 160.

27. Davidson, "Allen Tate," 16.

28. Wilson, "Tennessee Agrarians," 331.

29. Lillian Smith, *Killers of the Dream*, 225.

30. I'm indebted here to Filene's discussion of von Herder in *Romancing the Folk*, 10.

31. Frost, "Our Contemporary Ancestors," 318, 312.

32. Kephart, *Our Southern Highlanders*, 13, 17. Kephart's work evinces a preservationist ethos that extended to both the highlanders and their physical environment. His writings were instrumental in the campaign to establish Great Smoky Mountains National Park; he died in a car accident in 1931, three years before the dedication of the park.

33. Frank, *Our America*, 9, 10.

34. Greeson, *Our South*, 1. Italics in original.

35. John Charles Campbell, *Southern Highlander*, 20.

36. "A Unique History," John C. Campbell Folk School, www.folkschool.org/index.php?section=articles&article_cat_id=5&article_id=5 (accessed November 6, 2016).

37. Glen, *Highlander*, 17.

38. Lorence, *Hard Journey*, 29.

39. Ibid., 30.

40. Glen, *Highlander*, 20.

41. See Miller, *Segregating Sound*; Nunn, "Folk."

42. Horton, *Highlander Folk School*, 304, n.83.

43. Austin, "American Folk," 287.

44. Dundes, "What Is Folklore?" 2. Italics in original.

45. Susman, *Culture as History*, 155.

46. Dorson's take on Botkin and the midcentury study of American folklore more broadly is contained in "Theory for American Folklore," 197–215.

47. Hegeman, *Patterns for America*, 4.

48. Robin D. G. Kelley, "Notes," 1402.

49. Rourke, "Significance of Sections," 148.

50. Ibid., 148–49.

51. Marx and Engels, *Communist Manifesto*, 36.

52. Soja, *Thirdspace*, 206.

53. Berwick, "Farming in the Year 2000 A.D.," 570. This in pointed contrast with William Morris's novel *News from Nowhere* (1890), which countered *Looking Backward*'s disregard for rural spaces and labor by setting its utopia in an agrarian society of common ownership and joyful labor.

54. Not surprisingly, Cash has a less enthusiastic reading of the influence of the southern landscape on its inhabitants. The "wide fields and blue woods and flooding yellow sunlight" created "a world in which horses, dogs, guns, not books, ideas, and art" prevailed. *Mind of the South*, 96.

55. Banta, *Taylored Lives*, 6.

56. See Bergson, *Time and Free Will*, 59–94.

57. Kazin, *On Native Ground*, 443; Lilla, *Shipwrecked Mind*, xiii.

58. Cash, *Mind of the South*, 305–6.

59. Marx and Engels, *Communist Manifesto*, 39–40.

60. It's worth remembering that Nixon's left-leaning politics likely guided his diction. To this end, it's also important to remember that he was the group's political outlier: Bingham and Underwood label him a "New Deal liberal in the company of classical conservatives." See Introduction, *Southern Agrarians*, 7.

61. Sullivan, "Mr. Lytle," 63.

62. Adorno, "Free Time," 187.

63. Gray, *Writing the South*, 135.

64. Cash, *Mind of the South*, 30.

65. For more on the complexity of these networks, the density of their mathematical logic, and the ways that such complexity manifest in literary productions of both privileged and marginal southerners, see Taylor, *Disturbing Calculations*.

66. Kirby, *Rural Worlds Lost*, 27. The global agricultural market's ability to expand modernity through nominally isolated areas is a specialty of Daniel, in *Breaking the Land* and *Standing at the Crossroads*.

67. Grantham, Foreword, viii.

68. Pells, *Radical Visions*, 104.

69. Quoted in Wapshott, *Keynes Hayek*, 231.

70. Bone, *Postsouthern*, 13.

71. Ransom, "What Does the South Want?" 181. As Conkin tells it in *Southern Agrarians*, when Ransom came to recognize the practical blind spots of *I'll Take My Stand*, he tried to reeducate himself as a "lay economist, giving himself as fully to his new mistress as he had given himself to poetry in the early twenties" (101).

72. Cash, *Mind of the South*, 384.

73. Bissett, *Agrarian Socialism in America*, 7. Although the contrast between the STFU's evangelical flavor and the Agrarians'—particularly Allen Tate's—high church aspirations falls outside the range of this project, it is a promising topic for future studies. For more on the southern evangelical presence in organized labor during the Depression, see Gellman and Roll, *Gospel of the Working Class*.

74. See Bissett's discussion of the decline of the Socialist Party of Oklahoma in *Agrarian Socialism*, 142–73.

75. Rawe, "Agriculture," 50. Italics in original.

76. Davidson, "A Study of the Race Problem," 6.

77. Though it's tempting to dismiss Davidson as an outlier, Murphy claimed that one consequence of his outsized influence in the southern academy is that his thinking reverberated throughout the twentieth century at a higher frequency than that of his peers in the movement: "It was Davidson who was crucial to transforming

Agrarianism into a form of traditionalist conservatism after World War II." Murphy, *Rebuke*, 8.

78. Robin D. G. Kelley, *Hammer and Hoe*, 7.
79. Quoted in Lorence, "Mobilizing the Reserve Army," 60.
80. Gilmore, *Defying Dixie*, 30.
81. Ibid., 43.
82. See Griggs's novel *Imperium in Imperio* and Delany's tract on black separatism, *Condition, Elevation, Emigration*.
83. Suspicions about communism, interracial alliances, and agricultural community in the South came to a head in the succeeding decades when the state of Georgia launched investigations into alleged Communist activities at Koinonia Farm, a utopian agricultural commune launched by biblical scholar and Christian activist Clarence Jordan outside of Americus, Georgia. For more on Koinonia's continuing ministry, see www.koinoniapartners.org.
84. Duncan, *Fugitive Theory*, 2.
85. Rupert Vance, "Is Agrarianism for Farmers?" 57.
86. Scarry, *On Beauty and Being Just*.
87. Dorman, "Revolt of the Provinces," 2–3.
88. "Highlander Research and Education Center," http://highlandercenter.org (accessed December 2, 2016).
89. Benjamin, *Arcades Project*, 893.

Chapter 4. Disinherited Speech Acts

1. Mittleman, "Volkswagen to Appeal."
2. Greenhouse, "At a Nissan Plant," B1. In August 2017 Canton's Nissan workers voted to reject unionization.
3. "New Cotton Machines," *STFU News*, n.p.
4. Fiskio, "Unsettling Ecocriticism," 302.
5. Ibid., 310.
6. Ibid., 302.
7. Comentale, *Sweet Air*, 36.
8. Berlant, "National Brands/National Bodies," 176. I'm indebted to Flately's *Affective Mapping* for this quotation.
9. Acknowledgments to Aboul-Ela for unpacking the global implications of the "other South" in *Other South*.
10. Ayers, *Promise*, 266. See also Postel's argument about the unappreciated "modern" dimension of early twentieth-century populism in *Populist Vision*.
11. Ayers, *Promise*, 254–55.
12. Marx and Engels, *Communist Manifesto*, 57.
13. For an elegant treatment of the Alabama Communist Party, see Robin D. G. Kelley, *Hammer and Hoe*. The most comprehensive examination of the STFU remains Grubbs, *Cry from the Cotton*. Kester's *Revolt among the Sharecroppers*, originally published in 1936, provides a firsthand account of the rise of the STFU. Sharecropping

conditions were the subject of several other contemporaneous studies. See Thomas, *Plight*; Charles S. Johnson, *Collapse*; Raper, *Preface to Peasantry*.

14. "An Open Letter," 1936.
15. Denning, *Cultural Front*, 271.
16. Isenberg, *White Trash*, 315.
17. Jay Watson, *Reading for the Body*, 21.
18. Certeau, *Practice of Everyday Life*, 145.
19. Stott, *Documentary Expression*, 209.
20. Robin D. G. Kelley, *Hammer and Hoe*, 57–78.
21. T. E. W. to Dr. John N. Taylor. Quoted in Woodward, *Tom Watson*, 405.
22. White, *Man Called White*, 49.
23. Marx and Engels, *Communist Manifesto*, 42.
24. Rowe, *New American Studies*, 138.
25. In his account of the Alabama Communist Party, Kelley notes the importance of another set of publications: *The Southern Worker*, *The Daily Worker*, and *Working Woman* (*Hammer and Hoe*, 46). *The Sharecroppers' Voice* was replaced by the monthly newsletter *STFU News* when it suspended publication in 1938.
26. Lepore, *These Truths*, 435.
27. Cohen, Coyle, and Lewty, Introduction, 2.
28. Loviglio, *Radio's Intimate Public*, 6.
29. "First Show," 1940.
30. Roosevelt's support for youth groups such as the American Youth Congress and the American Student Union during the 1930s created plenty of controversy, particularly as the AYC began criticizing the New Deal from the left in the mid-1930s. Roosevelt also played an important role in publicizing and defending the National Youth Administration, a branch of the WPA devoted to helping high school and college students find work during the Depression. The first lady's broadcast on "Youth and Youth Organizations" was an installment in *Mrs. Eleanor Roosevelt's Own Program*, which began its run in 1940 and thus postdates the vast majority of the letters in Cohen's anthology. See "Youth and Youth Organizations."
31. Avery, *Radio Modernism*, 38.
32. James A. Connor, "Radio Free Joyce," 20.
33. Roosevelt's widely syndicated newspaper column *My Day* was produced with similar intent. But on the evidence of *Dear Mrs. Roosevelt*, the radio shows seem to have found a broader audience.
34. Multiple entries also importune Roosevelt to help the writer's family secure a radio (183, 184).
35. Fraser, "Rethinking the Public Sphere," 67.
36. Warner, *Publics and Counterpublics*, 12.
37. Bakhtin, *Dialogic Imagination*, 84.
38. On use-value, see Marx, *Capital*, 48–54.
39. The quotas, a key feature of 1933's Agricultural Adjustment Act, cut surpluses and raised prices in order to bolster the agricultural industry at large. The result was a windfall for landowners, who simply scaled back production, effectively strand-

ing many of their sharecroppers and tenant farmers. Daniel calls this condition the "southern enclosure." See Daniel, *Breaking the Land*, 155–83.

40. Hilmes, *Radio Voices*, 133.
41. Peters, *Speaking into the Air*, 214.
42. Altieri, *Painterly Abstraction*, 14.
43. Steven Connor, "Violence," 80.
44. Certeau, *Practice of Everyday Life*, 31.
45. Scarry, *Resisting Representation*, 3.
46. Barthes, *Camera Lucida*, 4.
47. Ibid., 27.
48. Sekula, "Body and the Archive," 345. Italics in original.
49. Sontag, *On Photography*, 156.
50. North, *Camera Works*, 4.
51. McLuhan, *Understanding Media*, 189.
52. See Benjamin's celebrated discussion of aura in "Work of Art," 223–24.
53. Butler, *Notes*, 83.
54. Stott, *Documentary Expression*, 60.
55. Allred's discussion of *You Have Seen Their Faces* appears in *American Modernism*, 133–66.
56. Hegeman, *Patterns for America*, 179.
57. Agee and Evans, *Let Us Now Praise*, 10.
58. Ibid., 5.
59. Garner, "Grievous Angel," 94.
60. Hegeman, *Patterns for America*, 191.
61. A more straightforward and forthrightly political account of Agee's subject, the actual manuscript of the *Praise*-originating article commissioned by *Fortune*, was rediscovered and published in 2013 as *Cotton Tenants: Three Families*.
62. In a private letter from the 1980s, Boyle provided the following biography: "I was born in 1910 in Grand Forks, N.D. and moved to Ithaca in 1918. In '31, I graduated from Vassar College, and after some fruitless job hunting, studied photography at the New York Institute of Photography in N.Y. City. After practicing photography in Ithaca, I switched to editing at the Cornell University Press. I still try to find the relationship between words and images." Boyle, Private letter.
63. Boyle, "Looking Back," n.p.
64. The book project never reached completion: among Boyle's papers in the STFU files at Cornell's Kheel Center is a rejection letter and reader's report from Temple University Press, which faults the manuscript's organization but praises Boyle's photographs. Multiple drafts of contributions to the project by both Boyle ("Looking Back") and Robertson ("Visit to an Arkansas Sharecropper") are available in Cornell's Catherwood Library archives.
65. Payne's contributions include "Lady Was a Sharecropper" and an entry on Lawrence in *Notable American Women*. She also presented a talk entitled "Fighting Sharecropper as Icon" at the Organization of American Historians and National Council on Public History in 2006. My discussion of Lawrence is best understood as a response to Payne's pioneering work on the topics.

66. Robertson, "Visit to an Arkansas Sharecropper," 3.
67. Ibid., 3.
68. Boyle, "Looking Back," n.p.
69. Henninger, *Ordering the Façade*, 7.
70. Lawrence, letter from Myrtle Lawrence to Louise Boyle.
71. Payne, "Lady Was a Sharecropper," 23.
72. Payne, "Myrtle Terry Lawrence," 373.
73. Payne, "Lady Was a Sharecropper," 5. For the "adrift hayseed," see Caroline Meeber of Dreiser's *Sister Carrie* (1900). The "earth mother" is embodied in Cather's Alexandra Bergson of *O Pioneers!* (1913) and Ántonia Shimerda of *My Ántonia* (1918). Alternately, Thea Kronborg of *Song of the Lark* (1915) stands as a rural woman who finds her greatest success as an opera singer when she moves to Chicago. In a different register, look to Mammy Yokum from Al Capp's *Li'l Abner* comic strip (1934–77) for a prominent image of the "brash country wife." These examples are obviously not exhaustive.
74. Roach, *Cities of the Dead*, 3.
75. Bachelard, *Poetics of Space*, 6.
76. Edith Summers Kelley, *Weeds*, 246.
77. Entin, *Sensational Modernism*, 4.
78. Benjamin, "Little History," 512.
79. Sontag, *On Photography*, 17.
80. Sutton, *Photography, Cinema, Memory*, 157. Deleuze's discussion of the time image originates in *Cinema 2*.
81. Phelan, *Unmarked*, 3.
82. Žižek, *Violence*, 45.
83. Payne, "Fighting Sharecropper as Icon."
84. Grubbs, *Cry from the Cotton*, 128.
85. Quoted in Mark Allan Jackson, *Prophet Singer*, 216.
86. Hagood, *Mothers of the South*, 5.
87. Ibid., 3.
88. Ibid., 242.
89. Ibid., 3.
90. Lepore, "Historians," 133.
91. Benjamin, "Theses," 263.
92. Robertson, letter from Priscilla Robertson to Michael Ames, n.p.
93. For a direct comparison between land reform proposals by the STFU and the Agrarians, see Brown and Gilbert, "Alternative Land Reform," 351–69. A recent example of the Nashville Agrarians as an alternative foodways touchstone is in Vernon, "Problematic History," 337–52. Edge directly relates The Farm—an agricultural commune started by Stephen Gaskin in 1971 and based in Lewis County, Tennessee—to the principles of *I'll Take My Stand* in *Potlikker Papers*, 105–6.
94. Daniels, *Southerner Discovers the South*, 9–10. Daniels's book includes a visit to Nashville and a mixed review of the Agrarian movement that deeply unnerved Davidson; he called Daniels a "speed artist," among other things, in a 1939 response published in the *Southern Review*. See Davidson, "Class Approach," 132–46.
95. H. L. Mitchell, "The Other South," n.p.

Chapter 5. Station to Station

1. Huber has recently claimed, "Most of the earliest hillbilly recordings were made in New York City" (*Linthead Stomp*, 26). The city's centrality continued beyond the hillbilly era: the most vibrant template for the urban folk revival of the 1950s and 1960s, the six-volume *Anthology of American Folk Music* compiled by Harry Smith in a West Forty-Seventh Street apartment, circled like a talisman throughout Greenwich Village. See Pankake, "Brotherhood of the Anthology." Collector and producer Ian Nagoski's recent work, in compilations such as *To What Strange Place: The Music of the Ottoman-American Diaspora, 1916–1929* (Tompkins Square Records, 2011), complicates the picture: focusing on recordings made by Eastern European immigrants in New York City of the 1910s and 1920s, Nagoski's goal is to show how American folk music is a more varied, more meaningfully global affair than is generally recognized.

2. Dinerstein, *Swinging the Machine*, 18. *The Rise and Fall of Paramount Records*, vol. 2, a 2014 collaborative release by Revenant–Third Man Records, makes explicit connections between the Machine Age, industrial aesthetics, and race and hillbilly records. A compilation of blues, old-time, gospel, and hot jazz recordings made by the Paramount label in the late 1920s and early 1930s, it features an elaborate Art Deco design that suggests the extent to which an increasingly mechanized America made the dispersal of these "country" artifacts possible.

3. Comentale, *Sweet Air*, 7. Mancini deftly argues for the categorization of old-time recordings as examples of "anthological modernism," expressive objects bound up in early twentieth-century matrices of mechanical reproduction, technologies of representation, and mobility. See "'Messin' with the Furniture Man,'" 208–37.

4. The resonance with J. Dillon Brown's "migrant modernism" is unintentional—his study focuses specifically on postwar novels by West Indian writers in London—but I do share his interest in the use of modernist aesthetic techniques to examine experiences of dislocation.

5. The standard examination of migration narratives in literary studies remains Griffin's *"Who Set You Flowin'?"* Her expansive study includes perceptive readings of canonical writers (Ellison, Wright, Toomer) as well as nonliterary sources such as the hip-hop group Arrested Development and painter Jacob Lawrence's Migration Series. A less-celebrated but similarly valuable resource is Rodgers's *Canaan Bound*. Rodgers's analysis may not be as adventurous as Griffin's, but his readings of unheralded migration texts such as Attaway's *Blood on the Forge* (1941) and West's *Living Is Easy* (1948) are a major contribution.

6. Gaonkar, "On Alternative Modernities," 1–23.

7. Jameson, *Geopolitical Aesthetic*, 163.

8. Woolf, *Mrs. Dalloway*, 184.

9. Faulkner, *Light in August*, 213.

10. Hurston, *Mules and Men*, 183.

11. Briggs, *New Negro*.

12. Huber, *Linthead Stomp*, 131.

13. Middleton, *Voicing the Popular*, 51. For more on nostalgia as a symptom of modernity and modernism, see *Modernism and Nostalgia*, ed. Clewell.

14. Huber covers the mass production of the banjo in Poole's world in *Linthead Stomp*, 113.

15. Dubois, *Banjo*, 212.

16. See Rorrer's liner notes to *Charlie Poole with the Highlanders*. In another turn toward the city, it's no stretch to imagine that Poole—a baseball aficionado whose distinctive three-finger banjo style evolved from an injury sustained in a barehand-fastball accident—named his group after the New York Highlanders, predecessors of the modern-day Yankees. The identification with Scots-Irish traditions in the Piedmont region is another possibility.

17. Mendelson and Prochaska, *Postcards*, xii.

18. I'm indebted to Gerard for this concept: *Jazz in Black and White*, 102–3. My thanks to Adam Gussow for pointing it out.

19. Pratt, "Arts of the Contact Zone," 34.

20. Griffin, *"Who Set You Flowin'?"* 48–99.

21. Arnesen, Introduction, *Black Protest*, 1.

22. See Lemann, *Promised Land*, 6. A more recent addition is Wilkerson's acclaimed *Warmth of Other Suns*. Like Lemann, Wilkerson relies more heavily on personal interviews than existing scholarship, and the sweep of her analysis is vast, taking in the multiple stages and geographic loci of the Great Migration from the 1910s into the 1970s. Hahn's *Nation under Our Feet* provides an even more comprehensive view, tracking the political consequences of black mobilities from the antebellum period to the middle of the twentieth century. Contemporaneous studies of the Great Migration include Scott, *Negro Migration*; Woodson, *Century of Negro Migration*; Nearing, *Black America*.

23. The first two chapters of Griffin's study begin with analyses of Lawrence's work (13–15, 48–49). From April to September 2015, the Museum of Modern Art featured a highly regarded exhibit (*One-Way Ticket: Jacob Lawrence's Migration Series*) that displayed all sixty panels alongside other important artifacts from the period.

24. J. W. Johnson, *Black Manhattan*, 152–53. In *Omni-Americans*, Murray sees the issue in an altogether different light: "[S]omeday students of machine-age culture in the United States may find that Negro slaves in the cotton field had already begun confronting and evolving esthetic solutions for the problems of assembly line regimentation, depersonalization, and collectivization" (63). In Murray's view, the labor conditions of the rural South and the legacies of slavery created subjects uniquely prepared to confront the challenges of industrial modernity with grace and with a distinctive sense of style.

25. Richardson, *Black Masculinity*, 15.

26. Locke, "Enter the New Negro," 631.

27. Locke, "Harlem," 630.

28. Variations on this reading are part of larger arguments posted by both Duck, *Nation's Region*, 118; and Parrish, *Flood Year 1927*, 7.

29. Charles S. Johnson, "New Frontage," 295.

30. See Storey, *Rural Fictions, Urban Realities*.

31. Mehroff uses the phrase "phenomenology of place" as the title of an article about the "human intentionality" of landmark architecture. Our subjects don't over-

lap much, but I do agree with his contention that "understanding of place as a total phenomenon necessarily encompasses the highly subjective dimensions of human cognition." I take this as another way of stating an important, if obvious, fact: human sensory response to a place plays a determining role in our experience of that place. See Mehroff, "Phenomenology of Place," 9–14. Tuan's *Space and Place* is a fine-grained examination of the ways in which human subjects orient themselves, both physically and psychically, using the senses and their relationship to emotion and thought.

32. Baptist, *Half Has Never Been Told*, 322.
33. Ibid., xviii–xx.
34. Glaeser, "Urban Colossus," 12–13.
35. Ibid., 12–13.
36. Singer's *New York and Slavery* is designed to correct incomplete state history curricula, and, despite its less-than-formal tone, it contains well-documented, essential information, such as the Moses Taylor connection mentioned above (31).
37. Ibid., 12. See also Philip Foner, *Business and Slavery*.
38. Burrows and Wallace, *Gotham*, 336.
39. Beckert, *Monied Metropolis*, 87.
40. Ibid., 87.
41. Beckert, *Empire of Cotton*, 222.
42. Burrows and Wallace, *Gotham*, 336. See also Walter Johnson, *River of Dark Dreams*, 280–302; "To Remake the World," 11, 13–31, 143.
43. Hobsbawm, *Industry and Empire*, 34.
44. Benjamin, *Arcades Project*, 3, 546.
45. See Fohlen, *L'industrie textile*, 284, 514. Acknowledgments to Beckert's *Empire of Cotton* for uncovering this source (243).
46. Ibid., 831.
47. Benjamin, "Theses," 261.
48. Kettell, *Southern Wealth*, 10.
49. Benjamin, "Theses," 256.
50. Ibid., 255.
51. White, "Paradox of Color," 363.
52. Ibid., 364. Although the exact number of white southern migrants in New York City during the period is difficult to gauge, Gregory notes a revealing cultural marker—membership in the Daughters of the Confederacy. According to data compiled at the 1932 *Annual Convention of the Daughters of the Confederacy Incorporated*, New York had the third most members of any nonsouthern state, surpassed only by Missouri and California. Gregory, *Southern Diaspora*, 158. See United Daughters, *Minutes*, 333, 312.
53. Johnson's *Autobiography of an Ex-Colored Man*, published anonymously in 1912 and then under the author's name in 1927, also prefigures this chapter's migration narratives as its geographic frame veers from the rural South to turn-of-the-century New York.
54. Stuart Hall, *Race*.
55. The biblical resonance of these stories is difficult to miss: "City of Refuge" alludes to the six cities in the Kingdoms of Judah and Israel that extended asylum to people—

like King Solomon Gillis—who had committed manslaughter. Of course, Gillis may not face legal recourse for killing a southern policeman, but he's saddled with a whole other set of problems in the urban North. And the Promised Land offered as a home to Israel in exile becomes a narrow space of confinement, unrest, and violence for African American exiles in Fisher's "The Promised Land."

56. Sante, *Low Life*, 40.
57. Quoted in Boyer, "The Hot Bach—II," 34.
58. According to Tuan, the whole concern of phenomenology is this very idea of "essences." See Tuan, "Geography," 181–92.
59. Yaeger, *Dirt and Desire*, 63.
60. Tschumpeter coined the phrase "creative destruction" as an extrapolation of Marx's attention to capitalism's tendency to manufacture obsolescence as it creates new markets. It is the guiding trope in *Capitalism, Socialism, and Democracy*. A variety of thinkers have since adapted Tschumpeter's model. For Harvey and Berman, this account of economic history offers an important optic for viewing twentieth-century capitalism's uneven development and its economic casualties. See Harvey, *Condition of Postmodernity*, 16–18; Berman, *All That Is Solid*, 98–104.
61. Rushdie, *Satanic Verses*, 8.
62. Morrison, "Rootedness," 62.
63. Griffin, *"Who Set You Flowin'?"* 5.
64. Rodgers, *Canaan Bound*, 25–31.
65. Hubbs, "William Faulkner's Rural Modernism," 464.
66. Carpio and Sollors, "Newly Complicated."
67. Reed and Warren, Introduction, viii. For instance, Carby's seminal *Reconstructing Womanhood* frequently makes "folk" synonymous with rural. See especially her discussion of Hurston and Nella Larsen (163–76).
68. Michaels, *Our America*, 16. Italics in original.
69. Lott, "Double-V, Double-Time," 245.
70. Gates, *Signifying Monkey*, 191–92.
71. Labov, *Language*, 8.
72. Cash, *Mind of the South*, 49–50.
73. Spivak, translator's preface, liv.
74. Duck, *Nation's Region*, 117.
75. Ibid., 117–18.
76. North, *Dialect of Modernism*, 185.
77. Carby, "Politics of Fiction," 30.
78. Baldwin, *Go Tell*, 192.
79. Baldwin, *Fire Next Time*, 54.
80. Certeau, *Heterologies*, 4.
81. Du Bois, *Darkwater*, 2.
82. I'm indebted to Jacquelyn Dowd Hall for the term "the long civil rights movement." See "Long Civil Rights Movement."
83. Harvey, *Urban Experience*, 117.
84. Gregory, *Southern Diaspora*, 15.
85. Kirby, "Southern Exodus," 600. When considering the sweep of the entire twen-

tieth century, the proportions are even more lopsided: "close to 8 million black southerners, nearly 20 million white southerners, and more than 1 million southern-born Latino southerners participated in the diaspora." Gregory, *Southern Diaspora*, 16. Berry's *Southern Migrant, Northern Exile* offers a rich exploration of white migrations that occur between the Appalachian regions of the South and the Midwestern industrial centers.

86. Gregory, *Southern Diaspora*, 5.

87. Ibid., 17. Gregory has also produced a probing examination of the spread of southern/southwestern culture through the dustbowl migration of the 1930s. See *American Exodus*.

88. Other examples of white characters that move from the hinterlands to New York City include lapsed minister Theron Ware's desperate lunge at the city in the dénouement of Harold Frederic's *Damnation of Theron Ware*. More to the point perhaps is Basil Ransom, from Henry James's *Bostonians*, a native Mississippian who moves to New York City to practice law and ends up competing with his cousin for the attentions of a talented young reformer in Boston's women's rights movement. Decades later, Edward Anderson's *Hungry Men* provides an exemplary fiction of Great Depression dislocation in the story of Acel Stecker, an unemployed musician "on the bum" who wanders the country with prominent stops in both New York and the rural South.

89. Proust, *Remembrance*, 51.

90. It's important to note how frequently Washington, D.C., has figured in this discussion: as a landmark in Charlie Poole's tourist fantasy, as the birthplace of both Fisher and Duke Ellington, as the market for Dorinda's agricultural outputs. One reason might be the space's liminality. Geographically, it is suspended between the South and the North and partakes of both identities, often at once: the city is a bastion of American freedoms and federal power, but it was also populated by slaves in the antebellum period and segregated by Woodrow Wilson in the 1910s. As a metaphor for the vagaries of the U.S. political processes, it simultaneously fulfills and fails its own ideals.

91. Conlogue, *Working the Garden*, 83. For Weaks-Baxter, Dorinda most fully inhabits the yeoman ideal, albeit a model of yeomanry headed by a woman and that "carries the mark of outside influence." *Reclaiming the American Farmer*, 21. David Davis makes a connection between advancements in Great War technology and Dorinda's agricultural innovations in World War I, 158–62.

92. The echo of former Secretary of Agriculture Earl Butz's famous admonition that postwar farmers "get big or get out" is intentional.

93. Simmel, "Metropolis and Mental Life." See also Kracauer, *Mass Ornament*.

94. Benjamin, "Motifs in Baudelaire," in *Illuminations*, 165.

95. Deleuze, *Difference and Repetition*, 69.

96. Benjamin, "Central Park," 42.

97. Blackmar and Rosenzweig, *Park and the People*, 10. The brightest flashpoint in this debate centered on the reclamation effort tied to the draining of the Lower Reservoir, which lasted through the early decades of the twentieth century. The reservoir was finally drained to make way for the Great Lawn in 1930; it briefly served as a makeshift Hooverville during the Depression.

98. Postel, *Populist Vision*, 282.
99. Raymond Williams, *Country and the City*, 9–12.
100. See Foucault, *Birth of the Clinic*.
101. Harvey, *Urban Experience*, 17–58.
102. See Deleuze and Guattari, *A Thousand Plateaus*, 474–500.
103. Bill Brown, *Material Unconscious*, 4–5. For more on the archaeology of objects in American literature, see Brown's *Sense of Things*, which includes an innovative reading of "Regional Artifacts" in the New England fiction of Sarah Orne Jewett (81–135).
104. Butler, *Psychic Life of Power*, 133.
105. Schuyler, *Black No More*, 11.
106. See hooks, *Belonging*; Stack, *Call to Home*.
107. Romine, *Real South*, 1–17.
108. Eliot, *Knowledge and Experience*, 148.

Coda. Uneven Ground

1. Garner, "Lost in Literary History," C1.
2. Giesen, "Creating 'Nate Shaw,'" 163. See also Cantwell, "Christmas, 1932," 663–68.
3. By the time he tells his tale, though, Shaw recognizes that a shared set of material conditions ties together both black and white laborers: "The poor white man and the poor black man is sittin in the same saddle today—big dudes done branched em off that way" (489).
4. Flately, *Affective Mapping*, 32.
5. Giddens, *Consequences of Modernity*, 39.
6. Benjamin, "One-Way Street," 75–76.
7. Aguiar, "Making Modernity," 73.
8. Appiah, *Cosmopolitan*, 111.
9. Nixon, *Slow Violence*, 17.
10. Faulkner, *Go Down, Moses*, 113.
11. Gaonkar, "On Alternative Modernities," 18.
12. Marx and Engels, *Communist Manifesto*, 57–58.
13. Ibid., 36. Deleuze and Guattari's discussion of smooth versus striated space is contained in *A Thousand Plateaus*, 474–500.
14. Benjamin, "On Some Motifs," in *Illuminations*, 184.
15. Rorty, *Achieving Our Country*, 90. As the antiglobalist grievances of Trumpism ballooned throughout the country, the condition of the white, rural working class in the Midwest and the South became a subject of serious inspection. J. D. Vance's *Hillbilly Elegy* (2016), an account of the author's move from Appalachian environments of drug abuse and domestic dysfunction to the corridors of Yale Law School, became an unanticipated best seller. Whereas mechanization dispossessed large segments of the agricultural working class around the turn of the last century, and where many—especially many whites—responded by participating in anti-institutional populist movements, populist anger in the age of Donald Trump is sparked by similarly irreversible transformations: globalization, automation, the demographic inevitability of a white minority.

16. Beckert, *Empire of Cotton*, 431.
17. Wilkerson, "When Will the North Face Its Racism?" SR6.
18. Wilkerson, "Emmett Till and Tamir Rice," SR4.
19. Coates, "Case for Reparations," 54–71.
20. Raymond Williams, *Politics of Modernism*, 35.
21. Ibid., 35.

WORKS CITED

Aboul-Ela, Hosam. *Other South: Faulkner, Coloniality, and the Mariátegui Tradition.* Pittsburgh: University of Pittsburgh Press, 2007.

Adorno, Theodor W. "Free Time." 1977. In *The Culture Industry: Selected Essays on Mass Culture*, ed. J. M. Bernstein, 187–97. New York: Routledge, 2001.

Adorno, Theodor W., and Max Horkheimer. *Dialectic of Enlightenment*, ed. Gunzelin Schmidt Noerr, trans. Edmund Jephcott. 1944. Stanford, Calif.: Stanford University Press, 2002.

Agee, James. *Cotton Tenants: Three Families*, ed. John Summers. Brooklyn: Melville House, 2013.

Agee, James, and Walker Evans. *Let Us Now Praise Famous Men.* 1941. New York: Mariner Books, 2001.

Aguiar, Marian. "Making Modernity: Inside the Technological Space of the Railway." *Cultural Critique* 68 (2008): 66–85.

Albion, Robert. *The Rise of New York Port, 1815–1860.* Hamden, Conn.: Archon Books, 1961.

Ali, Omar. *In the Lion's Mouth: Black Populism in the New South, 1886–1900.* Jackson: University Press of Mississippi, 2010.

Allewaert, Monique. "Swamp Sublime: Ecologies of Resistance in the American Plantation Zone." *PMLA* 123, no. 2 (2008): 340–57.

Allred, Jeff. *American Modernism and Depression Documentary.* New York: Oxford University Press, 2012.

Altieri, Charles. *Painterly Abstraction in Modernist American Poetry: The Contemporaneity of Modernism.* New York: Cambridge University Press, 1989.

Ammons, Elizabeth. *Conflicting Stories: American Women Writers at the Turn of the Twentieth Century.* New York: Oxford University Press, 1991.

Anderson, Edward. *Hungry Men.* 1935. Norman: University of Oklahoma Press, 1993.

Anderson, Perry. "Modernity and Revolution." In *Marxism and the Interpretation of Culture*, ed. Cary Nelson and Lawrence Grossberg, 317–33. Urbana: University of Illinois Press, 1988.

Appiah, Kwame Anthony. *Cosmopolitan: Ethics in a World of Strangers.* New York: W. W. Norton, 2006.

Aptheker, Herbert. Introduction. In *Quest of the Silver Fleece*, viii–ix. Mineola, N.Y.: Dover, 1974.

Arnesen, Eric. Introduction. In *Black Protest and the Great Migration: A Brief History with Documents*, 1–43. New York: Bedford/St. Martin's, 2003.

Attaway, William. *Blood on the Forge.* 1941. New York: New York Review Classics, 2005.

Austin, Mary. "American Folk." In *Folk Say: A Regional Miscellany*, ed. Benjamin A. Botkin, 287–90. Norman: University of Oklahoma Press, 1930.

Avery, Todd. *Radio Modernism: Literature, Ethics, and the BBC, 1922–1938*. Burlington, Vt.: Ashgate, 2006.

Ayers, Edward. *The Promise of the New South: Life after Reconstruction*. New York: Oxford University Press, 1993.

Bachelard, Gaston. *The Poetics of Space*, trans. Maria Jolas. 1958. Boston: Beacon Press, 1969.

Baker, Houston A., Jr. *Modernism and the Harlem Renaissance*. Chicago: University of Chicago Press, 1989.

———. *Turning South Again: Re-Thinking Modernism, Re-Reading Booker T*. Durham, N.C.: Duke University Press, 2001.

———. *Workings of the Spirit: The Poetics of Afro-American Women's Writing*. Chicago: University of Chicago Press, 1993.

Bakhtin, Mikhail. *The Dialogic Imagination: Four Essays*, ed. Michael Holquist. Austin: University of Texas Press, 1981.

Baldwin, James. *The Fire Next Time*. 1963. New York: Vintage International, 1991.

———. *Go Tell It on the Mountain*. 1953. New York: Vintage International, 2013.

Banta, Martha. *Taylored Lives: Narrative Productions in the Age of Taylor, Veblen, and Ford*. Chicago: University of Chicago Press, 1993.

Baptist, Edward. *The Half Has Never Been Told: Slavery and the Making of American Capitalism*. New York: Basic Books, 2014.

Barthes, Roland. *Camera Lucida: Reflections on Photography*, trans. Richard Howard. 1980. New York: Hill and Wang, 2010.

Baucom, Ian. "Township Modernism." In *Geomodernisms: Race, Modernism, Modernity*, ed. Laura Doyle and Laura Winkiel, 227–44. Bloomington: Indiana University Press, 2006.

Beckert, Sven. *The Empire of Cotton: A Global History*. New York: Knopf, 2014.

———. *The Monied Metropolis: New York City and the Consolidation of the American Bourgeoisie, 1856–1890*. New York: Cambridge University Press, 2001.

Belifuss, Michael. "Ironic Landscapes and Beautiful Swamps: W. E. B. Du Bois and the Troubled Landscapes of the American South." *ISLE* 22, no. 3 (Summer 2015): 485–506.

Benjamin, Walter. *The Arcades Project*, trans. Howard Eiland and Kevin McLaughlin. Cambridge, Mass.: Belknap Press, 1999.

———. "Central Park." *New German Critique* 34 (1985): 32–58.

———. "A Little History of Photography." 1931. In *Selected Writings*, ed. Michael W. Jennings, Howard Eiland, and Gary Smith, trans. Rodney Livingstone et al., 2:507–30. Cambridge, Mass.: Belknap Press, 1999.

———. "One-Way Street (selection)." 1955. In *Reflections: Essays, Aphorisms, Autobiographical Writings*, trans. Edmund Jephcott, 61–94. New York: Schocken Books, 1978.

———. "Theses on the Philosophy of History." 1942. In *Illuminations: Essays and Reflections*, trans. Harry Zohn, 253–64. New York: Schocken Books, 1968.

Bennett, Michael. "Anti-Pastoralism, Frederick Douglass, and the Nature of Slavery." In *Beyond Nature Writing: Expanding the Boundaries of Ecocriticism*, ed. Karla Armbruster and Kathleen R. Wallace, 195–210. Charlottesville: University Press of Virginia, 2001.

Bergson, Henri. *Time and Free Will* (selections). In *Key Writings*, ed. Keith Ansell Pearson and John Mullarkey, 59–94. New York: Bloomsbury Academic, 2002.

Berlant, Lauren. "National Brands/National Bodies: *Imitation of Life*." In *The Phantom Public Sphere*, ed. Bruce Robbins, 173–208. Minneapolis: University of Minnesota Press, 1993.

———. "The Queen of America Goes to Washington City: Harriet Jacobs, Frances Harper, Anita Hill." *American Literature* 65, no. 3 (Sept. 1993): 549–74.

Berman, Jessica. *Modernist Commitments: Ethics, Politics, and Transnational Modernism*. New York: Columbia University Press, 2011.

Berman, Marshall. *All That Is Solid Melts into Air: The Experience of Modernity*. New York: Verso, 1982.

Berry, Chad. *Southern Migrant, Northern Exile*. Champaign: University of Illinois Press, 2000.

Berry, Wendell. *A Continuous Harmony: Essays Cultural and Agricultural*. New York: Harcourt, Brace, 1972.

———. *The Unsettling of America: Culture and Agriculture*. San Francisco: Sierra Club Books, 1977.

Berwick, Edward. "Farming in the Year 2000 A.D." *Overland Monthly* 15, no. 90 (1890): 569–73.

Bingham, Emily, and Thomas Underwood. Introduction. In *The Southern Agrarians and the New Deal: Essays After I'll Take My Stand*, 1–34. Charlottesville: University of Virginia Press, 2001.

Bisset, Jim. *Agrarian Socialism in America: Marx, Jefferson, and Jesus in the Oklahoma Countryside, 1904–1920*. Norman: University of Oklahoma Press, 1999.

Blackmar, Elizabeth, and Roy Rosenzweig. *The Park and the People: A History of Central Park*. Ithaca, N.Y.: Cornell University Press, 1992.

Blackmon, Douglas. *Slavery by Another Name: The Re-Enslavement of Black Americans from the Civil War until World War II*. New York: Anchor, 2008.

Blight, David W. *Race and Reunion: The Civil War in American Memory*. Cambridge, Mass.: Belknap Press, 2001.

Bloch, Ernst. *The Principle of Hope*, trans. Neville Plaice, Stephen Plaice, and Paul Knight. Vol. 1. 1954. Cambridge, Mass.: MIT Press, 1995.

Bluemel, Kristin, and Michael McCluskey. *Rural Modernity in Britain: A Critical Intervention*. Edinburgh: Edinburgh University Press, 2018.

Bone, Martyn. *The Postsouthern Sense of Place in Contemporary Fiction*. Baton Rouge: Louisiana State University Press, 2005.

Boyer, Richard O. "The Hot Bach—II." *New Yorker*, July 1, 1944.

Boyle, Louise. "Looking Back." Collection no. 5859, Box 1, Folder 26. Southern Tenant Farmers' Union Research Files, Kheel Center for Labor-Management Documentation & Research, Cornell University.

———. Private letter. Collection no. 5859, Box 1, Folder 1. Southern Tenant Farmers' Union Research Files, Kheel Center for Labor-Management Documentation & Research, Cornell University.

Braidotti, Rosi. *Nomadic Subjects: Embodiment and Sexual Difference in Contemporary Feminist Theory*. New York: Columbia University Press, 1994.

———. *The Posthuman*. Malden, Mass.: Polity Press, 2013.

Breselor, Sara. "The Pigford Case: Justice for Black Farmers on Hold." *Salon*, April 8, 2010, www.salon.com/2010/04/08/john_boyd_pigford_glickman_settlement.

Briggs, Gabriel. *The New Negro in the Old South*. New Brunswick, N.J.: Rutgers University Press, 2015.

Brinkmeyer, Robert. *The Fourth Ghost: White Southern Writers and European Fascism, 1930–1950*. Baton Rouge: Louisiana State University Press, 2009.

Brodwin, Stanley. "The Veil Transcended: Form and Meaning in W. E. B. Du Bois' *The Souls of Black Folk*." *Journal of Black Studies* 2, no. 3 (1972): 303–21.

Brooker, Peter, and Andrew Thacker, eds. *Geographies of Modernism*. New York: Routledge, 2005.

Brown, Bill. *The Material Unconscious: American Amusement, Stephen Crane, and the Economics of Play*. Cambridge, Mass.: Harvard University Press, 1996.

———. *A Sense of Things: The Object Matter of American Literature*. Chicago: University of Chicago Press, 2003.

Brown, J. Dillon. *Migrant Modernism: Postwar London and the West Indian Novel*. Charlottesville: University of Virginia Press, 2013.

Brown, Steve, and Jess Gilbert. "Alternative Land Reform Proposals in the 1930s: The Nashville Agrarians and the Southern Tenant Farmers' Union." *Agricultural History* 55 (1981): 351–69.

Bruyn, Frans de. "From Georgic Poetry to Statistics and Graphs: Eighteenth-Century Representations and the 'State' of British Society." *Yale Journal of Criticism* 17, no. 1 (Spring 2004): 107–39.

Buell, Lawrence. *The Environmental Imagination: Thoreau, Nature Writing, and the Formation of American Culture*. Cambridge, Mass.: Belknap Press, 1996.

Burrows, Edwin, and Mike Wallace. *Gotham: A History of New York City to 1898*. New York: Oxford University Press, 1999.

Butler, Judith. *Notes toward a Performative Theory of Assembly*. Cambridge, Mass.: Harvard University Press, 2015.

———. *The Psychic Life of Power: Theories in Subjection*. Stanford, Calif.: Stanford University Press, 1997.

Byerman, Keith. "Race and Romance: *The Quest of the Silver Fleece* as Utopian Narrative." *American Literary Realism* 24, no. 2 (1992): 58–71.

Campbell, Jane. *Mythic Black Fiction: The Transformation of History*. Knoxville: University of Tennessee Press, 1986.

Campbell, John Charles. *The Southern Highlander and His Homeland*. New York: Russell Sage Foundation, 1921.

Cannon, Gus. "Can You Blame the Colored Man?" Paramount Records 12571, 1927.

Cantwell, Robert. "Christmas, 1932." In *A New Literary History of America*, ed. Greil Marcus and Werner Sollors, 663–68. Cambridge, Mass.: Belknap Press, 2009.

Carby, Hazel. "The Politics of Fiction, Anthropology, and the Folk: Zora Neale Hurston." In *History and Memory in African-American Culture*, ed. Genevieve Fabre and Robert O'Meally, 28–44. New York: Oxford University Press, 1994.

———. *Reconstructing Womanhood: The Emergence of the Afro-American Woman Novelist*. New York: Oxford University Press, 1987.

Carpio, Glenda, and Werner Sollors. "The Newly Complicated Zora Neale Hurston." *Chronicle of Higher Education,* January 2, 2011, www.chronicle.com/article/The-Newly-Complicated-Zora/125753.

Carr, Elston L., Jr. "Minstrelsy and the Dialect Poetry of Paul Laurence Dunbar." In *We Wear the Mask: Paul Laurence Dunbar and the Politics of Representative Reality,* ed. Willie J. Harrell Jr., 49–58. Kent, Ohio: Kent State University Press, 2010.

Cartwright, Keith. *Sacral Grooves, Limbo Gateways: Travels in Deep Southern Time, Circum-Caribbean Space, Afro-creole Authority.* Athens: University of Georgia Press, 2013.

Casey, Janet. *A New Heartland: Women, Modernity, and the Rural Ideal in America.* New York: Oxford University Press, 2009.

Cash, W. J. *The Mind of the South.* 1941. New York: Vintage International, 1991.

Castronovo, Russ. *Necro Citizenship: Death, Eroticism, and the Public Sphere in the Nineteenth-Century United States.* Durham, N.C.: Duke University Press, 2001.

Certeau, Michel de. *Heterologies: Discourse on the Other,* trans. Brian Massumi. 1986. Minneapolis: University of Minnesota Press, 1997.

———. *The Practice of Everyday Life,* trans. Steven F. Rendall. 1980. Berkeley: University of California Press, 2011.

Chakrabarty, Dipesh. *Provincializing Europe: Postcolonial Thought and Historical Difference.* Princeton, N.J.: Princeton University Press, 2000.

Chesnutt, Charles W. *Chesnutt: Stories, Novels, and Essays,* ed. Werner Sollors. New York: Library of America, 2002.

Child, Benjamin. "Astonishing Byblows: Rurality, Snopesism, and Populist Modernization in Faulkner's Frenchman's Bend." *Modern Fiction Studies* 62, no. 2 (2018): 286–310.

———. "The Magical Real and the Rural Modern in Cinema Novo: *Vidas Secas* and *Black God, White Devil.*" *South Central Review* 31, no. 1 (2014): 55–73.

Ching, Barbara, and Gerald Creed. "Recognizing Rusticity: Identity and the Power of Place." In *Knowing Your Place: Rural Identity and Cultural Hierarchy,* ed. Ching and Creed, 1–38. New York: Routledge, 1997.

Chu, Patricia. *Race, Nationalism, and the State in British and American Modernism.* New York: Cambridge University Press, 2006.

Cimbala, Paul. *Under the Guardianship of the Nation: The Freedmen's Bureau and the Reconstruction of Georgia, 1865–1870.* Athens: University of Georgia Press, 2003.

Cloud, N. B. *American Cotton Planter* 1 (1853).

Clukey, Amy. "Plantation Modernity: *Gone with the Wind* and Irish-Southern Culture." *American Literature* 85, no. 3 (2013): 505–30.

Coates, Ta-Nehisi. "The Case for Reparations." *Atlantic,* June 2014.

———. *We Were Eight Years in Power: An American Tragedy.* New York: One World, 2017.

Cobb, James. *Away Down South: A History of Southern Identity.* New York: Oxford University Press, 2007.

———. *Industrialization and the Southern Society, 1877–1984.* Lexington: University of Kentucky Press, 2004.

———. *The Most Southern Place on Earth: The Mississippi Delta and the Roots of Regional Identity.* New York: Oxford University Press, 1992.

Coclanis, Peter. "The Wizard of Tuskegee in Economic Context." In *Booker T. Washington and Black Progress: Up from Slavery 100 Years Later*, ed. W. Fitzhugh Brundage, 81–106. Gainesville: University Press of Florida, 2003.

Cohen, Debra Rae, Michael Coyle, and Jane Lewty. Introduction. In *Broadcasting Modernism*, 1–7. Gainesville: University Press of Florida, 2009.

Cohen, Jeffery Jerome, and Lowell Duckert, eds. *Elemental Ecocriticism: Thinking with Earth, Air, Water, and Fire*. Minneapolis: University of Minnesota Press, 2015.

Cohn, Deborah, and Jon Smith. "Introduction: Uncanny Hybridities." *Look Away! The U.S. South in New World Studies*, 1–24. Durham, N.C.: Duke University Press, 2004.

Comentale, Edward. *Sweet Air: Modernism, Regionalism, and American Popular Song*. Champaign: University of Illinois Press, 2013.

Conkin, Paul. *The Southern Agrarians*. Knoxville: University of Tennessee Press, 1988.

Conlogue, William. *Working the Garden: American Writers and the Industrialization of Agriculture*. Chapel Hill: University of North Carolina Press, 1992.

Connor, James A. "Radio Free Joyce: *Wake* Language and the Experience of Radio." In *Sound States: Innovative Poetics and Acoustical Technologies*, ed. Adalaide Morris, 17–51. Chapel Hill: University of North Carolina Press, 1997.

Connor, Steven. "Violence, Ventriloquism, and the Vocalic Body." In *Psychoanalysis and Performance*, ed. Patrick Campbell and Adrian Kear, 75–93. New York: Routledge, 2001.

Cooper, Anna Julia. *A Voice from the South*. 1892. New York: Oxford University Press, 1988.

Cowley, Malcolm. "The Grammar of Facts." *New Republic* 109, no. 4 (1943): 113–14.

Crèvecoeur, J. Hector St. John de. *Letters from an American Farmer*. 1782. New York: Penguin Classics, 1986.

Cronon, William. *Nature's Metropolis: Chicago and the Great West*. New York: W. W. Norton, 1991.

Cruse, Harold. *The Crisis of the Negro Intellectual: A Historical Analysis of the Failure of Black Leadership*. 1967. New York: Quill, 1984.

Daniel, Pete. *Breaking the Land: The Transformation of Cotton, Tobacco, and Rice Cultures since 1880*. Champaign: University of Illinois Press, 1986.

———. *Standing at the Crossroads: Southern Life in the Twentieth Century*. Baltimore, Md.: Johns Hopkins University Press, 1996.

Daniels, Jonathan. *A Southerner Discovers the South*. New York: MacMillan, 1938.

Davidson, Donald. "Allen Tate: The Traditionalist as Modern." Box 25, Folder 20. Donald Grady Davidson Papers, Special Collections, Jean and Alexander Heard Library, Vanderbilt University.

———. "The Class Approach to Southern Problems." 1939. In *The Southern Agrarians and the New Deal*, ed. Emily S. Bingham and Thomas A. Underwood, 132–46. Charlottesville: University Press of Virginia, 2001.

———. "A Study of the Race Problem." *Nashville Banner*, September 7, 1945. Box 26, Folder 37. Donald Grady Davidson Papers, Special Collections, Jean and Alexander Heard Library, Vanderbilt University.

Davis, David A. "Southern Modernists and Modernity." In *The Cambridge Companion to the Literature of the American South*, ed. Sharon Monteith, 88–103. New York: Cambridge University Press, 2013.

———. *World War I and Southern Modernism*. Jackson: University Press of Mississippi, 2017.
Deans, Gary, dir. *Toni Morrison Uncensored*. Princeton, N.J.: Films for the Humanities and Social Sciences, 1998.
Dear Mrs. Roosevelt: Letters from Children of the Great Depression, ed. Robert Cohen. Chapel Hill: University of North Carolina Press, 2002.
Delany, Martin. *Blake, or the Huts of America*. 1859–61. New York: Beacon, 1971.
———. *The Condition, Elevation, Emigration, and Destiny of the Colored People of the United States, Politically Considered*. 1852. Amherst, N.Y.: Humanity Books, 2004.
Deleuze, Gilles. *Cinema 2: The Time-Image*, trans. Hugh Tomlinson and Robert Galeta. 1985. Minneapolis: University of Minnesota Press, 1989.
———. *Difference and Repetition*, trans. Paul Patton. New York: Columbia University Press, 1994.
Deleuze, Gilles, and Guattari, Félix. *A Thousand Plateaus: Capitalism and Schizophrenia*, trans. Brian Massumi. 1980. Minneapolis: University of Minnesota Press, 1987.
Denning, Michael. *The Cultural Front: The Laboring of American Culture in the Twentieth Century*. New York: Verso, 1997.
———. *Noise Uprising: The Audiopolitics of a World Musical Revolution*. New York: Verso Books, 2015.
Dinerstein, Joel. *Swinging the Machine: Modernity, Technology, and Culture between the World Wars*. Amherst, Mass.: University of Massachusetts Press, 2003.
The Disinherited Speak: Letters from Sharecroppers. New York: Workers' Defense League, 1936.
Dollard, John. *Caste and Class in a Southern Town*. 1937. Madison: University of Wisconsin Press, 1987.
Donahue, Brian, Sara M. Gregg, and Edwin C. Hagenstein, eds. *American Georgics: Writings on Farming, Culture, and Land*. New Haven, Conn.: Yale University Press, 2011.
Dore, Florence. "The Modernism of Southern Literature." In *A Concise Companion to American Fiction, 1900–1950*, ed. Peter Stoneley and Cindy Weinstein, 228–52. New York: Blackwell, 2005.
Dorman, Richard. "Revolt of the Provinces: The Regionalist Movement in America, 1920–1945." In *The New Regionalism*, ed. Charles Reagan Wilson, 1–18. Jackson: University Press of Mississippi, 1998.
Dorson, Richard. "A Theory for American Folklore." *Journal of American Folklore* 72, no. 285 (1959): 197–215.
Douglass, Frederick. *A Narrative of the Life of Frederick Douglass, an American Slave*. 1845. New York: Penguin Classics, 2013.
Doyle, Laura, and Laura Winkiel, eds. *Geomodernisms: Race, Modernism, Modernity*. Bloomington: Indiana University Press, 2005.
Du Bois, W. E. B. *Black Reconstruction in America*. 1935. New York: Free Press, 1998.
———. "The Criteria of Negro Art." 1926. In *African American Literary Criticism, 1773–2000*, ed. Hazel Arnett Ervin, 39–43. New York: Twayne, 1999.
———. *Darkwater: Voices from Within the Veil*. 1920. New York: Washington Square Press, 2004.

———. Du Bois to Liberty Hyde Bailey, November 23, 1908. Liberty Hyde Papers, Cornell University Library. http://rmc.library.cornell.edu/bailey/commission/commission_3.html.

———. *Dusk of Dawn: An Essay toward an Autobiography of a Race Concept*. 1940. New York: Oxford University Press, 2007.

———. "The Negro in the Black Belt: Some Social Sketches." U.S. Bureau of the Census, *Bulletin* 4 (May 1899): 401–17.

———. "The Negro Farmer." U.S. Bureau of the Census, *Bulletin* 8 (1904): 69–98.

———. "The Negro Landholder of Georgia." U.S. Bureau of Labor, *Bulletin* 35 (June 1901): 647–777.

———. "The Negroes of Farmville, Virginia: A Social Study." U.S. Bureau of Labor, *Bulletin* 14 (January 1898): 1–38.

———. *The Quest of the Silver Fleece*. 1911. New York: Oxford University Press, 2014.

———. "The Rural South." *Publications of the American Statistical Association* 13, no. 97 (March 1912): 80–84.

———. *The Souls of Black Folk*. 1903. New York: W. W. Norton, 1999.

———. "The Talented Tenth." In *The Negro Problem: A Series of Articles by Representative American Negroes of To-day*, ed. Booker T. Washington, 31–76. New York: James Pott, 1904.

Dubois, Laurent. *The Banjo: America's African Instrument*. Cambridge, Mass.: Belknap Press, 2016.

Duck, Leigh Anne. *The Nation's Region: Southern Modernism, Segregation, and U.S. Nationalism*. Athens: University of Georgia Press, 2006.

———. "Peripatetic Modernism, or Joe Christmas' Father." *Philological Quarterly* 90, no. 2–3 (2011): 255–80.

Dunbar, Paul Laurence. *The Collected Poetry*. Charlottesville: University of Virginia Press, 1999.

———. *Folks from Dixie*. New York: Dodd, Mead, 1898.

———. *In Old Plantation Days*. New York: Dodd, Mead, 1903.

Duncan, Christopher. *Fugitive Theory: Political Theory, the Southern Agrarians, and America*. New York: Lexington Books, 2000.

Dundes, Alan. "What Is Folklore?" In *The Study of Folklore*, ed. Dundes, 1–3. Englewood Cliffs, N.J.: Prentice-Hall, 1965.

Dungy, Camille T., ed. *Black Nature: Four Centuries of African American Nature Poetry*. Athens: University of Georgia Press, 2009.

Duvall, John. "Regionalism in American Modernism." In *The Cambridge Companion to American Modernism*, ed. Walter Kalaidjian, 242–60. New York: Cambridge University Press, 2005.

Edge, John T. *The Potlikker Papers: A Food History of the Modern South*. New York: Penguin, 2017.

Eliot, T. S. *Knowledge and Experience in the Philosophy of F. H. Bradley*. 1964. New York: Columbia University Press, 1989.

Ellis, R. H. "The Calhoun School, Miss Charlotte Thorn's 'Lighthouse on the Hill' in Lowndes County, Alabama." *Alabama Review* 37, no. 3 (1984): 183–201.

Ellison, Ralph. "Change the Joke and Slip the Yoke." 1964. In *Shadow and Act*, 45–59. New York: Vintage International, 1995.

Emerson, Ken. *Doo-Dah: Stephen Foster and the Rise of American Popular Culture*. New York: Da Capo Press, 1998.

Emmons, Ebenezer. *Agriculture*. Part 2 of *North Carolina Geological Survey*. Raleigh, N.C.: W. W. Holden, 1860.

Entin, Joseph. *Sensational Modernism: Experimental Fiction and Photography in Thirties America*. Chapel Hill: University of North Carolina Press, 2007.

Fanon, Frantz. *The Wretched of the Earth*, trans. Richard Philcox. 1961. New York: Grove Press, 2005.

Farland, Maria. "Modernist Versions of Pastoral: Poetic Inspiration, Scientific Expertise, and the 'Degenerate' Farmer." *American Literary History* 19, no. 4 (2007): 905–36.

———. "W. E. B. Du Bois, Anthropometric Science, and the Limits of Racial Uplift." *American Quarterly* 58, no. 4 (2006): 1017–44.

Farmer-Kaiser, Mary. *Freewomen and the Freedmen's Bureau: Race, Gender, and Public Policy in the Age of Emancipation*. New York: Fordham University Press, 2010.

Faulkner, William. *Absalom, Absalom!* 1936. New York: Vintage International, 1990.

———. *Go Down, Moses*. 1942. New York: Vintage International, 1990.

———. *Light in August*. 1932. New York: Vintage International, 1990.

Filene, Benjamin. *Romancing the Folk: Public Memory and American Roots Music*. Chapel Hill: University of North Carolina Press, 2000.

"First Show." *Mrs. Eleanor Roosevelt's Own Program*, April 30, 1940, www.oldtimeradiodownloads.com/historical/mrs-eleanor-roosevelts-own-program.

Fisher, Rudolph. *The City of Refuge: The Collected Stories of Rudolph Fisher*. Columbia: University of Missouri Press, 2008.

Fiskio, Janet. "Unsettling Ecocriticism: Rethinking Agrarianism, Place, and Citizenship." *American Literature* 84, no. 2 (2012): 301–25.

Flately, Jonathan. *Affective Mapping: Melancholia and the Politics of Modernism*. Cambridge, Mass.: Harvard University Press, 2008.

Flemons, Dom. "Can You Blame Gus Cannon?" *Oxford American* 83 (December 2013): 128–37.

Fohlen, Claude. *L'industrie textile au temps du Second Empire*. Paris: Librairie Plon, 1956.

Foner, Eric. *Reconstruction: America's Unfinished Revolution, 1863–1877*. 1988. New York: HarperPerennial, 2002.

Foner, Philip. *Business and Slavery: The New York Merchants and the Irrepressible Conflict*. New York: Russell and Russell, 1941.

Fortune, T. Thomas. *Black and White: Land, Labor, and Politics in the South*. 1884. New York: Washington Square Press, 2007.

Foster, Stephen. "My Old Kentucky Home, Good-Night!" In *Stephen Foster & Co.: Lyrics of America's First Great Popular Songs*, ed. Ken Emerson. New York: Library of Congress, 2010.

Foucault, Michel. *The Birth of Biopolitics: Lectures at the Collège de France, 1978–79*, ed. Michel Senellart, trans. Graham Burchell. New York: Palgrave Macmillan, 2008.

———. *The Birth of the Clinic: An Archaeology of Medical Perception*, trans. Allan Sheridan. 1963. New York: Vintage International, 1994.

Frank, Waldo. *Our America*. New York: Boni & Liveright, 1919.

Fraser, Nancy. "Rethinking the Public Sphere: A Contribution to the Critique of Actually Existing Democracy." *Social Text* 25, no. 26 (1990): 56–80.

Frederic, Harold. *The Damnation of Theron Ware*. Chicago: Stone & Kimball, 1896.

Friedman, Susan Stanford. "Definitional Excursions: The Meanings of *Modern/Modernity/Modernism*." *Modernism/modernity* 8, no. 3 (2001): 493–513.

Frost, William Goodell. "Our Contemporary Ancestors in the Southern Mountains." *Atlantic Monthly* 83 (1899): 311–19.

Fussell, Paul. *The Great War and Modern Memory*. New York: Oxford University Press, 1975.

Gaither, Gerald H. *Blacks and the Populist Movement: Ballots and Bigotry in the New South*. Tuscaloosa: University of Alabama Press, 2005.

Gaonkar, Dilip. "On Alternative Modernities." In *Alternative Modernities*, ed. Gaonkar, 1–23. Durham, N.C.: Duke University Press, 2001.

Garner, Dwight. "Grievous Angel: The Unruly James Agee." *Harper's*, November 2005. 91–96.

———. "Lost in Literary History: A Tale of Courage in the South." *New York Times*, April 18, 2014.

Gates, Henry Louis, Jr. *The Signifying Monkey: A Theory of Afro-American Literary Criticism*. New York: Oxford University Press, 1988.

Gellman, Erik S., and Jared Roll. *The Gospel of the Working Class: Labor's Southern Prophets in New Deal America*. Champaign: University of Illinois Press, 2011.

Genovese, Eugene. *The Southern Tradition: The Achievement and Limitations of American Conservatism*. Cambridge, Mass.: Harvard University Press, 1996.

Gerard, Charles D. *Jazz in Black and White: Race, Culture, and Identity in the Jazz Community*. Westport, Conn.: Praeger, 1998.

Giddens, Antony. *The Consequences of Modernity*. Stanford, Calif.: Stanford University Press, 1990.

Giesen, James C. "Creating 'Nate Shaw': The Making and Re-Making of *All God's Dangers*." In *Reading Southern Poverty between the Wars*, ed. Richard Godden and Martin Crawford, 163–78. Athens: University of Georgia Press, 2006.

Gilman, Charlotte Perkins. *Women and Economics*. 1898. Mineola, N.Y.: Dover, 1997.

Gilmore, Glenda. *Defying Dixie: The Radical Roots of Civil Rights, 1919–1950*. New York: W. W. Norton, 2008.

Gilroy, Paul. *The Black Atlantic: Modernity and Double-Consciousness*. Cambridge, Mass.: Harvard University Press, 1993.

Glaeser, Edward. "Urban Colossus: Why Is New York America's Largest City?" *FRBNY Economic Policy Review* 11, no. 2 (2005): 7–24.

Glasgow, Ellen. *Barren Ground*. 1925. New York: Mariner Books, 1985.

Glave, Dianne D. *Rooted in the Earth: Reclaiming the African American Environmental Heritage*. Chicago: Chicago Review Press, 2010.

Glen, John M. *Highlander: No Ordinary School*. 2nd ed. Knoxville: University of Tennessee Press, 1996.

Goodman, Kevis. *Georgic Modernity and British Romanticism: Poetry and the Mediation of History.* New York: Cambridge University Press, 2004.

Gorky, Maxim. "Comrade." *The Social Democrat* 10, no. 8 (1906): 509–12.

Gottlieb, Robert, and Anupama Joshi. *Food Justice.* Cambridge, Mass.: MIT Press, 2013.

Grandison, Kenrick. "Landscapes of Terror: A Reading of Tuskegee's Historic Campus." In *The Geography of Identity,* ed. Patricia Yaeger, 334–67. Ann Arbor: University of Michigan Press, 1996.

Grant, Ulysses S. *Personal Memoirs.* 1885. New York: Penguin Classics, 1999.

Grantham, Dewey. Foreword. In *Cry from the Cotton: The Southern Tenant Farmers' Union and the New Deal,* by Donald Grubbs, vii–x. Chapel Hill: University of North Carolina Press, 1971.

———. *The South in Modern America: A Region at Odds.* Fayetteville: University of Arkansas Press, 2001.

Gray, Richard. *Writing the South: Ideas of an American Region.* Baton Rouge: Louisiana State University Press, 1998.

Greenblatt, Stephen. *The Swerve: How the World Became Modern.* New York: W. W. Norton, 2012.

Greene, J. Lee. Introduction. In *Jule,* by George Wylie Henderson, vii–xix. 1946. Tuscaloosa: University of Alabama Press, 1989.

Greenhouse, Steven. "At a Nissan Plant in Mississippi, a Battle to Shape the U.A.W.'s Future." *New York Times,* October 7, 2013.

Greeson, Jennifer Rae. *Our South: Geographic Fantasy and the Rise of National Literature.* Cambridge, Mass.: Harvard University Press, 2010.

Gregory, James. *American Exodus: The Dustbowl Migration and Okie Culture in California.* New York: Oxford University Press, 1991.

———. *The Southern Diaspora: How the Great Migrations of African American and White Southerners Transformed America.* Chapel Hill: University of North Carolina Press, 2005.

Griffin, Farah Jasmine. *"Who Set You Flowin'?": The African-American Migration Narrative.* New York: Oxford University Press, 1996.

Griggs, Sutton. *Imperium in Imperio: A Study of the Negro Race Problem.* 1899. New York: Modern Library Classics, 2004.

Grubbs, Donald. *Cry from the Cotton: The Southern Tenant Farmers' Union and the New Deal.* Chapel Hill: University of North Carolina Press, 1971.

Gussow, Joan Dye. *This Organic Life: Confessions of a Suburban Homesteader.* New York: Chelsea Green, 2002.

Guthrie, Woody. "This Land Is Your Land." In *This Land Is Your Land: The Asch Recordings.* Vol. 1. Smithsonian Folkways Records, 1997.

Hagood, Margaret Jarman. *Mothers of the South: Portraiture of the White Tenant Farm Woman.* 1939. New York: Arno Press, 1972.

Hahn, Steven. *A Nation under Our Feet: Black Political Struggles in the Rural South from Slavery to the Great Migration.* Cambridge, Mass.: Belknap Press, 2003.

Hale, Grace Elizabeth. *Making Whiteness: The Culture of Segregation in the South, 1890–1940.* New York: Random House, 1998.

Hall, Jacquelyn Dowd. "The Long Civil Rights Movement and the Political Uses of the Past." *Journal of American History* 91, no. 4 (2005): 1233–63.

Hall, Stuart. *Race: The Floating Signifier*, dir. Sut Jhally. The Media Foundation, 1996.

Handley, George. "A New World Poetics of Oblivion." In *Look Away! The U.S. South in New World Studies*, ed. Jon Smith and Deborah Cohn, 25–51. Durham, N.C.: Duke University Press, 2004.

———. *Postslavery Literatures in the Americas: Portraits in Black and White*. Charlottesville: University Press of Virginia, 2000.

Handy, W. C. *Father of the Blues: An Autobiography*. New York: Macmillan, 1941.

Harding, Desmond. *Writing the City: Urban Visions and Literary Modernism*. New York: Routledge, 2003.

Harper, Frances E. W. *Iola Leroy, or Shadows Uplifted*. New York: Penguin Classics, 2010.

Harvey, David. *The Condition of Postmodernity*. New York: Wiley-Blackwell, 1991.

———. *The Urban Experience*. Baltimore, Md.: Johns Hopkins University Press, 1989.

Hearn, Lafcadio. *Lafcadio Hearn's America: Ethnographic Sketches and Editorials*, ed. Simon J. Bronner. Lexington: University Press of Kentucky, 2002.

Hegeman, Susan. *Patterns for America: Modernism and the Concept of Culture*. Princeton, N.J.: Princeton University Press, 1999.

Henninger, Katherine. *Ordering the Façade: Photography and Contemporary Southern Women's Writing*. Chapel Hill: University of North Carolina Press, 2007.

Herring, Scott. *Another Country: Queer Anti-Urbanism*. New York: New York University Press, 2010.

Hersey, Mark D. *My Work Is That of Conservation: An Environmental Biography of George Washington Carver*. Athens: University of Georgia Press, 2011.

Hickman, Jared. *Black Prometheus: Race and Radicalism in the Age of Atlantic Slavery*. New York: Oxford University Press, 2017.

Hicks, Scott. "W. E. B. Du Bois, Booker T. Washington, and Richard Wright: Toward an Ecocriticism of Color." *Callaloo* 29, no. 1 (2006): 202–22.

"Highlander Research and Education Center," http://highlandercenter.org (accessed March 1, 2018).

Hilmes, Michele. *Radio Voices: American Broadcasting, 1922–1952*. Minneapolis: University of Minnesota Press, 1997.

Hobsbawm, Eric. *Industry and Empire: The Birth of the Industrial Revolution*. New York: New Press, 1999.

Hobson, Fred. *Serpent in Eden: H. L. Mencken and the South*. Baton Rouge: Louisiana State University Press, 1974.

———. *Tell about the South: The Southern Rage to Explain*. 1983. Baton Rouge: Louisiana State University Press, 1996.

Holiday, Billie. "Strange Fruit." Commodore Records, 526A, 1939. Lyrics and music by Abel Meeropol.

hooks, bell. *Belonging: A Culture of Place*. New York: Routledge, 2008.

Horton, Aimee Isgrig. *The Highlander Folk School: A History of Its Major Programs, 1932–1961*. New York: Carlson, 1989.

Hubbs, Jolene. "William Faulkner's Rural Modernism." *Mississippi Quarterly* 61, no. 3 (2008): 461–75.

Huber, Patrick. *Linthead Stomp: The Creation of Country Music in the Piedmont South.* Chapel Hill: University of North Carolina Press, 2008.

Hurston, Zora Neale. *The Complete Stories.* New York: HarperPerennial, 1995.

———. *Mules and Men.* 1935. New York: HarperPerennial, 1990.

Ingram, Tammy. *Dixie Highway: Road Building and the Making of the Modern South, 1900–1930.* Chapel Hill: University of North Carolina Press, 2014.

Isenberg, Nancy. *White Trash: The 400-Year Untold Story of Class in America.* New York: Viking, 2016.

Jabavu, D. D. T. "My Tuskegee Pilgrimage." 1913. D. D. T. Jabavu Papers, Documentation Center for African Studies, University of South Africa. http://uda.unisa.ac.za/cdm/singleitem/collection/JC/id/53/rec/15.

Jackson, Mark Allan. *Prophet Singer: The Voice and Vision of Woody Guthrie.* Jackson: University Press of Mississippi, 2007.

Jackson, Zakiyyah Iman. "Outer Worlds: The Persistence of Race in Movement 'Beyond the Human.'" *GLQ: A Journal of Lesbian and Gay Studies* 21, no. 2–3 (June 2015): 215–18.

Jacques, Geoffrey. *A Change in the Weather: Modernist Imagination, African American Imagery.* Amherst, Mass.: University of Massachusetts Press, 2009.

James, Henry. *The Bostonians.* London: Macmillan, 1886.

Jameson, Fredric. *The Geopolitical Aesthetic: Cinema and Space in the World System.* Bloomington: Indiana University Press, 1992.

———. *Postmodernism, or, The Cultural Logic of Late Capitalism.* Durham, N.C.: Duke University Press, 1991.

Johnson, Charles S. *The Collapse of Cotton Tenancy: Summary of Field Studies and Statistical Surveys, 1933–35.* Chapel Hill: University of North Carolina Press, 1935.

———. "The New Frontage on American Life." In *The New Negro*, ed. Locke, 278–99.

Johnson, James Weldon. *The Autobiography of an Ex-Colored Man.* 1912/1927. New York: Penguin Classics, 1990.

———. *Black Manhattan.* 1930. New York: Da Capo Press, 1991.

———. Preface. *The Book of American Negro Poetry*, vii–xlviii. New York: Harcourt, Brace, 1922.

Johnson, Kimberly. Introduction. In *The Georgics: A Poem of the Land*, by Virgil, xi–xxii. New York: Penguin Classics, 2011.

Johnson, Walter. *River of Dark Dreams: Slavery and Empire in the Cotton Kingdom.* Cambridge, Mass.: Belknap Press, 2013.

———. "To Remake the World: Slavery, Racial Capitalism, and Justice." *Boston Review* Forum 1: Race, Capitalism, Justice (2017): 11, 13–31, 143.

Jones, Gavin. *Strange Talk: The Politics of Dialect Literature in Gilded Age America.* Berkeley: University of California Press, 1999.

Jones, Suzanne W., and Sharon Monteith, eds. *South to a New Place: Region, Literature, Culture.* Baton Rouge: Louisiana State University Press, 2002.

Kazin, Alfred. *On Native Ground: An Interpretation of Modern Prose Literature.* 1942. New York: Harcourt Brace, 1970.

Keats, John. To George and Tom Keats, December 21, 27, 1817. In *Selected Letters of John Keats: Based on the Texts of Hyder Edward Rollins*, ed. Grant F. Scott, rev. ed. Cambridge, Mass.: Harvard University Press, 2005.

Kelley, Edith Summers. *Weeds*. 1923. New York: Feminist Press, 1997.
Kelley, Robin D. G. *Hammer and Hoe: Alabama Communists during the Great Depression*. Chapel Hill: University of North Carolina Press, 1990.
———. "Notes on Deconstructing 'The Folk.'" *American Historical Review* 97, no. 5 (1992): 1400–1408.
Kephart, Horace. *Our Southern Highlanders*. New York: Outing, 1913.
Kester, Howard. *Revolt among the Sharecroppers*. 1936. Knoxville: University of Tennessee Press, 1997.
Kettell, Thomas P. *Southern Wealth and Northern Profits*. New York: George W. and John A. Wood, 1860.
Kingsolver, Barbara. *Animal, Vegetable, Miracle: A Year of Food Life*. New York: HarperPerennial, 2007.
Kirby, Jack Temple. *Rural Worlds Lost: The American South, 1920–1960*. Baton Rouge: Louisiana State University Press, 1986.
———. "The Southern Exodus, 1910–1960: A Primer for Historians." *Journal of Southern History* 49 (Nov. 1983): 585–600.
Kracauer, Siegfried. *The Mass Ornament: Weimar Essays*, trans. Thomas Y. Levin. Cambridge, Mass.: Harvard University Press, 1995.
Kreyling, Michael. *Inventing Southern Literature*. Jackson: University Press of Mississippi, 1998.
Kreymborg, Alfred, Lewis Mumford, and Paul Rosenfield, eds. *American Caravan IV*. New York: Macaulay, 1931.
———. *The New American Caravan*. New York: Macaulay, 1929.
Kunkel, Thomas. *Man in Profile: Joseph Mitchell of* The New Yorker. New York: Random House, 2015.
Labov, William. *Language in the Inner Cities: Studies in Black English Vernacular*. Philadelphia: University of Pennsylvania Press, 1973.
LaFraniere, Sharon. "U.S. Opens Spigot after Farmers Claim Discrimination." *New York Times*, April 25, 2013.
Latour, Bruno. *We Have Never Been Modern*, trans. Catherine Porter. Cambridge, Mass.: Harvard University Press, 1993.
Lawrence, Myrtle. Letter from Myrtle Lawrence to Louise Boyle. Collection no. 5859, Box 1, Folder 33. Southern Tenant Farmers' Union Research Files, Kheel Center for Labor-Management Documentation & Research, Cornell University.
Lee, Maurice. "Du Bois the Novelist: White Influence, Black Spirit, and *The Quest of the Silver Fleece*." *African American Review* 33, no. 3 (Autumn 1999): 389–400.
Lemann, Nicholas. *The Promised Land: The Great Black Migration and How It Changed America*. New York: Knopf, 1991.
Leopold, Aldo. *A Sand County Almanac*. New York: Oxford University Press, 1968.
Lepore, Jill. "Historians Who Love Too Much: Reflections on Microhistory and Biography." *Journal of American History* 88, no. 1 (2001): 129–44.
———. *These Truths: A History of the United States*. New York: W. W. Norton, 2018.
Letwin, Daniel. "Labor Relations in the Industrializing South." In *A Companion to the American South*, ed. John Boles, 424–43. Malden, Mass.: Blackwell, 2004.

Levine, Lawrence. *Black Culture and Black Consciousness: Afro-American Folk Thought from Slavery to Freedom.* New York: Oxford University Press, 1977.

Lilla, Mark. *The Shipwrecked Mind: On Political Reaction.* New York: New York Review Books, 2016.

Limerick, Patricia Nelson. *The Legacy of Conquest: The Unbroken Past of the American West.* New York: W. W. Norton, 1987.

Locke, Alain. "Enter the New Negro." *Survey Graphic* 4, no. 6 (1925): 631–34.

———. "Harlem." *Survey Graphic* 4, no. 6 (1925): 629–30.

Logan, Rayford. *The Negro in American Life and Thought: The Nadir, 1877–1901.* New York: Dial Press, 1954.

Lorence, James. *A Hard Journey: The Life of Don West.* Urbana: University of Illinois Press, 2007.

———. "Mobilizing the Reserve Army: The Communist Party and the Unemployed in Atlanta, 1929–1934." In *Radicalism in the South since Reconstruction*, ed. Chris Green, Rachel Rubin, and James Smethurst, 57–82. New York: Palgrave Macmillan, 2006.

Lott, Eric. "Double-V, Double-Time: Be-Bop's Politics of Style." In *Jazz among the Discourses*, ed. Krin Gabbard, 243–55. Durham, N.C.: Duke University Press, 1995.

———. *Love and Theft: Blackface Minstrelsy and the American Working Class.* New York: Oxford University Press, 1993.

Loviglio, Jason. *Radio's Intimate Public: Network Broadcasting and Mass-Mediated Democracy.* Minneapolis: University of Minnesota Press, 2005.

MacKethan, Lucinda Hardwick. *The Dream of Arcady: Place and Time in Southern Literature.* Baton Rouge: Louisiana State University Press, 1999.

Mancini, J. M. "'Messin' with the Furniture Man': Early Country Music, Regional Culture, and the Search for Anthological Modernism." *American Literary History* 16, no. 2 (2004): 208–37.

Mao, Douglas, and Rebecca L. Walkowitz. "The New Modernist Studies." *PMLA* 123, no. 3 (2008): 737–48.

Mariani, Paul. *William Carlos Williams: A New World Naked.* New York: W. W. Norton, 1990.

Marx, Karl. *Capital: A Critique of the Political Economy*, trans. Samuel Moore and Edward Aveling. Vol. 1. 1867. New York: Modern Library, 1901.

———. *Economic and Philosophical Manuscripts of 1844*, trans. Martin Milligan. Amherst, N.Y.: Prometheus Books, 1988.

Marx, Karl, and Friedrich Engels. *The Communist Manifesto.* 1848. New York: Pathfinder, 2008.

May, Herbert L., and Dorothy Petgen. *Leisure and Its Use: Some International Observations.* New York: A. S. Barnes, 1928.

McCarthy, Jeffrey M. *Green Modernism: Nature and the English Novel, 1900–1930.* New York: Palgrave Macmillan, 2015.

McInnis, Jarvis C. "'Behold the Land': W. E. B. Du Bois, Cotton Futures, and the Afterlife of the Plantation in the U.S. South." *Global South* 10, no. 2 (2016): 70–98.

McKay, Claude. *Banjo.* New York: Harcourt Brace, 1929.

McKibben, Bill. *Deep Economy: The Wealth of Communities and the Durable Future.* New York: St. Martin's Griffin, 2007.

McLuhan, Marshall. *Understanding Media: The Extensions of Man.* 1964. Cambridge, Mass.: MIT Press, 1994.

Mehroff, W. Arthur. "The Phenomenology of Place." *Humanities Education* (June 1990): 9–14.

Mendelson, Jordana, and David Prochaska. Introduction. In *Postcards: Ephemeral Histories of Modernity*, xi–xix. College Station: Pennsylvania State University Press, 2010.

Michaels, Walter Benn. *Our America: Nativism, Modernism, and Pluralism.* Durham, N.C.: Duke University Press, 1995.

Middleton, Richard. *Voicing the Popular: On the Subjects of Popular Music.* New York: Routledge, 2006.

Miller, Karl Hagstrom. *Segregating Sound: Inventing Folk and Pop Music in the Age of Jim Crow.* Durham, N.C.: Duke University Press, 2010.

Mitchell, H. L. "The Other South." January 1946. American Press Associates, No. 10. Collection no. 5204, Box 1, Folder 11. Southern Tenant Farmers' Union Research Files, Kheel Center for Labor-Management Documentation & Research, Cornell University.

Mitchell, Joseph. "Brewers." In *American Caravan IV*, ed. Alfred Kreymborg, Lewis Mumford, and Paul Rosenfield, 274–78. New York: Macaulay, 1931.

———. "Cool Swamp and Field Woman." In *New American Caravan*, ed. Alfred Kreymborg, Lewis Mumford, and Paul Rosenfield, 133–39. New York: Macaulay, 1929.

———. "Days in the Branch." *New Yorker*, December 1, 2014.

———. *Up in the Old Hotel.* New York: Pantheon, 1992.

Mitchell, Margaret. *Gone with the Wind.* 1936. New York: Simon & Schuster, 1997.

Mitchell, Theodore R. *Political Education in the Southern Farmers' Alliance, 1887–1900.* Madison: University of Wisconsin Press, 1987.

Mittleman, Melissa. "Volkswagen to Appeal NLRB Ruling on Tennessee Union Election." *Bloomberg*, April 25, 2016, www.bloomberg.com/news/articles/2016-04-25/volkswagen-to-appeal-nlrb-ruling-on-tennessee-union-election.

Modernism and Nostalgia: Bodies, Locations, Aesthetics, ed. Tammy Clewell. New York: Palgrave MacMillan, 2013.

Moffitt, Anne Faye Hirsh. "Reviving the Rural: The Modernist Poetics of the Twentieth-Century Rural Novel." Ph.D. diss., Princeton University, 2012.

Moglen, Seth. *Mourning Modernity: Literary Modernism and the Wounds of American Capitalism.* Stanford, Calif.: Stanford University Press, 2007.

Morrison, Toni. *Beloved.* 1987. New York: Vintage International, 2004.

———. "Rootedness: The Ancestor in African American Literature." In *What Moves at the Margin: Selected Nonfiction*, 56–64. Jackson: University Press of Mississippi, 2008.

Morton, Timothy. *Ecology Without Nature: Rethinking Environmental Aesthetics.* Cambridge, Mass.: Harvard University Press, 2007.

———. *Hyperobjects: Philosophy and Ecology after the End of the World.* Minneapolis: University of Minnesota Press, 2013.

Murphy, Paul V. *The Rebuke of History: The Southern Agrarians and American Conservative Thought*. Chapel Hill: University of North Carolina Press, 2001.
Murray, Albert. *The Omni-Americans: Black Experience and American Culture*. New York: Da Capo, 1970.
Myrdal, Gunnar. *An American Dilemma: The Negro Problem and Modern Democracy*. 2 vols. 1944. New York: Routledge, 1995.
Nearing, Scott. *Black America*. New York: Vanguard Press, 1929.
"New Cotton Machines." *STFU News* 1, no. 1 (1938): n.p. Collection no. 5204, Box 1, Folder 13. Southern Tenant Farmers' Union Research Files, Kheel Center for Labor-Management Documentation & Research, Cornell University.
A New Literary History of America, ed. Greil Marcus and Werner Sollors. Cambridge, Mass.: Belknap Press, 2009.
The New Negro: Voices of the Harlem Renaissance, ed. Alain Locke. 1925. New York: Touchstone, 1997.
Nicholls, David. *Conjuring the Folk: Forms of Modernity in African America*. Ann Arbor: University of Michigan Press, 2000.
Nixon, Rob. *Slow Violence and the Environmentalism of the Poor*. Cambridge, Mass.: Harvard University Press, 2013.
Norrell, Robert J. *Up from History: The Life of Booker T. Washington*. Cambridge, Mass.: Belknap Press, 2009.
North, Michael. *Camera Works: Photography and the Twentieth-Century Word*. New York: Oxford University Press, 2005.
———. *The Dialect of Modernism: Race, Language, and Twentieth-Century Literature*. New York: Oxford University Press, 1994.
Nunn, Erich. "Folk." In *Keywords for Southern Studies*, ed. Scott Romine and Jennifer Rae Greeson, 189–99. Athens: University of Georgia Press, 2016.
———. *Sounding the Color Line: Music and Race in the Southern Imagination*. Athens: University of Georgia Press, 2015.
Nurhussein, Nadia. *Rhetorics of Literacy: The Cultivation of American Dialect Poetry*. Columbus: Ohio State University Press, 2013.
Oliver, Lawrence J. "W. E. B. Du Bois and the Dismal Science: Economic Theory and Social Justice." *American Studies* 52, no. 2 (2014): 49–70.
"An Open Letter to the President of the United States." Nov. 20, 1936. Collection no. 5204, Box 1, Folder 11. Southern Tenant Farmers' Union Research Files, Kheel Center for Labor-Management Documentation & Research, Cornell University.
Osborne, Peter. *The Politics of Time: Modernity and Avant-Garde*. New York: Verso, 1995.
Oubre, Claude. *Forty Acres and a Mule: The Freedmen's Bureau and Black Land Ownership*. 1978. Baton Rouge: Louisiana State University Press, 2012.
Outka, Paul. *Race and Nature from Transcendentalism to the Harlem Renaissance*. New York: Palgrave Macmillan, 2012.
Ownby, Ted. *American Dreams in Mississippi: Consumers, Poverty, and Culture, 1830–1998*. Chapel Hill: University of North Carolina Press, 1999.
Page, Thomas Nelson. *Red Rock: A Chronicle of Reconstruction*. New York: Charles Scribner's Sons, 1898.
Pankake, Jon. "The Brotherhood of the Anthology." In *A Booklet of Essays, Apprecia-

tions, and Annotations Pertaining to the Anthology of American Music, ed. Harry Smith, 26–28. Washington, D.C.: Smithsonian Folkways Records, 1997.

Parrish, Susan Scott. *The Flood Year 1927: A Cultural History*. Princeton, N.J.: Princeton University Press, 2017.

Payne, Elizabeth. "The Fighting Sharecropper as Icon: Myrtle Terry Lawrence and the Southern Tenant Farmers' Union." Organization of American Historians and National Council on Public History, Washington, D.C., April 20, 2006.

———. "The Lady Was a Sharecropper: Myrtle Lawrence and the Southern Tenant Farmers' Union." *Southern Cultures* 4, no. 2 (1998): 5–28.

———. "Myrtle Terry Lawrence." In *Notable American Women: A Biographical Dictionary, Completing the Twentieth Century*, ed. Susan Ware, 372–73. Cambridge, Mass.: Belknap Press, 2004.

Pellicer, Juan Christian. "Pastoral and Georgic." In *The Oxford History of Classical Reception in English Literature*, ed. David Hopkins and Charles Martindale, 3:287–322. New York: Oxford University Press, 2012.

Pells, Richard. *Radical Visions and American Dreams: Culture and Social Thought in the Depression Years*. New York: Harper Torchbooks, 1973.

Perkell, Christine. *The Poet's Truth: A Study of the Poet in Virgil's* Georgics. Berkeley: University of California Press, 1989.

Peters, John Durham. *Speaking into the Air: A History of the Idea of Communication*. Chicago: University of Chicago Press, 1999.

Phelan, Peggy. *Unmarked: The Politics of Performance*. New York: Routledge, 1999.

Pickert, Kate. "When Shirley Sherrod Was First Wronged by the USDA." *Time*, April 23, 2010, http://content.time.com/time/nation/article/0,8599,2006058,00.html (accessed January 30, 2018).

"The *Pigford* Cases: USDA Settlement of Discrimination Suits by Black Farmers." Congressional Research Service. May 29, 2013.

Piketty, Thomas. *Capital in the Twenty-First Century*. Cambridge, Mass.: Belknap Press, 2014.

Pollan, Michael. *The Omnivore's Dilemma*. New York: Penguin, 2006.

Porter, Carolyn. "*Gone with the Wind* and *Absalom, Absalom!*" In *New Literary History*, ed. Werner Sollors and Greil Marcus, 705–10. Cambridge, Mass.: Belknap Press, 2012.

Posnock, Russ. "Going Astray, Going Forward: Du Boisian Pragmatism and Its Lineage." In *The Revival of Pragmatism: New Essays on Social Thought, Law, and Culture*, ed. Morris Dickstein, 176–89. Durham, N.C.: Duke University Press, 1998.

Postel, Charles. *The Populist Vision*. New York: Oxford University Press, 2007.

Powdermaker, Hortense. *After Freedom: A Cultural Study in the Deep South*. 1939. Madison: University of Wisconsin Press, 1993.

Pratt, Mary Louise. "Arts of the Contact Zone." *Profession* (1991): 33–40.

Proust, Marcel. *Remembrance of Things Past*, trans. Scott Moncrieff and Terence Kilmartin. Vol. 1. 1913, 1919. New York: Vintage International, 1982.

Purdy, Jedediah. *After Nature: A Politics for the Anthropocene*. Cambridge, Mass.: Harvard University Press, 2015.

Quijano, Aníbal, and Immanuel Wallerstein. "Americanity as a Concept, or the Americas in the Modern World-System." *International Social Sciences Journal* 134 (1992): 549–57.

Raine, Anne. "Du Bois's Ambient Poetics: Rethinking Environmental Imagination in *The Souls of Black Folk*." *Callaloo* 36, no. 2 (Spring 2013): 322–41.

Rampersad, Arnold. *The Art and Imagination of W. E. B. Du Bois*. 1976. New York: Schocken Books, 1990.

Ransom, John Crowe. "The South: Old or New?" *Sewanee Review* 36, no. 2 (1928): 139–47.

———. "What Does the South Want?" In *Who Owns America? A New Declaration of Independence*, ed. Herbert Agar and Allen Tate, 178–93. New York: Houghton Mifflin, 1936.

Raper, Arthur. *Preface to Peasantry: A Tale of Two Black-Belt Counties*. Chapel Hill: University of North Carolina Press, 1936.

Rawe, John C. "Agriculture and the Property State." In *Who Owns America?*, ed. Agar and Tate, 36–51.

Reed, Adolph, and Kenneth Warren. Introduction. In *Renewing Black Intellectual History*, ed. Reed and Warren, vii–xi. Boulder: Paradigm, 2009.

Report on the Commission of Country Life. 1911. New York: Sturgis & Walton, 1917.

Richardson, Riché. *Black Masculinity in the U.S. South*. Athens: University of Georgia Press, 2007.

Roach, Joseph. *Cities of the Dead: Circum-Atlantic Performance*. New York: Columbia University Press, 1997.

Robbins, Hollis. Introduction. In *Iola Leroy, or Shadows Uplifted*, by Frances Harper, xiv–xxix. New York: Penguin Classics, 2010.

Robertson, Priscilla. Letter from Priscilla Robertson to Michael Ames. Collection no. 5859, Box 1, Folder 46. Southern Tenant Farmers' Union Research Files, Kheel Center for Labor-Management Documentation & Research, Cornell University.

———. "A Visit to an Arkansas Sharecropper in 1937." Collection no. 5859, Box 1, Folder 47. Southern Tenant Farmers' Union Research Files, Kheel Center for Labor-Management Documentation & Research, Cornell University.

Robinson, Cedric. *Black Marxism: The Making of the Black Radical Tradition*. Chapel Hill: University of North Carolina Press, 1984.

Robinson, Zandria. "Listening for the Country." *Oxford American* 95 (Winter 2016): 84–97.

———. *This Ain't No Chicago: Race, Class, and Regional Identity in the Post-Soul South*. Chapel Hill: University of North Carolina Press, 2014.

Rodgers, Lawrence. *Canaan Bound: The African-American Great Migration Novel*. Champaign: University of Illinois Press, 1997.

Romine, Scott. *The Real South: Southern Narrative in the Age of Cultural Reproduction*. Baton Rouge: Louisiana State University Press, 2008.

Ronda, Margaret. "'Work and Wait Unwearying': Dunbar's Georgics." *PMLA* 127, no. 4 (2012): 863–78.

Rorrer, Kinney. Liner notes. *Charlie Poole with the Highlanders: The Complete Paramount and Brunswick Recordings, 1929*. San Francisco: Tompkins Square Records, 2013.

Rorty, Richard. *Achieving Our Country: Leftist Thought in Twentieth-Century America.* Cambridge, Mass.: Harvard University Press, 1999.

Rosengarten, Theodore. *All God's Dangers: The Life of Nate Shaw.* New York: Random House, 1974.

Rosenthal, Caitlin. *Accounting for Slavery: Masters and Management.* Cambridge, Mass.: Harvard University Press, 2018.

Rosetti, Gina M. "Turning the Corner: Romance as Economic Critique in Norris's Trilogy of Wheat and Du Bois's *The Quest of the Silver Fleece.*" *Studies in American Naturalism* 7, no. 1 (2012): 39–49.

Rothman, Joshua. "The Contours of Cotton Capitalism: Speculation, Slavery, and Economic Panic in Mississippi, 1832–1841." In *Slavery's Capitalism: A New History of American Economic Development,* ed. Sven Beckert and Seth Rockman, 122–45. Philadelphia: University of Pennsylvania Press, 2016.

Rourke, Constance. "The Significance of Sections." *New Republic,* September 1933.

Rowe, John Carlos. *The New American Studies.* Minneapolis: University of Minnesota Press, 2002.

Ruffin, Kimberly N. *Black on Earth: African American Ecoliterary Traditions.* Athens: University of Georgia Press, 2010.

Rushdie, Salman. *The Satanic Verses.* New York: Random House, 2008.

Saint-Amour, Paul. *Tense Future: Modernism, Total War, and Encyclopedia Form.* New York: Oxford University Press, 2015.

Sanneh, Kalefa. "Out of the Office." *New Yorker,* June 22, 2009.

Sante, Luc. *Low Life: Lures and Snares of Old New York.* New York: Vintage International, 1991.

Saunders, Steven. "The Social Agenda of Stephen Foster's Plantation Melodies." *American Music* 30, no. 3 (Fall 2012): 275–89.

Scarry, Elaine. *On Beauty and Being Just.* Princeton, N.J.: Princeton University Press, 2001.

———. *Resisting Representation.* New York: Oxford University Press, 1994.

Scheiber, Andrew. "The Folk, the School, and the Marketplace: Locations of Culture in *The Souls of Black Folk.*" In *Post-Bellum, Pre-Harlem: African American Literature and Culture, 1877–1919,* ed. Barbara McCaskill and Caroline Gebhard, 250–67. New York: New York University Press, 2006.

Schmidt, Peter. *Sitting in Darkness: New South Fiction, Education, and the Rise of Jim Crow Colonialism.* Jackson: University Press of Mississippi, 2008.

Schoen, Brian. *The Fragile Fabric of Union: Cotton, Federal Politics, and the Global Origins of the Civil War.* Baltimore, Md.: Johns Hopkins University Press, 2009.

Schuyler, George S. *Black No More.* 1931. New York: Penguin Classics, 2018.

Scott, Emmett J. *Negro Migration During the War.* New York: Oxford University Press, 1920.

Sekula, Allan. "The Body and the Archive." In *The Contest of Meaning: Critical Histories of Photography,* ed. Richard Bolton, 343–89. Cambridge, Mass.: MIT Press, 1989.

Shaw, Stephanie J. *W. E. B. Du Bois and* The Souls of Black Folk. Chapel Hill: University of North Carolina Press, 2013.

Sherrod, Shirley. *The Courage to Hope: How I Stood Up to the Politics of Fear.* New York: Simon & Schuster, 2012.

Siemerling, Winfried. "W. E. B. Du Bois, Hegel, and the Staging of Alterity." *Callaloo* 24, no. 1 (Winter 2001): 325–33.
Silber, Nina. *The Romance of Reunion: Northerners and the South, 1865–1900*. Chapel Hill: University of North Carolina Press, 1993.
Simmel, Georg. "The Metropolis and Mental Life." 1903. In *The Blackwell City Reader*, ed. Gary Bridge and Sophie Watson, 12–19. Malden, Mass.: Wiley-Blackwell, 2002.
Simpson, Lewis. *The Dispossessed Garden: Pastoral and History in Southern Literature*. Baton Rouge: Louisiana State University Press, 1983.
Singal, Daniel. *The War Within: From Victorian to Modernist Thought in the U.S. South, 1919–1945*. Chapel Hill: University of North Carolina Press, 1982.
Singer, Alan J. *New York and Slavery: Time to Teach the Truth*. Albany: State University of New York Press, 2008.
Slavery's Capitalism: A New History of American Economic Development, ed. Sven Beckert and Seth Rockman. Philadelphia: University of Pennsylvania Press, 2016.
Slotkin, Richard. *Regeneration through Violence: The Mythology of the American Frontier, 1600–1860*. Norman: University of Oklahoma Press, 2000.
Smethurst, James. *The African American Roots of Modernism: From Reconstruction to the Harlem Renaissance*. Chapel Hill: University of North Carolina Press, 2011.
Smith, Jon. *Finding Purple America: The South and the Future of American Cultural Studies*. Athens: University of Georgia Press, 2013.
———. Review of *The Postsouthern Sense of Place in Contemporary Fiction*, by Martyn Bone. *Mississippi Quarterly* 52, no. 2 (2006): 369–73.
Smith, Jon, and Deborah Cohn, eds. *Look Away! The U.S. South in New World Studies*. Durham, N.C.: Duke University Press, 2004.
Smith, Kimberly K. *African American Environmental Thought*. Lawrence: University Press of Kansas, 2007.
Smith, Lillian. *Killers of the Dream*. 1949. New York: Anchor Books, 1963.
Smith, Paul Chaat. *Everything You Know about Indians Is Wrong*. Minneapolis: University of Minnesota Press, 2009.
Soils and Men: An Agricultural Yearbook 1938. United States Department of Agriculture. Washington, D.C.: United States Government Printing Office, 1938.
Soja, Edward. *Thirdspace: Journeys to Los Angeles and Other Real-and-imagined Places*. Oxford: Blackwell, 1996.
Sontag, Susan. *On Photography*. 1977. New York: Anchor Books, 1990.
Spivak, Gayatri Chakravorty. *Death of a Discipline*. New York: Columbia University Press, 2003.
———. "Subaltern Studies: Deconstructing Historiography." In *The Spivak Reader: Selected Works of Gayatri Chakravorty Spivak*, ed. Donna Landry and Gerald MacLean, 203–35. New York: Routledge, 1996.
———. Translator's preface. In Jacques Derrida, *Of Grammatology*, trans. Spivak, ix–lxxxvii. Baltimore, Md.: Johns Hopkins University Press, 1999.
Stack, Carol B. *Call to Home: African-Americans Reclaim the Rural South*. New York: Basic Books, 1998.
Stecopoulos, Harilaos. *Reconstructing the World: Southern Fictions and U.S. Imperialism, 1898–1976*. Ithaca, N.Y.: Cornell University Press, 2008.

Stewart, Jeffrey. *The New Negro: The Life of Alain Locke*. New York: Oxford University Press, 2018.

Storey, Mark. *Rural Fictions, Urban Realities: A Geography of Gilded Age American Literature*. New York: Oxford University Press, 2013.

Stott, William. *Documentary Expression and Thirties America*. 1973. Chicago: University of Chicago Press, 1986.

Sullivan, John Jeremiah. "Mr. Lytle: An Essay." In *Pulphead*, 55–78. New York: Farrar, Straus and Giroux, 2012.

Sundquist, Eric. *To Wake the Nations: Race in the Making of American Literature*. Cambridge, Mass.: Belknap Press, 1993.

Susman, Walter. *Culture as History: The Transformation of American Society in the Twentieth Century*. New York: Pantheon Books, 1984.

Sutton, Damian. *Photography, Cinema, Memory: The Crystal Image of Time*. Minneapolis: University of Minnesota Press, 2009.

Sweet, Timothy. *American Georgics: Economy and Environment in Early American Literature*. Philadelphia: University of Pennsylvania Press, 2002.

Tate, Allen. *Collected Poems, 1919–1976*. New York: Farrar, Straus and Giroux, 2007.

———. *The Fathers*. 1938. Athens, Ohio: Swallow Press, 1984.

Taylor, Melanie Benson. *Disturbing Calculations: The Economics of Identity in Postcolonial Southern Literature, 1912–2002*. Athens: University of Georgia Press, 2008.

Thomas, Norman. *The Plight of the Share-Cropper*. New York: League for Industrial Democracy, 1934.

Timrod, Henry. *The Poems of Henry Timrod*. New York: E. J. Hale & Son, 1872.

Toll, Robert. *Blacking Up: The Minstrel Show in Nineteenth-Century America*. New York: Oxford University Press, 1974.

Tourgée, Albion W. *A Fool's Errand: By One of the Fools*. 1879. Cambridge, Mass.: Belknap Press, 1961.

Tschumpeter, Joseph. *Capitalism, Socialism, and Democracy*. 1942. New York: HarperPerennial, 2008.

Tuan, Yi-Fu. "Geography, Phenomenology, and the Study of Human Nature." *Canadian Geographer* 15, no. 3 (1971): 181–92.

———. *Space and Place: The Perspective of Experience*. Minneapolis: University of Minnesota Press, 1977.

Twelve Southerners. *I'll Take My Stand: The South and the Agrarian Tradition*. 1930. Baton Rouge: Louisiana State University Press, 1978.

Underwood, Thomas. *Allen Tate: Orphan of the South*. Princeton, N.J.: Princeton University Press, 2000.

United Daughters of the Confederacy. *Minutes of the Fiftieth Annual Convention of the Daughters of the Confederacy Incorporated Held in Memphis, Tennessee*. November 15–19, 1932.

U.S. Census Reports 1900, vol. 6, Agriculture. Washington: United States Census Office, 1902.

Value of Swamp Lands, or How to Make Unproductive Black Soils More Valuable. New York: German Kali Works, 1907.

Van Wienan, Mark, and Julie Kraft. "How the Socialism of W. E. B. Du Bois Still Matters: Black Socialism in *The Quest of the Silver Fleece*—and Beyond." *African American Review* 41, no. 1. (2007): 67–85.

Vance, J. D. *Hillbilly Elegy: A Memoir of a Family and Culture in Crisis*. New York: Harper, 2016.

Vance, Rupert. "Is Agrarianism for Farmers?" *Southern Review* 1, no. 1 (1935): 41–57.

Veblen, Thorstein. *The Theory of the Leisure Class: An Economic Study of Institutions*. New York: Macmillan, 1905.

Vernon, Zackary. "The Problematic History and Recent Cultural Reappropriation of Southern Agrarianism." *ISLE: Interdisciplinary Studies in Literature and Environment* 21, no. 2 (Spring 2014): 337–52.

Virgil. *The Georgic: A Poem of the Land*, trans. Kimberly Johnson. New York: Penguin Classics, 2011.

Wagner-McCoy, Sarah. "Virgilian Chesnutt: Eclogues of Slavery and Georgics of Reconstruction in the *Conjure Tales*." *ELH* 80, no. (2013): 199–220.

Walkowitz, Rebecca L. *Cosmopolitan Style: Modernism beyond the Nation*. New York: Columbia University Press, 2006.

Wallerstein, Immanuel. *World-Systems Analysis: An Introduction*. Durham, N.C.: Duke University Press, 2004.

Wapshott, Nicholas. *Keynes Hayek: The Clash That Defined Modern Economics*. New York: W. W. Norton, 2011.

Warner, Michael. *Publics and Counterpublics*. Brooklyn: Zone Books, 2002.

Washington, Booker T. Booker T. Washington to Beno von Herman auf Wain, September 20, 1900. Booker T. Washington Papers, Manuscripts Division, Library of Congress, Washington, D.C., www.historycooperative.com.

———. Booker T. Washington to Edna Dow Littlehale Cheney, 15 October 1895. In *Booker T. Washington Papers*, ed. Louis R. Harlan, 4:56–57. Champaign: University of Illinois Press, 1978.

———. *The Farthest Man Down: A Record of Observation and Study in Europe*. New York: Doubleday, Page, 1912.

———. *My Larger Education: Being Chapters from My Experience*. New York: Doubleday, Page, 1911.

———. "A Speech before the Boston Unitarian Club, 1888." In *The Booker T. Washington Papers*, ed. Louis R. Harlan, 2:503–4. Urbana: University of Illinois Press, 1972.

———. *Up from Slavery*. 1901. New York: W. W. Norton, 1996.

———. *Working with the Hands; Being a Sequel to* Up from Slavery *Covering the Author's Experiences in Industrial Training at Tuskegee*. New York: Doubleday, Page, 1904.

Watson, Jay. *Reading for the Body: The Recalcitrant Materiality of Southern Fiction, 1893–1985*. Athens: University of Georgia Press, 2012.

———. *William Faulkner and the Faces of Modernity*. New York: Oxford University Press, 2020.

Watson, Thomas. T. E. W. to Dr. John N. Taylor, April 23, 1910. Quoted in C. Vann Woodward, *Tom Watson: Agrarian Rebel* (1938; New York: Oxford University Press, 1963).

Weaks-Baxter, Mary. *Reclaiming the American Farmer: The Reinvention of a Regional Mythology in Twentieth-Century Southern Writing*. Baton Rouge: Louisiana State University Press, 2006.

Weber, Max. *Economy and Society*. 1922. Berkeley: University of California Press, 2013.

Weheliye, Alexander. *Habeas Viscus: Racializing Assemblages, Biopolitics, and Black Feminist Theories of the Human*. Durham, N.C.: Duke University Press, 2014.

——. *Phonographies: Grooves in Sonic Afro-Modernity*. Durham, N.C.: Duke University Press, 2005.

Wells, Ida B. "Southern Horrors: Lynch Law in All Its Phases." In *Southern Horrors and Other Writings: The Anti-Lynching Campaign of Ida B. Wells, 1892–1900*, ed. Jacqueline Jones Royster, 49–72. New York: Bedford/St. Martin's, 1996.

West, Don. *No Lonesome Road: Selected Prose and Poems*, ed. Jeff Biggers and George Brosi. Urbana: University of Illinois Press, 2004.

West, Dorothy. *The Living Is Easy*. 1948. New York: Feminist Press, 1995.

West, Michael R. *The Education of Booker T. Washington: American Democracy and the Idea of Race Relations*. New York: Columbia University Press, 2006.

White, Walter. *A Man Called White: The Autobiography of Walter White*. 1948. Athens: University of Georgia Press, 1995.

——. "The Paradox of Color." In *The New Negro*, ed. Locke, 361–68.

Wilkerson, Isabel. "Emmett Till and Tamir Rice, Sons of the Great Migration." *New York Times*, February 14, 2016.

——. *The Warmth of Other Suns*. New York: Random House, 2010.

——. "When Will the North Face Its Racism?" *New York Times*, January 11, 2015.

Williams, Eric. *Capitalism and Slavery*. 1944. Chapel Hill: University of North Carolina Press, 1994.

Williams, Raymond. *The Country and the City*. New York: Oxford University Press, 1973.

——. *Keywords: A Vocabulary of Culture and Society*, Rev. ed. New York: Oxford University Press, 1983.

——. *The Politics of Modernism*. New York: Verso, 1989.

Williamson, Joel. *The Crucible of Race: Black/White Relations in the American South since Emancipation*. New York: Oxford University Press, 1984.

——. *A Rage for Order: Black/White Relations in the American South Since Emancipation*. New York: Oxford University Press, 1986.

——. "W. E. B. Du Bois as a Hegelian." In *What Was Freedom's Price?*, ed. David G. Sansing, 21–50. Jackson: University Press of Mississippi, 1978.

Wilson, Edmond. "Tennessee Agrarians." 1931. In *The American Earthquake: A Documentary of the Twenties and Thirties*. Garden City, N.Y.: Doubleday Anchor, 1958.

Witt, Susan, and Robert Swann. "Land: Challenge and Opportunity." In *Rooted in the Land: Essays of Community and Place*, ed. William Vitek and Wes Jackson, 244–52. New Haven, Conn.: Yale University Press, 1996.

Woods, Clyde. *Development Arrested: The Blues and Plantation Power in the Mississippi Delta*. New York: Verso, 1998.

Woodson, Carter G. *A Century of Negro Migration*. Washington D.C.: Association for the Study of Negro Life and History, 1918.

Woodward, C. Vann. *The Origins of the New South*. 1951. Baton Rouge: Louisiana State University Press, 1971.
Woolf, Virginia. *Mrs. Dalloway*. 1925. New York: Harcourt, 1981.
Wright, Gavin. *Old South, New South: Revolutions in the Southern Economy since the Civil War*. Baton Rouge: Louisiana State University Press, 1971.
Yaeger, Patricia. *Dirt and Desire: Reconstructing Southern Women's Writing, 1930–1990*. Chicago: University of Chicago Press, 2000.
"Youth and Youth Organizations." In *Mrs. Eleanor Roosevelt's Own Program*, May 9, 1940. www.oldtimeradiodownloads.com/historical/mrs-eleanor-roosevelts-own-program/youth-and-youth-organizations-1940-05-09.
Zimmerman, Andrew. *Alabama in Africa: Booker T. Washington, the German Empire, and the Globalization of the New South*. Princeton, N.J.: Princeton University Press, 2010.
Žižek, Slavoj. *Violence: Six Sideways Reflections*. New York: Picador, 2008.

INDEX

Page numbers in italics refer to figures.

Absalom, Absalom! (Faulkner), 45, 161
abstraction, 10, 15, 23, 25, 113–14, 123–27;
    materiality and, 53, 62, 131, 136–39, 153–54
accommodation, 28, 49, 52, 54, 111, 159, 164
Adorno, Theodor, 112, 217n44
aesthetics, 154; ethics and, 119–20; modernism
    and, 9–10, 95, 108
African Americans: advancement, 62–63,
    66, 71, 77, 80, 111, 167–68; autonomy, 52,
    59, 70, 82, 128, 227n88; ecologies, 15;
    killed by police, 212; labor, 173–74, 215n16,
    227n105 (*see also* black agricultural labor);
    masculinity and, 210; passing as white,
    36–37; women, 36–44, 54–55, 78, 81–82.
    See also black bodies; blackness; nadir;
    race; racism; segregation
Agamben, Giorgio, 26
Agee, James, 234n61; *Let Us Now Praise
    Famous Men* (with Evans), 16, 47, 143–45,
    207
agrarianism: conservativism and, 91–92;
    Jeffersonian, 51, 102, 153; modernism
    and, 94–103; neo-, 7, 92; place and, 122;
    progressive, 92, 96; in southern studies,
    229n6; use of term, 228n1. *See also* labor
    agrarianism; leisure agrarianism
Agrarians. *See* Nashville Agrarians
Agricultural Adjustment Act (1933), 151,
    233n39
agricultural collectives. *See* communal
    agriculture
agricultural labor: mechanization of, 122;
    modernity and, 5–6, 11–13; quotas and,
    233n39; standardization of, 194; types
    of, 96. *See also* black agricultural labor;
    black agropolitics; labor; plantations;
    sharecroppers; squireocracy; tenant
    farmers; yeoman farmers
agricultural movements, 5. *See also* labor
    agrarianism; Southern Tenant Farmers'
    Union
Aguiar, Marian, 206
airshafts, in Harlem, 176–77
Alabama, 73, 84
Alabama Sharecroppers' Union, 129, 201
"Alabama Tenant Farmer Wife" (Evans), 147
Albany Movement, 225n52
alienation, 107, 127, 160, 181
Allen, James Lane, 83
Allewaert, Monique, 78
All God's Dangers (1974), 17, 201–4, 206–10,
    208, 212
Allred, Jeff, 142
Altieri, Charles, 136
American Exodus (Lange and Taylor), 144
Ammons, Elizabeth, 43
ancestry, 98–101, 178–79, 198, 230n25
Anderson, Edward, 240n88
Anderson, Perry, 6–7, 97
Anderson, Sherwood, 2
"Antebellum Sermon, An" (Dunbar), 21
Anthology of American Folk Music, 107, 236n11
Appalachian culture, 93, 104–8, 189, 241n15.
    See also Highlander Project / Highlander
    Folk School
Appiah, Kwame Anthony, 206
Aptheker, Herbert, 73, 227n104
Ardoin, Amédé, 159
Arkansas, 144
Arnesen, Eric, 166
Arnow, Harriette, 189
As I Lay Dying (Faulkner), 179
Atlanta, 117
Atlanta Compromise speech (Washington),
    56, 62, 162
Atlanta Riot (1906), 43
Austin, Mary, 106, 210
Autobiography (Du Bois), 73

autonomy: black, 52, 59, 70, 82, 128, 227n88; food independence and, 56–57; standardization and, 165
Avery, Todd, 132
Ayers, Edward, 42–43, 123

Bachelard, Gaston, 148, 151
backwardness, 3, 11, 156
Bailey, Liberty Hyde, 79
Baker, Houston A., Jr., 39, 54, 58, 71, 88, 220n21, 224n30
Bakhtin, Mikhail, 135
Baldwin, James, 187
banjos, 34, 162–63, 221n45
Banta, Martha, 109
Baptist, Edward, 170, 171
Barren Ground (Glasgow), 17, 160, 190–98
Barthes, Roland, 16, 139, 141, 152
Baucom, Ian, 57
Baudelaire, Charles, 165, 172, 192–93, 210
Baudrillard, 193
Beckert, Sven, 83, 171, 211
Belifuss, Michael, 63, 71, 227n85
Bellamy, Edward, 109
Benjamin, Walter: fragmentation and, 210; on history, 28, 154; migrancy and, 165; "One-Way Street," 205; Paris arcades and *die Moderne*, 6, 26, 120, 172, 192–93, 197, 205–6; on photography, 141, 151
Bennett, Michael, 46
Berlant, Lauren, 123, 221n50
Berlin, Irving, 34
Berman, Jessica, 95
Berman, Marshall, 59, 216n30, 239n60
Berry, Chad, 240n85
Berry, Wendell, 7, 25, 229n3
Berwick, Edward, 109
Between the Plough Handles (West), 94
Beverly Hillbillies, The (television show), 189
Bingham, Emily S., 231n60
Birth of a Nation, The (1915), 85
Bissett, Jim, 115
black agricultural labor, 14–16, 22, 26–50; Du Bois and, 62–88; formerly enslaved persons and, 63–65; georgic mode and, 23–26, 42, 44–48, 50, 63; labor agrarianism and, 155–56; Social Security Act and, 222n76; subjecthood and, 22, 26–27, 78, 84–85, 88; value of, 203; Washington and, 50–62; women and, 36–44, 54–55. *See also* sharecroppers; tenant farmers
black agropolitics, 22–26, 35, 38, 41, 72, 81, 88, 116
Black Belt states, 12, 61, 65, 73, 87, 227n92
black bodies, 25–26; agricultural labor and, 61 (*see also* black agricultural labor); nonhuman world and, 30–31; sharecropping and, 128; soil and, 71
black English, 180–88
Black Man, The (magazine), 131
Blackmar, Elizabeth, 193
"black modernism," 224n30
blackness, 42, 46, 76, 198; abject, 167–68; communism and, 116–17, 232n83; double-voiced discourse and, 173–74; folk and, 182, 186
black rapist, image of, 30, 85
Black Reconstruction in America (Du Bois), 215n16
black vernacular culture, 74–76, 84, 163, 226n83
Blight, David, 28
Bloch, Ernst, 47, 216n30
blood, 31–32, 36, 85, 98–100, 104, 118, 191, 198. *See also* ancestry
bodies: class and, 124; language and, 133–39; photographs of, 139–55; of sharecroppers, 124–30; soil and, 100–101; speech acts and, 146; technologies of writing and, 126. *See also* black bodies
Bone, Martyn, 114
Book of American Negro Poetry, The (1922), 27
Botkin, Benjamin, 107
bourgeoisie, 23, 80, 112, 120, 128
Bourke-White, Margaret, 142–43, *144*, 155
Boyd, John, 47
Boyle, Louise, 16, 144–50, *147*, *149*, *151*, 153, 154, 234n62, 234n64
Braidotti, Rosi, 7
bricks and brickmaking, 69–70, 225n61
Briggs, Gabriel, 68, 162
Brinkmeyer, Robert, 97
Brodwin, Stanley, 69, 70
Brown, Bill, 196
Brown, J. Dillon, 236n4
Brown, Michael, 212
Brown, Sterling, 98
Bruyn, Frans de, 220n37

Buell, Lawrence, 9, 24
Burley, Dan, 180
Burroughs, Allie Mae, 147
Burrows, Edwin, 171
Butler, Judith, 197
Butz, Earl, 240n92

Caldwell, Erskine, 1, 142–43, 155
Calhoun Colored School, 74
Calloway, Cab, 180
Campbell, John C., 105
Cannon, Gus (Banjo Joe), 53–54
"Can You Blame the Colored Man?" (Cannon), 53–54, 223n16
capitalist modernity, 17; agricultural labor and, 42 (*see also* agricultural labor; black agricultural labor); economic inequality and, 116, 150, 153, 202–4, 212–13; migration and, 161; regional distinctions and, 108; slavery and, 3–4, 170–73 (*see also* slavery); technology and, 191; urban, 179, 195, 197. *See also* cotton economy; industrial capitalism; mechanization
Carby, Hazel, 42, 186, 239n67
Carpio, Glenda, 180
Carson, Fiddlin' John, 159
Carter Family, 159
Carver, George Washington, 56
Casey, Janet, 4
Cash, W. J., 111, 113, 115, 184, 231n54
cash crops, 13, 23, 54–57, 67, 122, 148, 150. *See also* cotton economy; sharecroppers
cash economy, 113, 164–65
Cassell, Charles Eugene, 2
Castronovo, Russ, 40
Cather, Willa, 95, 235n73
Census of Agriculture (1900), 67
center, 6, 10, 14, 53. *See also* core-periphery relations
Certeau, Michel de, 126, 137, 187
Chakrabarty, Dipesh, 7
Chaplin, Charlie, 165
Chesnutt, Charles W., 25, 220n34
Chicago, 161, 166–67
children, 133–34. *See also Dear Mrs. Roosevelt*
Ching, Barbara, 8
Chu, Patricia, 9, 94
Cimbala, Paul, 64
cities. *See* urban modern

citizenship: black, 22, 24, 36, 88, 221n50; settlement and, 122
"City of Refuge" (Fisher), 160, 169, 173–75, 178, 181, 238n55
civil rights movement, 108, 117, 120, 188, 225n61
Civil War, 28, 38
Clarksville, Tenn., 99
cleanliness, 61–62
"Clodhopper" (West), 118
Clods of Southern Earth (West), 94, 103
Clukey, Amy, 12
Coates, Ta-Nehisi, 212
Cobb, James, 66
Cobb, Ned, 17, 201, 207, *208*, 213
Coclanis, Peter, 61
code-speaking, 38, 221n50
Cohen, Robert, 124, 126, 131. See also *Dear Mrs. Roosevelt*
Cohn, Deborah, 217–18n52
collectivity, 95, 102, 129. *See also* communal agriculture
colonialism, 6–7, 12
colonization, 15, 51–53, 57–58, 68, 223n9
Colored Agricultural Wheel, 22
Colored Farmers' Alliance, 15, 22, 65
"Colored Soldiers, The" (Dunbar), 31
colorism, 41–42, 222n54
color line, 14–15, 64–65, 71, 74, 86–87
Comentale, Edward, 122, 159
Commission on Country Life, 79
commodification, 55, 197
communal agriculture, 59, 64–65, 81–82, 129, 230n53, 232n83
communal land ownership, 152–53
communism, 111, 210; blackness and, 116–17, 232n83. *See also* socialism
Communist Manifesto (Marx and Engels), 109, 112, 123, 210
Communist Party, 81, 96, 108, 116–17, 233n25
communities: black, 38, 42, 44, 59, 76, 176–77, 221n50; interracial cooperation and, 118; postal communication and, 130; public addresses and, 134
Confederacy, 31, 37, 53, 77–78, 86, 101, 117, 170; neo-, 29, 199
Conjure Man Dies, The (Fisher), 169
Conkin, Paul, 228n3, 231n71
Conlogue, William, 191
Connor, James A., 132

INDEX   271

Connor, Steven, 137
conservatism, 7, 91–92, 110–11, 115, 155–56, 197, 229n3, 229n7
consumption, 57–58, 122, 164, 179, 209
convict-lease system, 30
"coon songs," 34
Cooper, Anna Julia, 81
Cooperative Union, 22
core-periphery relations, 6–7, 11–12, 53, 197. *See also* center; marginality
Cotton, Ben, 74–75
cotton economy: alternatives to, 82; capitalist modernity and, 3–4, 6, 83, 215n19; global, 83–84, 113; mechanization and, 122; monocrop cultivation, 55–57, 67; New York City and, 162, 170–73; in *The Quest of the Silver Fleece*, 72–73; sharecropping and, 13, 57, 203–4; swamplands and, 78
Cotton Triangle, 17
counterpublics, 38, 40–41, 44, 133–34
Country Life movement, 194
Cowley, Malcolm, 2
Crab-Grass (West), 94
Crawford, Matthew, 91
creative destruction, 178, 209, 239n60
Creed, Gerald, 8
Crèvecoeur, J. Hector St. John de, 217n45; *Letters from an American Farmer*, 10–11
crime, 29, 41, 43
"Criteria of Negro Art, The" (Du Bois), 81
"Critique of the Philosophy of Progress, A" (Lanier), 111
Croft, Henry, 125, 129
Cronon, William, 216n20
crop-lien system, 57, 67, 82, 227n99. *See also* tenant farmers
Crummell, Alexander, 21
Cruse, Harold, 225n61
culture, 77, 127; definition of, 218n53; dissemination of, 132; Western, 80–81. *See also* Appalachian culture; vernacular music
Cummings, E. E., 1
Cuney, William Waring, 98

Daniel, Pete, 234n39
Daniels, Jonathan, 156, 235n94
Darkwater (Du Bois), 188
Darwinism, 10

Daughters of the Confederacy, 238n52
Davidson, Donald, 96, 99, 116, 117, 156, 228n3, 231n77, 235n94; "A Mirror for Artists," 103–4
Davis, David A., 215n10, 215n19
Davis, Thadious, 4
Dear Mrs. Roosevelt (Cohen, ed.), 124, 126, 131–39, 153, 155, 233n33
debt slavery, 30, 59, 204
decline, 33, 92, 97, 100–101
decolonization, 51–52
Delany, Martin R., 117
Deleuze, Gilles, 152, 193, 196, 210, 235n80
Delta Cooperative Farm, 141–42, *142*, *143*
Denning, Michael, 84, 124
Department of Agriculture, U.S., 47, 67
Derrida, Jacques, 185
"Deserted Plantation, The" (Dunbar), 32–36
Dewey, John, 110
dialect, 38, 41, 43, 180–88, 221nn39–40
difference, 38, 107; folk, 104–8; Nashville Agrarians and, 116; racial, 75–76, 118, 128; regional, 10, 108, 156, 195–99; standardized time and, 110
Dillingham, Mabel, 74
Dinerstein, Joel, 159
dirt, 30–31; Du Bois's representations of, 50, 68–72; Washington's representations of, 61–62, 69. *See also* soil
Disinherited Speak, The (1937), 124–30, 137, 139, 146, 153, 155, 213
dislocation, 160, 167, 187
dispossession, 114, 118, 147, 241n15
Dixon, Thomas, Jr., 85
documentary photography, 141–55
domestic labor, 127–28, 146–50, 154
Dore, Florence, 216n20
Dorman, Richard, 119
Dorson, Richard, 107
double-voiced discourse, 21, 43, 54; blackness and, 173–74; letters and, 137–38
Douglas, Aaron, 169
Douglass, Frederick, 37, 210
Dubois, Laurent, 163, 221n45
Du Bois, W. E. B.: background, 68; colorism and, 222n54; dirt and soil, images of, 68–72; Dunbar and, 27; "talented tenth," 39; urban modernity and, 46; Washington and, 15, 36, 49, 225n61

—works: *Autobiography*, 73; *Black Reconstruction in America*, 215n16; "The Criteria of Negro Art," 81; *Darkwater*, 188; *Dusk of Dawn*, 63, 73; "The Negro in the Black Belt," 72; "The Negro Landholder of Georgia," 72, 81, 226n68; *The Philadelphia Negro*, 72; *The Quest of the Silver Fleece*, 15, 49, 72–88, 167, 226nn71–72, 226n76, 227n100; "The Rural South," 72; *The Souls of Black Folk*, 15, 21, 22, 32, 37, 43, 49–50, 62–71, 74, 86–87, 227n105, 228n113
Duck, Leigh Anne, 5, 185, 196
Dunbar, Paul Laurence: georgic tradition and, 15, 25–26; plantation and farm poems, 22, 25–36, 42, 45–48; soil and, 100
—works: "An Antebellum Sermon," 21; "The Colored Soldiers," 31; "The Deserted Plantation," 32–36; *Folks from Dixie*, 220n33; "Goin' Back," 35–36; "The Haunted Oak," 29–31; *In Old Plantation Days*, 220n33; "The Party," 21; *The Sport of the Gods*, 174; "To Booker T. Washington," 21, 221n38; "To the Eastern Shore," 32; "To the South—On Its New Slavery," 30; "Tuskegee Song," 32, 221n38; "When de Co'n Pone's Hot," 21; "When Malindy Sings," 21
Dundes, Alan, 106
Dusk of Dawn (Du Bois), 63, 73
Dutch folk schools, 105

Eclogues (Virgil), 25
ecocriticism, 8–9, 15, 23, 25, 46
ecologies, 14, 56–57; swamp, 78–79
economic inequality, 116, 150, 153, 202–4, 212–13
economies, 14, 55; national, 10–11, 225n61
Edge, John T., 224n20, 234n93
education, 37, 40, 42, 49; advancement and, 77, 79–82
Elaine Massacre, 129
Eliot, T. S., 95, 96, 99, 127, 199, 230n22
Ellington, Duke, 176, 240n90
Ellison, Ralph, 75, 76
"Emblems" (Tate), 98–101
Emerson, Ken, 221n40
Emmett, Dan, 34
Engels, Friedrich, 53, 130, 170; *Communist Manifesto* (with Marx), 109, 112, 123, 210

enslaved people. *See* formerly enslaved persons; slavery
Entin, Joseph, 150
environmentalism, 206
epistemology, 76
Eurocentrism, 97
European consciousness, 26
Evans, Walker, 13, 143; "Alabama Tenant Farmer Wife," 147; *Let Us Now Praise Famous Men* (with Agee), 16, 143–45, 147, 207
exchange, systems of, 17
exploitation, 30–31, 41; modernization and, 205–6
"Ezekiel" (Fisher), 174
"Ezekiel Learns" (Fisher), 174

Fanon, Frantz, 51–53, 57, 223n9
Farland, Maria, 5, 219n10, 226n72, 226n76
Farmer-Kaiser, Mary, 225n44
Farmers' Alliance, 65
Farmers' Conference, 227n99
Farm Securities Administration, 124
Farthest Man Down, The (Washington), 52
Fathers, The (Tate), 230n25
Faulkner, William, 1, 2, 11, 95, 210; *Absalom, Absalom!*, 45, 161; *As I Lay Dying*, 179; *Go Down, Moses*, 161, 207, 241n10; *Light in August*, 45, 161; *Mosquitoes*, 161; *Pylon*, 161; *The Reivers*, 161; *Sanctuary*, 161
femininity, 43, 78. *See also* women
feminism, 39, 228n1
Finnegans Wake (Joyce), 1, 132
Fire!!! (1926), 169
Fisher, Rudolph, 16–17, 167–69, 171, 173–80, 197, 240n90; "City of Refuge," 160, 169, 173–75, 178, 181, 238n55; *The Conjure Man Dies*, 169; "Ezekiel," 174; "Ezekiel Learns," 174; "The Promised Land," 160, 174–79, 200, 239n55; "Ringtail," 174; "The South Lingers On," 160, 174–75, 179; "Vestiges," 174
Fiskio, Janet, 122
Fisk Jubilee Singers, 69, 74
Fitzgerald, F. Scott, 2, 95
Flately, Jonathan, 74, 204
Flemons, Dom, 223n16
folk, 16; blackness and, 182, 186; leisure agrarianism and, 103–8; mobility and, 188; rural, 239n67; urban, 186

folk memory, 104, 107
folk music, 74, 107, 236n1. *See also* vernacular music
Folks from Dixie (Dunbar), 220n33
Foner, Eric, 44, 65, 225n44
Foner, Philip, 171
food, consumption of, 122
food independence, 54–57, 224n20
formerly enslaved persons, 28–29, 39, 63–65. *See also* slavery
Fortune, T. Thomas, 59
Fort-Whiteman, Lovett, 117
Foster, Stephen, 33–36, 221n40, 221n43
Foucault, Michel, 26, 42, 195
fragmentation, 9, 13, 199–200, 207, 210
Franch, Ellen, 128
Frank, Waldo, 104
Fraser, Nancy, 133
Frazer, James, 96
Frederic, Harold, 240n88
Freedmen's Bureau, 63–65, 225n45
freedom, 36, 37, 39–40, 120, 188. *See also* formerly enslaved persons
free labor, 65
Freud, Sigmund, 10, 187
Friedman, Susan Stanford, 27, 97
frontier, 10, 229n6
Frost, Robert, 11
Frost, William Goodell, 104–5
Fugitives, 92
futurity, 31, 94, 101

Gaonkar, Dilip, 6–7, 27, 94, 209, 216n30
Garner, Dwight, 17, 145, 201–2
Garner, Eric, 212
Gates, Henry Louis, Jr., 32–33, 183
Gatewood, D., 125
gender roles, 11, 210, 228n1. *See also* women
Genovese, Eugene, 229n3
Georgia, 73, 232n83
"Georgia Wanted Me Dead or Alive" (West), 96
georgic mode: black agricultural labor and, 23–26, 42, 44–48, 50, 63; Du Bois and, 63, 70; Dunbar and, 15, 220n38; in England, 220n37; Harper and, 39, 42; modernism and, 23–26; Washington and, 53, 61–62
Georgics (Virgil), 24, 25, 31–32, 53, 84, 219n18, 220n37
German Kali Works, 84

Giddens, Anthony, 204–5
Giesen, James C., 201–2
Gilman, Charlotte Perkins, 11
Gilmore, Glenda, 117
Gilroy, Paul, 43, 62, 70, 71
Glaeser, Edward, 170–71
Glasgow, Ellen, 17, 160, 190–98
Glen, John M., 93
"Glossary of Harlem Slang" (Hurston), 168
Gobbler's Knob, N.C., 164–66
Go Down, Moses (Faulkner), 161, 207, 241n10
"Goin' Back" (Dunbar), 35–36
Gone with the Wind (Mitchell), 7, 12, 45, 202
Goodman, Kevis, 70
Grandison, Kenrick, 60
Grantham, Dewey, 113
Gray, Richard, 113
Great Depression, 114, 117, 240n97; images of rural life in, 139–55
Great Migration, 160, 166–68, 187, 189–90, 212
Greenblatt, Stephen, 217n45
Greene, J. Lee, 73
Greeson, Jennifer Rae, 105
Gregory, James, 189–90, 218n69, 238n52, 240n85
Griffin, Farah Jasmine, 160, 166, 178, 236n5
Griffith, D. W., 85
Griggs, Sutton, 117
Grubbs, Donald, 153
Guattari, Félix, 196, 210
Gussow, Joan Dye, 91
Guthrie, Woody, 124, 133; "This Land Is Your Land," 153

Hagood, Margaret Jarman, 154
Hahn, Steven, 237n22
Hale, Grace Elizabeth, 13, 218n60
Hall, Jacquelyn Dowd, 239n82
Hall, James Jefferson Davis, 2
Hall, Stuart, 174
Hamer, Fannie Lou, 224n20
Handcox, John, 124
Handley, George, 29, 38
Handy, W. C., 75
Harding, Desmond, 216n24
Harlem: black southern migrants in, 166–68, 173–78, 220n27; jive, 180–88
Harlem Renaissance, 160, 167, 169, 174, 186, 189

Harper, Frances E., 15, 22; *Iola Leroy*, 15, 22, 26, 36–48, 75, 167, 221n50
Harvey, David, 7, 188, 195, 239n60
"Haunted Oak, The" (Dunbar), 29–31
H. D., 95
Hearn, Lafcadio, 226n83
Hegel, Georg Wilhelm Friedrich, 66, 69, 70, 77, 80
Hegeman, Susan, 107, 144–45
Hemingway, Ernest, 2, 95
Henderson, George Wylie, 73
Henninger, Katherine, 146
Herder, Johann Gottfried von, 103
Herring, Scott, 216n34
Hersey, Mark D., 56
Hickman, Jared, 216n29, 217n45
Hicks, Scott, 56
Highlander Project / Highlander Folk School (HFS): folk and, 103–8; leisure agrarianism and, 16, 93–97, 110, 112, 115; racial integration and, 118–20; rural poverty and, 114. *See also* West, Don
Highlander Research and Education Centers, 120
Highlanders / Allegheny Highlanders (musical group), 163
hillbilly recordings, 236nn1–2. *See also* vernacular music
hillbilly stereotype, 189
Hillhouse, Miss., 141–42, *142*, *143*
Hilmes, Michelle, 135
history, 120, 127, 154–55; progress and, 110–11. *See also* memory; nostalgia
Hobsbawm, Eric, 171
Holiday, Billie, 220n34
hooks, bell, 46–47, 198
Horkheimer, Max, 217n44
horseshoe-shaped migration, 189–98
Horton, Myles, 92–93, 105–6
Howard, O. O., 64–65, 225n45
Hubbs, Jolene, 179
Huber, Patrick, 163, 236n1
Hughes, Langston, 95, 98, 169, 190
Hurston, Zora Neale, 11, 95, 167, 169, 210; "Glossary of Harlem Slang," 168; *Mules and Men*, 162; "Now You Cookin' with Gas," 160, 181–87; "Story in Harlem Slang," 17, 160, 180–87; *Their Eyes Were Watching God*, 183

identity: collective, 95; language and, 182–84; migration and, 182–84, 199–200; mutability of, 155; national, 107; rusticity as, 160, 165; slavery and, 209–10; Trumpism, 211–12, 241n15
I'll Take My Stand (Twelve Southerners), 15–16, 91–97, 104, 106, 108, 109, 111–13, 119, 127–28, 150, 155–56, 229n3, 231n71. *See also* Nashville Agrarians
imperialism, 68. *See also* colonization
independence, 10, 39, 41–42, 55, 57, 82
indigenous peoples, 51, 218n59
industrial capitalism, 9–10; agrarianism and, 95, 97, 112, 114–15; agriculture and, 94; time and, 109–10. *See also* capitalist modernity; mechanization
In Old Plantation Days (Dunbar), 220n33
insurrection, 227n88
interracial cooperation, 124, 154–56
interregional marriage, 86
Iola Leroy (Harper), 15, 22, 26, 36–48, 75, 167, 221n50
Irish modernists, 27, 220n27
Isenberg, Nancy, 124
Ives, Charles, 76

Jabavu, D. D. T., 59–60
Jackson, Zakiyyah Iman, 26
Jacques, Geoffrey, 26
James, Henry, 240n88
Jameson, Fredric, 23, 160–61, 199
jazz, 159, 236n2
Jefferson, Thomas, 10
Jeffersonian agrarianism, 51, 102, 153
Jim Crow, 14, 42–44, 128, 173, 175, 188–89. *See also* segregation
jive, 180–88
Johnson, Andrew, 67
Johnson, Charles S., 168, 238n53
Johnson, James Weldon, 27, 167, 179
Johnson, Kimberly, 24, 26, 28, 171
Johnson, Walter, 38
Jones, Gavin, 221n39
Jordan, Clarence, 232n83
Joyce, James, 1, 132

Kazin, Alfred, 98, 110
Kelley, Edith Summers, 148–49
Kelley, Robin D. G., 108, 116, 128–29, 233n25

INDEX 275

Kentucky, 111–12
Kephart, Horace, 104–5, 230n32
Kettel, Thomas P., 172
Keynesian economics, 114
Kimbrell, Elroe, *151*
Kimbrell, Lucille, *151*
King, Martin Luther, Jr., 224n30
Kingsolver, Barbara, 91
Kirby, Jack Temple, 113, 189
"Knotts County" (West), 111–12
Koinonia Farm, 232n83
Kreyling, Michael, 15, 91, 228n3
Kuznets, Simon, 203–4

labor, 210; deadening effects of, 149–50; gendered divisions of, 148; leisure and, 112–13, 149–50 (*see also* leisure agrarianism); organized, 117; race and, 12–17 (*see also* black agricultural labor); unionization, 121–31. *See also* agricultural labor; domestic labor
labor agrarianism, 16, 121–56; bodies of protest and, 121–39; cultural products of, 94; photography and, 139–55
Labov, William, 184
Lacan, Jacques, 141
"Land!" (Ransom), 114–15
Land of the Free (1938), 16
land ownership: by African Americans, 39–40, 82, 222n52; communal, 152–53; control over space and, 128–30; private, 152–53; quotas and, 233n39; redistribution of, 115–16; wealth and, 202–3. *See also* plantation owners
Lange, Dorothea, 13, 141–42, *142*, *143*; *American Exodus* (with Taylor), 144; "Migrant Mother," 147
language, 43; black English, 180–88; bodies and, 133–39; subjectivity and, 182–84; unrest and, 130–31. *See also* dialect
Lanier, Lyle, 110–11, 128; "A Critique of the Philosophy of Progress," 111
Larsen, Nella, 198
Latin American migrant workers, 155–56
Latour, Bruno, 22–23, 78
Lawrence, Icy Jewel, *151*
Lawrence, Jacob, 166–67
Lawrence, Myrtle, 16, 144–55, *147*, *149*, *151*, 154, 213, 234n65

Lawrence, Sylvia, *149*
Lee, Maurice, 86
leftists, 91–93
Lehman Brothers, 170
leisure: labor and, 112–13, 149–50; political action and, 109
leisure agrarianism, 16, 91–120; definition of, 93–94; folk and, 103–8; Nashville Agrarians, 108–20, 150; political action and, 114–20; progress and, 109–14
Lemann, Nicholas, 166–67
Leopold, Aldo, 59
Lepore, Jill, 131, 154
letters, 130–39. *See also Dear Mrs. Roosevelt*; *Disinherited Speak, The*
Letters from an American Farmer (Crèvecoeur), 10–11
Let Us Now Praise Famous Men (Agee and Evans), 16, 143–45, 147, 207
Levine, Lawrence, 38
Light in August (Faulkner), 45, 161
Li'l Abner (comic strip), 189, 235n73
Lilla, Mark, 110–11
Limerick, Patricia, 229n6
Lincoln, Abraham, 129
literacy, 37, 38, 40, 77, 126, 130–31
localism, 91–92, 228n1
Locke, Alain, 27, 168, 169, 220n27; *The New Negro*, 168, 173, 174
Lorence, James, 105–6, 116–17
lost cause fiction, 85–86
lost causism, 7
Lott, Eric, 33, 183
Loviglio, Jason, 132
Lucretius, 217n45
Lunsford, Bascom Lamar, 107
lynching, 24, 29–30, 111, 114, 169, 212, 220n34
Lytle, Andrew, 104, 111, 112

MacLeish, Archibald, 144
Macon, Uncle Dave, 159
mail and mailboxes: letters, 130–39; postcards, 164; as private space, 130
Mancini, J. M., 159, 236n3
marginality, 6, 10, 14, 53, 165. *See also* core-periphery relations
marriage plot, 86
Martí, José, 216n29, 223n9
Marx, Karl, 53, 108, 130, 239n60; *Communist*

276 INDEX

Manifesto (with Engels), 109, 112, 123, 210
Marxism, 10, 28, 44–45
Mason, Bobbie Ann, 189
materiality: abstraction and, 53, 62, 131, 136–39, 153–54; poverty and, 127–28, 137–39. *See also* bodies
May, Herbert L., 93
McCarthy, Jeffrey, 24
McDonald, Luella, 128
McInnis, Jarvis, 82, 226n71, 227n100
McKay, Claude, 221n45
McKenney, E. B., 131
McKibben, Bill, 91
McLuhan, Marshall, 140
mechanization, 10, 127, 195; of agricultural labor, 122; dispossession and, 241n15; domestic labor and, 148–49
Mehroff, W. Arthur, 237n31
melancholy, 35, 99, 197
memory, 28, 100; folk, 104, 107. *See also* nostalgia
Memphis, 161
Mencken, H. L., 11
metropolitanism, 68; values of, 106–7. *See also* urban modern
Michaels, Walter Benn, 182
Micheaux, Oscar, 166
microhistory, 154
Middleton, Richard, 163
"Migrant Mother" (Lange), 147
migration: black, 44, 160, 166–68, 187, 189–90, 197, 198–99, 212; identity and, 182–84, 199–200; psychological effects of, 180, 183, 194
migratory modernism, 16–17, 159–200; banjo music and, 162–66; black southern migrants in North, 168–80; dialect and, 180–88; fragmentation and, 199–200; horseshoe-shaped migration and, 189–98
Miller, Karl Hagstrom, 106
minstrelsy, 34, 35, 54, 74–75, 163, 164, 166, 221n43
"Mirror for Artists, A" (Davidson), 103–4
"miscegenation," 14, 31
Mitchell, H. L., 124, 126–27, 130, 155–56
Mitchell, Joseph, 1–3
Mitchell, Margaret, 7, 12, 45, 202
Mitchell, Theodore R., 65
mixed-race identity, 14, 36, 42

mobility, 37, 44, 55, 160, 188. *See also* migration
modern, definition of, 217n45
modern-in-the-rural, 17, 205, 207–13
modernism: backward-looking, 94; definitions of, 6, 9–10, 27, 204; despair and, 95; psychology of, 160–61; radio and, 132–33; redemption and, 95; rurality and, 3–8; southern, 3–7; turbulence of cultural rupture and, 97; urban life in, 1–3. *See also* rural modern; urban modern
modernity, definition of, 6, 9–10, 205
modernization, definition of, 9–10
modern world-system, 11
Moglen, Seth, 95, 99, 229n14
morality, 41, 115, 161, 210, 226n71
Morris, William, 230n53
Morrison, Toni, 87, 178, 224n39
Morton, Timothy, 8–9, 83
Mosquitoes (Faulkner), 161
mothers, 154, 235n73. *See also* domestic labor
"Mountain Boy" (West), 100–101
Mountain Dance and Folk Festival (Asheville), 107
Mrs. Eleanor Roosevelt's Own Program, 132, 233n30
"mulatto modernism," 224n30
Mules and Men (Hurston), 162
Murphy, Paul V., 228n3, 229n7, 231n77
Murray, Albert, 237n24
My Day (Roosevelt column), 233n33
My Larger Education (Washington), 223n10
"My Old Kentucky Home" (Foster), 33–36, 221n40, 221n43
"My South" (West), 109

NAACP, 73, 129
nadir (of American race relations), 23–25, 28, 36, 52, 212; use of term, 219n8
Nagoski, Ian, 236n1
Nashville, Tenn., 162
Nashville Agrarians, 7, 24, 228n3; community and, 118; conservatism of, 155–56, 197, 229n7; critiques of, 101–3, 235n94; difference and, 116; folk and, 103–8; idealism of, 122; leisure agrarianism and, 108–20, 150; modernism and, 94–103; rural spaces and, 99
—works: *I'll Take My Stand*, 15–16, 91–97, 104, 106, 108, 109, 111–13, 119, 127–28, 150, 155–56,

INDEX 277

Nashville Agrarians, works (*continued*) 229n3, 231n71; *Who Owns America?*, 16, 115–16
National Farm Labor Union, 156
national identity, 107
national institutions, 130; national economies, 10–11, 225n61
National Negro Business League, 225n61
nature, definition of, 23, 218n53
"Negro in the Black Belt, The" (Du Bois), 72
"Negro Landholder of Georgia, The" (Du Bois), 72, 81, 226n68
Negro World (magazine), 131
neo-agrarianism, 7, 92
neo-Confederacy, 29, 199
New Communities, 225n52
New Critical modernism, 92, 94–95
New Deal, 204
New Domesticity movement, 228n1
New Negro, 167–68, 178, 180, 186
New Negro, The (Locke, ed.), 168, 173, 174
New Orleans, 161–62
"New River Train" (fiddle tune), 164
New York City, 1, 16–17, 159–62; black southern migrants in, 160, 166–88; slavery and cotton trade, 162, 170–73; white migrants in, 160, 162–66, 189–98
Niagara Movement, 73, 222n1
Nicholls, David, 56
Niebuhr, Reinhold, 93
Nixon, Herman, 112, 231n60
Nixon, Rob, 63, 206–7, 210
"No Room for a Tramp" (Poole), 165
Norrell, Robert J., 51
Norris, Frank, 83
North, Michael, 140, 186
nostalgia, 28, 66, 110–11, 163, 180; modernity and, 163
"Now You Cookin' with Gas" (Hurston), 160, 181–87
Nunn, Erich, 106

"Ode to the Confederate Dead" (Tate), 101
Olsen, Tillie, 95
"one-drop rule," 31
organized labor, 117; unionization, 121–31
Osborne, Peter, 2
otherness, 14, 155–56. *See also* difference
Oubre, Claude, 225n44

Outka, Paul, 45, 219n10
ownership. *See* land ownership; plantation owners
Owsley, Frank, 104, 107, 109, 113

Page, Thomas Nelson, 7, 86, 228n113
Parchman, Lula, 128
Paris Arcades, 6, 26, 172, 197
Parks, Rosa, 120, 188
"Party, The" (Dunbar), 21
pastoral mode, 24, 44–46, 194, 219n10
Patton, Charley, 159
Payne, Elizabeth, 16, 146–48, 152–53, 234n65
Pelham, John, 77
Pellicer, Juan Christian, 34
Pells, Richard, 114
Peoples, Nathan, 125
periphery. *See* core-periphery relations; marginality
Perkell, Christine, 25, 219n18
Peters, John Durham, 136
Petgen, Dorothy, 93
Phelan, Peggy, 152
Philadelphia Negro, The (Du Bois), 72
photography, 124, 139–55
Pierce, Marie, 127
Pigford v. Glickman (1999), 47, 225n52
Piketty, Thomas, 17, 202–4, 211, 212
place, 122; phenomenology of, 192, 237n31; sense of, 135–36, 228n3. *See also* space
plantation owners (white planter class), 36, 51, 65, 84–85, 96, 99, 111–15, 123, 171. *See also* squireocracy
plantation romances, 7, 40, 85
plantations: abandoned, 42, 64–65; black labor and, 25–36, 45; as geography of oblivion, 29, 36; idyllic, 33; modernity and, 11–12, 87–88; as proscenium, 81; in *The Quest of the Silver Fleece*, 79–81; slavery on, 12–14, 28–36
Plato, 80
Plessy, Homer, 188
political action, 123; folk and, 107; language and, 130–31; radical, 117, 120; rural, 94. *See also* communism; labor agrarianism; leisure agrarianism; socialism; Southern Tenant Farmers' Union; unionization
Pollan, Michael, 91
Poole, Charlie, 160, 162–66, 189, 199, 237n16,

240n90; "No Room for a Tramp," 165; "A Trip to New York," 163–66
populist movements, 123, 241n15
postcards, 164
postcolonialism, 7, 160, 209
posthumanism, 25–26, 88
postmodernism, 4, 199, 204, 212–13
Pound, Ezra, 11, 95, 229n22
poverty, 119; children in, 133–34; material bodies and, 137–39; photographs of, 142–43; rural, 13, 113–14, 127–28, 152; urban, 11; white farmers, 113–14, 155–56, 165, 179; women and, 127. *See also* economic inequality
Pratt, Mary Louise, 6, 166
primitivism, 216n29
privacy, 130
production, 23, 25, 54–57, 59, 64–65, 209; exploitation and, 205–6; landowners and, 129, 135; space and, 42; time and, 110; urban, 179. *See also* capitalist modernity; cash crops; cotton economy; labor
progress, 66, 81, 210; leisure agrarianism and, 109–14. *See also* racial progress / racial uplift
Progressive Era fiction, 82–83
Progressive Farmers and Household Union of America, 129
proletariat, 108, 120
"Promised Land, The" (Fisher), 160, 174–79, 200, 239n55
protest, 131; labor agrarianism and, 121–39. *See also* political action
Providence Cooperative Farm, 141–42
psychological dualism, 43, 71
psychology, 3, 10, 36, 45, 85, 152, 169; migration and, 180, 183, 194; of modernism, 160–61, 190–91
publics, 132–35. *See also* counterpublics
Purdy, Jedediah, 23, 79
Pylon (Faulkner), 161

Quest of the Silver Fleece, The (Du Bois), 15, 49, 72–88, 167, 226nn71–72, 226n76, 227n100
Quijano, Aníbal, 11
quotas, 233n39

race, 14; indigenous peoples and, 218n59; labor and, 12–17; "one-drop rule," 31; rural modern and, 4. *See also* African Americans; blackness; nadir; whiteness
racial integration, 31, 118–19, 154–56
racial progress / racial uplift, 37, 39–41, 61, 62–63, 66, 71, 77, 80, 111, 167–68
racial unrest, 212
racism, 65, 116–17; dialect and, 221n39; fear of communism and, 116–17. *See also* lynching; segregation; white supremacy
radio, 131–33
railroads, 206
Raine, Anne, 63, 87
Rampersad, Arnold, 82
Ransom, John Crowe, 113; "Land!," 114–15; "The South—Old or New?," 97; "What Does the South Want?," 119, 231n71
Rawe, John C., 116
reclamation, 22, 24–26, 28, 79, 85, 240n97
reconciliation, 38, 42, 44
Reconstruction era, 2, 37, 45, 51, 63–65, 69, 225n44
Reed, Adolph, 182
reflexivity, 205
regional difference, 10, 108, 156, 195–99
regionalism, 12, 108, 197, 213
Reivers, The (Faulkner), 161
reparations, 212
Republic, The (Plato), 80
restitution, 38
Rice, Tamir, 212
Richardson, Riché, 46, 167, 219n3
"Richmond" (fiddle tune), 164
"Ringtail" (Fisher), 174
Roach, Joseph, 148
Robbins, Hollis, 38
Robertson, Priscilla, 144–45, 155
Robeson County, N.C., 2
Robinson, Cedric J., 4
Robinson, Lester, 125, 128
Rodgers, Lawrence, 160, 179, 236n5
Romine, Scott, 199
Ronda, Margaret, 15, 25, 33, 220n38
Roosevelt, Eleanor, 16, 124; *Mrs. Eleanor Roosevelt's Own Program*, 132, 233n30; *My Day* (newspaper column), 233n33; prominence of, 136–39; radio and, 132; support for youth groups, 233n30; working class and, 133. See also *Dear Mrs. Roosevelt*
Roosevelt, Franklin D., 222n76

INDEX 279

Roosevelt, Theodore, 54, 79
Rorrer, Kinney, 237n16
Rorty, Richard, 211
Rosenzweig, Roy, 193
Rourke, Constance, 108
Rowe, John Carlos, 130
Rukeyser, Muriel, 130–31
Rural Electrification Act, 5
rurality: black georgic and, 44–48; definition of, 8; marginalization and, 136, 165
rural modern, 3–17; modern-in-the-rural, 17, 205, 207–13; rural-in-the-modern, 17, 205–7. *See also* black agricultural labor; Du Bois, W. E. B.; Dunbar, Paul Laurence; labor agrarianism; leisure agrarianism; migratory modernism; Washington, Booker T.
"Rural South, The" (Du Bois), 72
rural values, 106–7
Rushdie, Salman, 178
rusticity, as identity marker, 160, 165

Sanctuary (Faulkner), 161
Sanneh, Kelefa, 91
Sante, Luc, 176
Saunders, Steven, 221n43
Scarry, Elaine, 119, 138–39
Scheiber, Andrew, 68
Schmidt, Peter, 42, 80
Schoenberg, Arnold, 76
Schuyler, George S., 198
Scottsboro Boys, 188, 210
segregation, 12–14, 43, 119, 218nn60–61; Agrarians and, 92; Farmers' Alliance and, 65; in Harlem, 177; Washington and, 50, 223n2. *See also* Jim Crow
Sekula, Allan, 139–40
sense of place, 135–36, 228n3
sharecroppers, 13; agrarianism and, 122; black, 201–4; bodies of, 124–30; cotton farming and, 13, 57, 203–4; labor agrarianism and, 94; photographs of, 146–55; white, 113–14. *See also* Southern Tenant Farmers' Union; tenant farmers
Sharecroppers' Union, 124
Sharecroppers' Voice (magazine), 131
Shaw, Nate, 201–4, 206–10
Shelton, Allen, 77–78
Sherrod, Shirley, 225n52

Silber, Nina, 44
Simmel, Georg, 192
Simms, William Gilmore, 45
Simpson, Lewis, 45
Sinclair, Upton, 83
Singer, Alan, 238n36
slavery, 15, 50, 188; code-speaking and, 38; colonization and, 51–53; economy and, 111; identity and, 209–10; legacies of, 128, 237n24; memory and, 28. *See also* formerly enslaved persons; plantations
Slotkin, Richard, 32
slow violence, 63
Smethurst, James, 26, 43, 49, 71
Smith, Harry, 107, 236n1
Smith, Jon, 8, 217–18n52
Smith, Lillian, 13–14, 102–3
Smith, Paul Chaat, 218n59
Smith-Lever Act (1914), 194
socialism, 81, 115–16, 118, 129, 229n3. *See also* communism
Socialist Party of Oklahoma, 124
Social Security Act (1935), 222n76
soil, 8, 36; aesthetics and, 119; bodies and, 100–101; in Dunbar's poems, 30–32; progress and, 109–14; in swamps, 84–85; Washington and, 61. *See also* dirt
soil exhaustion, 67
Soja, Edward, 109
Sollors, Werner, 180
Sontag, Susan, 16, 140, 152–53
Souls of Black Folk The (Du Bois), 15, 21, 22, 32, 37, 43, 49–50, 62–71, 74, 86–87, 227n105, 228n113
South: as backward, 3, 11, 156; highlanders, 104–5; identity and, 199–200; modernism, 3–7; obsolescence and, 196; "other South" and, 155–56; as region, 12; urban, 161–62
southern diaspora, 17, 218n69
Southern Folk School and Libraries, 93
Southern Labor School, 146
southern studies, 3–5, 12
Southern Tenant Farmers' Union (STFU), 5, 16, 115, 231n73; cooperative farms, 141–42; documentary photographs and, 144–55; failure of, 152–53; interracial cooperation in, 124, 128, 154–56; women in, 128. See also *Disinherited Speak, The*

"South Lingers On, The" (Fisher), 160, 174–75, 179
"South—Old or New?, The" (Ransom), 97
space, 99, 128–30, 135–36. *See also* place
speech acts, 131; embodied, 146
Spencer, Herbert, 80
Spivak, Gayatri, 68, 124, 185, 216n29, 223n9
Spivey, Donald, 51
Sport of the Gods, The (Dunbar), 174
squireocracy, 96, 99, 102, 110, 113. *See also* plantation owners
Stack, Carol B., 198
standardization, 10, 110, 165, 194, 199–200, 217n44
static reality, 132–33, 138
Stecopoulos, Harilaos, 12
Stewart, Jeffrey, 27
STFU. *See* Southern Tenant Farmers' Union
Storey, Mark, 5, 168
"Story in Harlem Slang" (Hurston), 17, 160, 180–87
Stott, William, 126, 142
Stowe, Harriet Beecher, 227n88; *Uncle Tom's Cabin*, 33
"Strange Fruit" (Holiday), 220n34
subaltern populations, 12; bodies of, 123
subjectivity, 95; language and, 182–84
Sullivan, John Jeremiah, 112
Sundquist, Eric, 74
Susman, Walter, 107
Sutton, Damian, 152
swamps, 2, 50, 72–82, 84, 87, 227n85, 227n88
Synge, John Millington, 27

Tallapoosa County, Ala., 201–4, 207
Tate, Allen, 110, 116, 119, 150, 231n73; "Emblems," 98–101; *The Fathers*, 230n25; "Ode to the Confederate Dead," 101; *Who Owns America?* (ed., with Agar), 16, 115–16
Taylor, Frederick Winslow, 109–10
Taylor, John, 84
Taylor, Moses, 170, 238n36
Taylor, Paul, 144
technologies, 10, 22, 58–59; capitalist modernity and, 191; communication, 127, 135; dangers of, 165; protest and, 131; radio and, 132
television, 137
tenant farmers, 12–15, 17, 50, 116; Agrarians and, 229n3; bodies of, 124–30; debt-slavery and, 59, 67, 82; labor agrarianism and, 94; material concerns and, 127–28; mechanization and, 122; photographs of, 142–55, *143*, *144*, *147*, *149*, *151*; private space and, 128–29. *See also* sharecroppers; Southern Tenant Farmers' Union
Tennessee Valley Authority, 5
Their Eyes Were Watching God (Hurston), 183
"They Take Their Stand" (West), 102–3
"This Land Is Your Land" (Guthrie), 153
Thompson, Florence Owens, 147
Thorn, Charlotte, 74
Thurman, Wallace, 169
time, 109–10, 120, 135, 185
Timrod, Henry, 31
Tin Pan Alley, 34
"To Booker T. Washington" (Dunbar), 21, 221n38
Toil and Hunger (West), 94, 103
Toomer, Jean, 1, 95, 210
"To the Eastern Shore" (Dunbar), 32
"To the South—On Its New Slavery" (Dunbar), 30
Tourgée, Albion W., 69, 222n52, 225n61
tradition, 110–11, 154
translation, 22–23, 78
"Trip to New York, A" (Poole), 163–66
Trotter, William Monroe, 222n1
Truman, Harry, 114
Trump, Donald, 211–12, 241n15
Tschumpeter, Joseph, 178, 239n60
Tuan, Yi-Fu, 238n31, 239n58
Tukabahchee County, Ala., *208*
"Turkey in the Straw" (fiddle tune), 164
Turner, Frederick Jackson, 104, 229n6
Tuskegee Institute, 15, 21, 28, 32, 43, 50–52, 54–60, 82
"Tuskegee Song" (Dunbar), 32, 221n38
12 Million Black Voices (1941), 16, 144
Twelve Southerners. *See* Nashville Agrarians

Uncle Tom's Cabin (Stowe), 33
Underwood, Thomas, 99, 231n60
unionization, 121–31
United Auto Workers (UAW), 121
Up from Slavery (Washington), 3, 15, 21, 22, 39, 43, 49–62, 69–70, 72–73, 81–82, 86–87, 220n21, 223n2, 223n9, 223n16, 225n61

uplift. *See* racial progress / racial uplift
urban folk, 186
urban modern, 1–11, 14, 43; capitalism and, 179, 195, 197; migration and, 160; as periphery, 53; progress and, 210; southern cities, 161–62; time and, 185

Value of Swamp Land (German Kali Works), 84
values, 106–7, 128
Vance, J. D., 241n15
Vance, Rupert, 119
vaudeville dialects, 221n39
Veblen, Thorstein, 93, 112
vernacular landscape, 206–7
vernacular-lyric modernists, 98
vernacular music: black, 74–76, 84, 163, 226n83; New York and, 159–60; white, 106
"Vestiges" (Fisher), 174
violence, 14–15, 29–32, 223n9; black-on-white, 181; bodies and, 125–26; neo-Confederacy and, 199; police killings, 212; racial, 24, 85, 129; slavery and, 63; slow, 63; in South, 187–88. *See also* lynching
Virgil: *Eclogues*, 25; *Georgics*, 24, 25, 31–32, 53, 84, 219n18, 220n37
Virginia Minstrels, 34
vocational training, 51
Volkswagen, 121

Wagner-McCoy, Sarah, 25
Walker, Frank, 163
Walkowitz, Rebecca L., 216n24
Wallace, Mike, 171
Wallerstein, Immanuel, 11
Warner, Michael, 16, 78, 133–34
Warren, Kenneth, 182
Warren, Robert Penn, 1
Washington, Booker T.: as accommodationist, 49, 52, 54; agriculture and, 12, 49–62, 67; antagonists, 222n1; Atlanta Compromise speech, 162; black autonomy and, 70; on cleanliness, 61–62; colorism and, 222n54; dirt and soil images and, 61–62, 69; Du Bois and, 15, 36, 49, 222n1, 225n61; Dunbar and, 27, 32, 220n38; economic nationalism, 225n61; industrial education and, 73–74, 80; progress and, 66; Tuskegee Institute and, 28, 50–52, 54–60, 82
—works: Atlanta Compromise speech, 56, 62, 162; *The Farthest Man Down*, 52; *My Larger Education*, 223n10; *Up from Slavery*, 3, 15, 21, 22, 39, 43, 49–62, 69–70, 72–73, 81–82, 86–87, 220n21, 223n2, 223n9, 223n16, 225n61; *Working with the Hands*, 50, 54–55, 57, 58, 60, 61–62, 82, 227n99
Washington, D. C., 164, 240n90
Watson, Jay, 124
Watson, Tom, 129
Weaks-Baxter, Mary, 96, 112, 240n91
wealth, 11, 202–4, 207, 212; redistribution of, 138
Weber, Max, 217n44
Webern, Anton, 76
Weheliye, Alexander, 26
Wells, Ida B., 14, 218n61
Wesley, Charles H., 116
"We Southerners Have a Rendezvous with Destiny" (West), 97
West, Don, 16, 92–98, 109, 117, 154, 213; *Between the Plough Handles*, 94; "Clodhopper," 118; *Clods of Southern Earth*, 94, 103; *Crab-Grass*, 94; "Georgia Wanted Me Dead or Alive," 96; "Knotts County," 111–12; "Mountain Boy," 100–101; "My South," 109; "They Take Their Stand," 102–3; *Toil and Hunger*, 94, 103; "We Southerners Have a Rendezvous with Destiny," 97
West, Michael R., 50, 224n33
Western frontier, 229n6
"What Does the South Want?" (Ransom), 119, 231n71
What the Negro Wants, 116
"When de Co'n Pone's Hot" (Dunbar), 21
"When Malindy Sings" (Dunbar), 21
White, Walter, 129, 173
Whitecaps, 65
whiteness, 36–37, 45, 198
whites: industrial education and, 73–74; migration, 189–98; rural working class, 113–14, 155–56, 165, 179, 241n15. *See also* plantation owners
white supremacy, 44, 57, 66, 85, 102
white women, 86, 181
Whitman, Walt, 104
Who Owns America? (Agar and Tate, eds.), 16, 115–16. *See also* Nashville Agrarians
Wilkerson, Isabel, 212, 237n22

Williams, Eric, 4
Williams, Raymond, 8, 24, 70, 212–13, 219n10
Williams, Spencer, 166
Williams, William Carlos, 1, 95, 229n22
Williamson, Joel, 51, 65
Wilson, Edmund, 100
Wolcott, Marion Post, 13
women: access to public life, 132, 135; autonomy of, 128; black, 36–44, 54–55, 78, 81–82; education and, 79–81; as labor agrarians, 16; poverty and, 127; rural modern and, 4; white, 86, 181
Wood, Fernando, 170
Woods, Clyde, 4, 215n17
Workers Defense League, 124

working class, 39, 42, 86–87, 97–98, 103–8, 120, 133, 155, 241n15
Working with the Hands (Washington), 50, 54–55, 57, 58, 60, 61–62, 82, 227n99
Wright, Richard, 56, 144, 161

Yaeger, Patricia, 70, 177
Yeats, W. B., 27
yeoman farmers, 96, 104, 110, 113, 115, 240n91
You Have Seen Their Faces (1937), 16, 142–43, *144*
Young, Stark, 113

Zimmerman, Andrew, 51
Žižek, Slavoj, 152

The New Southern Studies

The Nation's Region: Southern Modernism, Segregation, and U.S. Nationalism
BY LEIGH ANNE DUCK

Black Masculinity and the U.S. South: From Uncle Tom to Gangsta
BY RICHÉ RICHARDSON

Grounded Globalism: How the U.S. South Embraces the World
BY JAMES L. PEACOCK

Disturbing Calculations: The Economics of Identity in Postcolonial Southern Literature, 1912–2002
BY MELANIE BENSON TAYLOR

American Cinema and the Southern Imaginary
EDITED BY DEBORAH E. BARKER AND KATHRYN MCKEE

Southern Civil Religions: Imagining the Good Society in the Post-Reconstruction Era
BY ARTHUR REMILLARD

Reconstructing the Native South: American Indian Literature and the Lost Cause
BY MELANIE BENSON TAYLOR

Apples and Ashes: Literature, Nationalism, and the Confederate States of America
BY COLEMAN HUTCHISON

Reading for the Body: The Recalcitrant Materiality of Southern Fiction, 1893–1985
BY JAY WATSON

Latining America: Black-Brown Passages and the Coloring of Latino/a Studies
BY CLAUDIA MILIAN

Finding Purple America: The South and the Future of American Cultural Studies
BY JON SMITH

The Signifying Eye: Seeing Faulkner's Art
BY CANDACE WAID

Sacral Grooves, Limbo Gateways: Travels in Deep Southern Time, Circum-Caribbean Space, Afro-creole Authority
BY KEITH CARTWRIGHT

Jim Crow, Literature, and the Legacy of Sutton E. Griggs
EDITED BY TESS CHAKKALAKAL AND KENNETH W. WARREN

Sounding the Color Line: Music and Race in the Southern Imagination
BY ERICH NUNN

Borges's Poe: The Influence and Reinvention of Edgar Allan Poe in Spanish America
BY EMRON ESPLIN

Eudora Welty's Fiction and Photography: The Body of the Other Woman
BY HARRIET POLLACK

Keywords for Southern Studies
EDITED BY SCOTT ROMINE AND JENNIFER RAE GREESON

The Southern Hospitality Myth: Ethics, Politics, Race, and American Memory
BY ANTHONY SZCZESIUL

Navigating Souths: Transdisciplinary Explorations of a U.S. Region
EDITED BY MICHELE GRIGSBY COFFEY AND JODI SKIPPER

Where the New World Is: Literature about the U.S. South at Global Scales
BY MARTYN BONE

Red States: Indigeneity, Settler Colonialism, and Southern Studies
BY GINA CAISON

The Whole Machinery: The Rural Modern in Cultures of the U.S. South, 1890–1946
BY BENJAMIN S. CHILD

Look Abroad, Angel: Thomas Wolfe and the Geographies of Longing
BY JEDEDIAH EVANS

www.ingramcontent.com/pod-product-compliance
Lightning Source LLC
Chambersburg PA
CBHW021851230426
43671CB00006B/343